The Revolutionary Imagination in the

Americas and the Age of Development

A book in the series

Latin America Otherwise: Languages, Empires, Nations

SERIES EDITORS: Walter D. Mignolo, Duke University;

Irene Silverblatt, Duke University; Sonia Saldívar-Hull,

University of California at Los Angeles

MARÍA JOSEFINA SALDAÑA-PORTILLO

The Revolutionary Imagination in the

Americas and the Age of Development

DUKE UNIVERSITY PRESS   Durham and London   2003

2nd printing, 2005

© 2003 DUKE UNIVERSITY PRESS

Printed in the United States of America

on acid-free paper ∞

Typeset in Scala by Keystone Typesetting, Inc.

Library of Congress Cataloging-in-Publication

Data appear on the last printed page of this book.

Este libro está dedicado primero y siempre, al pueblo

nicaragüense, generoso y valiente—por diez años su

revolución

fue la mejor universidad del mundo

a mis padres—

Miguel, quien me enseñó ser intelectual, marxista y feminista

Fina, quien me enseñó ser feliz con su fuerza para sobrevivir

a mi querida sobrina Rebeca—

amiga, hermana, compañera

¿cómo es que te fuiste y me dejaste tan sola?

Contents

Latin America Otherwise: Languages, Empires, Nations is a critical series. It aims to explore the emergence and consequences of concepts used to define "Latin America" while at the same time exploring the broad interplay of political, economic, and cultural practices that have shaped Latin American worlds. Latin America, at the crossroads of competing imperial designs and local responses, has been construed as a geocultural and geopolitical entity since the nineteenth century. This series provides a starting point to redefine Latin America as a configuration of political, linguistic, cultural, and economic intersections that demands a continuous reappraisal of the role of the Americas in history, and of the ongoing process of globalization and the relocation of people and cultures that have characterized Latin America's experience. *Latin America Otherwise: Languages, Empires, Nations* is a forum that confronts established geocultural constructions, that rethinks area studies and disciplinary boundaries, that assesses convictions of the academy and of public policy, and that, correspondingly, demands that the practices through which we produce knowledge and understanding about and from Latin America be subject to rigorous and critical scrutiny.

By linking development rhetoric toward Latin America from the United States (in complicity with local governments) with revolutionary uprisings in Latin America during the Cold War, Saldaña offers a very detailed analysis of the dialectic between "regulation" and "emancipation," between "having to be developed by global forces" and "wanting alternatives to development" implied in revolutionary uprisings and social movements. But more than a detailed analysis, *The Revolutionary Imagination in the Americas and the Age of Development* provides a new departure from the now old debate between literary and cultural studies, on the one hand, and the old paradigm of area studies (e.g., Latin American Studies in both its social sciences and cultural versions). Its first contribution emanates from looking simultaneously at the dialectics between local histories (Latin American countries) and global designs (U.S. foreign policy and rhetoric). Saldaña's reading of Rigoberta Menchú is a refreshing departure from both narrow literary analysis of *testimonio* and empiricist ethical reading of her narrative. The second contribution is a look inside the United States at the responses of the civil rights movement in the local history of the country that was implementing development rhetoric and policies toward Latin America and designing new forms of internal control of the population. As a consequence, Josefina Saldaña-Portillo (of Mexican descent and teaching in an English department) brings a new design for understanding the Americas in the global order after the end of the Cold War. A truly Latin America Otherwise book.

Acknowledgments

This book has been in progress since before I even knew that I was going to write it. Thus, I would like to begin by thanking all of my friends and colleagues in Nicaragua who are responsible for my profound interest in the intersection of revolution and development, feminism, and ethnic identity. *Alrededor de una mesa de trago o un juego de naipes discutimos cada aspecto del proceso revolucionario. Gracias a* Amy Bank, Judy Butler, Larry Boyd, Heriberto Castillo, Myra Guillen, Joan Kirkwood, Carlos Molina, Orlando Morales, Carolina Obando, David Oliver, Edwin Paredes, Paul Rice, Esperanza Rivas, Otto Rojas Aguilar, Michael Saperstein, Richard Staller-Schultz, Lois Wessel, Joel Zúniga *y especialmente* Freddy Quesada Pastrán and Mary Talbot. There was never a solution for which Freddy could not figure out a problem, and there was never a problem for which Mary could not figure out a solution. If not for the intellectual engagement and revolutionary commitment of all these people, this project would not have been hatched.

As an academic, I have had the good fortune of wonderful mentorship throughout my career, and I thank them all. Regina Gagnier, Mary Louise Pratt, Renato Rosaldo, Stefano Varese, and Sylvia Winter, each in their own way, modeled a feminist teaching practice and politically engaged intellectuality for me during my time at Stanford. Norma Alarcón, Sandra Drake, Akhil Gupta, and Ramón Saldívar shepherded this project through its first incarnation with endless generosity, wit, and wisdom. While I was in the University of California system, a number of colleagues challenged and inspired my work, and provided me with innumerable opportunities for intellectual exchange: Inderpal Grewal, Caren Kaplan, Gwen Kirkpatrick, Francine Masiello, Lisa Lowe, David Lloyd, and Denise Segura. Of course, the love and friendship of my dear friends at University of California, Santa Barbara—Avery Gordon, Beth Merchant, Chris Newfield, Rafael Perez-Torres, and Chela Sandoval—kept me centered and sane. The Latin American Subaltern Studies Group has left an indelible intellectual stamp on this project, and I am very much indebted to John Beverly, John Kraniauskas, Walter Mignolo, Alberto Moreiras, Ileana Rodríguez, José Rabasa, Patricia Seed, and Gareth Williams for their own scholarship and their brilliant insights into my work. Finally, I would like to thank all my colleagues at Brown University for their support and friendship, especially Nancy Armstrong, Laura Chrisman, Jose Itzigsohn, and my partner-in-crime, Daniel Kim. I thank my research assistant Asha Nadkarni. She has not only been an excellent interlocutor on issues of development but a veritable sleuth with the bibliography. Naomi Reed I thank for her indexing and proofreading of the final proof. I thank Jane Donnelly, Lorraine Mazza, Suzie Nacar, Marilyn Netter, and Ellen Viola for their endless administrative support.

Multiple institutions contributed to the completion of this project with their financial support. I thank the Ford Foundation for its generous Dissertation Fellowship, as well as the Stanford Humanities Center. The UC President's Postdoctoral Fellowship program allowed me to conduct extensive research in Chiapas, Mexico, while the UC Humanities Research Institute provided me with the opportunity to share my research in the "Cultures of the Americas, Narratives of Globalization" Research Group.

I want to thank my family, who were so patient during the entire writing process, from my mom (¿Cuándo acabarás ese mentado libro mija?), to my dear sister Ana (page police), to my cousins Ana, Sara, and David ("Just pick a year, any year. Anything that happened to the Zapatistas after that, too bad."): they were always full of suggestions and support; the Flores women for being such excellent role models, starting with my Tía Nena: intelligent, independent, talented, extremely funny, and beautiful; my brothers and sisters and their spouses, who have loved me throughout all our political differences; my nieces and nephews, especially Elizabeth Semmelman— twenty shining stars, this is for each and every one of them; all my uncles and aunts, but especially my sweet Tía Graciela Hernandez, who is always so loving and in my corner with unwavering support, and my beloved Tía Irene Saldaña, for always supporting my education financially, and for always inspiring me with her example and her faith in me. Special thanks to Alice McGrath, the aunt of my political imaginary, who models engagement in the social with grace and wit.

I also want to thank my comadres, Alicia Arizon, Alicia Schmidt-Camacho, Claudia Carrillo, Ines Salazar, and most especially mi hermana de espiritu Teresa Carrillo: with your love and support there is nothing I can't face. Paco Guajardo I thank for a long list of things: friendship, love, financial support, faith, and handy carpentry skills. I want to thank my personal "team" of editors, my dearest friends Madhu Dubey and Shay Brawn, who answered my calls at all hours, listened to me recite endless arguments over the phone, and read this manuscript so conscientiously for form and content. Shay, of course, is my fourth sister because twenty-five years of friendship are as thick as blood. I also thank David Eng, Miranda Joseph, and Fred Moten, each of whom read sections of this book with meticulous care and gave extraordinary feedback. If something in this book sounds like David, Miranda, or Fred, that's because it probably is. Thanks for the intellectual input and for your loving friendship. Finally, Ed Cohen, Laura Harris, Anahid Kassabian, Ira Livingston, Kevin Sullivan, Leo and Maral Svendsen, Mary Talbot (still solving problems), Livia Tenzer, and Jyotsna Uppal provided much of the love and support in New York City, making me believe I belong there, even if it's not *Califas*. Thank you for big hearts and sharp wit.

Friendships in Sevilla provided the *arte y duende* that has sustained my intellectual life. Evelina Krone and Jill Snow generously invited us into their homes and into their flamenco community, providing us with countless music-filled evenings and wondrous adventures. These two women, with their courage for living life fully, provide me with a model for living mine: *"¡una copa más!" para Evelina y Jill*. Geórgia Gugliotta and Miguel Aragón—*amigos queridos y artistas que conmueven con su baile, toque y cante—gracias por tantas aventuras* and for providing much needed comic relief and a touch of Latin America in Sevilla. *A mi maestra, la artista Juana Amaya, quien me hace olvidar todo dolor con su genio musical incomparable, le doy las gracias por ese olvido y también por enseñarme a ser mejor maestra*.

Lastly and especially, I thank David Kazanjian for every goofy face he made to entertain me during the writing of this book, for the pages of notes he took while I clarified my ideas out loud, for drying tears of frustration and joy, for the freedom and independence he has always given me in pursuing my intellectual endeavors, for covering for me with my family when my research got me into sticky situations in Chiapas, for believing in me and in this book even when I didn't. He read every word with love. The trace of David's intellectual contribution can be found on every page. Most importantly, though, David knows all the hiding places of my soul and I thank him for this.

Part I

Introduction

One year ago today I proposed that the people of this hemisphere join in an *Alianza para el Progreso*—a continent-wide cooperative effort to satisfy the basic needs of the American people for homes, work and land, for health and schools, for political liberty and the dignity of the spirit. Our mission, I said, was "to complete the revolution of the Americas, to build a hemisphere where all men can hope for a suitable standard of living and all can live out their lives in dignity and freedom."
—President John F. Kennedy, 14 March 1962, commemorating the "Alliance for Progress" Initiative

Pedimos tu participación decidida apoyando este plan del pueblo mexicano que lucha por *trabajo, tierra, techo, alimentación, salud, educación, independencia, libertad, democracia, justicia y paz.* Declaramos que no dejaremos de pelear hasta lograr el cumplimiento de estas demandas básicas de nuestro pueblo formando un gobierno de nuestro país libre y democratico. [We ask your resolute participation in supporting this plan of the Mexican people, which struggles for work, land, housing, food, health, education, independence, liberty, democracy, justice, and peace. We declare that we shall not stop fighting for the fulfillment of these basic demands of our people, forming a government for our free and democratic country.]
—General Command, Zapatista National Liberation Army, Declaration from the Lacandón Jungle, December 1993

Thirty-two years after President Kennedy told the Latin American diplomatic corps in Washington, D.C., that he "look[ed] forward to the day when the people of Latin America will take their place beside the United States and Western Europe as citizens of industrialized and . . . increasingly abundant societies," that day had failed to arrive (Kennedy 18). Instead, on 1 January 1994, the Zapatista National Liberation Army (EZLN) issued their declaration of war against the Mexican government, timing their insurrection to coincide—in protest—with the inauguration of the North American Free Trade Agreement (NAFTA), the latest articulation of Kennedy's promise of "increasingly abundant societies" for Latin America. What joins these remarkably similar performative speech acts, uttered by such seemingly incongruous subjects?

How is it that a leader of the self-declared "free world" of capitalist political economies found himself calling for the completion of revolution in the Americas? How is it that a group of Marxist-inspired, subaltern insurgents found themselves reiterating the principles of his development plan thirty years later? Why is it that development projects and revolutionary movements persist long after both development and revolution have been declared "failures" by their critics both on the right and on the left? What accounts for the striking resemblance between these presumably opposed and enduring narratives of liberation? These questions about the imbrication of development and revolution inspire the writing of this book. *The Revolutionary Imagination in the Americas and the Age of Development* is an interrogation of the conjunctures and disjunctures between two narratives of progress that, in one way or another, captured the imagination of three generations of nationalists in the Americas in the second half of the twentieth century.

The convergence between late-twentieth-century discourses of development and revolution cannot be explained by a mechanistic derivation of one from the other, for developmentalist and revolutionary speech acts are constitutive of each other. For instance, a reading of Kennedy's historical reasoning as "neocolonialist" would dismiss his call for the completion of the revolutionary project in the Americas as simple rhetorical posturing in the interest of solidifying U.S. hegemony in the region at the height of the Cold War. There is some validity in this argument, as development aid was a powerful weapon in the arsenal of Cold War politics, rewarded to those economies adhering to the principles of laissez-faire capitalism, denied to those economies straying from these principles. However, although the liberal discourse of development that emerged after World War II was clearly part of a strategy for the containment of communism, that alone cannot account for the extent to which the nationalist leaders of newly decolonized countries and of previously sovereign nations, such as those in Latin America, embraced development theory and its practice. More important, reading the development-revolution convergence as neocolonialist cannot account for the powerful hold that developmentalism had on the imagination of the post–World War II revolutionary movements, which were themselves the origin of the "communist" threat to which Kennedy alludes. The central argument of this book is that a discourse of development captured the imagination of these revolutionary movements, often to the detriment of the constituencies these movements sought to liberate through their anti-imperialist struggle.

Alternately, reading this convergence from the vantage point of postcolonial theory might interpret such revolutionary developmentalism as compelled by the mimetic desire of colonial relations, or it might interpret revolutionary nationalism as derivative, predicated on a repetition, albeit with a difference, of Western development.[1] However, while mimetic desire and derivative nationalism play a role in the imbrication of revolution and development, such a reading cannot account for the fact that Kennedy seemed compelled to articulate his developmentalism in revolutionary terms, or that development policy was itself compelled by revolutionary movements. After all, Kennedy does not mention export-led growth or free trade, the backbones of World Bank development projects. Instead he reiterates the social and economic demands—work, land, housing, education, health care—that have animated revolutionary movements in Latin America since the first articulation of these demands as rights in the 1917 Mexican constitution.

Let me be clear. I am not interested in conflating post–World War II revolutionary movements and development strategies, for neither is monolithic through time, and these two discursive formations are not merely the same. Since World War II, First World agencies and think tanks have put forth complex and various development strategies, often in direct response to revolutionary analyses and challenges, as we shall see in chapter 2. In turn, revolutionary movements and development strategies in the Americas attempted to institute substantially different models of economic and political sociality, with substantially different consequences for the populations that have come under their sway.

Nor am I advocating an antidevelopmental position that would reject in general and absolute terms the imperative to develop embodied in both development and revolutionary ideologies. In the last fifteen years, several excellent poststructuralist critiques of the "age of development" have been published (Ferguson; Sachs; Escobar, *Encountering Development;* Apffel-Marglin and Marglin; Gupta; Hewitt de Alcántara, *Boundaries and Paradigms*). These authors do not merely question the validity of different models of development (GNP growth, growth with equity, basic needs approach, sustainability, etc.); they also critique development's entire discursive and institutional apparatus—exposing it, as a discourse, to history. If the problem with the age of development lies in its rendering as "natural" certain normative concepts of growth, progress, and modernity, as these authors make clear, then in the spirit of their critiques we should not respond by, in turn, uncritically privileging indigeny, tradition, and antiprogressive models of futurity. For if one continues to recognize a need for revolutionary change in the aftermath of what fifty years of "development" have wrought—if one's sympathies continue to lie with the revolutionary movements committed to challenging capitalist development, as mine do—then one accepts that some model of progress pertains. Thus I argue that the problem lies not with the idea of progress per se but with the *mode* of progressive movement—indeed, with the theory of human agency and model of subjectivity—that has underwritten the discursive collusion between the age of development and the revolutionary movements therein.

To clarify the complex relationship between revolutionary movements and development paradigms of the last half century, it is important to distinguish between two relatively distinct modalities of developmentalism. For much of the post–World War II period, First World development paradigms subscribed to the idea that societies moved through stages of development. Let us consider this the first modality of development. The second modality of developmentalism is expressed in the idea that this movement of societies is contingent on the development of the members of these societies into free, mature, fully conscious, and self-determining individual subjects. While it is by now evident that most, if not all, twentieth-century revolutionary movements subscribed to a developmentalist model of history (the first modality of developmentalism), the impact of the second modality of developmentalism on revolutionary politics over the last century has been less recognized. It is the theoretical elaboration of this second modality of development by revolutionary movements in the Americas with which my book is concerned. Indeed, it is my contention that the revolutionary movements under consideration subscribed not only to a developmentalist model of history but—more damning to the everyday practice of radical politics—to a developmentalist model of revolutionary subjectivity, consciousness, and agency.

Thus, rather than positing a mechanistic relationship of parody or derivation between the two speech acts presented in this chapter's epigraphs, as the neocolonial and postcolonial readings I sketched might do, I suggest that they are both animated by a particular theory of subjectivity. Not only do these two discursive terms depend on each other dialectically for their mutual constitution as historical alternatives (i.e., as vying ideological accounts of the first modality of developmentalism), but *both* revolutionary and development discourses also depend on colonial legacies of race and gender in their theoretical elaborations of subjectivity, agency, consciousness, and change (developmentalism's second, less evident, modality). Even as revolutionary movements in the Americas constituted themselves against the capitalist models of national development prescribed by U.S. and international agencies, those movements nevertheless articulated a liberal, developmentalist model of revolutionary subjectivity and consciousness in response. Similarly, even as Cold War development paradigms defined themselves in contradistinction to revolutionary movements, they nevertheless articulated the requirement for revolutionary agency and change in the American nations.

A normative theory of human transformation and agency, then, is at the heart of the discursive collusion between revolutionary and development discourses. Why might this be so? As narratives of liberation, both discourses share an origin in imperial reason: in those Enlightenment doctrines of progress, evolution, and change that were historically articulated with the practice of European colonialism and colonial capitalism. Thus, even as post–World War II discourses of development and revolution were specifically articulated *against* colonial and neocolonial relations of power, both shared a theory of human perfectibility that was itself a legacy of the various raced and gendered subject formations animating colonialism. It is precisely the prevalence of this meliorist model of subjectivity and theory of agency in revolutionary movements that, I argue, contributed to the "failure" of decolonization and liberation struggles in Latin America and the United States in the late twentieth century. In this meliorist theory of subjectivity, transformation, and agency, the formation of revolutionary consciousness was predicated on the transcendence of a premodern *ethnos*. The attainment of the universal(ized) condition of revolutionary agency, as I argue in chapters 3 and 4, was repeatedly (inevitably?) figured as the leaving behind of one's own particularity, as leaving behind the feminized ethnos of indigenous, peasant, or urban black cultural identity. The complex imbrication of development and revolution compels us as cultural critics, then, to reread the narratives of liberation by minority or marginal subjects in this postwar period. We cannot simply read revolutionary movements of the period as against colonial and neocolonial capitalism. We must also read them as *within* a racialized and gendered developmentalism. In an attempt to do so, this book proceeds in three parts.

The shared meliorist theory of subjectivity and human agency is not a stable, transhistorical formation. Although this mode of subjectivity and agency was discursively related to modes of subjectivity produced by imperial reason and colonial subalternization in the Americas, it was also discretely new and historically contingent. In part I, I argue that a new mode of subjectivity emerged as the transformative agent for the age of development in the aftermath of World War II and decolonization struggles. Chapter 2, "Development and Revolution: Narratives of Liberation and Regimes of Subjectivity in the Postwar Period," is an account of First World intellectual efforts expended to construct an appropriate subject of labor for capitalist expansion in the Third World, wherever development might cast its eye. In examining this new subjectivity's emergence within hegemonic First World development paradigms, I engage in a discursive analysis of the implied subject of (under)development, investigating the principles of human activity and the model of historical consciousness implied by the discourse of development and its policies.

During the age of development there have been several moments of crisis over the very meaning of development, with each epistemic crisis producing a plethora of new development strategies in response. I am not suggesting that these complex and various development paradigms shared a singular vision of development or relentlessly reiterated a singular recipe for producing it across Third World countries. However, I am suggesting that a strikingly similar theory of subjectivity and agency underwrites most of these paradigm shifts. More precisely, I observe that a particular set of metaphors, tropes, and themes accompanies the theorization of development and its agent/object across quite different development strategies— indeed, even across ideological and political lines. By analyzing some of the foundational moments in the formation of the development apparatus, as well as some important texts in development theory, I identify these key recurring themes, tropes, and metaphors.

Specifically, I trace the arc of the age of development through the rhetorical formation of its subject across a series of historical flash points: its beginnings at the Bretton Woods conference, its ascent into Cold War hegemony through President Harry Truman's Four Point Program, its apex in W. W. Rostow's modernization theory under presidents Kennedy and Johnson, and its cusping in the critical light of dependency theory during Robert S. McNamara's reign at the World Bank.[2] I consider the continuities and discontinuities between colonial categories of subjectivity and developmental categories of national citizenship: how race is relativized within the domain of cultural attitudes that must be overcome, how gender is allegorized within the domain of active and reactive nationalisms, and how hierarchical and exploitative relations of exchange in a global capitalist system are reorganized into normative levels of productivity that must be achieved. I argue that the discourse of development requires an epochal change in its subject. It requires the subject to become an agent of transformation in his own right, one who is highly ethical, mobile, progressive, risk taking, and masculinist, regardless of whether the agent/object of a development strategy is a man or a woman, an adult or a child.

To illustrate the discursive coincidence between this subject of development and the subject of revolution, part 2 goes on to examine the models of subjectivity and agency embedded both in the autobiographical texts of two revolutionary icons of the 1960s and 1970s and in the discourse of Sandinista agricultural policy. Together, these two chapters theorize the effect this development-revolution convergence had on the national liberation struggles under consideration. Revolutionary movements in the United States, Mexico, and Central America, I argue, have met with resistance from the very people these movements intended to liberate—women and men of color, indigenous peoples, and the land-poor peasantry—because of their adherence to an ahistorical teleology of human subjectivity and agency as revelation, transformation, and transcendence.

In chapter 3, "The Authorized Subjects of Revolution: Ernesto 'Che' Guevara and Mario Payeras," I analyze the impact that Ernesto "Che" Guevara's theory of human transformation has had on revolutionary leaders in Latin America and, more specifically, on peasant subalternity and ethnic particularity. Through an analysis of their diaries and political essays, I argue that Guevara and subsequent Latin American revolutionary leaders such as Guatemalan Mario Payeras represent revolutionary transformation as an epochal conversion experience, as the epistemic death of a prior subject, the subject of a prerevolutionary and premodern consciousness. I suggest that Guevara and Payeras each experience an epochal conversion to become transformative agents in their own lives and the lives of others. In doing so, these revolutionary heroes represent indigenous peoples and peasant subalterns as the horizon of their messianic, revolutionary errands, as the agents/objects of a revolutionary developmentalism. Furthermore, these two men represent themselves as catalysts for the transformation of subaltern consciousness, a transformation that inevitably entails the transcendence of ethnic, subaltern particularity.

These masculinist narratives of self-development bear a metaphoric, thematic, and tropological resemblance to the implied subject of (under)development I elaborate in chapter 2. However, I argue that the very act of representing themselves as autonomous, self-determining subjects unsettles the bourgeois development discourse. Although First World development theory appears to mandate this form of subjectivity for Third World denizens, it ultimately withholds its promise. Thus the performative acts of these autobiographical texts—their taking development discourse at its word—hold the possibility of a limited subversion even today.

After coming to power, the Sandinista National Liberation Front (FSLN) was constrained in making policy decisions by the model of dependent development imposed by the Somocistas and their U.S. allies. In chapter 4, "Irresistible Seduction: Rural Subjectivity under Sandinista Agricultural Policy," I suggest, however, that the dependency was not only economic but also epistemic. The Sandinistas were committed to transforming their country from an underdeveloped nation into a developed one. While certainly the economic exploitation of Nicaragua motivated the Sandinistas' desire for change, the discourse of development's imperative to economic growth produced effects in spheres beyond such economic considerations. Hence, when the Sandinista party made decisions about development and agriculture based on narrow models of subjectivity and national sovereignty, their decisions had negative impacts on the enfranchisement and political representation of Nicaraguan citizens. Committed to extending agro-industrial development nationwide through state farms and cooperatives, the party's view of revolutionary national development was based on an episteme that privileged proletarian and collective consciousness over the consciousness of the smallholding peasantry making up the majority of Nicaragua's rural population.

While the peasantry is not racialized as indigenous within Nicaragua, the Sandinistas nevertheless viewed peasant consciousness as a "premodern" ethnos, as an obstacle to a model of development that would better serve both the peasants' own interests and the economic growth of the nation. On that basis, the FSLN denied sectors of the peasantry the avenues of political representation that the party made available for other sectors of the rural population. Instead the Sandinistas took it on themselves not only to decide the interest of the peasants but to enact paternalistic and coercive policies in agriculture to assist the peasants in their revolutionary transformation of consciousness, much as liberal development schemes would have done.

In part 3, I turn my attention to the insurgent subalterns who have so often been both the intended beneficiaries of revolutionary activity in the Americas and the targets of economic development: the indigenous and peasant classes of Mexico and Central America. In chapters 5 and 6, I examine the textual production, autonomous articulations, and public performance of subjectivity by Rigoberta Menchú and the members of the Zapatista National Liberation Army. Both Menchú and the EZLN, I contend, retheorize the model of human subjectivity and agency put forth by their revolutionary predecessors. By theorizing how ethnicity and class function historically as mutually constituting categories in the Americas, these subaltern insurgents reject the ahistorical developmentalism of a revolutionary transformation based on the transcendence of ethnic and gendered particularity.

In chapter 5, "Reiterations of the Revolutionary 'I': Menchú and the Performance of Subaltern *Conciencia*," I consider the autobiographical *testimonio* of feminist and indigenist revolutionary Rigoberta Menchú. In *Me llamo Rigoberta Menchú y así me nació la conciencia*, Menchú strategically vacillates between the position of the autonomous liberal subject and the position of the primitive and underdeveloped Other. She does so, I suggest, to manipulate the Western reader (and her Ladino revolutionary counterparts) into a critique of modernization and development, a critique launched from Menchú's specific gender, class, and ethnic position. Menchú borrows the Western form of the authorial "I" to critique the revolutionary teleologies of consciousness privileged by the masterful "I" of her Ladino guerrilla predecessors. In Menchú's narrative, I argue, the process of coming to consciousness is not represented as epochal or revelatory, as it is in the narratives of Guevara and Payeras. Rather, an understanding of exploitation accrues through her experience with the mundane—the territory of women, of indigenous peoples, and of peasants. In previous narratives of revolution, this mundane consciousness was typically represented as a premodern ethnic formation that had to be superseded for nationalist change to occur. Menchú, to the contrary, posits a "nonmodern" positionality for indigenous subalterns, a positionality that allows the K'iche' Indians to negotiate a limited participation in the developmentalist discourse that encroaches on them from all sides. It is this authority over one's experience that Menchú demands, on behalf of K'iche' Indians, from any revolutionary model of development as well.

In contrast to Menchú's model of limited K'iche' participation in modernity and the nation-state, the Zapatistas began their insurrection in southern Mexico by demanding full participation in national development and in statist forms of government. In chapter 6, "The Politics of Silence: Development and Difference in Zapatismo," I analyze the communiqués issued publicly by the EZLN, the peace negotiations between the Institutional Revolutionary Party (PRI) and the Zapatistas, as well as the demand for autonomy by the Zapatistas and other indigenous organizations, as attempts by subaltern indigenous subjects to constitute themselves as "citizens of the nation" and as global economic agents. The Zapatista insurrection, I argue, demands the reconstitution of the Mexican state and economy. As such, it interrupts the rhetoric of progress for Mexico as a "developing" nation. I analyze how the Zapatistas reconceptualize the meaning and practice of citizenship through a critique of *mestizaje,* the PRI's model for citizenship. The Zapatista critique exposes the inherent developmentalism in the term "mestizaje" as it is predicated on the erasure of the indigenous subject in favor of the tropologically more advanced mestizo subject. In addition, the Zapatistas threaten the triumph of neoliberalism and globalization represented by NAFTA by demanding control over economic resources for indigenous people. They do so, however, not to exclude themselves from a national development process. Rather, the Zapatistas claim the role of the state for themselves to dictate the terms of a development project in which they are already fully implicated. Together, chapters 5 and 6 demonstrate alternative indigenous approaches to the constant negotiation with nationalism and modernity that development and globalization demand from all subjects. They also demonstrate how indigenous movements are rewriting revolutionary projects in the Americas to include indigenous people as authorities over their own experience.

Indeed, the indigenous/peasant cultural and political production of Menchú and the EZLN exceeds the terms of the revolution/development dialectic. Rejecting developmentalist notions that interpret their indigenous and peasant subject positions as premodern, they instead offer a model of revolutionary consciousness predicated on the global politics of local "everyday life." Thus, I argue, these insurgent subalterns challenge a model of revolutionary subjectivity and a theory of agency not from a position of indigenous purity but from an indigenous and peasant subject position simultaneously produced by modernity and in reaction to its developmentalism. As such, they force us to rethink the deployment of the categories of universalism and particularism so central in Western political thought. Also, these subaltern interventions require a rethinking of mestizaje. Thus, in the epilogue I suggest we can no longer uncritically celebrate mestizaje in Chicana/o and other social formations as a positionality of radical, postmodern hybridity but must recognize it as a racial ideology with its own developmentalist history, one that has underwritten revolutionary movements in North and South America prior to the age of development.

My methodological approach combines the ethnographic study of social movements with the literary analysis of the textual production of revolutionaries. And so in yet another way, the reader will find in this book the juxtaposition of what might seem incongruous objects of study and types of evidence in terms of the usual academic divides among literary studies, history, anthropology, and development studies: modernization and dependency theory during the Cold War; agricultural policy under the Sandinista government in Nicaragua; autobiographies of Malcolm X, Che Guevara, Mario Payeras, and Rigoberta Menchú; energy development policies in Mexico; EZLN communiqués, negotiations for autonomy, and political rallies; mestizaje in queer Aztlán. However, it is my contention that when one is studying the theorization of human subjectivity and agency in post–World War II revolutionary movements, one must place such diverse objects alongside one another. The problematic I identify is the ideological collusion between developmentalist and revolutionary models of subjectivity. The project of development begins within the confines of economic policy to effect a specific political consequence. However, development's goal is necessarily two-fold: producing "developed" capitalist national economies and thereby "developed" liberal citizens therein. Revolutionary movements similarly seek to transform their national economies from a condition of dependent development and neocolonial exploitation to a condition of sovereign and independent development, thereby transforming dependent and exploited classes into freed revolutionary subjects/citizens.

I focus my analysis on public economic policy and literary production because in *any* revolutionary movement, these are the two areas dedicated to the task of transforming subjectivity and consciousness. While agricultural policy, industrial diversification, and autonomy projects provide the model for the revolutionary transformation of the national economy (with its implied economic subject), autobiographies model revolutionary subjectivity for a reading public by offering exemplary narratives of personal transformation. If the underlying problematic unifying this book is a certain collusion between revolutionary and development projects, thematically each chapter focuses on the production of revolutionary subjectivity, whether it be in agricultural, industrial, and autonomy projects, or in autobiography. The combination of these various kinds of evidence enables the reader to see the coordinated effort to interpellate national, revolutionary subjectivity across governmental policy and literary production. I elaborate on the details of how I conducted my ethnographic research within the relevant chapters.

Finally, before proceeding with a historical and rhetorical analysis of the subject of (under)development, I would like to specify the interventions I hope to make with this book, especially because the nature of my interventions defies the usual divisions of academic fields. Minoritarian revolutionary movements in the United States are most often interpreted within a narrowly nationalist paradigm, while revolutionary movements in Mexico, Central America, and South America have traditionally been interpreted according to the reductivist East/West paradigm of the Cold War. By contrast, I bring U.S. minority and Latin American revolutionary movements together to examine their discursive and historical connections, both to each other and to the history of revolution in the Americas. While it is undoubtedly true that the Soviet Union and China financed and influenced the formation of national liberation struggles in Latin America, including revolutionary models of national development, a particularly conservative strain of Latin American studies disregards the rich history of revolutionary struggle in the Americas. At the same time, U.S. exceptionalism in American studies has extended to the area of Ethnic studies, which often interprets minority racial formations only within the constraints of U.S. borders.

Instead, I traverse the historical divide between Latin American studies and U.S. American studies through the comparative analysis of revolutionary movements in the Americas. I contend, first, that the U.S. Revolution of 1776 and the Mexican Revolution of 1910 are the primary intellectual influences of American revolutionary movements in the late twentieth century.[3] I argue that the legacy of colonialism in the Americas—including the independence movements by white settlers in the United States and Latin America—profoundly influenced the discursive formations of development *and* revolution in the second half of the twentieth century. This book offers a comparative analysis of the influence that colonial legacies of race and gender had on the construction of twentieth-century revolutionary agency. I suggest that on both sides of the Mexico–U.S. border, revolutionary agents in the late twentieth century unwittingly appropriated Spanish and Anglo-American colonial quest narratives in their struggles for liberation. Although the distinct racial legacies of Anglo-American and Spanish colonialism produced some variations in the revolutionary appropriations of figures such as Malcolm X and Che Guevara, the subjectivities prescribed in the autobiographies of these revolutionaries were nevertheless predicated on a remarkably similar sense of compromised racial masculinity. In this resemblance to Spanish and Anglo racial legacies, and to each other, these appropriations by Guevara and Malcolm X reinforce the model of an autonomous, self-determining subject imagining the world in his own image, albeit a "revolutionary" one. Similarly, the appropriation of mestizaje by Chicana/o nationalists in their attempt to fend off discriminatory practices in the United States borrows heavily from the colonial register of Indian subalternization under Spanish colonialism, making coalition across indigenous and Chicano movements difficult, if not impossible. This appropriation continues to haunt even the antinationalism of contemporary queer Aztlán.

In addition, I place the texts of U.S. minority subjects in dialogue with the texts of revolutionary subjects in Latin America because the global deployment of the discourse of development necessitates such a transnational focus. By placing these texts in dialogue, however, I am not positing a simple equivalence between these Latin Americans and U.S. minorities. On the contrary, I examine their differential relations within the discursive practices of development and revolution. As the major neocolonial power in the Americas in the postwar period, the United States brings U.S. minority and Latin American subaltern subjects together on the terrain of resistance. As the major proponent of the development paradigm in the Americas, however, the United States also depends on a strict differentiation between First World and Third World subjects on the terrain of labor. Although shared models of racialized and masculinist subjectivity join together revolutionary movements across the Americas, the differentiated positionalities of U.S. minority and Latin American subaltern subjects across the international division of labor confounds simple models of Third World revolutionary unity.

For all of these reasons, the reader will find Malcolm X's autobiography and texts from queer Aztlán alongside Che's diary and EZLN communiqués. My study of the revolutionary imagination is by no means exhaustive, but no such study would be complete without these kinds of connections. In my unorthodox traversing of the geographic divide of the literary and cultural field, I am answering recent calls for the further inclusion of Latino studies within Latin American studies, as well as the call for a truly "American" studies in the United States. As such, I bring postcolonial and minority discourse analysis to bear on the cross-pollination of transnational raced and gendered ideologies in the Americas. But I am answering another call as well, a call made by the texts themselves, for they were all written in an anticolonialist spirit that has brought the Americas together as often as neocolonialism has rent them asunder. It is a call I hope the reader will hear echoing in the analysis I offer. It is my sincere hope that my effort toward a comparative analysis of the impact of colonial legacies on revolutionary models of human subjectivity and agency, as well as on development schemata of human differentiation, might allow us to theorize anew the possibility of such revolutionary unity across the Americas.

Development and Revolution:

Narratives of Liberation and Regimes of

Subjectivity in the Postwar Period

It was in the struggle of the British bourgeoisie against the remnants of feudalism that the idea of development was born. There is, then, a connection between the conception of development and the development of specific social conflicts.
—Jorge Larrain, *Theories of Development*

We have reached this evening a decisive point. But it is only a beginning. We have to go out from here as missionaries, inspired by zeal and faith.
—John Maynard Keynes, on the ratification of the Articles of Agreement for the World Bank at the closing Bretton Woods Plenary, 1944

Although development has occurred throughout history and across civilizations, its formal, self-conscious articulation as a necessary and self-evident social process is of fairly recent elaboration, as Jorge Larrain, an intellectual historian of development, suggests, dating back to the rise of the British bourgeoisie, to classical economists' theories of "progress," and to Marx and Engels's theory of the development of social classes and productive forces (Larrain 1–2). The modern elaboration of the concept of "development-as-progress" in the late eighteenth century through the mid-nineteenth, however, is quite distinct from the twentieth-century concern with the engineered economic development of entire "peripheral" and "semiperipheral" areas. In Larrain's assessment, even the neoclassical and imperialist theories of capitalist expansion, elaborated during the height of colonial acquisition (1860–1945), were fairly indifferent toward the developmental effects of capitalist penetration on the periphery. Instead, these theories focused almost exclusively on the effects of colonialism on the economies of empire nations (6–10). However, when theorists of the period turned their attention to the periphery, it was generally agreed by neoclassical and anti-imperialist theorists alike—Walras, Jevons, Menger, Marshall, on the one hand;

Bukharin, Luxemburg, Hilferding, Lenin, on the other—that colonial penetration enhanced capitalist development in the periphery.[1]

While genealogically related to Enlightenment doctrines of imperial reason, development's contemporary usage as the modernization of national economies dates back only to the beginning of the twentieth century. Immanuel Wallerstein places the origin of the idea of "national development" at 1917, in the "great ideological antinomy of the twentieth century, Wilsonianism vs. Leninism," as both the United States and the Soviet Union expressed their desire for the liquidation of European empires on the basis of the right to self-determination of peoples (Wallerstein, *After Liberalism* 108–9). Indeed, Wallerstein credits Woodrow Wilson with universalizing the individual's right to self-determination during his administration by extending this right to entire colonized "peoples" in the international arena. Likewise, Lenin saw the condition of sovereignty as a necessary step for all nations or peoples on the road toward the creation of a universal world proletariat (110). According to Wallerstein, this early articulation by competing ideologies of the right to self-determination with the need for political and economic integration of the periphery permanently wed nationalism to development and, in turn, national development to anticolonial struggle.

National Development as the Promise of a Postcolonial Era

The historical record bears this out. Roosevelt's purported condition for entering World War II on behalf of the Allied forces was the dismantling of empires following the war. He demanded the guarantee of equality of peoples and of free trade among them. In his memoir about his father, *As He Saw It*, Elliot Roosevelt writes that the president made this demand explicit to Churchill during their historic meeting in August 1941, which resulted in the Atlantic Charter. According to his son, President Roosevelt made the postwar abrogation of special trade agreements between the British empire and its colonies a condition for U.S. assistance (George and Sabelli 23).[2] Roosevelt attributed the cause of the war to monopolistic colonial relations, territorial rivalries, and currency devaluations associated with colonial competition, a position shared by U.S. government officials, political pundits, and economists of the period. Even before the war was formally over, the United States spearheaded the implementation of Roosevelt's conditions by hosting the United Nations Monetary and Financial Conference. More commonly known as the Bretton Woods conference after the quiet New Hampshire town that hosted it in July 1944, this conference was a preparatory meeting for the foundation of the International Monetary Fund (IMF) and the International Bank for Reconstruction and Development (IBRD). After its mission of reconstructing Europe was fulfilled, the IBRD became what is today the World Bank (WB). In the documents produced in preparation for, and in the aftermath of, the Bretton Woods conference, "free trade among free nations" was repeatedly cited as the blueprint for peace and prosperity in a postwar era.[3] The Bretton Woods conference sought to create structures that would put this principle into practice. It was the birthplace of modern development as social engineering on a global scale.

This new commitment to the right of sovereignty for colonized nations in the periphery dovetailed nicely with the economic interests of the United States. Government officials rightly perceived a looming crisis in U.S. capitalist expansion, as the booming war economy would need to find new outlets for its greatly expanded productive capacity (George and Sabelli 23). Roosevelt's administration, then, saw no contradiction between undertaking the humanitarian mission of assisting in the development of decolonizing spaces and expanding the network of trade for the United States. In a U.S. Treasury Department document explaining the Bretton Woods Accord to the public, a section on the IBRD states simply:

> The need for developmental loans is perhaps less urgent [than loans for reconstruction], though equally important from the standpoint of promoting trade expansion. The underdeveloped countries offer immense stores of raw materials that the more advanced countries, including the United States, need to supplement their own exhaustible resources. They also offer the prospect of a substantial market for manufactured goods. Their first need, however, is for machinery, tools, and heavy equipment, all of which will have to be imported and largely paid for with borrowed funds. (U.S. Treasury Department 16)[4]

The point here is not that the United States was simply or only operating out of the ulterior motive of solidifying its neocolonial power, for benevolent intentions and self-serving economic interests are hopelessly intertwined. Rather, my purpose is to illustrate that, at its inception, development is inextricably linked to managing a crisis in capitalist production precipitated equally by the exhaustion of colonial capitalism's expansive capacities and by the greatly expanded productive capacity of the U.S. postwar economy. As a globalizing system, capitalism has always relied on supplementary discourses for its perpetuation and extension. Development, as it took shape in the fields of diplomacy and political economy, under the auspices of the

United Nations, the IMF, the IBRD/WB, and the U.S. Treasury Department, began as precisely such a supplementary discourse. Development replaced the "civilizing mission" of the age of colonialism with the imperatives of self-determination, independence, free trade, industrialization, and economic growth in a postcolonial era.

The United States has arguably been the primary beneficiary of the invention of development as a management tool for capitalist production crises. However, at Bretton Woods, the U.S. delegation was primarily concerned with solidifying U.S. economic hegemony by institutionalizing the IMF as the vehicle for stabilizing currency exchange rates among Western nations and financing the (relatively) free trade of manufactured goods and raw materials globally (George and Sabelli 27–29). According to Susan George and Fabrizio Sabelli, the U.S. delegation had not contemplated institutionalizing the concept of developing decolonized economies under the auspices of a world development bank. Thus, when U.S. treasury secretary Henry Morgenthau accepted the nomination as conference president, his speech at the first plenary of Bretton Woods referred only once to the constitution of the future IBRD. After impugning currency disorder and the lack of free trade as the causes of war, he talked at length about the formation and functions of the IMF. Finally, toward the end of his speech, he made some brief comments on the role of the would-be bank, ending with a dismissive comment: "The technicians have prepared the outline of a plan for an International Bank for Postwar Reconstruction which will investigate the opportunities for loans of this character" (George and Sabelli 28). George and Sabelli suggest that the U.S. delegation had little interest in expanding the bank's purpose or longevity beyond the short-term goal of reconstructing Europe. As the joint authors point out: "The word 'development' in particular had not been pronounced. 'Postwar Reconstruction' was what Morgenthau had said and it was what he meant: the reconstruction certainly of Europe—possibly China and Japan as well, but he was looking no further. . . . The conference lasted three weeks and for most of that time, the bank remained the poor relation [of the IMF], relegated to the background" (28).

Instead, it was John Maynard Keynes, as chairman of "Commission II" for the establishment of the bank, who explicitly introduced the word "development" into the bank's title and into articles of its constitution. As my chapter epigraph makes clear, Keynes had in mind a much broader vision of the bank's mandate than the reconstruction of Europe; indeed, he proposed a moral and ethical "mission" for the bank, requiring the "zeal" of devout purpose and the universalist horizon of a "faith." In his initial discussions of the bank's future role, he implored the members of his commission to look beyond its initial mandate for the reconstruction of Europe: "The field of reconstruction from the consequences of war will mainly occupy the proposed Bank in its early days. But as soon as possible, and with increasing emphasis as time goes on, there is a second primary duty laid upon it, namely to develop the resources and productive capacity of the world, with special attention to the less developed countries, to raising the standard of life and the conditions of labour everywhere, to make the resources of the world more fully available to all mankind" (George and Sabelli 34).

Development as a "primary duty" of this international agency has supplanted what British imperial theorist J. A. Hobson identified as England's "public duty" during the great age of empire (Hobson 231). While the British empire is dwarfed in comparison with the bank's proposed purview ("to make the resources of the world more fully available to all mankind"), the bank's purpose is not so far removed from the purpose of British imperial reason in Hobson's worldview: "It is the great practical business of the country to explore and develop, by every method which science can devise, the hidden natural and human resources of the globe" (229). The social Darwinism invoked by Hobson's humanist imperialism, however, which characterized British colonial subjects as belonging to the "lower races," has been banished in Keynes's estimation of the bank's mandate; gone are the references to the "indolence and torpor of character" of tropical populations (Hobson 227). In their stead we have a nonbiological, evolutionary sociology of "less developed countries," and a universalized "productive capacity" of all world citizens. Development has also banished compulsory labor under colonial administrations, replacing it with free wage labor and a concern for "raising the standard of life and the conditions of labour everywhere."

It might be tempting to think of development as little more than warmed-over colonialism, given its role in managing a crisis in capitalist production; or to think of it as a complete break from colonialism, given its putative claim to deliver on liberal democracy's promise of liberty and prosperity for all. However, it is important to see development's *difference from* colonialism, rooted in its action as a vehicle for facilitating decolonization, and its *links to* colonialism, rooted in its redeployment of colonialism's logics and structures. (Indeed, it is quite stunning that suddenly, at least for the moment, all nations in both the First World and the Third World—those destroyed by war in Europe and those "hindered" by a lesser development in decolonized and decolonizing spaces—existed on the equal footing of "aid recipient," standing within a single "everywhere" in need of improved conditions of labor and living.) Even as development emerged in concert with the universal right to national self-determination, it nonetheless carried within it the traces of imperial reason, of an evolutionary hierarchy and racialized subordination. Thus, on one hand, development reformulates a racialized theory of human perfectibility and progress. Even as it dispenses with references to the "lower races" and genetically determined indolence, the traces of these categories remain in its concept of "less developed countries" with impaired productive capacities. Perhaps more significant, though, what lingers almost imperceptibly is the religiously ordained nature of the civilizing mission. As the passive construction of Keynes's phrase "a primary duty is laid upon it" implies, the bank's duty to develop the world is mandated by a higher principle or power than mere economic interest, and it requires the fervor of faith to implement this divine principle. This trace of religious mission also inhabits development's liberatory promise to deliver "mankind" from need.

On the other hand, however, developmentalism far exceeds the scope of colonialism, bringing the entire world under the surveillance of a few international agencies. Indeed, colonialism is rendered anachronistic by development. It is precisely the marriage of development and decolonization that discursively legitimates the extraction of resources and productive capacity in a way the civilizing mission of colonialism never could. The extraction of resources and productive capacity is ordained as the principal course of action for a decolonized nation to achieve and maintain sovereignty. Even as development articulates the liberatory promise of delivering decolonized nations from need, it simultaneously re-creates it by recognizing the "less developed countries" as being *in need* of assistance to carry out this dual process of extraction. In this manner, development aid and agencies insinuate themselves "everywhere."

Wolfgang Sachs, Gustavo Esteva, and Arturo Escobar have all identified Harry Truman's inaugural address on 20 January 1949 as the dawn of the age of development, as the initiation of a new era of power/knowledge in world affairs (Sachs 2; Esteva 6–7; Escobar, *Encountering Development* 3). I locate its emergence before this historic speech, in the negotiations for a postwar order that began with Roosevelt's conditions for entering the war. There is no need, however, to quibble over an ever-receding origin point (Wilson and Lenin? Smith and Marx?) of this new power/knowledge system, because at whichever point we locate it, what is important for my argument is that its emergence is marked by the articulation of a set of discursive signifiers ("equality of peoples," "self-determination," "less developed countries," "free trade," "limited productive capacity," "prosperity," "need") with a new set of filial institutions (the IMF and the WB) dedicated, in turn, to the financing of trade and the financing of national development geared toward trade. Development's discursive emergence was thus, paradoxically, *both* a liberatory strategy for decolonizing the world *and* a "neutral" rearticulation of racialized colonial categories as national difference. Development rendered formal colonialism obsolete, but it also gave imperial knowledge production a new lease on life. Thus I seek to elucidate the continuities and discontinuities between what I would suggest are the two great organizing tropes of imperial reason in what Giovanni Arrighi has called "the long twentieth century": *civilization* and *development*.

If we look to these tropes, and to the set of discursive signifiers through which development mobilizes, then we see that by Truman's 1949 inaugural address, this discursive deployment of development had become hegemonic. Rehashing the 1947 "Truman Doctrine," the president's inaugural address proposed, as an alternative to "that false philosophy of Communism," a four-point program for increasing the prosperity of the United States and the rest of the world in tandem. After outlining the three points of his program pertaining to the domestic sphere, the Marshall Plan, and the foundation of NATO, Truman turned his attention to the world outside of Europe and the United States. In his fourth point, he insisted the United States "must embark on a bold new program for making the benefits of our scientific advances and industrial progress available for the improvement and growth of underdeveloped areas." He lamented that half of the world's population lived in such areas, often "in conditions approaching misery. Their food is inadequate. They are victims of disease. Their economic life is primitive and stagnant. Their poverty is a handicap and a threat both to them and to more prosperous areas. For the first time in history humanity possesses the knowledge and the skill to relieve the suffering of these people" (Truman 293, 296). What is remarkable, as Escobar points out, is not that Truman made such a statement, but that such statements "made perfect sense" to domestic and international audiences alike (Escobar, *Encountering Development* 4). From former colonizing elites to independence leaders in Africa and Asia, from liberal economists in the United States to revolutionary leaders in Latin America, all had come to understand in a span of a few years the Southern Hemisphere and its inhabitants as existing in a condition of "underdevelopment."[5] More remarkable still, many of these same leaders believed the proper application of development aid in the fields of "scientific advances" and "industrial progress" would rapidly remake the world in the image of the United States.

Truman's inaugural address recognizes half the world's population as "primitive" and "stagnant" "victims of disease," but more crucially for the purposes of this project, it also rhetorically reconfigures the interior space of the individual subjects living in these "underdeveloped areas."[6] Truman's speech thus registers a swerve in development discourse toward subjectivity, a move we can see clearly in his closing remarks, which shift the target of development from national economies to individuated subjectivities:

> The old imperialism—exploitation for foreign profit—has no place in our plans. What we envisage is a program of development based on the concepts of democratic fair-dealing. . . . Only by helping the least fortunate of its members to help themselves can the human family achieve the decent, satisfying life that is the right of all people. Democracy alone can supply the vitalizing force to stir the peoples of the world into triumphant action, not only against their human oppressors, but also against their ancient enemies—hunger, misery, and despair. . . . Slowly but surely we are weaving a world fabric of international and growing prosperity. We are aided by all who wish to live in freedom from fear—even by those who live today in fear under their own governments. We are aided by all who want relief from the lies of propaganda—who desire truth and sincerity. We are aided by all who desire self-government and a voice in their own affairs. We are aided by all who long for economic security—for the security and abundance that men in free societies can enjoy. We are aided by all who desire freedom of speech, freedom of religion, and freedom to live their own lives for useful ends. (Truman 297)

Aiding the "underdeveloped areas" of the world becomes completely intertwined with fighting communism as U.S. development aid to the "least fortunate" of the "human family" is aided, in turn, by those who oppose unnamed tyrannical governments and the "lies of propaganda." Certainly these closing remarks are aimed at the citizens of the Soviet Union. They are also, however, directed at all those involved in revolutionary struggles "against their ancient enemies—hunger, misery, and despair," those who might be inspired by communism in this pursuit.

What is noteworthy beyond this imbrication of development, anticolonialism, and anticommunism, however, is the new terrain on which the battle both *for* development and *against* communism will be fought. Whereas Keynes was concerned with national "standards of living" and indexes of "productive capacity," with industrialization and infrastructure in "less developed" economies, Truman is concerned with a set of *attitudes*, including an attitude toward freedom from want: development is aided by "all who *long* for economic security—for . . . security and abundance." With Truman's speech, the desire for development-as-freedom is implanted within (under-developed) subjectivity, evinced by "wishes," "desires," "voice," "longing," and, ultimately, choice. It is no longer simply the "less developed countries" that may or may not embrace national development; it is now the millions of "despair[ing]" individuals who *desire* development, who would willingly choose it as the means for making "useful ends" of their own lives. The target of development is no longer only the "less developed countries," but now also the less developed subjects of the "human family."

That the Point Four Program was principally concerned with the desired/desiring subject of (under)development is underscored by the type of aid dispensed under its auspices. On 5 June 1950, Congress implemented Truman's Point Four Program by passing the Act for International Development, allocating $35 million in direct foreign aid for such projects as adult literacy in India, education on disease prevention in children in Burma, and a vocational school in Libya (Lott 297). Compared to the lending capacity of the IBRD and the U.S. Export-Import Bank, which in 1951 jointly extended more than $1 billion in loans to "developing" nations, the sum allotted for implementation of the Point Four Program seems minuscule (Hayes 12). Arguably, the discrepancy in funding suggests that the Point Four Program was largely symbolic, part of a U.S. Cold War propaganda campaign abroad. However, I would argue that the direction of the funding points us toward a significant *augmentation* in the discourse of development. While IBRD loans, especially those made in the early years, were directed toward national economies, toward building appropriate communication, transportation, and energy infrastructures at the national level, the Point Four Program made the target of aid the national citizen. Its aid was directed at constructing appropriate subjects for national development, at reforming the illiterate Indian, the diseased Burmese, the unskilled Libyan. Because its development was ideological more than economic, because its addressees were individual subjects more than national economies, the Point Four Program, with its microfunding for small-scale programs, made *individuals* available for development.[7]

Like Truman before him, John F. Kennedy responded to revolutionary movements in the Third World with a dual strategy of military intervention and development aid. Indeed, Kennedy's "covert" involvement in Cuba and Vietnam strategically, tactically, and geographically mirrors Truman's involvement in Korea and Guatemala. Nevertheless, under Kennedy's administration, development aid became a far more prominent aspect of U.S. foreign policy than in the two previous administrations, especially with regard to Latin America. Kennedy's Alliance for Progress greatly surpassed Truman's Point Four Program in scope. More than $1 billion in development aid and loans were extended to Latin America in the program's first year.[8] Devised under the advisement of economic historian W. W. Rostow, the Alliance for Progress was a response to communist-inspired national liberation movements.[9] Rostow saw himself as a member of an intellectual vanguard of economic historians and theorists in the battle to contain communism. His *Stages of Economic Growth: A Non-Communist Manifesto* is both an explicitly anticommunist treatise on national liberation (as the title attests) and a foundational text in "modernization theory" of the Pax Americana postwar period.

Development theory was initially formulated by economists strongly influenced by Keynes; however, intellectual historian Colin Leys has pointed out that "by the end of the 1950s . . . the original optimism that this approach would yield rapid results had begun to evaporate, and the limitations of development economics as a theory of development were beginning to be exposed" (8). As such, a second generation of development theorists responded to the failure of Keynesian economics to produce immediate results in the decolonizing world. Alternately called modernization theorists or structural functionalists, these men attempted to provide sociological, psychological, and cultural explanations for the failure of development economics to take hold in any given Third World society. With this second generation, development theory moved beyond the realm of economics into the disciplines of political science, sociology, anthropology, and psychology.[10] Although many proponents of modernization theory or structural functionalism were "Cold War warriors" such as Gabriel Almond, Edward Shils, Lucien Pye, and Samuel Huntington, who were clearly positioned on the U.S. side of a polarized geopolitics, it is also true that this second generation of development theorists gained intellectual ascendancy fairly quickly (Leys 10). As Larrain has argued, "the first mainstream post-war theories of development within the capitalist world were born as modernization theories, that is to say, as theories of the processes and stages through which traditional or backward societies were bound to go during their transition to modern society. These processes and stages were to be determined by looking at the history of developed societies. The assumption was that newly developing societies must repeat the same experience" (85–86). This mainstreaming of modernization theory in the development establishment, and particularly in the U.S. academy, dehistoricized the evolution of global capitalism. While Keynesian economists saw development as at least in part a response to the ill effects of colonialism, modernization theorists naturalized development's emergence into a series of discrete stages inevitably traversed by all *national* economies. With its sociological and cultural variants as explanations for why development occurred in some places and not in others, modernization theory and structural functionalism displaced the scene of its emergence onto the terrain of attitudes held by national citizens, of choices made by national societies.[11] Rostow's *Stages of Economic Growth* is an ideal text for tracing the effect of this displacement, because the key themes, metaphors, and tropes he employs—indeed, the entire chain of discursive signifiers he constructs—will accompany the subject of (under)-development across subsequent generations of development strategies, and even across the ideological divides of the Cold War.

I am not suggesting that *Stages of Economic Growth* was the definitive blueprint for all future development discourses and practices. However, it does exemplify the swerve of development theory from the terrain of national economies toward that of human subjectivity initiated by Truman. In the chain of discursive signifiers accompanying Rostow's (under)developed subject, we will find traces of colonialism's racial legacy. We will also recognize the reiterative force of this chain of signification as it is reformulated time and again across the age of development. In addition, as director of policy and planning in the U.S. State Department under Kennedy and as chief adviser on Vietnam to President Lyndon B. Johnson, Rostow had a direct impact on the discursive imbrication of development aid (Alliance for Progress) and revolutionary movements (Cuba, Vietnam).

From Territory to Interiority:
The Desiring Subject of Development

In my readings of Keynes and Truman, I have suggested that some of the tropes of civilization were incorporated into the idiom of development in the 1950s and 1960s. From that incorporation emerged two new manifest subjects: the modern, fully developed subject and its premodern, underdeveloped counterpart. These subjects are *manifest* because their level of development appears as self-evident. What needed to be explained was not *whether* these subjects were developed but rather *how* the developed subject came to be so, and how the underdeveloped subject might follow in his path. This section focuses, then, on modernization theory as precisely one such explanation.

For Rostow and other modernization theorists, the path to national development was beautiful in its linear simplicity. Rostow's *Stages of Economic Growth* distills from the histories of Europe, the United States, Russia, China, and Japan five universal stages of development for all societies en route to becoming modern, secular nations: traditional society, preconditions for takeoff, takeoff, the drive to maturity, and high mass consumption. In the preface to the second edition, Rostow states that he is explicitly idealist in his transhistorical, transsocietal survey of development: "*Stages of Economic Growth* is an effort to map a large problem. It is not an encyclopedia of economic history" (ix). Rostow thus dispenses with the use of economic evidence (GNP, per capita income indicators, sectoral indicators) early on in his comparative survey.[12]

Indeed, this "how-to" book on modernization is not a study of national economics at all but a study of the culture of free will. Although he periodically discusses overhead capital investment, investment-to-income ratios, or industrial sectors conducive to compounded growth, Rostow inevitably returns to culture as the true indicator of whether or not modernization will take root in a society: "In surveying now the broad contours of each stage-of-growth we are examining, then, not merely the sectoral structures of economies, as they transformed themselves for growth, and grew; we are also examining a succession of *strategic choices made* by various societies concerning the disposition of their resources which include *but transcend* the income- and price-elasticities of demand" (16, italics mine). In this way, Rostow emphatically disassociates his inherently economic project from the economic ("which include *but transcend*"), and it is in this disassociation that subjectivity as the terrain of development enters the scene of modernization. It is within these "broad contours of each stage-of-growth" that we spot the manifest subject of development.

When Rostow theorizes the economic growth of presumed modern nations as the consequence of a series of "strategic choices made" at transitional points in history, he displaces development onto a question of freely executing the proper will. He universalizes the uneven and heterogeneous Euro-American trajectories of development across "various societies," deriving *all* trajectories from a prescriptive model of an autonomous, self-conscious, self-controlling subject constituted by his ability to make proper choices. Development here is precisely an extension of such an imagined subjectivity. It is the expression of a *collective, social disposition* for making the right choices, free of any imaginable material or historical constraints. Indeed, such a collective culture of free will transcends even the base motivations of profitability and competition, as "income" and "demand" are dispensed within the collective calculus of what to do with "resources."

This theme of reducing development and progress to a matter of making the "proper choice," free of material or historical constraint, recurs later in diverse third-generation development paradigms such as the "basic needs approach" and "sustainable development." In the case of a "basic needs approach," a Third World society is called on to choose, freely and suddenly, to radically alter the distribution of profit among its classes, so that the "basic needs" of its poorest members may be fulfilled. In the case of the "sustainable development" paradigm, an impoverished local community is called on to choose to privilege the long-term sustainability of the environment over its own immediate need, for instance, to deforest an area for planting cash crops. In both theoretical models, the politics of dictatorial regimes, oligarchies, death squads, unjust land tenure systems, and internal migration patterns are all relegated to the margins, rather than figured as central factors in determining the possibility for development and change.

While these three development models—modernization, basic needs, sustainable—are not the same, neither equally viable nor desirable, all three fall under the sway of a particular discursive formation, that of the individual and collective subject of free will, capable of transcending material, political, and historical constraints and choosing to become developed. More noteworthy than this, however, is the recurrence of these discursive signifiers in revolutionary theory. Revolutionaries, adhering to specifically socialist or "Second World" development paradigms, nevertheless represented their personal transformations in a similar rhetoric of transcendence, representing themselves and others as just such autonomous, self-controlling, and self-determining individuals freely choosing to become revolutionaries, as we shall see in part 2.

Returning to Rostow and his chain of discursive signifiers, the content of the collective culture of free will he describes is curiously bifurcated in his chapter entitled "The Preconditions for Take-Off." This chapter describes the transitional stage between the traditional society and the takeoff into self-sustained growth, and for Rostow, this is *the* pivotal stage in the modernization process. Here, once again, he eschews merely economic explanations. Though Rostow sardonically agrees with the "modern economist" that takeoff into self-sustained growth begins when a society's overall investment rate reaches 10 percent of the national income, this simple indicator fails to explain *why* investment rates might rise in the first instance (19–20). Hence Rostow once again locates the preconditions for increased rates of investments in "effective attitude":

> But to get the rate of investment up some men in the society must be able to manipulate and apply . . . modern science and useful cost-reducing inventions.
>
> Some other men in the society must be prepared to undergo the strain and risks of leadership in bringing the flow of available inventions productively into the capital stock.
>
> Some other men in the society must be prepared to lend their money on long term, at high risk, to back the innovating entrepreneurs . . . in modern industry.
>
> Some other men in the society must be prepared to accept training for—and then operate—an economic system whose methods are subject to regular change, and one which also increasingly *confines* the individual in large, disciplined organizations allocating to him specialized *narrow, recurrent* tasks.
>
> In short, the rise in the rate of investment—which the economist conjures to summarize the transition—requires a radical shift in the society's *effective attitude* toward fundamental and applied science; toward the initiation of change in productive technique; toward the taking of risk; and toward *the conditions and methods of work.* (20, italics mine)

On the one hand, Rostow's phrase "must be prepared," which he repeats three times in the passage, suggests that before compounded growth can occur, men must be ready either to assume leadership in industry and in banking or to take their place on the factory floor. Once again, modernization depends on a certain shift in cultural attitude: on a society of men *at the ready,* asserting themselves as free subjects making responsible choices at pivotal historical conjunctures. Some choose leadership positions as risk-taking entrepreneurs, and others choose to embrace industrial "conditions and methods of work" as laborers. *Stages of Economic Growth,* however, is also a "how-to" treatise on development. Thus, on the other hand, "must be prepared" can also be read imperatively: men must be made ready to be ready, in an Althusserian sense. The development imperative once again aims for the interiority of subjectivity: some men must be made ready to be ready to become the risk-taking, innovating subjects of capital, while others must be made ready to be ready to become the disciplined subjects of monotonous wage labor. The imperative of development is also a regime of "subjection"—that "process of becoming subordinated by power as well as the process of becoming a subject"—aimed at making "underdeveloped" populations available to capital as never before (Butler, *The Psychic Life of Power* 2). The vast majority of the men of these "traditional societies" in transition "must be prepared" to accept the routinized, narrow, and confining "conditions and methods of work" offered by industrial specialization. Development aid must be geared toward precipitating this transition in subjectivity at a national scale, thereby "making ready" the laboring population of an entire underdeveloped country for capital investment.

Importantly, while Rostow writes his treatise explicitly against Marx—and particularly against Marx's bifurcation of classes into antagonistic capital and labor—he nevertheless returns us to a bifurcated society that resembles Marx's in his analysis of the "sociological and psychological changes . . . at the heart of the creation of the preconditions for take-off" (26).[13] While in the above passage a dissimulating Rostow derives modernization from a society of men acting in concert to attain a mutually desired and equally beneficial goal, a few pages later he reduces these multiple roles to just two: "It would be widely agreed that a new élite—a new leadership—must emerge and be given scope to begin the building of a modern industrial society. . . . And more generally—in rural as in urban areas . . . men must become prepared for a life of change and specialized function" (26). Thus we arrive at a society constituted by a vanguard leadership on one hand, and a mass population subject to the whims of "change and specialized function" on the other.

Here we catch a glimpse of a disturbing resemblance between the regimes of subjection under developmentalism and under revolutionary movements. Although the content of working-class culture could not be more different under the two theoretical models of discursive signification —and that is a *key* difference, as we will see—both oddly depend on vanguard leadership to make men ready either for development or for revolution. Indeed, behind the *foquismo* of the first wave of Latin American revolutionary movements is precisely such a belief in the incendiary leadership possibilities of a vanguard among the masses. Ideally in revolutionary theory (though certainly not always in practice), this vanguard leadership is derived from the masses themselves. Nevertheless, foquismo unwittingly reproduces a developmentalist model of hierarchy and subordination in its theory of subjection. In part 2, I explore at greater length the consequences of this for *foquista* and post-*foquista* revolutionary movements.

Rostow insists that the emergence of a leadership elite is a universal condition that must be achieved by all societies poised for takeoff. The leadership elite he describes, however, is endowed with a particular ethos. This ethos turns out to be, surprisingly enough, the Protestant ethic, even though Rostow goes out of his way to deny that the Protestant ethic as such is a necessary origin of that ethos: "while the Protestant ethic by no means represents a set of values uniquely suitable for modernization, it is essential that the members of this new élite regard modernization as a possible task, serving some end they judge to be ethically good or otherwise advantageous" (26). The rhetorical structure of disavowal, of denying the unique suitability of the Protestant ethic for the task of modernization while nevertheless acknowledging its suitability, precisely serves to solidify it as the Ur-text of modernization, as a key discursive signifier of what one may judge to be "ethically good or otherwise advantageous" within the age of development. Indeed, what is presupposed by the freely executed choices implied in a "basic needs approach" or in "sustainable development" if not a universally agreed on criteria for the "ethically good or otherwise advantageous"?

Thus Rostow repeatedly prescribes a Protestant "set of values" for this emerging bourgeoisie: "The income above minimum levels of consumption, largely concentrated in the hands of those who own land, must be shifted into the hands of those who will spend it on roads and railroads, schools and factories rather than on country houses and servants, personal ornaments and temples" (19). Later Rostow paraphrases Adam Smith for the reader, insisting that "surplus income derived from ownership of land must, somehow, be transferred out of the hands of those who would sterilize it in prodigal living into the hands of the productive men who will invest it in the modern sector and then regularly plough back their profits as output and productivity rise" (24). Given Rostow's rhetoric, this set of values is not simply Protestant but almost puritanical.

In Rostow's transhistorical analysis, the ancien régimes of Japan, China, Russia, and France ("country houses and servants"), as well as the economies of present-day indigenous cultures ("ornaments and temples"), are rendered equally "sterile" before the vigor of the universal "productive men" of nineteenth-century Britain, the United States, and Canada. Indeed, Rostow specifies the four countries in the world who were singly "born free" of the constraints of traditional society: the United States, Australia, New

Zealand, and Canada. These four white-settler nations essentially skip the first two stages of development entirely and are "born" in the takeoff stage, according to Rostow, because "they are created mainly out of a Britain already far along in the transitional process" (17). According to Rostow, the nonconformists of these new worlds, like their British ancestors, are uniquely unencumbered by the prejudices of caste or clan, of superstition or intuition, afflicting the rest of Europe and the world. This discursive binary between prodigal premodern men and productive fully modern ones recurs, as we shall see, in Guevara's and Payeras's diaries, as well as in Malcolm X's autobiography and in Sandinista agrarian policy. All four revolutionary texts represent political consciousness among indigenous peasants or urban blacks as dangerously contaminated by premodern prodigal tendencies and in need of reformation.

In his "Preconditions for Take-Off" chapter, amid the discussion of the formation of extractive industries and social overhead capital, Rostow runs through the gamut of attitudes in a traditional society that must be transformed in order for takeoff to occur—those toward clan and region, toward children, toward work, toward nature. Rostow insists that these cultural factors are more important than the economic factors. And yet, toward the end of the chapter, Rostow observes that even these changes in societal values remain insufficient for bringing about the preconditions for takeoff:

> While in no way denying the significance of some such changes in attitude, value, social structure and expectations, we would emphasize, in addition, the role of the political process and of political motive in the transition.
>
> As a matter of historical fact a reactive nationalism—reacting against intrusion from more advanced nations—has been a most important and powerful motive force in the transition from traditional to modern societies, at least as important as the profit motive. Men holding effective authority or influence have been willing to uproot traditional societies not, primarily, to make more money but because the traditional society failed—or threatened to fail—to protect them from humiliation by foreigners. (26–27)

Rostow illustrates the positive effect of this reactive nationalism with the examples of nineteenth-century Germany, Russia, Japan, and China. However, European imperialism and postwar nationalist liberation movements are also clearly invoked by this passage.

Rostow's reading of reactive nationalism has two important implications. First, his description of reactive nationalism is homoerotically gendered. Nationalism reacts to an "intrusion," to a penetration by a more powerful nation. As such, traditional society is feminized, rendered incapable of resisting this penetration. "Men holding effective authority" over these traditional societies nevertheless renounce them because of this emasculation, because they were incapable of warding off "humiliation by foreigners." As such, reactive nationalism in Rostow's account is implicitly a condition of aggrieved masculinity. Given Rostow's schema, in which most transitions to modernity are the effect of this reactive nationalism, only a chosen few countries exist in a condition of unaggrieved masculinity. European countries that constitute the "advanced nations" perpetrating the intrusion (Britain, France, and the Netherlands), and those few countries "born free," are the sole purveyors of a fully masculine modern nationalism. Far from renouncing the decolonizing nationalisms fueling postwar communist-inspired liberation struggles, Rostow's development theory embraces them as *the* determinant factor in the transition to modernity by folding them into a hierarchical structure of gendered nationalisms.

Second, as a consequence of this homoeroticized desire for the Other's full masculinity, colonialism is rendered a benign initiation into modernity. Immediately following his discussion of reactive nationalism, Rostow explicitly addresses contemporary imperialism, suggesting that the "colonial areas of the southern half of the world" benefited from the "dual demonstration effect" of colonialism (27). While imperial policies "did not always optimize the development of the preconditions for take-off," they did transform "thought, knowledge, institutions and the supply of social overhead capital which moved the colonial society along the transitional path . . . the reality of the *effective power* that went with *an ability to wield modern technology* was demonstrated and *the more thoughtful local people drew appropriate conclusions* . . . and a concept of nationalism, *transcending the old ties to clan or region*, inevitably crystallized around an accumulating resentment of colonial rule" (27–28, italics mine). The manly "effective power" of the colonizer teaches "thoughtful" local people to *desire* it—to desire "an ability to wield modern technology," to emulate the father's knowledge/power.

With the use of phallic language like "intrusion," "humiliation," "effective power," and "to wield," Rostow figures colonialism as, at best, an unsolicited seduction or, at worst, an auspicious rape. In either case, development of the nation is once again metaphorized through the interiority of subjectivity, with colonialism figured as a constitutive trauma initiating adulthood for the underdeveloped subject. Furthermore, this trauma individuates the subject, forcing him to reject vertical ties of a multigenerational "clan" in favor of the horizontal ties of the presumably abstract and egalitarian national community. If colonialism initiates the development of the underdeveloped, then the development process itself is necessarily inscribed by a "dual demonstration effect" of colonial gendering. Nations of the developed Northern Hemisphere are gendered as demonstrative of full masculinity. Meanwhile the emulative underdeveloped nations are gendered as demonstrative of aggrieved masculinity: "without the affront to human and national dignity caused by the intrusion of more advanced powers, the rate of modernization of traditional societies . . . would have been much slower than, in fact, it has been" (28).

Although Rostow explicitly writes his treatise *against* a Marxist-Leninist interpretation of development history, with its imputed outcome in revolution, Rostow nevertheless ends up once again echoing Marx in his evaluation of colonialism as humiliating, but ultimately beneficial, to the colonized country. In Marx's early texts on colonialism, he was, on one hand, harshly critical of the motives for colonialism and of the excesses associated with it, and yet, on the other hand, thoroughly convinced of its "historical necessity as the only means to liberate backward societies from their millennial stagnation and to initiate them in the path of capitalist industrialization and development" (Larrain 46). While Larrain's analysis of Marx's critique of colonialism makes evident that Marx's views on the subject changed dramatically over time, we nevertheless find the following conclusions in key early texts by him:

> England, it is true, in causing a social revolution in Hindustan was actuated only by the vilest interests, and was stupid in her manner of enforcing them. But that is not the question. The question is, can mankind fulfill its destiny without a fundamental revolution in the social state of Asia? (*Surveys from Exile* 306–7; quoted in Larrain 46)

> England has to fulfill a double mission in India: one destructive, the other regenerating—the annihilation of old Asiatic society, and the laying of the material foundations of Western society in Asia. (*Surveys from Exile* 320; quoted in Larrain 46)

> I know that the English millocracy intends to endow India with railways with the exclusive view of extracting at diminishing expenses the cotton and other raw materials for their manufactures. But when you

have once introduced machinery into the locomotion of a country which possesses iron and coals, you are unable to withhold it from fabrication. . . . The railway system will therefore become, in India, truly the forerunner of modern industry. (*Surveys from Exile* 322; quoted in Larrain 46)

Just as Marx believed that the introduction of railroad technology would be the harbinger of a mimetic industrial development in India, so Rostow subsequently placed his faith in the mimesis provoked by "dual demonstration effect" of imperial development: "thoughtful people" will draw "appropriate conclusions." And though Marx may revile the violence of imperialist methods while Rostow glosses over them with phrases like "affront to dignity" or "failure to optimize . . . development," Rostow reiterates Marx's apologia for colonialism as a destructive force that is, in turn, the necessary precursor for regeneration through emulation of Western society. Indeed, Rostow's twentieth-century reactive nationalist who is busy overturning his traditional society's archaic values is the rhetorical descendent of Marx's nineteenth-century British colonizer who annihilates the "old Asiatic society" and its outdated mode of production, social relations, and value system. There is, of course, a difference in focus, as Marx is concerned with the evolution of forces for class struggle, while Rostow is concerned with the aggrieved entrepreneurial elite. There is also a difference in scope, as Marx understands the revolution in Indian productive forces that was caused by colonialism as imperative for global humanity, while Rostow is strictly concerned with the national development of decolonizing countries. Nevertheless, it is as if Rostow writes a redaction of Marx at key points, albeit one that clearly suited the ideological purposes of the Cold War. Thus it should not surprise us that Rostow's subtle and not-so-subtle racialization of the appropriate "ethos" for a nationalist elite would also echo the racialization in Marx's writings on the national question and on colonialism. As Larrain explains, "Difficult to believe as it may seem to some people, it is a fact that Marx and Engels refer rather contemptuously to certain nationalities and countries. Thus the Mexicans are said to be 'lazy,' the Montenegrins are labeled as 'cattle robbers,' the Bedouins are branded as a 'nation of robbers,' and there is reference to the 'hereditary stupidity' of the Chinese" (57).

Rostow's treatise shares more than a similar opinion of colonialism with Marx, however. As I have discussed in chapter 1, it is necessary to distinguish between two distinct *modalities* of developmentalism: the first suggests that all societies move through relatively universal and progressive stages of economic development; the second suggests that this first modality is homologous to (indeed, contingent on) the development of the individual members of society into free, mature, fully conscious, and self-determining subjects. Thus Rostow and Marx share a *structural* resemblance as vying theories of the stages entailed in the development of a universal history, that is, as vying theories of the first modality of developmentalism. Consequently, Rostow's stages of growth—his traditional society, preconditions for takeoff, takeoff, the drive to maturity, and high mass consumption—parallel Marx's mode of production theory of development in his preface to *A Contribution to the Critique of Political Economy*: "In broad outline, the Asiatic, ancient, feudal and modern bourgeois modes of production may be designated as epochs marking progress in the economic development of society. The bourgeois mode of production is the last antagonistic form of the social process of production—antagonistic not in the sense of individual antagonism but of an antagonism that emanates from the individuals' social conditions of existence—but the productive forces developing within bourgeois society create also the material conditions for a solution of this antagonism. The prehistory of human society accordingly closes with this social formation" (Marx, *Early Writings* 426). While Rostow's idealist interpretation of world history falls far from the mark of Marx's material analysis, Rostow nevertheless posits his "high mass consumption" stage precisely as an answer to the implied "solution" of communism in Marx. And just as Marx formulates communism as a social formation in which humanity is universally liberated from "antagonism," so too does Rostow suggest that the age of "high mass consumption" brings an end to antagonism through universalized purchasing power.

It is this teleological drive in Marx's writing on world development that orthodox Marxists adhere to and that Second World development theories issued from. Once again, Larrain provides us with a careful interpretation of Marx's historical materialism as elaborated by "the theoreticians of the Second International both from the German SPD and the Bolshevik party, and which was finally codified by Stalin":

> First, historical materialism is considered [by these theoreticians] to be an extension or application of the principles of dialectical materialism to the study of society and history. Second, consciousness is a reflection of material reality because being, the material world, is prior to and exists independently of consciousness. Third, productive forces tend to develop throughout history and are the chief determining factor of

changes in the economic structure and, through it, of changes in the rest of society. Fourth, history evolves through universal and necessary stages according to the progressive logic of natural-like laws which inevitably lead humankind toward the classless society. (31)

For this orthodox Second World interpretation of Marx's theory of history, the productive forces determine consciousness, historical agency, and change, as evidenced in the second, third, and fourth principles described in the extract. Arguably, this strain of Marxist thought—which sees all agency and change as invariably reflecting and deriving from the "universal and necessary stages" of growth in the productive forces—is as dehistoricizing and idealist as Rostow's attribution of progress to a manly leadership class making the proper choices. Once again we spot the development-revolution convergence of these ideologically opposed, yet similarly deterministic, theories of history represented by Rostow and Second World development principles. Whereas in liberal development's theory of history, thoughtful men direct the transformation of productive forces, in Second World development's theory of history, consciousness merely reflects the productive forces around it, which progress according to "natural-like laws." While in one case unencumbered subjects boldly lead productive forces and in the other unselfconscious subjects simply reflect them, both cases exhibit a *deterministic* relationship between the transformation of subjectivity and the evolution of the productive forces: one irrevocably follows the other.

Larrain admits that there is a strong basis for this orthodox interpretation of historical materialism in Marx's corpus. Indeed, he concedes that the preponderance of Marx's writing asserts the primacy of the productive forces in determining consciousness, agency, and change. Nonetheless Larrain insists that we reject this version of Marx in favor of the Marx who saw the relationship between productive forces and agency as dynamic and dialectical. There are "some essential tensions in Marx's thought," according to Larrain, that are expressed in "the opposition between, on the one hand, a unilinear and universal conception of history which inexorably leads to a preordained end, and, on the other, a conception which is based on human practice and which rejects the interpretation of history as 'a metaphysical subject of which the real human individuals are merely the bearers'" (Larrain 39). Thus Larrain insists that even if the textual evidence in Marx may have supported the Second World's deterministic theories of development, for social critics today, these "tensions in Marx's thought" "must be resolved in favour of a conception which underlines the increasing scope of human practice and rejects the idea of an immanent drive which leads history toward an inevitable end [of revolution]" (39).

Larrain refuses to capitulate to a Second World teleology of history. Instead, his analysis allows us to see the convergence of developmentalism in both Second World socialist and First World liberal orthodoxies. What is interesting about Larrain's analysis is that while he refuses to capitulate to the teleology of historical development in Marx's own writings, and subsequently in orthodox and Second World development theory, Larrain nevertheless accedes to Marx's teleology of consciousness. Larrain rejects the determinism in Marxist interpretations of the first modality of developmentalism, but he quite willingly participates in the deterministic impetus behind Marx's approach to the universal evolution of human consciousness, the second modality of developmentalism. Thus, while Larrain dismisses the stagelike development implied by Marx's "Asiatic, ancient, feudal and modern bourgeois modes of production" narrative, he nonetheless agrees with Marx that there is a schematic evolution of human consciousness that occurs at the moment of the transition from precapitalist modes of production to the capitalist mode of production:

> Whereas in pre-capitalist modes of production based on landed property natural relations still predominate, in the capitalist mode of production "social, historically evolved elements predominate." This means that before capitalism human beings were far less capable of consciously altering the course of history and they were mostly driven by social and economic forces of which they were not aware and of which consequently they could not seek control.
>
> With capitalism on the other hand the possibility for conscious human participation in shaping the future of society is greatly increased. This means that the outcome of socio-political processes is not determined solely by natural relations but is shaped by conscious human intervention. True, even in pre-capitalist modes of production, human intervention was crucial because nothing in history can happen without human practice. But it was not a fully conscious human practice in that human beings were unable to understand the real causes of their actions and set themselves goals which could not be achieved. (Larrain 35–36)

Larrain insists on a "qualitative change" in consciousness, and I would agree that forms of consciousness are qualitatively different at different historical moments, or in different modes of production (39). For instance, slaves in ancient Greece struggled for different forms of freedom from different forms of oppression than do indigenous peasants in Guatemala who are tied to capitalist plantations through debt peonage and extraeconomic forms of coercion. However, in Larrain's assessment, such a change in consciousness is not so much qualitative as it is quantitative. While precapitalist subjects are "less capable" of historical intervention because they lack an "aware[ness]" of their own material circumstances, under capitalism subjects find their ability for historical intervention "greatly increased" because they are finally "fully conscious" of their own exploitation. The consciousness of which he speaks does not seem to change qualitatively; rather, human subjects simply have more or less of it depending on the historical era in which they live. Continuing with my example, can we confidently argue that slaves in ancient Greece were less aware of their particular form of servitude than indigenous peasant subalterns in Guatemala, or less innovative in their political and cultural struggles for their very different form of freedom? Thus I suggest that Larrain is participating in the second modality of developmentalism in his assessment of the universal transformations in consciousness that occur under different modes of production.[14] Not only is his less-to-more model of transformation idealist, but it is deterministic, as well, since capitalist relations of production inevitably produce "more" consciousness, a greater ability for self-reflection and for historical agency. Larrain ends up formulating a relationship between mode of production and subject formation that is as deterministic as the relationship proposed between productive forces and subjectivity in Second World or orthodox Marxist theories of history.

While Larrain's assessment of transitions in consciousness might appear to be a moot point, as we would be hard pressed to find a society today that had eluded the capitalist mode of production, he nevertheless makes available just such a conclusion. Therein lies the more disturbing, if unintentional, consequence of Larrain's formulation that human consciousness increases decisively in the transition from precapitalism to capitalism. Indeed, Ernesto Laclau has convincingly argued that capitalism *requires* the coexistence of other, seemingly precapitalist, modes of production for the rate of profit to continue to grow on a global scale. Accordingly a host of Third World nomadic farmers and subsistence producers could easily be classified as "precapitalist" formations, and indeed many rural societies have been classified as such by marauding development specialists of all ideological ilks. Thus Larrain's own representation of this transition in consciousness unwittingly participates in the inevitable racialization of "premodern" particularity, as he unintentionally opens the door for the subordination of peoples deemed to exist in precapitalist modes of production and to suffer from a "less[er] capab[ility]" for understanding and improving their situation. As I will discuss in the following chapters, rural subalterns were repeatedly seen as existing in isolated, premodern conditions by revolutionary nationalists in the Americas who were hell-bent on initiating the subaltern's entry into modern rationality according to a less-to-more model of consciousness. Although Larrain breaks free from the orthodoxy of Second World development's theory of history, he paradoxically succumbs to the orthodoxy of the second modality of developmentalism. Implicit in his view is the principle that men become more fully human with each subsequent stage of economic development. Furthermore, this blind spot in Larrain's own Marxist analysis allows us to see the seductive power of this second modality of developmentalism, for in the final analysis, First World liberal, Second World socialist, and even Western Marxist development paradigms all fall under its spell when theorizing a regime of subjection.

Continuing on, then, in our search for the discursive family of statements that accompany this regime of subjection across ideological divides, let us return to the manifest subject of liberal postwar development theory as evinced by Rostow. In his theory of history, after the crucial transition period in which the preconditions for takeoff are established by manly reactive nationalists, modernization evolves much as one might expect. During the "takeoff into self-sustained growth" stage, these risk-taking—if slightly prudish—"productive men" take the lead of a transitional society: transforming social and political institutions, plowing back profits into social overhead spending, expanding production, and creating wages that in turn create demand. During the "drive towards maturity," a nation invests in more social overhead spending, diversifies industries, creates *more* wages and *more* demand, until finally reaching a stage in which all citizens of the nation are engaged in high mass consumption.

Although Rostow's fourth chapter on the takeoff into self-sustained growth is the most often anthologized, it is this "Preconditions for Take-Off" chapter that best illustrates the age of development's new discursive regime of subjection for formerly colonized and neocolonized areas of the world. This new set of metaphors, themes, and tropes for the formation of modern subjectivity is deeply nationalist and vehemently egalitarian, as we have seen. Indeed, it is the prior sovereignty of the nation and dignity of all individuals that is presumably aroused by the violation of colonialism in Rostow's account of reactive nationalism. As a response to postwar national liberation movements, development's new regime of modern subjectivity must register the political affront of colonialism. Consequently, development promises to the periphery an alternative mode of integration, one that is predicated on national sovereignty and respects human equality—one that promises full masculinity to underdeveloped subjects. Indeed, a condition of aggrieved masculinity is a recurrent metaphor in the autobiographies of revolutionaries who, as we shall see, seek the promise of a fully masculine, modern nationalism for themselves and their societies through Marxist-Leninist or separatist revolutions.

Even as modernization theory advocated political sovereignty for the colonial world, it provided an alibi for European colonialism. Liberal development's new regime of subjection, illustrated in Rostow, bore the trace of colonialism's racial and sexual legacy. In its chain of discursive signification—in those recurrent metaphors, themes, and tropes identified by Rostow—we find that colonialism's differences in kind between the "white" race and the "lower" races were relativized and nationalized in development's domain of cultural attitudes conducive to good judgment and modernization. Although a Protestant ethos was not uniquely conducive to such good judgment, it became the baseline against which the character of all other *national* bourgeois would be judged. In turn, the discursive terms of gender and sexuality were reformulated. Under British and Anglo-American colonialism, the hyper-civilized races of Asia were seen as degenerative, while the African and New World races were eroticized for their excess sexuality. Under the new discursive regime of development, gendered sexuality has been allegorized through a hierarchy of nationalisms. The aggrieved masculinity of reactive nationalisms was subordinated to, and yet oddly enabled by, the full masculinity of the originary nationalisms. Thus we have left behind the social Darwinism of British and Anglo-American colonialism, in which evolution is determined by one's proximity to an appropriately potent whiteness, without fully abandoning its racial legacy. In its stead we have a model of development in which modernity was determined by one's proximity to this risk-taking, decision-making, frugal, nonornamental (i.e., elemental), productive, fully masculine, national subject. At the opposite end of the continuum of equally human subjects was the rule-bound, doctrine-led, adorned (i.e., supplemental), profligate, emasculated, clannish subject of the underdeveloped traditional societies.

It should not surprise us that development's regime of subjection dovetails with the capitalist mode of production of value (in its bifurcated culture of free will), or universalizes an Anglocentric experience (in its privileging of Protestant ethics). It is perhaps even expected that development discourse would retain the trace of colonialism's racialized discourse of civilization. What should surprise, however, is the remarkable resemblance between this subject of development and the subject of revolution put forth in the United States and Latin America during the 1970s and 1980s. Many of the metaphors, themes, and tropes identified in Rostow as the key discursive terms for developmentalist subjection appear as well in the texts of revolutionaries. In both revolutionary and developmentalist regimes of subjection, we find the prescriptive representations of agency as free will, of consciousness as autonomous and self-determining, of progressive transformation as transcendence over the restrictions of clan or caste (ethnos). Similarly—or rather consequently—in both we find a call to vanguard leadership predicated on a binary division between a mass of prodigal men in need of reformation and an elite of productive men at the ready to implement reform. Finally, in both models, we find that a condition of aggrieved masculinity compels the desire for transformation and reform. I am not suggesting revolutionary discourse is derivative of development. To the contrary, I am suggesting that both discursive models depend on a particular rendition of fully modern masculinity as the basis for full citizenship in either a developed or a revolutionary society. Further analysis of this discursive resemblance or coincidence between the promise of development and the promise of revolution—and its unfortunate consequences for the latter—is elaborated in the ensuing chapters.

For now let us consider what these reiterative gestures in Rostow's schema accomplish for the age of development. Rostow reduces development to a series of ethical choices made by a risk-taking vanguard leadership and a well-disciplined cadre of workers. At the moment when colonial powers were losing the practical control necessary for maintaining economic hegemony over vast populations and territories, the First World, I suggest, established ethical control over the decolonized spaces through development's discursive regime of subjection. I use the term *ethical* because, as a regime of subjection, development paradigms subsequently made "progress" a matter of individuated and collective choice outside of geopolitical or economic constraints: the choice of embracing technology (development through import substitution), the choice of shedding feudal mind-sets (demonstration-effect development), the choice to save money (export-led growth), the choice to be independent (import substitution), the choice to invest capital in social overhead costs (basic needs approach), the choice between clan and nation (dual societies models), and, most important, the choice to be productive rather than prodigal. As such, the discursive regime illustrated by Rostow paradoxically absolves the First World from responsibility for the consequences of colonialism, even as the First World is credited with inciting the desire to choose to enter the age of development.

In modernization theory, as in most second- and third-generation development paradigms, Third World countries were seen as traditional societies or as societies at Rostow's "preconditions for takeoff" stage. Thus these new nations were still cluttered on one end of the human continuum: outside of modernization or just on the brink of entering it. Tautologically, development theories themselves produced this diagnosis. Thus, Rostow and other development theorists claimed that traditional societies simultaneously occupied the contradictory positions of "self-sufficiency" and "limited productivity" (5). In what sense can a self-sufficient society also be said to be *limited* in its productivity? Limited for whom? This contradiction can only be resolved *outside* of a developmentalist narrative, in the interest of universal capitalism to bring this self-sufficient entity, with its limited productivity, into full production for the accumulation of capital on an international scale. That is, production can be viewed as limited only from the perspective of an expanding capitalism that this limited production eludes.

Early development theories like Rostow's placed "traditional" or "underdeveloped" nations outside the productivist discourse of modernization so that it could then become the joint mission of international and national development agencies to bring these new nations into discourse: to name the traditional, to define the conditions of underdevelopment, to demarcate underdevelopment geographically, to inspect it, to enact policy around it, to police it, to harness its productivity—in effect, to contain the anxiety produced by the Third World's decolonizing presence.

From Rostow to McNamara and Back Again

Decolonization alone was not the principal threat to the capitalist world system, as colonialism was fast becoming inefficient given the rise of multinational capitalism (Magdoff, "Imperialism" 11–39). The establishment of the Soviet Union as a superpower, however, with its consequent post–World War II realignment of global economic and ideological forces, did fundamentally threaten the extension and intensification of capitalism. The "free" capitalist world, and particularly the United States, countered the rise of communism in the decolonizing spaces not only militarily but also dialectically, with the birth of a new field and a new regime of subjection. On one hand, development discourse—of which modernization theory is just one, albeit important, early iteration—was simply a rearticulation of Enlightenment concepts of technological, progressive history and world-historical agency. On the other hand, it was something distinctly new. Development discourse recognized the gross economic inequality that exists between the First World and the Third World and *managed it,* just as Rostow's discursive regime of subjection recognized nationalist revolutionary fervor and accounted for it with an evolutionary narrative of progress.[15]

As a management strategy in the 1960s, 1970s, and 1980s, development discourse, with its various paradigms, well served the ends of a Cold War containment. Development paradigms from a wide spectrum of liberal orientations, and even across ideological divides, consistently rendered development synonymous with the founding of the nation-state in decolonizing spaces. Consequently, when Robert Strange McNamara took over as president of the World Bank in 1969, after serving as U.S. secretary of defense for eight years, he saw increased intervention in the internal affairs of a decolonized state and national sovereignty as entirely compatible, if such intervention took place under the guise of development. On 30 September 1968, in his first address to the WB's board of governors, in Washington, D.C., McNamara proposed expanding First World presence in the Third World under the bank's auspices:

> The work of the Bank will also be increased because in many of the countries in which we will now be investing, there is no well established Development Plan or Planning Organization. We shall try, in conjunction with other sources of funds, to help these countries to develop plans and to adopt wise and appropriate polices for development—in some cases by establishing resident missions . . . but always remembering that *it is their country, their economy, their culture and their aspirations which we seek to assist.* (McNamara 9)

Between 1969 and 1973, McNamara's WB "assisted" considerably in these sovereign aspirations. During his first five years as president, McNamara fully doubled the funds lent by the WB during the previous five years (McNamara 6).

By all accounts, McNamara transformed the bank and its mission during his tenure (1969–1981). He spent his first week as president poring over the bank's statistics for each borrowing country, demanding to know why so few funds were being disbursed, and why politically strategic countries in Asia and Africa were altogether overlooked. McNamara immediately ordered his staff to formulate a development plan for each borrowing country as if "the only limit on our activities [is] the capacity of our member countries to use our assistance effectively and to repay our loans" (McNamara, quoted in George and Sabelli 40–42).[16] During his first five years, the WB expanded its staff by 120 percent; it borrowed more funds on capital markets during that time than it had during the whole of its previous existence. Between 1947 and 1968, the WB had financed 708 projects at a total cost of $10.7 billion. In the five years between 1969 and 1973, McNamara's bank undertook 760 new projects costing $13.4 billion (McNamara 236; George and Sabelli 42).[17]

Not only did he significantly increase the funds and staff available for instituting development projects, but McNamara also reformulated the very concept of development. As George and Sabelli put it, "Never before had the Bank conceived of 'development's task' as relieving the poverty of severely deprived men and women, individually or *en masse*. Development's task had always been making sure that states had sufficient electrical power, transport, communications, et cetera, to become 'modern' and more like the already industrialized countries" (38–39). To implement this newly expanded mission of development, McNamara introduced the multiproject integrated development program, coordinating various levels of development intervention within one nation (George and Sabelli 43). These integrated development programs linked, for example, a national project for introducing green revolution technology in agro-industries to a regional dam project for restructuring irrigation patterns, and, in turn, linked these national and regional projects to communal loans for farmers reorienting their production, and to monies for female counterparts to develop artisan skills, thereby expanding the export capacities of each individual family. What George and Sabelli's historical research allows us to see is how, under McNamara's auspices, development as a decolonization management strategy, on the one hand, and development as a regime of subjection, on the other, were seamlessly conjoined and institutionalized in the bank's apparatus.

Under McNamara's new bank mandate, First World and Third World governments created national, regional, and local offices dedicated to studying the causes of underdevelopment, and to coordinating policies to combat it at every level of societal relation. Liberal economists, sociologists, anthropologists, missionaries, and freelancers—the bureaucrats and good Samaritans of the development apparatus—proliferated in both hemispheres, dedicating themselves with religious zeal to administering development projects, small and large, in decolonizing spaces. "Development studies" became a field of inquiry in all major First World and Third World universities. Meanwhile independent think tanks were founded across the globe to come up with development strategies as well, and nongovernmental aid organizations sprung up like weeds to assist in the efforts to implement them. Most of these disparate development efforts were coordinated under the auspices of international agencies with global reach, like the WB and the IMF, under the banner of sovereignty.

"Development Is Peace"? A Response from the Periphery

Upon becoming World Bank president, John McNamara declared that "as Secretary of Defense I had observed, and spoken publicly about, the connection between world poverty and unstable relations among nations; as a citizen of the world I had come to sense the truth in Pope Paul's dictum that 'Development is Peace.'" (3). By 1968, though, it was already apparent that development was producing anything but "peace." As noted scholar of Mexican development Cynthia Hewitt Alcántara has noted, "If economic 'backwardness' and social 'traditionalism' were really nothing more than the result of isolation from the mainstream of technological and socio-economic change associated with modernization in early industrial centers, as liberalism or structural functionalism held, there was no way to explain why the process of urbanization and industrialization moving with varying degrees of speed across the underdeveloped world from the 1940s onward was apparently not producing prosperous and relatively egalitarian industrial democracies, in which everyone received some relative material benefit from modernization, but rather increasingly polarized societies composed of an opulent 'modern' and an impoverished and excluded 'traditional' sector" (*Boundaries and Paradigms* 159–60). Thus, by the mid-1960s, early dependency theory was seriously challenging the liberalism of first- and second-generation development paradigms. And yet, as a diverse group of theorists from all over Latin America, they were not simply reacting to strategies like modernization theory or demonstration-effect development. Genealogies of development often represent dependency theorists strictly along a North-South axis of intellectual exchange, as emerging out of a Euro-U.S. Marxist tradition or as responding to liberal development theorists from the First World.[18] Although dependency theory constitutes a pivotal moment in the dialectical relationship between development discourse and revolutionary thought, the dependency critique grew out of a Latin American tradition of South-South intellectual exchange in the social sciences dating back to at least the *indigenismo* movement of the 1920s.

Just as dependency theory grew out of a South-South axis of intellectual exchange, it went on to inform the revolutionary thought of almost all Latin American national liberation struggles, as well as a considerable number of liberation struggles and postcolonial governments in Africa, Asia, and even the United States. This school of development theory was also highly influential with many of the progressive Latin American governments that came to power during this postwar period, such as Salvador Allende's Chile, and were subsequently deposed by U.S.-backed, right-wing military coups. Indeed, many dependency theorists, such as Fernando Henrique Cardoso, Enrique Dussel, and Enzo Falleto, wrote in exile, having fled the often deadly persecution of the military regimes in their home countries.

In this post–World War II period of intellectual fecundity for the international Left, dependency theory held sway over the perspectives of millions of political and guerrilla activists all over the Third World. Indeed, it is from dependency theory that the more popular paradigms of "neocolonialism" in Latin America and "internal colonialism" in the United States emerged and took their form. Thus I turn to dependency theory at this point in my analysis of the discursive regimes of subjection produced by development theory and revolutionary thought because dependency theory occupied a prominent position in both discourses. I suggest that dependency theory was a nodal point in the discursive imbrication of revolution and development. And while dependency theorists rarely, if ever, took poetic license in their analysis, as Rostow did with such idealist flourish, their materialist paradigm nevertheless implied a subject (or subjects) of development, and a subject (or subjects) of underdevelopment. Before proceeding to the analysis of dependency's models of subjectivity and consciousness, however, I begin with an analysis of their economic and epistemic critique of liberal development theories.

With most Latin American countries achieving independence in the first half of the nineteenth century, postcolonial modernization was well under way in the Americas by the beginning of the twentieth century. The first Latin American industrial boom took place between the world wars, before modernization policies found their formal articulation in development discourse. By the late 1940s, modernization in Latin America—import substitution industrialization, technology transfer, infrastructure building, urbanization, enclosure, proletarianization—was not only in full swing but also had already generated significant internal critique.

The dependency school's immediate intellectual predecessors, then, were not Keynes and Rostow but the Economic Commission for Latin

America (ECLA). As one of the first international development agencies created by the United Nations in the late 1940s, ECLA's mission was to promote modernization and industrialization throughout Latin America. As Larrain notes, under the chairmanship of Raúl Prebisch, ECLA began to theorize the limitations inherent in capitalist development for Latin American countries: "According to [ECLA's] analysis, the terms of trade are consistently deteriorating for raw material exporters because they sell their products at international prices which are below their real value, whereas central countries sell their industrial products at prices above their real value. There is therefore unequal exchange between the centre and periphery, a terminology which they were the first to introduce. This means that most developing countries must export an increased amount of raw materials each year in order to be able to continue to import the same amount of industrial goods" (13).

ECLA initiated an organic critique of the development processes that were already under way in several Latin American countries, especially those with more diversified economies, such as Argentina, Brazil, Chile, and Mexico. Following in ECLA's intellectual tracks, by the late 1950s, social sciences in Latin America had turned to the study of colonial relations as a way of understanding the economic and social similarities among independent states not only in Latin America but also throughout the decolonizing Third World. Dependency theory specifically investigated the *acceleration* of development that had occurred in Latin America between the world wars. Since at least the 1930s, many nationalist governments had followed the general formula of promoting export expansion for the accumulation of capital that would subsequently be invested in import substitution industry: the technical recipe for self-sustained growth. (In fact, despite the income disparities in promoting the *expansion* of the export of raw materials to fund the development of national industries made evident by their own analysis, ECLA nevertheless continued to recommend import substitution as the best avenue for economic development.) Thus, during the 1960s and 1970s, the dependency position gained political currency with both First World and Third World governments, as well as with development theorists and leftist intellectuals, because of the contradictions generated by the *practice* of modernization strategies—contradictions that dependency theorists addressed systematically.

Dependency theory challenged the essence of liberal development theories by asserting that the traditional and the modern, the underdeveloped and the developed, the periphery and the center, are not mutually exclusive categories. Development's progressivist history necessarily constituted the traditional system and the modern system as mutually exclusive and static categories that can be objectively described. In the United States, second-generation development theories like Rostow's had given rise to a proliferation of social science literature during the 1960s and 1970s based on the firm belief that "the traditional" was the primary obstacle to development.[19] Indeed, across the social science disciplines the traditional or underdeveloped society was described in terms similar to those observed in Rostow's theory. If modern or developed societies were highly differentiated, then the traditional or underdeveloped societies lacked differentiation. If developed societies consisted of highly specialized and autonomous social units operating in the economic, familial, political, and religious spheres, then underdeveloped societies had yet to even differentiate between these spheres. Once exposed to modernization, according to this second generation, the traditional societies moved toward the desired economic and social differentiation and specialization (i.e., the demonstration-effect principle in Rostow's reactive nationalism). Accordingly, the traditional needed to be fully displaced if modernization were to occur.

In contrast, for dependency theorists, the traditional and the modern were historically, economically, and epistemologically intertwined conditions. Dependency theory began by challenging development theory's fundamentally ahistorical treatment of change and community in Latin American rural areas. In the mid-1960s, Rodolfo Stavenhagen critiqued two operative fallacies in the sociology of underdeveloped nations that proceeded from the static understanding of the modern and the traditional as mutually exclusive categories (83–97).[20] According to Stavenhagen, sociologists of underdevelopment eclipse the complexity of Third World spaces by designating entire nations as "traditional" because of the predominance of a rural economy. This masks the national and international role of urban centers within these nations and leads to the misconclusion by some sociologists, as Stavenhagen notes, that "up to two-thirds of the world's population lives in static, archaic, change resistant folk societies" (84). Secondly, development theories deployed the concept of a "dual society," in which a modern and a traditional sector are said to exist independently of each other within a single national space (84). These alternate visions of reality served similar purposes. They offered the Third World two choices of national identity: one embryonic, one fractured.

Stavenhagen attributes these logical fallacies to the privileged "time-centric" gaze of early development theorists who saw change as a recent phenomenon in the lives of rural populations in Latin America:

> Many students of social change in underdeveloped areas not only suffer from an ethnocentric fallacy but also from a time-centric illusion. In fact, it is frequently thought that change is a recent phenomenon, perhaps dating from the end of the Second World War, that the so-called traditional communities are only just now, as Hoselitz (1964) puts it, "being drawn into a social framework with much more complex and more highly stratified structures." It is believed or at least implied, that before the present-day processes of "modernization," rural society was essentially static, and the term 'traditional' is used to refer to some sort of eternal or perhaps slowly drifting type of social organization which is only now awakening under the impact of external innovations. (85)

For first- and second-generation development theorists, change begins once capital fixes its gaze anew (after colonialism) on the periphery. This, in turn, dovetails with a refusal on the part of development agencies to recognize the consequences of colonialism, for decolonized or decolonizing societies have miraculously remained untouched until the arrival of postwar development agents.

By contrast, Stavenhagen interprets "modernization" in the Third World as a process that begins in the fifteenth century with the expansion of Europe and the integration of rural economies to the urban centers within and beyond the regional colonies. Subsistence economies of the period, he argues, were not closed economies, but economies that had been historically and intricately involved in national and international production. At the very least, subsistence economies are involved in capitalism through consumption. More often than not, however, subsistence economies developed as necessary corollaries to capitalist production. Indeed, as Stavenhagen's historical analysis makes clear, creating or maintaining subsistence economies was most often the official colonial or state policy, as in the case of colonial Spain *and* postcolonial Latin America (85). Subsistence economies thus continue to provide a flexible labor supply for monocultural commercial agriculture in need of seasonal labor. They also help depress wages on a national level by providing cheap food for urban centers, thereby keeping industrial costs artificially low (86). Variables between modern and traditional sectors, then, cannot be the result of isolation; rather, these differences result from a *single* process of global modernization: "Underdevelopment—not as a state-of-being but as a process—evolved hand in hand with development in these areas" (85).

Stavenhagen challenges the progressive character of modern technology, as well. The technology of colonial agriculture and cash cropping often displaced sophisticated techniques of irrigation and erosion control, as in pre-Hispanic America. Stavenhagen, however, does not romanticize peasant farmers of yore. Rather, his analysis emphasizes that most if not all of the indigenous farming communities in colonized America, Africa, and Asia have long since been exposed to cash cropping, wage labor, jeans, working women, radio, migration, and the disintegration of the extended family as the site of production, consumption, and authority. Stavenhagen, like dependency theorists to follow, disrupts development discourse's facile characterization of change, especially technological change, as progressive.

Stavenhagen's insistence on the simultaneity of the "traditional" and the "modern," foreshadowing hybridity theorists such as Néstor García Canclini, begins to undo the binary construction of primitive consciousness/ modern consciousness in development's regime of subjection as evidenced by Rostow. If the development of national export agriculture, industrialization, and urbanization has historically depended on the cheap labor and food goods provided by subsistence farming and impoverished rural communities, then "traditional societies" can no longer teleologically precede urban modernity. Instead, these two terms depend on each other discursively for their mutual constitution, and the entire chain of signification— development's regime of subjection—is broken. The narrative of progress implied by the polarization of the terms "traditional" and "modern" is interrupted by Stavenhagen's formulation, obviating the issue of choice and free will at the level of subjection. The (under)developed subject cannot simply choose to enter history, to cross over to the other side of the binary. The structure of colonial modernization processes constrains him. More importantly, the subject of development is no longer an autonomous and self-controlling agent, as his very condition of modernity is enabled by the labor and production of the underdeveloped subject. The operative fallacies in development's masculinist regime of subjection are exposed.

Dependency theorists are credited with having clarified the structure of Third World economic dependence on the First World. However, they also exposed the developed First World's economic *and discursive* dependence on the underdeveloped Third World. Whereas Stavenhagen focused on the legacy of colonialism inherent in the urban-rural relationship within the contemporary national setting, subsequent dependency theorists, such as Theotonio Dos Santos, Celso Furtado, Fernando Henrique Cardoso, Ernesto Laclau, and André Gunder Frank, considered colonialism's effect on the (underdeveloped) national economy within the (developed) international capitalist system.

In his often anthologized "The Development of Underdevelopment," for example, Frank inverts the terms of development discourse. Exposure to colonial development inevitably led to gross stagnation for the colony, he argues. Frank enumerates the various contemporary examples of "ultra-underdevelopment": the sugar-exporting West Indies and northeastern Brazil, for example; or the former mining regions of Minas Gerais in Brazil, the highlands in Peru and Bolivia, or Guanajuato and Zacatecas in Mexico. Like Stavenhagen before him, Frank argues convincingly that this condition of underdevelopment resulted precisely from intensive early contact, rather than lack of contact, with the "modern" world (27–28). Each of these regions, existing in conditions of extreme economic stagnation and poverty during the 1960s, had experienced a "golden age" in colonial times. They had each sustained thriving commercial economies in the sixteenth and seventeenth centuries, equipped with the most sophisticated technologies for growing, processing, and mining available at that time. Elites in these regions engaged in trade relations on a global scale with European metropoles in England, Spain, Portugal, and France.

These currently underdeveloped regions were once famous worldwide for their sugar and silver and had "provided the life blood of mercantile and industrial capitalist development—in the metropolis" (28). However, these same regions were also the site of extraeconomic forms of labor exploitation (the latifundium) and of an extraction of surplus so complete that this development for export prevented the creation of a wage economy and the reinvestment of capital necessary for diversification.[21] For Frank, it was this experience of hyper-exposure to the most sophisticated technologies and extractive markets of the colonial period that generated the conditions of underdevelopment in the contemporary period.[22] Once the markets for these goods had ceased to exist, or a permanent drop in the prices for these goods decreased profitability, local economies stagnated. Much like Stavenhagen before him, Frank determined that the underdevelopment in these regions is thus not a lack of development but a *development of development*.

Frank's "development of underdevelopment" was particularly influential with those nationalists in the United States who were concerned with understanding the impoverished conditions of African American, Latino, Native American, and Asian American minorities. The "internal colonialism" model borrowed heavily from Frank's theoretical model in explaining the poverty and stagnation in the South's former cotton belt and in the abandoned mining regions of the Southwest. Robert Blauner's "Colonized and Immigrant Minorities" borrowed directly from Frank, and theorists and activists such as Stokely Carmichael and Charles Hamilton were clearly influenced by the general circulation of Frank's ideas in their groundbreaking *Black Power: The Politics of Liberation*.

Still, economic and social theorists like Theotonio Dos Santos, Fernando Henrique Cardoso, Enzo Faletto, and Celso Furtado critiqued Frank's construction of underdevelopment as the unqualified condition of Latin American economies. Indeed, it was this group of theorists who coined the term "dependent development" and fully elaborated its operative premises. They argued that Frank's model of underdevelopment made colonial and neocolonial imperialism a never-ending cycle of penetration by foreign capital for the extraction of raw materials and surplus, involving temporary periods of growth followed by increased stagnation. Dependent development presented a far more dynamic interpretation of capitalist development in the periphery, with a complex rendering of the contradictory interests of foreign and national bourgeois, civilian and military states, and the proletarian and peasant classes.

In his famous article "Dependency and Development in Latin America," as in his similarly titled book coauthored with Enzo Faletto, Cardoso reconsiders the relevance of the dichotomy between development and underdevelopment in the contemporary global capitalist economy: "Foreign investment no longer remains a simple zero-sum game of exploitation as was the pattern in classical imperialism. . . . it is not difficult to show that *development* and *monopoly penetration* in the industrial sectors of dependent economics are not incompatible. The idea that there occurs a kind of development of under-development, apart from the play on words, is not helpful. In fact, *dependency, monopoly capitalism* and *development* are not contradictory terms: there occurs a kind of *dependent capitalist development* in the sectors of the Third World integrated into the new forms of monopolistic expansion" (Cardoso 89). Cardoso remaps Lenin's theory of imperialism from the perspective of the periphery, one already deeply inculcated in the classically defined terms of modernization. With rapidly industrializing urban sectors, technologically sophisticated "traditional" sectors, participation by local bourgeois in multinational capitalist enterprise, and the formation of a working-class elite with expanded consumption capacity, the periphery is no longer simply a *complementary* mode of economic production to capitalism in the core. In Lenin's treatment of imperialism, expansion is fueled by the impossibility of reproducing capital within the confines of a core nation-state in which conditions of monopoly capitalism have taken hold. Internal limits to capital investment drive capital abroad, and this capital is invested primarily in industry for the extraction of raw materials necessary for the reproduction of capital in the center. For Cardoso, however, the periphery is no longer simply the site of extraction for raw materials. The periphery also contains markets, import substitution industry, and even export industries.

This transformation in the periphery does not mark a significant departure from imperialist relations for Cardoso, though it does reconfigure the terms of the First World's domination over Latin American economies. In a Latin American dependent economy—which is already an industrialized economy—capital cannot complete the cycle of its own reproduction without returning to the metropole. Cardoso argues that Latin American capital must always return to the metropole to purchase the technology (i.e., improvements in capital goods, new production methods, etc.) on which increased profit margins and further industrialization hinge. Either as license fees, as joint venture costs, or as direct purchase costs, capital generated by businesses in the periphery returns to corporations in the center to purchase technology that Latin American industry cannot produce on its own. This First World monopoly on technology not only siphons off this much needed capital from the Latin American economies but also becomes a method of control. Thus development theory's universal plea for the underdeveloped world to accept technology from the First World functions as a policing technique, as an administered technological obsolescence that determines the terms of dependence.

Dependency theorists destabilize all the established criteria of development discourse: underdevelopment and development are simultaneously modern; underdevelopment is neither original (precursor) nor traditional (quaint); development is neither autonomous nor nationally bounded; the diffusion of technology from the core to the periphery neither is a benevolent gesture nor holds the promise of independence. Dependency theory denaturalizes capitalist development by disrupting the linear progress of the stages of development narrative and denationalizes development theory by insisting on a truly global analysis. Nations are no longer destined to pass from one stage to another like Aristotle's acorn destined to become a tree, nor do they go forth in their own development independently.

As such, dependency theorists did more than intervene in idealist historiography. From Stavenhagen's early formulations to Cardoso's fully articulated paradigm, dependency theorists also implicitly challenged the derivative nature of development's discursive regime of subjection. Dependency theory exposed the complex, intertwined relationship between developed and underdeveloped subjects. No longer is the underdeveloped consciousness expected to formulaically emulate developed consciousness as an avenue to modernity. And instead of a relationship of unilateral derivation, the very agency and model of consciousness of the subject of First World is fully dependent on that of the Third.

Beyond its discursive reach, dependency theory influenced the economic policy of a number of reformist and revolutionary governments in Latin America. Castro's Cuba, Allende's Chile, Michael Manley's Jamaica, Cheddi Jagan's Guyana, Maurice Bishop's Grenada, and the Sandinistas in Nicaragua all incorporated some degree of its analysis into their national development plans for breaking the cycle of dependence. Many of the school's preeminent theorists held government posts in these administrations before they were overthrown by U.S.-backed right-wing military coups. Indeed, the vehemence of the United States' multiple and costly counterinsurgency campaigns betrays the perceived danger of dependency theory. Paradoxically, even U.S.-backed military dictatorships, such as Brazil's in the 1970s, found themselves using dependency theory in their efforts to "catch up" with the First World technologically.

Given its geopolitical influence as a form of revolutionary analysis in Latin America, dependency theory compelled a dialectical reformulation in the discursive terms of development. Indeed, according to development theorist and intellectual historian Colin Leys, the development apparatus was compelled to incorporate the terms of the dependency critique:

> The early 1970s thus became—briefly—an era of dependency theory. Or, to be more accurate, in intellectual circles, especially among students in Europe and in Third World countries, dependency theory held the initiative; and eventually even the international "development community" felt obliged to accommodate some of its perspectives: for instance, the International Labour Office's 1972 call for "redistribution with growth" and the World Bank's adoption in 1973 of the principle of meeting "basic needs" were both influenced by the (unacknowledged) impact of dependency thinking. (11–12)

By exposing the deleterious consequences of "demonstration-effect" development on Latin America, the dependency school indirectly ushered in a third phase of development theory. Case study after case study by dependency theorists thoroughly illustrated that despite impressive GNP growth because of rapid industrialization, structural inequalities not only persisted but were aggravated during the first "decade of development" in the 1960s. Income disparity between rich and poor countries increased during this decade, as did income disparities between bourgeois classes and the working and peasant classes within Latin American countries. Consequently, by his 1973 address to the World Bank's board of governors, McNamara had explicitly recognized "the need to reorient development policies in order to provide a more equitable distribution of the benefits of economic growth" (McNamara 243). Alternately called "basic needs approach," "growth with equity," or "redistribution with growth," a third generation of development theories and paradigms required new modes of assessing social "maladies" (illiteracy, malnutrition, population growth), and new indices for measuring growth and development (access to credit, to public services, to potable water) (McNamara 243–56).

If McNamara incorporated some of the dependency critique during his second five-year term as president of the World Bank, he necessarily missed the point of its conclusions: that monopolistic tendencies within global capitalism will forever limit the potential of industrial development in the Third World, as well as skew its benefits to national and international elites. Instead, McNamara reiterated his faith in the WB and in development as liberation. Indeed, he repeatedly chided the developed world for hampering the WB in this effort by failing to contribute sufficient funds for lending, most notably in his 1973 address:

> I have heard it said in the developed countries—in the United States and elsewhere—that their domestic problems are so pressing that they require exclusive claim on the immense incremental wealth which will accrue to their societies. . . . But I believe that such critics of additional assistance to the poorer nations, when citing the needs of their own cities and countryside, fail to distinguish between two kinds of poverty: what might be termed relative poverty and absolute poverty.
>
> Relative poverty means simply that some countries are less affluent than other countries, or that some citizens of a given country have less personal abundance than their neighbors. . . . But absolute poverty is . . . a condition of life so limited as to prevent realization of the potential of genes with which one is born; a condition of life so degrading as to insult human dignity—and yet a condition of life so

common as to be the lot of some 40% of the peoples of the developing countries. And are not we who tolerate such poverty, when it is within our power to reduce the number afflicted by it, failing to fulfill fundamental obligations accepted by civilized men since the beginning of time? (238–39)

In his 1968 address to the board of governors, McNamara had been positively ebullient in his vision of what the bank could accomplish. Just five years later, in his 1973 address, McNamara was suffering from battle fatigue. Although he had accomplished much of his first five-year plan in the interim between these two speeches, his rhetoric in the 1973 speech registers a profound sense of frustration with development's failure to deliver on its promise of liberating Third World peoples from need. His construction of the subject of underdevelopment in this passage has all but forgotten the strident and emulative reactive nationalist from Rostow's chain of discursive signifiers. Instead McNamara returns us to the abject masses of Truman's Point Four Program awaiting liberation "by civilized men."

Perhaps McNamara's reiterative return to this genetically abject, underdeveloped subject is a periodic necessity for the constitution of the discourse itself. Indeed, Rostow's reactive nationalist and McNamara's abject masses are discursive doubles, and the entire discourse of development depends on their recursive reiteration, for both are subjects-in-waiting. The mimetic subject of reactive nationalism, as an originary stage of history, awaits completion. Meanwhile the abject masses simply await their own rescue.

If these are the recursive subjects of development discourse exposed by a decade of critique, who are the subjects of dependency theory? On the one hand, capitalist and working-class subjects in the center depend on the periphery to purchase First World technology and capital goods (the products, after all, of free capital and free labor). These First World subjects also continue to depend on the periphery for certain necessary inputs and consumer products—minerals, foodstuffs, and inexpensively manufactured goods. On the other hand, we have the implied subjects of the periphery. These are local bourgeois elites—the comprador class—who benefit from their relationship with monopolistic corporate interests in the First World. Then we have the victims of that relationship: the generalized urban and rural masses who suffer the consequences of dependent development in the periphery. Thus, although dependency critique *did* challenge the many binaries in development discourse, especially the binary of primitive and modern consciousness, it nevertheless re-created its own determinant binary.

Dependency theory, in the final analysis, also constructs two kinds of subjects in the periphery who oddly resemble the recursive subjects of underdevelopment: bourgeois elites (reactive nationalists) and victims of their machinations (abject masses). There are significant differences, of course. In dependency theory, the interests of the elites lie in direct contradiction with the interests of the masses. Indeed, the elites, with their bifurcated loyalties, assist in producing dependent development and its structural inequities. But just as the recursive subjects of development discourse await liberation, so too do the generalized masses of dependency await that possibility. Dependency theorists still entertain the possibility of independent development, of fully sovereign nations on the horizon. Thus we are not outside the discursive imbrication with which we began this chapter. In dependency theory, the popular classes await a system that will break them free from bourgeois elites and ultimately bestow on them independence as national producers. These popular classes are still imminently national subjects because although the goods they produce flow across international boundaries, and international corporations bring factory floors to them, their hopes and aspirations are tied to the possibility of their nations breaking free from a cycle of dependency.

Indeed, in the final analysis, dependency theory generates a binary model for peripheral economies that is just as intractable as Frank's development of underdevelopment, for what will break the cycle of Third World dependence on the First World? What will break the cycle of an administered technological obsolescence for the periphery? Given the intractability of the system of dependent development, only an epochal break from this system holds the promise of liberation. The subjects of dependency theory are still effects of development's regime of subjection. These underdeveloped subjects are still subjects-in-waiting: they await revolution.

Part II

The Authorized Subjects of Revolution:

Ernesto "Che" Guevara and Mario Payeras

I do not intend here to forget that, to become viable projects, revolutions need money-capital, which is very scarce in poor societies. Neither do I want to gloss over questions relative to wars—questions we cultural critics often neglect but with which the social scientists relentlessly grapple. *I simply want to assert that revolutions are also questions of words and wordings.* Political leaders often have argued that revolutions are the paramount expressions of culture. Therefore, disengaging pronouns becomes a grammatical issue impinging on representation and power mainly when, as the 1960s slogan asserted, all power (has not been given) to the people.

—Ileana Rodríguez, *Women, Guerrillas, and Love* (italics mine)

In the spirit of Latin American literary scholar Ileana Rodríguez's critique, I consider revolutions from different angles: from the perspective of the dependent economy in search of new means of capital accumulation, and from the perspective of revolutionaries in search of new modes of being, new forms of cultural production. The previous chapter introduced the reader to the subjects of development, tracing the historical emergence of a model of subjectivity under the regime of development. This chapter traces the emergence of a model of revolutionary subjectivity through the autobiographical speech acts of two of the most renowned Latin American revolutionary heroes of the post–World War II Americas: Ernesto "Che" Guevara and Mario Payeras. As Rodríguez observes, "the narrative of the revolution is a narrative of the construction of the self first as *guerrillero*, and then as vanguard, party, leader, and government" (*Women, Guerrillas, and Love* xvii).

My aim is to illuminate the failure of decolonization struggles in North and South America, to understand the loss of the revolutionary imagination in the Americas, by interrogating the effects of the disturbing resemblance between Guevara's and Payeras's recursive iterations of revolutionary subjectivity and the chain of discursive signifiers associated with the liberal subject of development. The literature of revolutionary subjection is complicit in this failure, for, as Latin American cultural critic Jean Franco has so succinctly put it, "Literature is a protagonist in this drama of loss and dislocation not only because it articulated the utopian but also because it is implicated in its demise" (*Decline and Fall* 1). The diaries of Che Guevara and Mario Payeras were deservedly models of revolutionary transformation for generations of activists and scholars in the Americas. Nevertheless it is imperative to interrogate the limits of their revolutionary vision if we are to move forward through the profound dislocation and loss of the post–Cold War, postrevolutionary period.

Resemblance-in-Difference

Gayatri Chakravorty Spivak has referred to the European subject's differentiation from colonized subjects during the "great age of imperialism" as "the 'worlding' of what is now called 'the Third World' " ("Three Women's Texts" 262). Spivak ties this worlding of the world and of the "native" to the colonial mission of "soul-making" and traces this mission to the "categorical imperative" formulated by Kant:

> I am using "Kant" . . . as a metonym for the most flexible ethical moment in the European eighteenth century. Kant words the categorical imperative, conceived as the universal moral law given by pure reason, in this way: "In all creation every thing one chooses and over which one has any power, may be used *merely as means;* man alone, and with him every rational creature, is an end in himself." It is thus a moving displacement of Christian ethics from religion to philosophy. As Kant writes: "With this agrees well the possibility of such a command as: *Love God above everything, and thy neighbor as thyself*. For as a command it requires respect for a law which *commands love* and does not leave it to our own arbitrary choice to make this our principle." (267)

Spivak argues that this categorical imperative, "travestied in the service of the state," turns terroristic when it "justif[ies] the imperialist project by producing the following formula: *make* the heathen into a human so that he can be treated as an end in himself" (267).[1] According to Spivak, this double displacement of the Christian ethic from the religious to the philosophical, from the philosophical to the state, reveals the double logic of colonial violence—benevolence coupled with instrumentality. With the Christian soul as the basis for the production of the human social subject, the "heathen," the "native," or the "Other" of colonial spaces is deftly placed *outside* of humanity, and it becomes the duty (the *command to love*) of the messianic colonizer to bring that Other into the family of (Christian) humanity. The colonial Other is prehuman to the protohumanity of the Western subject, who is making colonial history through a wilderness of prehistoric spaces. However, as Spivak notes, the Other, once placed outside humanity in the realm of "nature," also "may be used *merely as means*" toward the greater project—toward the end of making (Western) man and his world/empire. The discourses of Enlightenment and messianic Christianity, then, come together in the colonial process of structuring a feminized Other outside of (Christian) humanity.[2]

As chapter 2 demonstrates, the twentieth-century idiom of development and modernization gave us yet another worlding of the world. This time around, a Euro-U.S. subject responds to a new categorical imperative, but he still has a mission, a promised end, a possibility for profit. The "indigenous," the "peasant," and the categorized "Third World" have once again been removed from historicity, this time placed *outside* or *prior to* "development." Thus it becomes the task of a benevolent First World and its citizens to pull the Third World and its inhabitants into the family of developed nations—coincidentally justifying instrumental, neocolonial relations between the two. The "wilderness" of colonial space has been displaced onto the chaos of "underdeveloped" place (feudal countryside, informal sector), impinging ever more desperately on urban centers (*favelas, colonias*), but nevertheless suspended on the verge of history. If we are no longer concerned with soul making, as in the trajectory of the colonizing subject (and if the "we" now includes "native" party members and policy analysts), we *are* concerned with making the preindustrious into the industrious, the prodigal into the prolific.

For first-generation development theorists (indeed, even for many second-generation ones), the First World is ensconced as the central model of being (industrial, capitalist, democratic), with the Third World held in the abeyance of becoming (folk, pre-economic, despotic). The protagonist remains the protohuman of imperial reason that Norma Alarcón has described as the "autonomous, self-making, self-determining . . . subject of consciousness" (357). But in the age of development, the hero dons the garb of discursive signification specifically associated with its regime of subjection: he is a risk-taking, resolute, frugal, nonornamental, productive, fully masculine, fully national fellow. The antagonist is recast as the unruly, feminized, not-quite-human, but not quite/not human, traditional native, the object of perpetual instruction.[3]

Ernesto "Che" Guevara and Mario Payeras figured prominently as oppositional subjects within development's "worlding of the world." And yet many of the key metaphors, themes, and tropes of development discourse emerge in the diaries and political essays of Guevara and Payeras. Thus I suggest their narratives, in theorizing revolutionary subjection, also repeatedly figure the moment of achieving revolutionary consciousness as a transcendental moment of choice, with its attendant discursive binary of modes of being. As in the developmentalist narrative, the tropes of previous personal histories (ethnos, particularity) are figuratively nullified by this act of choice, with the subject reborn in/to revolution. Indeed, these two revolutionaries figure the transcendental moment as a moment that frees them from previous, sometimes painful, personal histories. For Guevara, this is the history of his bourgeois privilege and complicity, but also of a sense of compromised masculinity as a Third World subject. Consequently, Guevara repeatedly represents his personal transformation into revolutionary subjectivity in the language of spectacular revelation and renunciation, of sacrifice and deliverance. To illustrate how Guevara's formula of personal transformation is reproduced and resolutely adhered to in the lives and texts of subsequent Latin American revolutionaries, I engage in a comparative analysis of revolutionary subjection in Payeras's first diary, *Los dias de la selva*, as well as his essays on indigenism.[4]

However, a resemblance always presupposes a difference; the subject of revolution differs from the subject of development in two crucial ways. Beyond the transcendental choice made by the (under)developed subject lies the possibility of fully competitive capitalism, with risk-taking entrepreneurs on the one hand and disciplined, productive workers on the other. By contrast, beyond the transcendental choice made by revolutionaries lies the revolutionary imagining of the fullness of the collective community, a community not bifurcated by class, gender, or race, brought together in a participatory democracy deciding on the production and distribution of material goods. This is, of course, a fundamental difference, and it is in the interest of this difference that I launch my critique. However, it is precisely this difference that makes the similarity disturbing. There is a second, perhaps more critical, difference-in-resemblance between the subject of development and the subject of revolution. This difference-in-resemblance unfolds *within* revolutionary subjectivity, that is, within the interior narratives represented in the texts of Guevara and Payeras. For these two men, the moment of transcendental transformation is never fully completed. Painful and pleasurable histories return to haunt their stories, to hail these revolutionaries back to a prerevolutionary subjectivity that refuses to disappear. It is in the tension produced by the haunting loss of the "premodern," I believe, that we find the revolutionary possibility still animating their discourse.

Chronicle of a Death, Retold

In the second chapter of *Guerrilla Warfare*, Guevara instructs prospective revolutionaries: "We have already described the guerrilla fighter as one who shares the longing of the people for liberation and who, once peaceful means are exhausted, initiates the fight and converts himself into an armed vanguard of the fighting people. From the very beginning of the struggle he has the intention of destroying an unjust order and therefore an intention, *more or less hidden,* to replace the old with something new" (Guevara, *Guerrilla Warfare* 38; italics mine). He goes on to describe the guerrilla combatant as "an ascetic" with a "rigid self control that will prevent a single excess, a single slip" (39); as "striking like a tornado, destroying all, giving no quarter" (42); as "audacious . . . always ready to take an optimistic attitude toward circumstances" (42–43); as possessing a "degree of adaptability" and "instantaneous inventiveness" (43); as "an extraordinary companion" and physically "indefatigable" (43); as entirely self-contained, "carry[ing] his house on his back like a snail" (45). In his paradoxical string of adjectives and descriptive phrases, Guevara is "utilizing the terminology of Protestant personal repression," as Ileana Rodríguez has suggested (*Women, Guerrillas, and Love* 44). Indeed, Guevara's guerrilla subject bears a compelling tropological resemblance to the hero of development discourse: he is resolute, destructive *and* productive, a risk taker, an advantage seeker, flexible and highly mobile; he is loving, strong, frugal, and self-determining.

Yet the most striking attribute of this guerrilla combatant is that he comes to the people fully formed, "as a guiding angel who has fallen into the zone, helping the poor always" (39). In this "how-to" manual on revolutionary struggle, there is absolutely no indication of how this revolutionary is forged, of *how* he "converts himself into an armed vanguard of the fighting people." Instead, this manual gives us a clear and consistent picture of who the revolutionary *already is,* of what he should carry in his knapsack, of how he should pitch his tent and tend to his weapon. This representation of revolutionary subjectivity is important because it models most fully the ideal subject after a transcendental choice has been made and the revolutionary has left behind a prerevolutionary order of consciousness. However, it stands in dynamic contrast to the representation of revolutionary transformation in Guevara's diaries.

In *Pasajes de la guerra revolucionaria*, Guevara's first diary, he not only chronicles the triumph of the Cuban *guerrilla* under Fidel Castro's direction but also relentlessly frames the spectacle of his own rebirth from a bumbling, inept, asthmatic, would-be doctor into an authorized subject of insurrection. He repeatedly bears witness to his own transformation from Ernesto Guevara, the young, affluent Argentinean intellectual, into *El Che*, a weathered revolutionary who transcends the boundaries of nation and class. Guevara prefaces this entire tale of transformation with an account of his own personal moment of choice. By 1955 Castro is already in Mexico City preparing for the secret entry of his group of patriots into Cuba to fight the Batista regime. Guevara is also there, having fled Guatemala after the 1954 U.S.-backed military overthrow of Jacobo Arbenz Guzman's democratically elected government. Guevara tells us, "I met him [Fidel] on one of those cold Mexican nights, and I remember that our first discussion turned to international politics. Within a few hours that same night—by dawn—I was one of the future expeditionaries" (*Pasajes* 1).[5] "Within a few hours" Guevara makes an ethical choice, represented by him—given the alacrity with which he makes it—as unwavering and without hesitation.[6] Indeed, the moment of choice is not even represented in this quote, with Guevara moving swiftly and directly from "discussion" to "I was."

As a consequence of this epochal choice, Guevara leaves Mexico a year later, one of eighty-two men to arrive in Cuba on 2 December 1956. The guerrilla troop is immediately attacked by Batista's air force, and they take cover in a nearby swamp. After three days of hiding in this swamp to evade these forces, the guerrillas emerge into the light: "We were left on *firm ground, adrift,* stumbling, an army of shadows, of ghosts, that walked as if following some dark psychic mechanism. We had spent seven days of hunger and continuous seasickness in transit, plus three more terrible days on land [in the swamp]. Exactly ten days after our departure from Mexico, on 5 December at dawn, after a nocturnal march interrupted by fainting, exhaustion, and rest on the part of the troops, we arrived at a place named, paradoxically, Alegría de Pío [Joy of the Devout]" (*Pasajes* 4; italics mine). Clearly, Guevara's description of the troop as "an army of shadows, of ghosts" is attributable in part to their hunger and exhaustion. But they are also shadows or ghosts of their former selves because they have made an epochal choice in choosing to become guerrillas, and thus their former identities are figuratively eviscerated as a consequence of it. Nevertheless, the certainty of the choice they have made to be revolutionaries, that "dark psychic mecha-nism," guides them. They are delivered, paradoxically, onto *firm ground*, even though they are *adrift* and stumbling.

Guevara draws attention to the "paradoxical" name of Alegría de Pío, suggesting an incongruity in such an auspicious name, the *joy* of the devout, for such inauspicious beginnings, the *suffering* of the guerrillas. Yet a para-dox is precisely something that, while seemingly contradictory, also contains truth. Thus another reading of this paradoxical naming suggests that the troop had certainly arrived at the joy of devotion. After all, in a Christian model of faith, it is precisely the suffering entailed by sacrifice for one's belief that brings joy to the believer.

Pasajes is a compilation of a series of articles Guevara published between 1959 and 1964. The bulk of the entries were written between 1961 and 1964 for publication in *Verde Olivo,* the weekly magazine of the Cuban Revolu-tionary Armed Forces (FAR). However, the first and the last entries in *Pasajes* ("A Revolution Begins" and "Final Offensive: The Battle of Santa Clara") were originally published in 1959 for the Brazilian magazine *O Cruceiro.* Thus Guevara actually wrote two versions of this "origin story," one for *Verde Olivo* and one for *O Cruceiro* (Waters 30, 34–36). The *Verde Olivo* origin story, entitled simply "Alegría de Pío," provides a more dramatic and detailed account of the voyage and the guerrillas' first days in Cuba. The guerrillas' arrival in Cuba is again rendered in the language of transcen-dence and loss, of rebirth and baptism, of (re)creation and religious mis-sion: "We had landed on December 2, at a place known as Las Coloradas beach, losing almost all our equipment. . . . We had reached Cuba following a seven-day voyage across the Gulf of Mexico and Caribbean Sea, without food, in a boat in poor condition, with almost everyone plagued by seasick-ness, since we were unaccustomed to sea travel. . . . All that was left of our war equipment was the rifle, the cartridge, and some wet bullets. Our medi-cal supplies had disappeared, and most of our knapsacks had been left in the swamps" (*Pasajes* 5). I would suggest that this "leaving behind" of the knap-sacks, of a personal history, in the swamp is as necessary to the formation of this primary collectivity as the guns are to revolutionary struggle. The troop is reborn into a primitive egalitarianism in this passage through the experi-ence of loss. Each man is reborn into an equivalence with one another, suggested both by the abandoned knapsacks they leave behind and the gun each man rescues. They exist as comrades-in-arms, no more, no less.

Guevara then proceeds to render the scene of this primitive egalitarian-ism in slightly Edenic terms: "Due to our inexperience, we satisfied our hunger and thirst by eating sugarcane on the side of the road and leaving the peelings right there. But the soldiers didn't need such subtle hints, since our guide—as we found out years later—was the author of the betrayal and had brought them to us. . . . We should never have permitted our false guide to leave" (*Pasajes* 5). The men satiate their hunger by indulging in the sweet sugarcane growing freely on the side of the road. In Edenic innocence, they do not even bother to pick up after themselves. And yet no sooner has Guevara established this first idyllic moment of collective culture than it is threatened, violated, apparently from within—the guide will betray them. The guide, we find out some chapters later, is a peasant named Eutimio Guerra. With this foreshadowing early in the text, Guevara introduces the element of deception.

The effect is twofold. Not only is this primitive egalitarianism immediately undone, but the betrayal suddenly bifurcates the collective. The reader is tipped off: This group of men, having shed their previous attachments, are nevertheless *not* attached to the scene of their revolutionary errand. They indeed need a guide, and this guide clearly does not see himself as part of this primary egalitarianism, hence the betrayal. This initial distance between the guerrillas and the peasantry is certainly to be expected; and by the end of the war, hundreds of peasants will, in fact, come to understand themselves as part of this guerrilla collective. Nevertheless, by simultaneously introducing the elements of betrayal and of the peasant guide into the narrative, Guevara ties the peasantry to deception. Indeed, as we will see again, for the remainder of the narrative, Guevara repeatedly deploys a discursive binary of consciousness in his diaries, alternately representing the peasant classes as either notoriously deceptive or organically one with the guerrillas.

Pasajes is a conversion narrative. Not only does it tell the story of Guevara's conversion into a revolutionary, but it also tells of the conversion of individuated bourgeois subjects into a collective consciousness. True to the conventions of a conversion narrative, though the choice may be represented as once-and-for-all, the faith necessary to make this choice must repeatedly be tested. Throughout *Pasajes*, then, guerrilla collectivity is repeatedly tested, threatened with disintegration, and reestablished, until the group is forged into a victorious army. Similarly, Guevara recounts how the revolutionary mettle of each member of the troop, including himself, is tested. However, the outcome is rarely as fortuitous for the individual member as it is for the troop.

The first and most devastating test of the guerrillas comes just a few days after their arrival at Alegría de Pío. Guevara informs us that the troop spends the first five days marching, talking, and eating together. The tranquil, idyllic monotony of their primitive egalitarianism is brought abruptly to an end: "The *compañero* Montané and I were leaning against a tree trunk, talking about our respective kids; we were eating our meager rations—half a sausage and two crackers—when a shot went off; a difference of only seconds and a hurricane of bullets—or at least so it seemed to our anguished spirits during that test of fire—drizzled onto our group of eighty-two men. My gun was not one of the best; I had purposefully asked that it be this way because my physical condition was deplorable due to a long bout of asthma I sustained during our sea voyage, and I didn't want a valuable weapon to be wasted in my hands" (*Pasajes* 6). Guevara's decision to ask for an inferior rifle bespeaks his renowned sense of self-criticism and self-sacrifice. However, the pathos of "my physical condition was deplorable" also conveys a deeply personal sense of compromised masculinity on Guevara's part.

Indeed, it is the deplorable condition of his masculinity that is being tested in this first "test of fire." This "test" and subsequent ones are represented as a series of simple, straightforward, life-altering choices that he must make in combat. These choices inevitably boil down to a choice between surrendering to a former self, a former order, or embracing a new subjectivity forged in collectivity *and* a fully masculine nationalism. Thus Guevara specifically informs us that he and Montané were having a leisurely discussion about their *children* at the moment of the attack. The "hurricane of bullets" figuratively cuts them off from their progeny, as their individual roles as fathers must be forsaken in the name of their newly designated collective role as fathers-of-the-*patria*.[7]

In the full description of the attack, we find out not all the medicines had, in fact, perished during landing. The remaining medicine figures prominently in the first choice Guevara must make as part of his revolutionary transformation:

> At that moment a compañero left a box of bullets practically at my feet; I indicated this to him, and the man answered me with a face I remember perfectly, because of the anguish in it, something like "This is not the hour for boxes of bullets," and immediately he continued toward the cane fields (later he was assassinated by one of Batista's henchmen). Perhaps that was the first time that the dilemma of choosing between my dedication to medicine and my duty as a revolutionary soldier was placed *straightforwardly* before me. I had in front of me

a backpack full of medicines and a box of bullets, together they were too heavy to carry; I chose the box of bullets, leaving the backpack, to cross the clearing separating me from the cane fields. (*Pasajes* 6; italics mine)

Given that Guevara has just invoked his disabling asthma, the severity of his choice is painfully evident—he leaves the medicine that can alleviate his own illness in favor of the box of bullets to be shared with the entire troop. Again, Guevara represents this as a choice, at once self-evident and revelatory, between a previous personal order—his deplorable condition, his dedication as a doctor—and a new order of collective duty. He leaves the backpack and immediately crosses a clearing—suggesting his own clarity at this moment —to get to a cane field where the collective awaits him. He evacuates his former subject position so that he may come to be "an armed vanguard of the fighting people." Guevara asserts a revolutionary ethic of collective judgment in making his choice, and the correctness of the choice is underscored by the fact that the man who left the bullets behind is later killed, for the passage suggests the man later pays for his (in)decision with his life.

The next choice Guevara must make confronts him immediately after he reaches the cane fields and joins his compañeros, some of whom are firing back at the air force. Guevara and another guerrilla soldier are both hit by the same round of fire:

Arbentosa, vomiting blood through his nose, his mouth, with the enormous wound from the bullet of a .45, yelled something like "They killed me," and he started shooting crazily; well, you couldn't see anything at that moment. I said to Faustino, from the ground, "They finished me" (only I used a stronger word), Faustino looked at me in the middle of his task and told me that it was nothing, but in his eyes I read the death sentence my wound signified. I was left sprawled on the ground [*tendido*]; I fired a shot toward the woods, following the same dark impulse as the wounded soldier. Immediately I began to think about the best way to die in that moment when all seemed lost. I remembered an old story by Jack London, where the protagonist, leaning against the trunk of a tree, resigns himself to die with dignity, once he knows he will freeze to death in the Alaskan cold zones. It's the only image I remember. Someone, on his knees, was screaming that it was necessary to surrender, and a voice in the background, that I later learned was Camilo Cienfuegos, yelled, "Aqui no se rinde nadie . . ." (*Pasajes* 7)

Faustino, of course, turns out to be correct; we find out the bullet only grazed Guevara's neck. Guevara has a dark sense of humor in his writing, and this scene is at once grotesque, with its image of Arbentosa bleeding to death through various orifices as he wildly shoots his gun, and comical, with the image of Guevara led to do the same by the sheer power of persuasion and then retreating into a bizarre Londonian reverie over his own death. And yet it is precisely the farcical nature of Guevara's behavior that ends up structuring this choice between life and death as entirely a question of sheer will. Guevara resigns himself to death, indulging in boyhood dreams of adventure, until Camilo returns him to revolutionary life with the cry "Nobody surrenders here!" Across memory and time, the revolutionary hails Guevara—that isolated reader/adventurer, that pubescent bourgeois intellectual—and *El Che* responds, willing himself back to his new life.

As an instance of imagined insertion of the self into a drama of masculine striving, Guevara's identification with the protagonist of a Jack London story is particularly significant for my purposes. Not only does it foreground an identification with the rugged individualism of the lone adventurer always present in London's stories and novels, but it is also a double identification with a very "American" coming-of-age narrative. On the one hand, London's narrative portrays the lone Anglo adventurer in the Americas triumphing over adversity in wild and threatening nature. On the other hand, Jack London's books are most popular with preteens and adolescents, suggesting that reading these adventure stories is a formative act of subject constitution for a particular age-group and class stratum of readers across the continents. Thus a dual identification with London's stories suggests that Guevara must free himself from a sense of U.S./white colonial propriety over the American wilderness in order to free Latin America from the clutches of U.S. neocolonialism.

As such, Guevara represents this first confrontation with "scenes [that were] at times Dantesque and at times grotesque," as a necessary loss of innocence for the guerrillas (*Pasajes* 7). With its imagery of destruction and rebirth, it is a "baptism of fire . . . that forges what would one day be the *Ejercito Rebelde*," figuratively casting the guerrillas out of a false paradise (hence his reference to the *Inferno* and qualified descriptions of this time as a dystopia) of neocolonial relations (hence his reference to London) (*Pasajes* 7). Only eighteen of the eighty-two men survive this first attack, and these men are wounded, lost, dispersed into small groups, unaware of each other's presence. The terrain that will become the guerrillas' theater of operations—cane fields, mountains, and rain forest—is permanently refigured as a chaotic, hostile, indeed deadly, place. This is the Cuban guerrillas' wilderness, the tabula rasa on which a new revolutionary subjectivity and a new revolutionary culture will be inscribed.

As with any Edenic teleology (even this dystopic one), there are elements of prophecy and predestination evinced in Guevara's retroactive representation of this momentous transition for the troop and for its individual soldiers:

> By noon, unusual signs began to occur, when Piper aircraft and other types of small planes—owned by the military or privately—began circling nearby. Some of the members of the group tranquilly cut cane while the planes passed, without thinking of how visible they were, given the low altitude and slow speed at which the enemy planes flew. My job at the time as doctor of the troop was to cure the sores on wounded feet. I believe I remember my last patient on that day. The compañero was named Humberto Lamotte, and that was his last working day. A tired and anguished figure sticks in my mind, carrying in his hands the shoes he could not wear from my first-aid station to his post. (*Pasajes* 6)

Lulled into a dangerous, prelapsarian tranquility, these soldiers are incapable of reading even the most "unusual signs" of their coming expulsion from this false paradise—the military planes circling above. Just as the predestined loss of the troop's artificial innocence is foretold in this reconstruction of events, so is the fate of individual soldiers. Thus Guevara remembers his last patient's last day. In anguish, Humberto carries the shoes that no longer fit, prefiguring his death: the condition of revolutionary subjectivity is represented as something that does not "fit" just anyone. In other words, not everyone who has chosen this path will in turn be chosen to become *el nuevo hombre*, the new man. Once again, failure to make a decisive choice over one's new life—reflected in Humberto's "tired and anguished figure"—turns out to be fatal.

This brings us to yet a third choice the guerrillas face in this chapter, one Guevara and most of the survivors fail to make correctly. Even this failure, however, is ultimately represented as serving a greater purpose. Guevara interrupts his account of the massacre at Alegía de Pío to inform the reader that "later [he] learned that Fidel had tried vainly to get everybody together into the adjoining cane field, *which could be reached by simply crossing a line* [guardaraya]. But the surprise had been too great, the bullets too heavy" (*Pasajes* 6; italics mine). Of course, this passage primarily pays homage to

Castro, who attends to the troop even as this apocalyptic scene transpires all around him. Such representations of the commander in chief as loving caretaker are de rigueur in the literary representations of revolutionary struggle in *la montaña*.[8] However, Guevara also draws the reader's attention to the path not taken by the guerrillas by emphasizing the ironic failure to recognize the safe haven reachable by "simply crossing a line." The passage is tinged with remorse: the survivors fail to see the obvious and consequently are dispersed into small groups, separated from Castro and wandering around the cane fields for days. There can be only a twinge of remorse on Guevara's part, however, not just because the troop evidently went on to regroup and to win the revolution, but also, I would suggest, because there can only be slight regret given the predestined nature of these events. Indeed, the failure to make the correct choice ends up paradoxically being the right choice, a "fortunate fall" that reestablishes the collective on stronger terms in the subsequent chapter, appropriately entitled "Left Adrift."

This third chapter retraces the (mis)adventures of Guevara and four other survivors cut off from Castro's group by the first "baptism of fire." They are thirsty and hungry, wandering aimlessly through brush and over rocky hills. Making matters worse, the guerrilla soldier in charge of food rations, Benítez, inadvertently spills the contents of their one can of milk. The men come across a cave, offering a good defensive position, and decide to rest out of sight for the day. Guevara informs us that there, in the solemnity of the darkness, the five men made a formal vow "to fight to the death. Those of us who made this pact were Ramiro Valdés, Juan Almeida, Chao, Benítez, and your narrator. We all survived that terrible first experience with defeat and the subsequent battles" (*Pasajes* 8). The structure of Guevara's representation, with survival following directly on the heels of making a pact, once again suggests a causal relation between a decisive commitment to primary collectivity (after all, they make the vow *to each other*) and the possibility for futurity (as all five live to see the triumph of the revolution). The whole of this chapter, then, is dedicated to demonstrating how collectivity must be repeatedly reaffirmed and solidified.

At night, his group continues its march toward the Sierra Maestra, and Guevara uses his knowledge of astronomy to locate the North Star. Always humorously self-effacing, though, he tells the reader it was sheer luck that led them eastward, since he had identified the wrong star. During the march, Guevara's group is reunited with three other guerrilla survivors, including Camilo Cienfuegos. Together these eight men learn to find water in the crevices of rocks and to ration it with field glasses. They scavenge for food and share whatever they find (*Pasajes* 8–9). On more than one occasion, they narrowly evade Batista's army. Twice the group mistakenly identifies army soldiers as peasants.[9] Eventually the band of survivors does make contact with some actual peasants who prepare a feast for them. After eating until dawn the plentiful food that appears continuously before them, all eight of the guerrillas become violently ill, and the peasants' house becomes "an inferno" (*Pasajes* 11). Through their shared thirst and hunger, their shared bouts of vomiting and diarrhea, and their near-death encounters with the army and fraternal encounters with the peasants, these unlikely heroes learn to discuss their differences and reach consensus in a loving community. In other words, they are (re)born into collectivity with each infernal (mis)adventure.

The cane fields, mountains, and rain forests of Cuba are the scenes of their revolutionary transformation. Nevertheless the guerrillas must repeatedly rely on the peasants to guide them through their newfound wilderness. The peasants, of course, have known exactly where Castro is all the while. After the feast, they agree to lead our meandering heroes to him on the condition that the soldiers leave their weapons behind to avoid suspicion. Once again the peasants are not to be trusted, however. As if treachery is part of their essential nature, the peasants betray the guerrillas in spite of themselves: "We had just left the [peasant's] house when the owner *couldn't resist the temptation* to communicate the news to a friend to discuss where they might hide the arms; this friend convinced him to sell the weapons, and they entered into negotiations with a third guy. He denounced us to the army, and within a few hours after we left our first hospitable mansion in Cuba, the enemy burst in, taking Pablo Hurtado [a sick comrade] prisoner and capturing all the arms" (*Pasajes* 12; italics mine). Even the most hospitable peasant cannot resist the temptation to betray. The lesson is quite simple. Although they must repeatedly rely on the peasantry for guidance, sustenance, shelter, and ultimately to give their mission meaning, the guerrillas must never fully rely on their own trust in them.

Finally, after a few more nights of travel and days of hiding, the group of eight is reunited with Castro's troop. This is hardly cause for celebration, however. Guevara continues: "Our little troop presented itself [before Fidel] without uniforms and without weapons, since the two pistols were all we were able to salvage from the disaster. The meeting with Castro was very violent. During that whole campaign, and even today, we remember his admonitions: 'You have yet to pay for the error you have committed, because you pay with your life for leaving your gun [behind] in these circumstances;

the only chance of surviving you had, in the event of running into the army, would have been your weapon. Leaving them was a crime and a stupidity' " (*Pasajes* 12). In Castro's reaction, the reader recognizes the scolding but loving parent who berates a child for crossing a busy intersection without looking. It is this mixture of discipline and love that Guevara repeatedly uses to describe "Fidel," the indisputable commander in chief of the rebel army. Once "our little troop" is reunited with the remaining survivors, Castro whips the guerrillas into shape. No more wandering or wanderlust is permitted. Castro institutes order where order was sorely lacking in the days "left adrift." He instills discipline, establishes a training camp, orders target practice, and insists that the guerrillas bathe (13–14). Furthermore, it is Castro who establishes permanent relations with the local peasantry and ministers to the troop's frequent bouts of defeatism (15–16). Guevara's praise for him is lavish.

In Guevara's representation, the guerrillas learn to act in unison in a matter of weeks solely because of Castro's leadership. They go on to win a series of battles against the army, detailed in the subsequent chapters, with their success attributable almost exclusively to Castro's guidance. Time and again, the guerrillas "pass the test" of battle, until they figuratively arrive on the other side of the effort required to forge a guerrilla army: "[Ambushing the army] improved our spirits greatly, and allowed us to keep climbing the inaccessible woods all day long to escape persecution. . . . That is how we ended up on the other side of the mountain, walking parallel to Batista's troops . . . for two days our troop and the enemy troop marched almost together, without realizing it" (*Pasajes* 20). Under the disciplining love administered by Castro, the guerrillas "ended up on the other side of the mountain" and on a par with the army troops in strength, cunning, and speed. The passage suggests that the guerrillas achieve a full masculinity—walking parallel—through their successful confrontation with the army. Furthermore, under Castro's tender but firm hand, I would suggest, Guevara himself is reborn from the condition of compromised masculinity that shadowed him on the beach to an uncompromised masculinity achieved in the mountain. But what is the nature of the full revolutionary masculinity?

In effect, Castro's tender, loving care repeatedly threatens to tip into tyranny, and—foreshadowing his own ascent to platoon commander (and to commander in chief of the 1967 Bolivian guerrilla effort)—Guevara must repeatedly step in to temper Castro's tough love. Guevara informs us that the guerrillas passed various tests of unity. Nonetheless the collectivity of the group is also continuously undermined, most often by the wavering morale of individual members. Consequently Castro resorts to some unflattering tactics:

> There Manuel Fajardo approached, asking if it were possible that we would lose the war. Our reply, regardless of whether or not we were in the euphoria of victory, was always the same: indisputably, the war would be won. He explained that he had asked me because the *gallago* Morán had told him that it was no longer possible to win the war, that we were lost, and he had invited [Fajardo] to abandon the campaign. I let Fidel know these facts, but he told me Morán had already told him that he was just testing the morale of the troops. We agreed that this was not the best system, and Fidel made a short speech urging greater discipline and explaining the dangers that might arise if it were disregarded. He also announced the three crimes punishable by death: insubordination, desertion, and defeatism. (*Pasajes* 21)

Guevara convinces Castro that trickery and espionage might not be the best method to minister to the morale of the troop. Although partially successful in this effort, the tyranny behind Castro's *tendresse*, as Ileana Rodríguez has called it, nevertheless reemerges in the death threats issued by the commander in chief/loving caregiver.

Is "el Nuevo Hombre" la Nueva Mujer in Drag?

In *Women, Guerrillas, and Love: Understanding War in Central America*, Ileana Rodríguez elaborates on the gendering of Guevara's ideal of revolutionary subjectivity. Analyzing the feminization of subjectivity in the diaries and autobiographies of Latin American revolutionaries who posit the equation "new man = guerrilla leader," Rodríguez demonstrates that the terms in which these revolutionaries repeatedly characterize themselves and other guerrilla leaders are the same terms used to characterize the feminine in models of nineteenth-century domestic heroism: endurance, tenderness, discipline, love, sacrifice, surrender, suffering. Indeed, as I have also illustrated, these are precisely the terms Guevara uses to characterize the Cuban guerrillas, himself as a combatant, and particularly Fidel Castro. Through her analysis of Guevara's Bolivian diary and his *Guerrilla Warfare*, Rodríguez suggests that Guevara, in his relationship with his troops, not only is the leader but becomes a tangible example of Julia Kristeva's "virginal maternal." Guevara, that "model of the masculine desire for manliness," is also "mother as idealization of relations, as paradigm of the complex relation between the masculine (Christ/troops) and the feminine (tendresse) as a point of convergence of humanization; as representation of poverty, modesty, humility, devotion" (50, 54). Guevara embodies a feminized masculinity: "in formulating this image as paradigmatic, a concealed, perhaps even unconscious, convergence of maleness and femaleness was being proposed, an androgyny necessary for the building of a new society" (61). In his description of the formation of the guerrillas and their revolutionary leader, Guevara identifies in Castro and in himself the radical potential made available by this androgynous tendresse as a model for the new social subject.

Guevara's revolutionary androgyny appears to supersede the binary opposition put in play by development's discursive regime of subjection. This revolutionary androgyny appears to have synthesized, dialectically, the thesis of a fully masculine, developed subject moving forward universally through historical time and the antithesis of a feminized, underdeveloped subject who gets left behind in the particularity of domesticity once the choice for progress is made. The strength of Rodríguez's analysis, however, lies in her ability to contemplate the possibilities made available by the apparently contradictory tropes operating in revolutionary texts, or, as in the case of revolutionary androgyny, to complicate the seemingly consistent ones. Thus, for Rodríguez, at times the guerrilla troop indeed exists in the mountains as a utopian domestic community in which all the participants are men—a genuinely democratic space where the new man/collective subject can be socialized, where the absence of women seems to preclude certain patriarchal tyrannies from forming. This is precisely the condition of egalitarianism suggested by Guevara in the opening scenes of *Pasajes,* an egalitarianism into which the guerrillas must reiteratively be (re)born throughout the text. Rodríguez recognizes a revolutionary possibility in the blurring of gender dualities in the mountains. But the outcome of this possibility is less favorable, as Rodríguez notes, when time and again the feminine is introduced and appropriated by the new man in order that woman, as sign *and* as referent, may ultimately disappear entirely. Rodríguez's analysis permits us to see that rather than having a dialectical synthesis, we have the absorption of all difference by the primary term.

Rodríguez observes that while the mountains are repeatedly feminized in these revolutionary texts, they are nevertheless the scene where women are eliminated and men beget men, albeit feminized ones. The new man, in a way, is a new woman, better at representing her than his female counterpart is at being her. Not surprisingly, the new man gets tired of the role reversal rather quickly, and this domestic community "demonstrates male frustration at and within domesticity, lacking house and woman, someone to order about, somewhere to unload, 'repose' " (*Women, Guerrillas, and Love* 55). Woman as sign and referent has been banished, but her banishment does not eliminate relations of subordination and domination. To the contrary, her banishment simply displaces this hierarchy onto relationships between men. Tendresse, Rodríguez argues, inevitably becomes an alibi for the "new man's" uncontrolled exercise of power. As we saw in the threat of Castro's swift justice, sacrifice slips into punishment, discipline into repression, love into intransigence, becoming "increasingly oxymoronic" (46).

With regard to Guevara's troops, then, Rodríguez suggests that the guerrilla leader at times (inevitably?) slips from the eternal maternal into the mortal tyrannical. Again, Rodríguez's analysis allows us to see that the discursive binary deployed in development discourse has not disappeared. Rather, I suggest that it has been transposed onto the community of men, interiorized within each combatant, as these feminized subjects of underdevelopment strive to regain fully potent agency through revolutionary subjection. Indeed, this tendresse is the revolutionary's response to the imperative of mastery implied by a developmentalist model of unitary, self-determining, and determinant consciousness—the content of a fully masculine national subject. For what could be more masterful than a subjectivity that is able to slip effortlessly into all subject positions (masculine/feminine, peasant/urban, intellectual/revolutionary), apparently absorbing all difference into his system of total experience?

Rodríguez makes evident that for the guerrilla leader to become the new man, "woman" must be appropriated and excised. The entire chain of equivalencies underpinning this *nuevo hombre*, she argues, gets contaminated when tendresse proves necessarily incapable of absorbing all difference implied by the signifier "woman" into the sameness of revolutionary universalism. Furthermore, I submit that the guerrilla leader cannot *equal* his troops, then, and his troops cannot *equal* the masses, when equality means the absorption of particularity into a revolutionary homogeneity. There can be no smooth or simple transition within a revolutionary regime of subjection (in which such equivalencies are primary) from the masculine "I" of the guerrilla leader to the feminized, collective "we" of the popular subject. The same-equals-same chain of equivalence between leader/troops/masses is disrupted by the persistence of a difference in the feminine signifier. And yet there can be no greater goal for the revolutionary leader than to represent the masses, as Rodríguez amply demonstrates. Nothing, I suggest, proves more elusive. By extending Rodríguez's critique to the revolutionary regime of subjection imposed on the subaltern masses by guerrilla narratives, we see that the promise of equality suggested by this regime is impossible as long as it is predicated on a model of transcendence of difference.

As *Pasajes* continues, the interiorized binary of development indicated by Rodríguez's analysis of revolutionary tendresse is repeatedly displaced onto the objects of revolutionary agency, the peasant classes. In Guevara's multiple diaries, his representations of the peasant subaltern—the "masses" of la montaña—range from simplistic to sinister. In *Pasajes* Guevara's representation of the peasants moves increasingly toward a profound ambivalence over the place of the peasant in guerrilla struggle. This ambivalent representation, I suggest, reflects the displacement of a deep anxiety over his *own* personal revolutionary transformation. The arc of this ambivalence and displacement is best represented in two middle chapters of *Pasajes*, entitled "An Unpleasant Incident" and "The Struggle against Banditry."

Once Guevara is promoted to commander of his own platoon, it becomes *his* duty to instill discipline, dispense love, and administer justice. Castro sends Guevara's platoon to an adjacent region to extend the liberated zone: "Together with our newfound experience of independent life came new problems for the guerrillas. It was necessary to establish a rigid discipline, to designate ranks, and establish a General Command to ensure victory in upcoming battles. This was not an easy task given the poor discipline of the troops" (*Pasajes* 80). Following a less-than-successful first attack on Pino del Agua, Guevara decides to establish a disciplinary committee: "Lieutenant López's squadron had distinguished itself at Pino del Agua, and its members were serious boys. They were elected as the Discipline Committee, responsible for surveillance, for ensuring compliance with established norms of vigilance and discipline in general, for supervising cleaning of the camp, and for revolutionary morale. But the commission was short-lived, and was dissolved under tragic circumstances a few days after it was created" (91). Initially, the committee performs the mundane tasks that establish domestic order and community: designating cleaning chores, bolstering morale, enforcing the rules of communal living. Things go terribly awry, however, in the implementation of these feminine duties.

The committee's members are the target of relentless teasing and practical jokes by other members of the platoon who, like unruly adolescents, resist the committee's arbitrary power, "obliging it to take drastic measures" (*Pasajes* 98). Guevara does not describe the nature of the teasing, but it is quite likely that the ground for the teasing is the "feminine" nature of the tasks the committee performs or enforces. Indeed, only homophobic teasing could explain the extreme assertion of masculinity triggered as a response from a committee member, once again belying the failure of Guevara's revolutionary androgyny. Indeed, the response is "drastic," as Lalo Sardiñas "impulsively punished an undisciplined compañero by pistol-whipping him about the head when the gun accidentally went off and killed him instead" (98–99).

The troops in the rear guard of the platoon revolt over the incident, demanding the summary judgment and execution of Sardiñas. Although corporal punishment of guerrilla combatants is strictly forbidden, and this is not Sardiñas's first offense in this regard, Guevara cannot bring himself to execute Sardiñas. "It was a difficult situation," Guevara explains, "Sardiñas had been a brave combatant, a strict disciplinarian, and a man with a great spirit of sacrifice, while those who demanded the death penalty were by no means the best of the bunch" (*Pasajes* 99). "Strict discipline" and the "spirit of sacrifice" combine to produce tyrannical excess, which troubles Guevara, but he nevertheless represses this discomfort. First Guevara attempts to convince the troop that Batista is responsible rather than Sardiñas, for the comrade's death was attributable to "the conditions of struggle, to the very fact of war." Castro is then summoned to adjudicate the "unpleasant incident," and he attempts to shift the blame further. He waxes on for an hour, attempting to convince the platoon that culpability lies finally with the troops themselves, for it was their general lack of discipline that provoked the extreme act. Nevertheless, "despite his eloquence," Castro cannot convince the troops of the rear guard to desist in their demand for justice (99), and the troop decides to take a vote on Sardiñas's fate. His life is spared by a narrow margin; however, the next day, members of *both* the rear guard *and* the Disciplinary Committee resign from the guerrillas. Many of these, Guevara informs us, went on to join the counterrevolutionary troops after the triumph (100).

This incident provides a window onto the early machinations of revolutionary justice *en la montaña,* onto the inevitable slippage from the eternal maternal into the mortal tyrannical within this domestic community. The unruly behavior of both the undisciplined rank and file and the members of the Disciplinary Committee, however, gains its full significance when viewed in the context of Guevara's subsequent chapter, in which peasant "bandits" are also brought to revolutionary justice. Guevara has previously informed the reader that "the guerrillas and the peasantry had melded into *one single mass,* without anyone being able to say at exactly what moment in our long march this had occurred" (*Pasajes* 49; italics mine). For Guevara, it is his interaction with the Sierra peasants that transforms his "spontaneous and lyrical decision into a strong and serene conviction": "Those suffering and loyal inhabitants of the Sierra Maestra have no idea of the role they played in forging our revolutionary ideology" (49). In this passage, the peasants suffering at the hands of the Batista regime and their loyalty to the guerrillas perfectly mirror Guevara's own suffering as a guerrilla and his loyalty to revolutionary struggle. Indeed, the peasantry gives substance to Guevara's initial decision, turning spontaneous, transcendent choice into lasting "revolutionary ideology," notably without the peasants even being cognizant of it.

Nevertheless, in the beginning of "The Struggle against Banditry" chapter, Guevara must qualify his previous reflections on peasant loyalty, once again vacillating in his representation between their organic "oneness" with the guerrillas and their inherent duplicity. Although a broad swath of the Sierra Maestra is now liberated territory, Guevara describes the political situation as "precarious," in part because he has little confidence in the peasantry's commitment to the fight: "The political development of [the Sierra's] inhabitants was very superficial, and the presence of the threatening enemy army, a short distance away, prevented us from overcoming this deficiency. As the enemy's noose tightened once again, and there were signs of its new advance on the Sierra, the inhabitants of the zone became quite nervous, and the weakest among them sought the possibility of saving themselves from the feared invasion of Batista assassins" (*Pasajes* 102). These "weakest elements" of the peasantry resort to banditry to "save themselves," though Guevara never explains the apparent relation between fear and banditry. Guevara prefaces the chapter with this disclaimer, presumably to explain the actions his guerrilla troop then takes in the battle against banditry. In a matter of a few days during October 1957, Guevara's platoon brought dozens of "bandits" to justice, the majority of them of peasant extraction from the Sierra Maestra. These bands of peasants were guilty of a variety of crimes, from petty theft to rape and murder. Many of these "bandits" were or had been guerrillas, though. The reader is informed of this because it was particularly worrisome to Guevara, as their actions sullied the reputation of the guerrillas in the area. All the leaders of these bandit gangs were summarily executed, and their followers were subjected to various punishments, some quite severe, and most were reintegrated into the troop.

The juxtaposition of these parallel chapters on revolutionary justice, published just one month apart, reveals Guevara's anxiety over the inconsistent, at times contradictory, nature of revolutionary transformation. Although

Guevara repeatedly represents his own revolutionary transformation as self-willed and determinant, the behavior of those around him continuously undermines his developmentalist representation of revolutionary agency. However, rather than interrogate the evidently vexed and vexing nature of the transformation among the guerrilla combatants described in "An Unpleasant Incident," Guevara reduces it to a discursive binary displaced onto a feminized peasantry in "The Struggle against Banditry." Although Sardiñas evidently violates the tenets of proper guerrilla behavior, Guevara insists that Sardiñas is a model of discipline and revolutionary virtue, while he represents the rear guard as a rebellious mob. This troubling contradiction between the "disciplined" behavior of a vanguard member who inflicts grave bodily harm and the "unruly" behavior of the troops who demand justice is displaced onto the dichotomous, feminized representation of peasant consciousness. Guevara deflects his anxiety over the unruly aspects of revolutionary transformation onto the criminal excess of the peasantry because their unruly behavior can be swiftly and clearly adjudicated. Never mind the fact that many of these bandits identify as revolutionaries, or that their crimes bear a troubling resemblance to the actions of the guerrillas—stealing food, rustling horses, executing traitors.

What is "on trial" in these chapters is not just criminality but the internally contradicted nature of Guevara's representation of revolutionary subjectivity. And to reach the desired verdict, he displaces the contradiction onto a familiar binary between the productive, modern, fully developed and potent universal man, on the one hand, and the profligate, premodern, underdeveloped, and impotent traditional man, on the other. The peasant masses of the Sierra are alternately one with the guerrillas or the cause for the guerrillas' eternal vigilance. This discursive binary, though, also returns us to the vanguardist bifurcation of culture put forth in Rostow's modernization paradigm. Just as Lalo Sardiñas, Camilo Cienfuegos, and Che Guevara are made ready to be revolutionary leaders by Castro (their sins forgiven, their excesses tempered), the masses of peasants are made ready to submit to a revolutionary leadership whose tendresse gives way to tyranny at a moment's notice. Both representations of the peasant masses are ultimately feminizing, as the peasants are portrayed as either willingly submitting to revolutionary law or resisting it through willful excess. Meanwhile the centrality of the revolutionary subject is solidified as he remains the masculine hero who must, in either case, discipline the peasants' underdeveloped consciousness, drawing them forward toward revolutionary subjectivity.[10] Thus those peasant bandits who escape execution are nevertheless subjected to a mild form of psychological torture to ensure their reform. Indeed, revolutionary discipline works as a form of subjection, for Guevara tells us that most, if not all, of these men went on to become great combatants and leaders in their own right.

Guevara repeatedly offers a strict dichotomous representation of peasant subjectivity—at the expense of a more nuanced account of their heterogeneous subjectivities—to reinforce his representation of his own teleological transformation from the unruly, feminized subject of neocolonial underdevelopment into the disciplined, masculinist subject of revolutionary development. He desires a seamless narrative of revolutionary transformation and agency. For what is at stake in this strict binary representation of peasant subjectivity but an anxious desire to resolve it and, in doing so, to resolve the developmentalist binary of the developed subject of the First World and the underdeveloped subject of the Third? In addition, and perhaps more significantly, Guevara is moved to resolve any differentiation between the peasantry and the combatants. Just as the "new man" needs to fold feminine tendresse into masculine discipline for his personal transformation, so too do the guerrillas need to fold the peasantry's particularity into the universality of a revolutionary regime of subjection. However, the specificity of Cuban peasant culture is effaced in Guevara's attempt to resolve the binary.

This binary representation of peasant consciousness also returns us to Guevara's representation of the ideal combatant in *Guerrilla Warfare*: the one who demonstrates both rigid self-control and unending flexibility, who shows no mercy and is a loving companion, who is entirely self-contained and entirely dependent on the "longing of the people" for his own survival. What is the ideal combatant if not the masterful subject, effortlessly occupying all subject positions at once? In the arc of "An Unpleasant Incident" and "The Struggle against Banditry," in the shadows of the application of revolutionary justice, we witness Guevara's anxious attempt to transform differentiation—indeed, contradiction—into homogeneity. We witness, that is, his anxious desire for the ideal revolutionary subject who falls from the sky fully formed, transcending all differences in the process of forming a unified revolutionary consciousness.

Interrogating Guevara's (mis)representation of subaltern subjectivity and culture helps to illustrate the disturbing resemblance between developmental and revolutionary regimes of subjection. It also exposes this revolutionary model of transformation to scrutiny for its teleological and binary effects, allowing us to ask: What is at stake in such a narrative formulation of revolutionary subjectivity, consciousness, and agency? What gets preserved in the forward sweep of the "after" of revolutionary transformation, and what gets left behind in the brushing away of the "before" of "prerevolutionary" consciousness? How is the legacy of race in Latin America caught up in this revolutionary regime of subjection? How are both regimes of subjection—development and revolution—racialized in the aftermath of colonialism in the Americas? How are narratives of colonial subalternization preserved in these regimes of subjection?

Betwixt Ariel and Caliban:
A Small Arc of Historical Representation

Guevara's dichotomous representation of these peasants, of the combatants, and ultimately of himself, is not new. Rather, he borrows from a rich Spanish-colonial register for representing subalternity in Latin America. Roberto Fernández Retamar first elaborated on this colonial register in his 1971 essay "Caliban: Notes towards a Discussion of Culture in Our America." In his attempt to answer the perennial question "Does Latin American culture exist?" Fernández Retamar traces Shakespeare's literary representation of Ariel and Caliban in *The Tempest* back to Cristobal Colon's *Diario de navegacion*. In his collection of letters to the Spanish Crown, Colon describes the island peoples he first encounters in strictly binary terms, as the meek and docile *Arauacos* (Ariel), on the one hand, and the flesh-eating and ferocious *Canibas* or *Caribs* (Caliban), on the other.[11] According to Fernández Retamar, this initial representation of the indigenous population in the West Indies introduced a dichotomous set of terms that has been used to represent Latin America culture to this day. On the Arauaco/Ariel side of the binary, we have representations of elite Latin American culture as reasoned, civilized, and emulative of European modernity. On the Carib/Caliban side, we find representations of the popular culture of the masses as irrational, rebellious, and barbarous. Fernández Retamar traces this discursive dichotomy through the literary and political writing of renowned Latin American independence leaders, literary figures, proponents of modernity, and contemporary intellectuals. Since before independence, Fernández Retamar argues, Latin American politicians and intellectuals have inevitably privileged the Arauaco/Ariel trope as the protagonist of a progressive Latin American cultural history.

In contrast, Fernández Retamar rereads Caliban's barbarity as the organic revolutionary consciousness of the popular classes, as a reservoir of courage and honor in the face the submissive and sycophantic Ariel consciousness of Latin American elites, historically complicit with U.S. neocolonialism. In a reworking of Gramsci's distinction between traditional and organic intellectuals, Fernández Retamar analyzes the function of contemporary "Ariels" and "Calibans" in Third World national liberation struggles. Ariel is the traditional intellectual, generally of Creole extraction, whose economic dependence on the national and the international bourgeoisie is reflected in his philosophical dependence on classical European thought and culture. Meanwhile, it is the Calibans, drawn from the mass of "common men," who are the organic intellectuals of the Americas, the only men capable of bringing about true revolutionary change. During revolutionary times, a few Arielian intellectuals (like Fernández Retamar himself) will sever their ties with the bourgeois classes, breaking free of decadent European paradigms, joining the struggle on the side of the oppressed.

In this influential essay, Fernández Retamar suggests that the entire history of Latin American cultural production can be viewed through the lens of these binary forms of consciousness. Rather than subvert this binary construction, however, he replicates it by simply inverting the hierarchy of its terms, as did so much of the anticolonial writing of the period. Crucially, for my purposes, he closes the essay with a discussion of Che Guevara as the quintessential example of an Ariel intellectual, who, in casting his lot with the popular classes, transforms himself into a heroic Caliban: "[Guevara] proposed to Ariel, through his own luminous and sublime example if ever there was one, that he seek from Caliban the honor of a place in his rebellious and glorious ranks" (72). Fernández Retamar, like Guevara himself, represents Che's revolutionary transformation as a decisive move from emasculation to full potency, from submission to self-determination, from Ariel to Caliban.

In an effort to trouble Fernández Retamar's binarism, we can turn to subalternist historian Patricia Seed, who traces this discursive dichotomy to the Spanish Crown's *Requerimiento*. The Requerimiento was the document that Iberian colonizers read aloud to indigenous populations they encountered in the Americas. Written and read in Spanish, it required indigenous populations to make one of two choices before the Crown's representatives: submit to the Christian empire, in which case their needs and the needs of their wives and children would be taken care of by the empire, or resist the Crown, in which case the empire would wage a just and bloody war against them, their wives, and their children. Concludes Seed: "By establishing the opposite of obedience as insurgence, the Requirement [Requerimiento] es-

tablished resistance as proof-positive of opposition to imperial power and
. . . [as] one of the durable signals by which subalternity could be recognized
for aboriginal groups within Hispanic society. Resistance or rebellion
against authority signaled subalternity" (*Requirement for Resistance* 5).
Whereas to Fernández Retamar Caliban represents a rebellious overthrow
of Ariel's submission, to Seed the constitutive relationship between rebellion and submission forged by the Requerimiento—the inextricable relationship between Caliban and Ariel, if you will—transforms the indigenous
into the subaltern. That is, Spanish colonialism itself conditioned recognition of the indigenous, and thus indigenous subjectivity, on the stark choice
between rebellion and submission. By foreclosing any other modes of indigenous subjectivity, this Spanish colonial figure of the submissive or resistive
indigenous subject, echoed by Fernández Retamar, does not allow the indigenous to represent themselves. Rather, it speaks *for* the indigenous by requiring that the indigenous speak either as Caliban or Ariel.

Guevara's representation of the peasantry in *Pasajes*—either as submitting to revolutionary law or as becoming recalcitrant bandits—participates
in this very subalternizing discourse. By demanding that the peasants be at
once submissive and rebellious, Guevara's text issues its own Requerimiento, and in the process it effaces the heterogeneous specificities of peasant consciousness. *Pasajes* resolves this entanglement with the figure of
"Che" himself, who emerges, if furtively, as a self-determining, unitary,
masterful, and masculine revolutionary subject. Guevara's emergence models the transformation of an underdeveloped consciousness, represented
primarily by the abject devotion or resistive duplicity of the peasant, into a
fully developed consciousness, represented primarily by his own revolutionary universality, his tendresse and discipline. Guevara shows how the peasant classes must leave behind their particularity if they are to achieve revolutionary universality. This transformation is *the* key component of both
developmental and revolutionary regimes of subjection, or rather of a developmentalist, revolutionary regime of subjection.

Ultimately, *Pasajes* produces another knowledge of the dictatorship's reliance on repression to secure a particular economic and political order. The
political violence unleashed against the civilian population by the Batista
regime in response to armed struggle foreshadowed the genocidal counterinsurgency policies followed in the 1970s and 1980s by U.S.-backed
dictatorships determined to succeed against communist guerrillas where
Batista had failed. Once again turning to Jean Franco for an assessment of
the overall effect of this state-sponsored violence: "The secular project initi-

ated by the Enlightenment reached its culmination in the disenchanted world of these technologically advanced repressive states. When people found themselves looking for unmarked graves and attempting to identify their children or parents from piles of bones, they confronted the twisted nature of late capitalism's logic in which individual human life, especially in the Third World, is of little moment" (*Decline and Fall* 13). Dictatorial repression and torture undergird the post–World War II discourse of a supposedly peaceful, democratic, and free "development." Guevara's dystopia—the stages of violence and counterviolence described in *Pasajes*—divulges the secret cost of development discourse's Edenic teleology of societies moving progressively, and relatively painlessly, from one stage of modernization to another.

Nonetheless Guevara's dystopian utopia, with its model of revolutionary transformation, subjectivity, agency, and consciousness, participates in its own teleology of relatively effortless social progress from one revolutionary stage to another. In his representation of revolutionary subjection, we find many of the same key metaphors, themes, and tropes deployed by development's regime of subjection. Once again, we find the transition from one stage of consciousness to another figured as a self-willed choice. Guevara's representation of revolutionary transformation "leaves behind" a previously immature, complicit consciousness for a fully formed, collective one, resembling a model of development that "leaves behind" premodern forms of subjectivity and agency for thoroughly modern ones. Both models invariably "leave behind" the ethnic particularity of indigenous or peasant subjectivity, while carrying forward a racialized and masculinist understanding of fully modern, revolutionary agency. The full consequences of this troubling resemblance for ethnic particularity are borne out when Guevara's revolutionary formula is transposed onto the terrain of indigenous Guatemala in Mario Payeras's *Los dias de la selva*, as we will see in the next section, and in Rigoberta Menchú's response, the topic of chapter 5.

As I suggested earlier, however, resemblance also implies difference. We can locate the difference between revolutionary and developmental regimes of subjection precisely in Guevara's reiterative return to the moment of transformation in his serialized diary. This return to the moment of transcendent choice in chapter after chapter belies the *impossibility* of transcending internal differentiation. Guevara's narrative return to these scenes of adjudication expresses his agony over the excision of the unruly, an agony that exceeds the drive toward transcendence over subaltern particularity. It is in this reiterative return to the scenes of his own inevitably incomplete transformation that we can locate the revolutionary potential for the inclusion of difference *as difference* in any future model of revolutionary consciousness and resistance, despite the teleological drive that underwrites his narrative. In and of itself, his continued return to the problem of difference —both internal and external—holds the possibility for the radical inclusion of the difference that peasant subjectivity and culture represent for Guevara. I am reminded here of a photograph in *The Diary of Che Guevara, Bolivia: November 7, 1966–October 7, 1968*. Che Guevara, the famous guerrillero, sits in a tree at the end of the day, dressed in army fatigues, recording his thoughts in his diary. Who is this Ernesto "Che" Guevara if not Ariel *in* Caliban—the consummate, contemplative intellectual within and apart from the revolutionary activity transpiring all around him—resemblance-in-difference?

Che's Legacy: "We Announced Simply That We Were Going to Triumph"

Mario Payeras was a founding member of the Ejercito Guerrillero de los Pobres (Guerrilla Army of the Poor), one of the four groups of armed insurgents that went on to form the Unidad Revolucionaria Nacional Guatemalteca (URNG) (National Revolutionary Union of Guatemala). He was also a writer, poet, and scholar who spent the last fifteen years of his life as a political exile in Mexico. A Marxist intellectual and a committed revolutionary, Payeras epitomized the Latin American middle-class youth who followed Guevara's incendiary example in their attempt to liberate their countries from conditions of economic dependency and political dictatorship. As Rolando Moran, another URNG commander, states in his introduction to Payeras's *Los dias de la selva,*

> Por eso fuimos llamados "foquistas" y "guevaristas" por muchos, pero no rebatimos esos califacativos. Porque "foquistas" de hecho lo fuimos, aunque nunca consideramos el califactivo de "foquista" como una consideración estratégica ni ideológica, porque "guevaristas" en el sentido más amplio, que nosotros no consideramos eliminado con la muerte el Comandante Che Guevara en Ñancahuazo, lo hemos seguido siendo y lo demuestra que tenemos a su efige por insignia.
> [And so we were called "foquistas" and "guevaristas" by many, but we do not refute these designations. It is a given that we were foquistas, although we never adopted foquismo as a strategy or ideology, because

we continue to be "guevarista" in its broadest sense, in that we do not consider the Commander Che Guevara eliminated with his death at Ñancahuazo, and that is why we use his effigy as our insignia.]

Unlike Che Guevara, however, Payeras lived to see the outcome of the more than thirty years of revolutionary struggle in Latin America inspired by the Cuban revolution. Thus although Payeras never abandoned his revolutionary beliefs, he nonetheless had time to reflect on the errors committed by the revolutionary Left, as the arc of his writings demonstrates.

His thoughts on the relationship between indigenous identity and revolutionary struggle evolved dramatically over the course of his life. As Héctor Díaz Polanco, renowned scholar of American indigenous history and identity, has noted, Payeras was one of the first Latin American leftists to recognize Guatemala as a multiethnic society and to consider how race was intricately related to the oligarchic system of class exploitation. As Díaz Polanco rightly points out, Payeras attempts to move beyond the either/or impasse of assimilation and separatism in his 1982 essay *Los pueblos indígenas y la revolución guatemalteca* (Díaz Polanco, "Etnicidad y autonomía" 7–8). However, although Payeras recognizes the centrality of the "ethnonational" problem in this essay, he nevertheless characterizes the "ethnonationalist" consciousness of indigenous Guatemalans as fundamentally stunted, and their place in revolutionary struggle as strictly complementary to the motor force of the worker-peasant alliance (Payeras, *Los pueblos* 81, 83–84). By a 1992 interview with Concepción Villaverde, Payeras had changed his position by 180 degrees. He denounced the genocidal tendencies in all nationalisms, insisted on territorial autonomy for the indigenous populations of Latin America, and recognized that an indigenous-led struggle against racial discrimination was paramount to any successful class-based revolutionary struggle in Guatemala (*Los pueblos* 94, 96–97, 100).[12]

My aim here, however, is not to exhaustively analyze the arc of Payeras's intellectual and political growth, exemplary though it may be. Instead, my interest is far more delineated: I examine two of Payeras's early writings before his autocritical turn. Payeras's first diary and his early essay on the indigenous question, *Los pueblos indígenas y la revolución guatemalteca*, illustrate the degree to which guerrillas of this period modeled revolutionary transformation on Guevara's own transformation (a modeling that Rolando Moran makes clear). Revolutionaries like Payeras deployed a formula for revolutionary subjection in their interaction with the indigenous peasantry of Latin America that was conditioned by the same teleological, masculinist narrative of personal development we find in Guevara's diaries. The reliance on this regime of subjection by revolutionaries operating among the indigenous peasantry had deleterious effects that Payeras himself came to recognize. I choose Payeras instead of any of the other Latin American revolutionaries who have also documented their experiences in writing because, like Guevara, Payeras wrote about his experiences almost immediately after having them. Unlike Nicaragua's Tomás Borge, for example, the precritical Payeras did not have the benefit of ten years of hindsight that would have allowed him to temper the racial implications of his writing. Also, I have chosen Payeras because of his revolutionary and literary connection with feminist compatriot Rigoberta Menchú, whose autobiography is the topic of chapter 5.

On 9 January 1972, twenty-five years after Castro, Guevara, and their guerrilla troop landed on Cuba's beaches, fifteen revolutionaries entered Guatemala from Mexico through the Ixcán region of El K'iche'. These fifteen men founded the first of four new guerrilla organizations that would, in turn, form the Ejercito Guerrillero de los Pobres (EGP). Mario Payeras was one of these fifteen men. He recorded their early attempts to establish an armed guerrilla movement among the indigenous peasants of the Guatemalan highlands in his first diary, *Los dias de la selva*. Although Rolando declares that the EGP was both foquista and guevarista in his introductory remarks to Payeras's diary, the EGP's guerrilla strategy stood in fairly explicit contrast to Guevara's famous *foco* theory. Throughout the 1960s, foco guerrilla groups made up of ex-military men and middle-class youths opposed to the 1954 coup moved to the countryside and launched unsuccessful direct attacks against the Guatemalan military. The founders of the EGP learned from this history. Payeras's group sought to establish a social base among the peasantry and to recruit them into their ranks before engaging in combat with the army: "The defeat of the previous decade had been educational, and one of its principal lessons had been to caution us about the risks of impromptu actions" (*Los dias* 13–14).[13] Indeed, Payeras's description of his group's initial activities is a study in contrast to the harried arrival of Castro's guerrilla band on Cuban shores: "While the group at the ranch [on the Mexican side of the border] maintained appearances, we dug up arms, unpacked ammunition and supplies, set up the first camps deep inside [Guatemalan] territory. We were a caravan of ants that started working at dawn and didn't finish until the night" (*Los dias* 15). Payeras's choice of metaphor, a "caravan of ants" quietly working day in, day out, connotes patient and diligent organizational labor carried out in obscurity rather than the frontal assault of foquista tactics.

Although Payeras differentiates his group's tactics from previous efforts in the region, his representations of the Guatemalan jungle, of his revolutionary mission, of indigenous peasant consciousness, and of his own transformation nevertheless adhere to the formula Guevara established in *Pasajes*. Payeras proceeds with a description of the guerrillas' first few weeks in the Guatemalan jungle:

> It was an era in which the tracks of a tiger constituted a major event. By then, the splendid library we had collected over months had been ruined by the force of the elements. The tomes of social knowledge of the nineteenth century were perforated by the voracity of termites, or entire pages were discolored by the rain. *The First Year of the Russian Revolution, One Hundred Years of Solitude,* and *The Country of Long Shadows* were the only works to survive the disaster. The rest were abandoned to the rainy season. The law of minimum exertion began to govern our movements, and a system of priorities based on absolute realism resulted in a new hierarchy of value attached to the material goods in our lives. . . .
>
> These first days were spent learning the basic truths of the jungle. We had entered a sad world, where only with time did our intelligence learn the points of reference. Without these, our compass was a useless instrument. . . . Meanwhile, we learned to orient ourselves rudimentarily, using the light and the events of the land. For now, we did not often venture out into that silence of butterflies and fireflies. (*Los dias* 15–16)

As in the opening scenes of *Pasajes*, the EGP's theater of operations is first figured as a negation of a prior order, of a prior history, while a "new hierarchy of value" is established. Guevara's dystopic vision most often rendered the scene of negation and re-creation as a staccato of destruction and chaos, with prior personal identities rent asunder by dictatorial violence and reconstituted in revolutionary tendresse/tyranny. Meanwhile Payeras renders the scene of the negation as a lulling absence of activity, as a loss of language, as a forgetting of former knowledge and social meaning. In either Guevara's dystopic opening scenes or Payeras's utopic one, the effect is similar. The "law of minimum exertion" suggests a libidinal withdrawal that equals the death of a prior (bourgeois) subject. Previous forms of orienting oneself in space and time—of mapping identification—are "useless instruments" in the Guatemalan jungle, as "basic truths" must be relearned.

Not only does this place elude all previous forms of geographic and personal mapping, but it is positively hostile to all the trappings of imperial reason. Termites devour the "social knowledge" of its great age, the nineteenth-century books. Importantly, *One Hundred Years of Solitude* survives the elements, for as Franco has suggested, "García Márquez's Macondo only needed to be mentioned for people to understand that it was the fantasy of a liberated territory" (Franco, *Decline and Fall* 7). With the butterfly allusion, and with devouring termites referencing the devouring ants in *One Hundred Years of Solitude,* Payeras furthers the intertextual identification between the jungle and Macondo—that quintessential Latin American town that time forgot. The fantasy of Macondo as liberated territory is precisely the fantasy of it as a space that has escaped colonial and neocolonial modernity (Franco, *Decline and Fall* 8).[14]

The Guatemalan jungle, like Macondo, is free of the exploitative trappings of bourgeois modernity and subsequently frees the guerrilla combatants from their own bourgeois identifications, as "with time" their intelligence learns new "points of reference" in light and landscape. Once again, revolutionary transformation is figured as death and rebirth, as an almost religious transcendence over a prior, complicit subjectivity. Payeras even invokes Guevara's ghostly terms in his description of the Guatemalan guerrillas' transformation: "After having crossed half the jungle, we were a starving army, in rags. That peculiar pallor of someone deprived of light for long periods and the bad odor of accumulated sweat identified us as that *troop of shadows, moving by instinct*" (*Los días* 27; italics mine). Here we have a direct reference to Guevara's use of the phrase "army of shadows" to describe the Cuban guerrillas, and consequently to Guevara's revolutionary formula of death and rebirth. And again, although dead to their former selves, these new revolutionary subjects are nevertheless driven "by instinct," by the "dark psychic mechanisms" described by Guevara as the inner truth of revolutionary agency.

On the other hand, even if imperial reason and bourgeois civilization are "devoured" by the inhospitable jungle, another form of civilization survives—or rather arrives—with the Guatemalan guerrillas. After all, some knowledge does survive the jungle's hostility toward modernity. The jungle in *Días,* as the intertextual equivalent of Macondo, continues to represent the dependency theorist's dream of "an economically workable society freed from outside control" (Franco, *Decline and Fall* 8). In the representational foreshadowing of this economically independent social order, the guerrillas' revolutionary aspirations for the jungle—*The First Year of the Russian Revolution*—also survives. In both Guevara's dystopic and Payeras's utopic representations of the guerrillas' death and rebirth, the troops are "reborn" into a collectivity resembling a primitive communism that prefigures these aspirations. It is as if in both Guevara's and Payeras's revolutionary visions, the guerrilla community must move back in time to move forward toward revolutionary collectivity and egalitarianism.

Thus, throughout the first third of *Los dias*, we find the guerrillas engaged in what Payeras describes as a (re)settling of the jungle. For example, after a few months in the jungle, the guerrilla troop has reestablished contact with clandestine urban forces who are sending the guerrillas grains, foodstuffs, and industrial goods. They have also established some tentative contacts with peasants from isolated towns in the jungle. Despite this contact with the outside world, though, Payeras insists on representing this period as a preliminary stage in the mode-of-production narrative, with the guerrillas represented as transitioning from a hunter-gatherer society to an isolated agricultural society:

> The months for constructing huts in the woods [finally] arrived, and we stored enough grains for long periods, foreseeing the long winter and the eventual enemy offensive. One day, without us even noticing when exactly, the time of hunger passed, and the omnipotent powers of Atilio [a guerrilla member], that Robespierre of provisions, ceased. It was the *era of great inventions* and of apprenticeship in sedentary life. We *invented* bread, *discovered* the rubber boot, and learned the *art of navigating* on a raft. Jacobo, Jorge, and a few others who came from the coast or had lived in the countryside were able fishermen, and they would frequently go off at first light. They returned late at night, and the next morning daybreak would find them in the kitchen with a string of thirty or more fish. Our camps took on a different aspect, and for the first time we had time to read and to review some of our principal experiences. . . . We were the only ones living in thousands of square kilometers. Someone often said that we had the largest house [in the world], where water, light, and energy were free and we paid no rent. (*Los dias* 53; italics mine)

The guerrillas' nomadic wandering and hunger come to an end with the construction of the huts and the storage of goods. With this settlement, they come to exist as a community where egalitarian relations rule, since there is no hereditary status or authoritarian power. Instead the guerrillas share a collective right to the jungle's basic resources, to the "water, light, and energy" they may freely appropriate. Although some members of the community produce more because of their greater skill, all the goods are distributed fairly among the entire community, as is made evident in the example of the fishermen and their fish. Indeed, men not only hunt and fish but also cook and clean. The guerrillas learn to attend to each other's domestic needs. In other words, with the end of their wanderings, the guerrilla troop is finally established as a loving community existing in revolutionary tendresse: even Atilio backs off of his ironfisted approach to protecting and distributing the provisions. They exist in an unalienated relation to their labor, to each other, to their "feminine side," and to nature. And in Payeras's representation of this transition, they appear to accomplish this community all by their lonesome.

The language that Payeras uses to describe this period in the guerrillas' jungle life appears to be taken almost directly from Marx's description of this initial stage of development in his *Pre-capitalist Economic Formations:* "The earth is the great laboratory, the arsenal which provides both the means and the materials of labor, and also the location, the *basis* of the community. Men's relationship to it is naive: they regard themselves as its *communal proprietors,* and as those of the community which produces and reproduces itself by living labor. Only in so far as the individual is a member —in the literal and figurative sense—of such a community, does he regard himself as an owner or possessor" (208–9). The jungle is precisely the "great laboratory" of the guerrillas' "inventions," its free "water, light, and energy" their "arsenal" of "materials [for] labor." As Marx suggests, no single member of the guerrilla troop considers himself owner of the jungle's riches; rather, "they regard themselves as its *communal proprietors,*" reproducing themselves androgynously in loving tendresse. Payeras's representation of the guerrillas as existing in such a state is precisely what constitutes them as a community for the reader and, more importantly, for themselves.

If Payeras's jungle community at this point in the narrative represents a textbook case of Marx's definition of production for use value in primitive communism (Bottomore 445),[15] the passage is also rich in the language of a liberal and imperial discourse of development, coupling scientific mastery and colonial quest: The guerrillas invent things, and in the process of inventing these things, they remake themselves and the terrain around them. The guerrillas are the Robinson Crusoes of the Guatemalan jungle, introducing an imperial narrative of progress—*era, invention, discovery, art, navigation*— to a jungle constructed as awaiting their historical agency. The guerrillas are primary, independent, potent social beings who bring the jungle under their explicit control. Payeras's idea of development in this passage resembles the Kantian imperative: Everything exists to be used *merely as a means* by rational man; nature is rendered in his image. In a liberal model of political economy, the construction of the social privileges individual action and individual accumulation. As a Marxist-Leninist, however, Payeras constructs the social differently. Like Guevara before him, he fills this undeveloped space with a utopian vision of collective action and the satisfaction of material need in a boundless "house" capable of accommodating all. In this state of primitive communism, the guerrillas even have leisure time available for pleasurable intellectual activities, such as reading and self-reflection.

The imbrication of the modernization-through-stages narrative in liberal development discourse and the mode-of-production narrative in Marxism-Leninism is revealed in Payeras's diary even more so than in Guevara's. Stated more precisely, these vying narratives of progress are *reconciled* in the revolutionary regime for subjection put forth in Guevara and performatively reiterated by Payeras. While not relying on the liberal figure of the individual, Payeras's representation of the collective subject still relies on the construction of the jungle space as a primary lack in contrast to the evolving, technological presence of natural man. In both Guevara's and Payeras's representations of guerrilla collectivity as a primitive communism unfolding in this jungle space, the transformation into revolutionary subjectivity (individually and collectively) is foreseen as occurring through discrete, progressive stages. Guevara and Payeras, in their literary returns to an original collectivity in order to move forward toward revolutionary communalism, are simply resetting the historical clock in the hopes of obviating liberal stages of development with their own model of transformation and agency. What is far more problematic than their substitution of Marx's mode-of-production narrative for modernization's stages of development, however, is the dependence of *both* theories of history—and consequently of Third World revolutionary nationalism—on a disturbingly similar and normative model of consciousness and theory of human agency. It is this dependence on the second modality of developmentalism shared by First World, Second World, and Third World development paradigms that once again, in Payeras's text, bifurcates the community in which it transpires.

If Payeras represents the EGP as Guatemalan Robinson Crusoes—as a fundamental collectivity of men creating civilization in an uncivilized place—is there a Friday in this narrative? Is there a primitive inhabitant of this blank jungle space who functions as the necessary anterior to Payeras's primitive communism? In the first third of the book, the "native inhabitants" of this place are only present through their conspicuous absence. Payeras repeatedly tells us that the guerrillas progressively learned the ways of the jungle—which plants were edible, which were medicinal, which snakes were deadly, how to avoid getting lost. Yet he does not tell us *how* they attained so much knowledge in so little time. Payeras repeatedly uses the terms "discovery" and "accumulation" to describe the guerrillas' attainment of this knowledge. However, this kind of knowledge takes longer to accumulate than one or two months. The bearers of this cumulative knowledge, the "Fridays"—be they actual indigenous members of the guerrilla troop or indigenous peasants they may have encountered—must be erased in order to construct the guerrilla as the "original man" engaged in civilizing this jungle. As with Guevara, the terms Payeras uses to represent Guatemala's indigenous peasantry derive from his own aspirations for transformation.

Payeras references Guatemala's indigenous population exactly twice in his narrative of the guerrillas' first two months in the jungle. The first reference is in his description of the group's makeup. Four of the fifteen guerrillas, it turns out, are indigenous. Even as Payeras acknowledges this, however, indigenous identity is at once constructed as anterior to revolutionary history and as under erasure. Payeras describes the guerrillas' first weeks of marching deep into the jungle:

> We did not see the sun again, and we started to lose our sense of time. We were the first to pass through here in many centuries. Every once in a while, when we would dig up the humus to do our business, we would unearth indigenous pottery. It was a small testimony to the fact that at one point these latitudes had been the regular routes of the great human migrations of the past. We would get up at daybreak, with the universal gibberish of birds, and we would march all day in silence or speaking very little. We had plenty of time to think things over, to scrutinize our recondite class motivations. What was each one thinking during that interminable journey? We were a mosaic of bloods and class positions. Lacho, Jorge, Julián, and Mario belonged to the Cakchikel ethnic group. Despite the ties of language and culture, they did not form a group. The enigmas and misadventures of indigenous identity would keep Lacho up at night, in the midst of [another] culture at once hostile and desirable. The others were perhaps not so troubled by [these] matters, or more likely their thought focused on the elemental constant [*constatación elimental*] that men organize

themselves and fragment the world according to their material interests. (*Los dias* 24–25)

Indigenous identity is represented as doubly anterior to revolutionary subjectivity in this passage. Indigenous peoples are the historic ancestors of our revolutionary heroes, as the guerrillas retrace the steps of the "great human migrations" of yore. Even as Payeras references an image of the Maya's expansive and populous kingdom, with its dynamic trade and travel routes, this prior civilization is already disintegrated—reduced to broken pieces of earthenware rummaged from the dank and decomposing jungle soil.

Payeras then moves seamlessly from the late, great Maya empire *through* the mysterious and mystical ("recondite") class motivations of each guerrilla to a description of four living Indians divided *in their particularity.* Although the four Cakchikel Indians share a language and culture, "they did not form a group." Indeed, it is the laconic Lacho's racial perturbations that appear to divide the group, setting him apart from the three whose analysis is represented by Payeras as clearly more advanced. Jorge, Julian, and Mario understand the "elemental constant" that is class antagonism, the "material interests" that drive human history, and consequently they are not distracted by their own racial particularity. Indeed, Jorge's, Julian's, and Mario's class analysis frees them from the troubled sleep induced by Lacho's racial ruminations, which do not even rise to the level of "motivations" for struggle. Instead these "misadventures" appear to suspend him in taciturn, hostile, and inappropriate "desire."

The effect of this representation of ethnicity as doubly anterior to revolutionary subjectivity—in chronological time and historical consciousness—is to deracinate it. In the jungle "latitudes," indigenous empire is superseded by revolutionary order, just as among the guerrilla troops Lacho's ethnic identification must "give way" to the superior analysis and more fundamental solidarity of the three men who understand themselves according to their class position. The particularity of these Cakchikel Indians is, at best, auxiliary to their economic universality, given that Payeras represents Jorge, Julian, and Mario as, at best, indifferent to their own ethnic identity.

Payeras's essay *Los pueblos indígenas y la revolución guatemalteca* appeared anonymously in 1982 in *Compañero,* the EGP's international publication, which reached an audience beyond the group's militants (Díaz Polanco, *Etnicidad y autonomía* 7). As the title suggests, the essay is a position paper on the role that indigenous Guatemalans should play in the revolutionary movement. It is an elaborate analysis of the imbrication of racial discrimination and economic exploitation. In addition, Payeras theorized the causes for the demise of Guatemala's pre-Hispanic populations. According to Payeras's historical analysis, the indigenous populations of Latin America were on the verge of developing the "national consciousness" that would have facilitated accelerated economic development when the Spanish arrived. Hence in Guatemala the indigenous people were unable to resist colonization: "Lacking the unity and national consciousness necessary for forming an organized resistance that could successfully oppose the invader, the national liberation struggle was unable to develop, despite the initial resistance—dispersed and disorganized—by empires in disarray. The subsequent capitalist development made it so that the indigenous society, already in a process of decomposition, was penetrated by new contradictions, those of dependent capitalism" (*Los pueblos* 85).

In this description of the effect of colonialism on indigenous Guatemalans, Payeras richly echoes Rostow's discussion of reactive nationalism. Just as in Rostow's homoeroticized theory of colonialism, Payeras's "traditional" ancestors proved incapable of fending off colonial capitalism and its distorted development. Their nascent national resistance was impotent in the face of Spanish penetration. In an echo as well of the Requerimiento's terms of subaltern subjection, Payeras's Arielian ancestors are positively abject in their submission: they are in "a process of decomposition" even *before* capitalist penetration. Indeed, Payeras is Rostow's reactive nationalist, for Payeras marches in the footsteps of his defeated ancestors, responding with Calibanian resistance to humiliation, determined to rectify the damage caused by colonial capitalism with a new and improved national liberation struggle. So once again we see the tropes of developmentalist, revolutionary subjection reiterated in a distinctly *American* register of racial and gender categories.

Of course, even while ethnic identity is represented as secondary to class consciousness in Payeras's description of Lacho, Jorge, Julian, and Mario, indigenous peasants are absolutely primary to the revolutionary mission of the EGP. Payeras represents the guerrillas as self-determined and determining revolutionary agents in the jungle, and yet all the while they are searching for those who will be the target of their revolutionary errand. Thus we come to the second acknowledgment of the indigenous peasantry in Payeras's narrative. At the end of the first chapter, the guerrillas finally stumble on some native inhabitants, and—again in accordance with the formula for revolutionary subjection—the "Fridays" of Guatemala's uncivilized jungle-space must ultimately mirror the guerrillas' own transformation:

All we could distinguish of the town [at this distance] was an intense light in the clearing and here and there the old cuttings of axes. It was the hour of profound silence in the jungle, barely disturbed by the discreet movement of birds on the upper branches. We waited a long time, listening to the beating of our hearts. Then we heard the crowing of a cock from the direction of the town. It was the first time in months that we had heard that welcome trumpeting. We all exchanged a glance that held both *trepidation* and *joy* in it. *There they were, at last, the poor people of our country; but we were ignorant of what would be their response.* As time passed we distinguished new noises: chickens clucking, the distant hacking of machetes, familiar voices of women calling to birds to get back in their cages. All of the sudden, abruptly and intensely, dogs would bark. . . . As we approached the houses, a thin boy, with bushy eyebrows and a loud voice, without any wonder or surprise at our attire or at the guns held by those who approached him, said hello to us in a most familiar manner, adding immediately that they [the villagers] had just been talking about us. They were six families total that had recently settled in this small clearing, and they already knew of [our] activity on the border through their radio. They still didn't have maize, but they put what little they had at our disposal. That night we brought together the men of the village, and we explained extensively the reason for our struggle, and we announced simply that we were going to triumph. (29–30; italics mine)

The bright light beckoning them toward the town and the unusual silence that falls over the jungle set the scene as one of mystical, almost religious, arrival by the guerrillas. Indeed, there is a predestined quality to the encounter insinuated by the young boy's insouciant response to them and the villagers' anticipatory conversation. Payeras simultaneously constructs the peasants as awaiting a guerrilla force they *already know about* "through their radio" and as the horizon for guerrilla activity: *"There they were, at last, the poor people of our country."* Peasant desire ("already knowing") and guerrilla purpose ("there they were *at last*") are wed in his representation, though it is Payeras who displaces his desire onto the peasants when he represents their foreknowledge as a form of anticipation. It is the guerrillas who have been awaiting just such villagers in order that their mission may have meaning. Thus it is the guerrillas—and not the peasants —who are held in awe *("trepidation* and *joy")* by the surprising sight of the

Other. Just as it is the guerrillas who must performatively pronounce themselves into being before these subaltern witnesses: "we announced simply that we were going to triumph."

In this second passage, Payeras once again represents Guatemala's indigenous peasantry as doubly anterior to revolutionary subjectivity. They are anterior to revolutionary subjectivity in that they anticipate the coming of the guerrillas—the peasants know that the guerrilla troop is coming even before it arrives. But they are anterior to the guerrillas' revolutionary subjectivity ontologically as well, for the peasants are repeatedly represented in the passage in terms that equate them with their natural surroundings. First a cock speaks for the indigenous peasant villagers from the direction of the town. Then the clucking of chickens, the sounds of machetes, the barking of dogs, and the voices of women are all equated in this elliptical representation of the villagers as existing in a primordial, mythological oneness with nature. The villagers all but dissolve into the primitive wilderness of the jungle. Or more accurately put, the villagers resolve out of nature—that is, they come into resolution once spotted by the guerrillas.

What is fascinating about this passage is that the peasants are represented as at once emerging *out of* oneness with nature and emerging *into* oneness with the guerrillas. In other words, though their level of consciousness is represented as premodern, as organically emanating from their natural surrounding, it is also represented as organically "in tune" with the revolutionary consciousness of the guerrillas. Hence even though the villagers have no maize, "they put what little they had at our disposal." (Never mind that the fact of the villagers' hearing about the guerrillas through their radios could equally be read as contradicting both their apparent premodern condition and their intuitive connection with the troop.) The village, in its apparent isolation and organic community, *is* the distorted, precapitalist social formation Payeras discusses in his essay. Although this representation of precapitalist society may be drawn from Second World development theory, it is also homologous to the famously autarkic "traditional society" or "subsistence economy" of development discourse. In either interpretation, the villagers exist in a condition of protohumanity, from which revolutionary transformation must rescue them. These villagers, however, are also filled with anticipatory desire, with a prerevolutionary consciousness that awaits completion under the guiding hand of the guerrillas. In Rostow's terms of developmental subjection, the peasants are prepared to "be prepared" by the guerrillas; they are ready to be made ready (Rostow 20). Once again, indigenous peasant particularity is figured as doubly anterior to revolutionary universality. In both their "need" for evolutionary development of consciousness and their anticipatory desire, these native inhabitants are the condition of possibility for the guerrillas. The peasants are the anteriority that gives the guerrillas' mission meaning. Hence, like a beacon, the bright light from the village summons the guerrillas forth, into revolutionary being.[16]

Payeras elaborates on this double anteriority in *Los pueblos indígenas y la revolución guatemalteca*. Although the essay is written in an analytical, rather than literary, voice, the terms he uses to represent ethnic identity and indigenous consciousness are strikingly similar to those used in the diary:

> Indigenous subsistence farmers *(autoconsumidores)* and indigenous semiproletariats, for example, produce and think differently from each other, though they share the same sense of ethno-cultural identity; [they are] distinguished from each other by the ideological features [*rasgos*] that derive from their socioeconomic condition. Among the subsistence farmers there is a correspondence between the way in which they produce and their ethnic-national consciousness, given that they live and produce in the basic state of affairs of the pre-Hispanic, precapitalist society, [and] for that reason their cultural state of affairs is not in contradiction with the socioeconomic state of affairs in which they produce. But among the semiproletarian indigenous, the ethnic-national consciousness is permeated by political and ideological elements that are proper to the relations of production in which they find themselves, such as the nascent consciousness of [their own] exploitation, a *glimmer* of the class differentiation *that allows them to see* the rich indigenous [as their exploiters] and of class consciousness in relation to the Ladinos who are exploiters and Ladinos who are exploited, et cetera. (*Los pueblos* 81; italics mine)

Payeras's analysis also adheres to liberal development discourse. His description of indigenous subsistence farmers might appear in a development studies textbook as a case study of a "dual societies" paradigm. Payeras's premodern autoconsumidores are "subsistence economies" existing contiguous to, but in bounded isolation from, modern capitalist formations. Anxious as he is to liberate his country from its dependent development, Payeras is nevertheless oblivious to a fundamental tenet of dependency theory. After all, as I have discussed in chapter 2 as well, Stavenhagen dispenses with modernization theorists' facile characterization of rural communities as self-contained, insisting that such communities have not existed in Latin America since the conquest. Indeed, even the most remote indigenous peasant producers, such as those in the Péten, have been exposed to modernity. This is made evident by their very migration to the jungle, triggered by their dispossession in the densely populated highlands of Guatemala. However, for Payeras, Guatemala's indigenous peasantry continue to "live and produce in the basic state of affairs of the pre-Hispanic, precapitalist society." As such, they are not even familiar with social antagonism, according to Payeras's representation, since there is no contradiction between their culture and the prehistoric economic formation. Here Payeras's analysis is reminiscent of Larrain's analysis of subject formation, also discussed in chapter 2, for once again precapitalist forms of consciousness automatically give way to more enlightened forms of consciousness under capitalism. And again, as in Larrain's analysis, these "precapitalist" peasants presumably live in blissful ignorance of their own exploitation.

Therein lies a far more troubling implication in Payeras's teleological analysis with regard to revolutionary subjection. For Payeras, "ethnic-national consciousness" is conjoined with precapitalist formation. In his formulation in this passage, there is a "correspondence" between the two. In other words, their ethnic particularity and their purported precapitalist economic formation, for Payeras, are one and the same. Ethno-nationalism is a "sense" that autoconsumidores and semiproletarian Indians share, an ephemeral feeling. But in *thought* these two groups of Indians are divided. They are cleaved apart by ideological "rasgos," by the ideologically informed thought of a semiproletarian consciousness characterized in the privileged terms of greater mental acuity: "glimmer," "see." These semiproletarian Indians are leaving their emotive ethnic sentiment behind in the private sphere, while their class consciousness determines their future. Once again, revolutionary agency depends on a cultural deracination of the racialized subject.

This requirement for deracination in the revolutionary's regime of subjection is made most evident toward the end of the essay, when Payeras ruminates on what ethnic identity will look like after the revolution has triumphed. Payeras imagines the nation after a fully sovereign, independent, and socialist economy has supplanted Guatemala's dependent, distorted development:

> [In the] new multinational patria, it is unavoidable that new relations of production, established in our country upon having eliminated the exploitation of some men by others, will erode the culture originally

based on precapitalist relations of production. To propose the contrary would be the equivalent of denying our country the development of its productive social forces, of rejecting the conquests of science and the technology that humanity has acquired in its evolution. What our new multinational patria can and should aspire to is for the culture of indigenous peoples—what is timeless in it, valid, and valuable—to stop being the object of decomposition, distortion, and debasement by blind laws and the dehumanization of capitalism. (86)

Not only are the technological achievements of indigenous cultures somehow outside of the "conquests of science and the technology that humanity has acquired in its evolution," but indigenous culture is suspended at the vanishing point of a precapitalist dawn to the horizon of a socialist future for humanity. New productive forces will not only evolve into Marx's communist vision of a solution of class antagonism but also necessarily entail the erosion of ethnic particularity.

Payeras's analysis of the role that "ethno-nationalism" will play in Guatemala's national liberation struggle against U.S. neocolonialism subscribes to Lenin's view of the distinction between struggles of nationalist liberation from colonialism and struggles for national cultural autonomy. In "Resolution on the National Question," published in *Pravda* on 16 May 1917, Lenin firmly commits himself and the party to the right of nations to self-determination: "Only the recognition by the proletariat of the right of nations to secede can ensure complete solidarity among the workers of the various nations and help to bring the nations closer together on truly democratic lines" (*Selected Works* 111). But while Lenin decries the role of modern imperialism in "subjugat[ing] weaker nations" and supports national liberation movements in their struggles against it, he nevertheless adamantly opposes all forms of cultural nationalism: "The party of the proletariat emphatically rejects what is known as 'national cultural autonomy,' under which education, etc., is removed from the control of the state and put in the control of some kind of national diets. National cultural autonomy artificially divides the workers living in one locality, and even working in the same industrial enterprise, according to their various 'national cultures'; in other words, it strengthens the ties between the workers and the bourgeois culture of the nations, whereas the aim of the Social-Democrats is to develop the international culture of the world proletariat" (*National Question* 112). Thus, while nationalist identity is appropriate, and even necessary, in the struggle against capitalist imperial oppression, nationalist sentiment, or a sentimental attachment to the cultural trappings of one's national identity ("national diets"), is clearly inappropriate, divisive, and undesirable. Similarly, in his essay, Payeras distinguishes between two kinds of nationalisms in Guatemala. The "ethno-nationalism" of the indigenous minorities, associated, in his estimation, with precapitalist economic *and* cultural formations, is analogous to the sentimental attachment to nationalist culture that Lenin derides. Meanwhile the implied nationalism of the Guatemalan revolutionaries, who will have "eliminated the exploitation of some men by others," is analogous to the anti-imperialist nationalism of a simultaneously international proletariat. Hence these anti-imperialist nationalists would never participate in "denying our country the development of its productive social forces" by advocating the preservation of indigenous cultural forms. In sum, ethno-nationalism for Payeras can only ever play a supplementary role to the true nationalism of Guatemala's proletariat, and even this supplementary role must be diminished once the struggle for national liberation from U.S. imperialism has triumphed and new productive forces take root.

There are two misappropriations in Payeras's transposition of Lenin's analysis onto the American continent and context. First, what Payeras fails to see—indeed, what he cannot see from his Ladino position—is the possibility that Mayan ethno-nationalism could be interpreted, even under Lenin's schema, as precisely the basis for a continuing struggle against Spanish colonialism, its heirs, and its neocolonial, capitalist aftermath. Thus, rather than disagree with Lenin's position on the theoretical shortfalls and practical dangers of separatist ethnic movements, I would instead suggest that the pre-autocritical Payeras is incapable of recognizing ethno-nationalism as anything other than precapitalist and therefore secondary, when instead it may be a force of resistance to both colonial racialization and capitalist exploitation, as we shall see in chapter 5. Second, more problematically, Payeras's reading of indigenous attachment to ethnic particularity as the equivalent of reactionary attachments to "national cultural autonomy," evidenced by his insistence that only that which is "timeless in it, valid, and valuable" will be preserved, inevitably leads to a policy of ethnic deracination; for who gets to decide what constitutes "timeless," "valid," or "valuable"?[17] And how exactly does that which is invalid get excised and eliminated? Finally, we arrive at the crux of the matter: Payeras's "multinational patria" is paradoxically monocultural. If the indigenous population wants to participate in the revolutionary struggle, it must participate in a personal transformation that necessitates the transcendence of its own ethnic particularity. In the end, Payeras's regime of revolutionary subjection is not all that different from the nineteenth-century assimilation policies of liberal independence movements in Latin America, or from the twentieth-century rearticulation of assimilation under the guise of cultural indigenismo.

Payeras's early essay is published less than two years after the publication of his jungle chronicle, and one could thus assume that his observations on the topic of indigenous identity in Guatemala emerged out of his personal experience in the jungle with the indigenous peasantry. But I have also suggested that Payeras's representational terms for the indigenous peasants emerge from his personal desires and motivations, from a Spanish colonial narrative of conquest and legacy of race, and, most importantly, from a fundamentally developmentalist regime of revolutionary subjection. By representing his own revolutionary transformation as a transformation into an enlightened subject possessing full consciousness, into the central, self-determining, self-contained agent of transformation for the jungle, Payeras, like Guevara before him, concludes by privileging the modern, self-reliant subject as the model of oppositional consciousness—a model that is ultimately untenable in a modern world of multiple dependencies. Thus Payeras and the guerrillas mythically survive in the jungles and mountains of Guatemala by themselves. When the guerrillas do encounter the local inhabitants of the jungle, these inhabitants are represented as themselves in need of development, as agent/objects of a future revolutionary development who are presently trapped in the misleading and precapitalist consciousness of ethnic particularity. These indigenous peasants are represented as needing a transformation in consciousness that can only be actuated by the universal (deracinated), self-contained, self-reliant guerrilla subjects. Indeed, for Payeras, liberating the patria from underdevelopment requires liberating it from the very "precapitalist" indigenous particularity that, in his opinion, maintains the nation in a state of predevelopment vis-à-vis other Western nations. Thus even as his revolutionary ambitions for Guatemala are to liberate it and his countrymen from a condition of dependent development, he remains dependent on the second modality of developmentalism with regard to subjectivity, and thus his literary rendition of revolutionary subjection in the Guatemalan jungle and highland reproduces subalternization and subordination.

In sum, by adhering to this regime of revolutionary subjection, Guevara and Payeras illustrate the logic that has led to the impasse between Marxist-Leninist revolutionary movements and peasant classes or ethnic minorities in Latin America. Guevara and Payeras adhere to the orthodox Marxist-Leninist mode-of-production narrative. While it is unsurprising that these Latin American revolutionaries adhere to a Second World development theory of history, what I have been suggesting is that this theory of history also implies a regime of subjection that is remarkably similar to the regime of subjection under a liberal First World development discourse. Indeed, First World, Second World, and revolutionary Third World development theories all presuppose a teleology of the human subject in which the peasant formation or ethnic identity is a precursor to a higher form of consciousness. Consequently, Guevara's and Payeras's representations of indigenous/peasant subjectivity and consciousness subscribe to the same key metaphors, themes, and tropes for representing peasant and indigenous formations present in the post–World War II liberal discourse of development and progress. Payeras and Guevara proceed by bifurcating indigenous/peasant subaltern consciousness as primitive and reactionary, on the one hand, and as organically revolutionary, on the other. I have tried to demonstrate how this model of revolutionary transformation is structured around Payeras's and Guevara's own bifurcated desires for, and anxieties about, their personal transformations. They desire full masculinity, a pristine horizon in which this masculinity may unfold, and prerevolutionary subaltern subjects who not only bear witness to their personal transformations but also await their masculinist revolutionary agency. Simultaneously, Guevara and Payeras are anxious about the "completeness" of their own transformation, about the inherently duplicitous nature of the subaltern, and about the subaltern's "premodern" resistance to their revolutionary modernity. Guevara and Payeras participate in a discourse of development that necessitates the transcendence or repression of "preconsciousness" particularity in order to attain a revolutionary consciousness capable of founding a modern, developed nation. In addition, Guevara's and Payeras's representations of revolutionary subjection conform as well to the terms of colonial history in Latin America for representing indigenous peasants, and to the paradigmatic masculinity of imperial reason. These literary techniques of representation, however, have political consequences—"it is unavoidable"—as we will see in chapters 4, 5, and 6.

4

Irresistible Seduction:

Rural Subjectivity under

Sandinista Agricultural Policy

Now, women forget all those things they don't want to remember, and remember everything they don't want to forget. The dream is the truth. Then they act and do things accordingly.
—Zora Neale Hurston, *Their Eyes Were Watching God*

As I discussed in chapter 2, developmentalism constructed Third World nations as suspended in a preliminary stage of productivity and an elementary stage in the history of becoming modern, industrialized, capitalist nation-states.[1] It did so by inventing an underdeveloped, underproductive subject to be named, located, studied, theorized, and ultimately policed through development policy and projects. "Development colonized reality, became reality," as Arturo Escobar has succinctly stated. "Development proceeded by creating abnormalities ('the poor,' 'the malnourished,' 'the illiterate,' 'pregnant women,' 'the landless') which it would then treat or reform" ("Imagining a Post-Development Era?" 25). Once located and enumerated, these subjects could presumably benefit from development projects imparted from above by governments under the direction of international agencies.

This teleology of progress not only provided an alibi for colonialism's role in forging the conditions in which decolonized and decolonizing nations found themselves but also provided the conditions for continued surveillance of peripheral nations and their citizens. Categories of need abstracted by this discourse warranted development projects that extended the opportunity for exploitative economic and social relations into every corner of the globe. The promise of development was to bring these benighted subjects of the Third World into the epochal history of the modern nation—into full productivity—with the subsequent rights and privileges available to the productive citizen of an international family of nations.[2] From Pinochet to the Zapatistas, this promise of full productivity, this horizon of political evolution, this discourse of development, has seduced the Right and the Left in Latin America for more than forty years.

Development as a discursive phenomenon and as a policy field quickly assumed a stubbornly "nonideological" character. James Ferguson, in his case study of livestock development projects in Lesotho, has suggested that international development agencies and state bureaucracies become "anti-politics" machines because they continually reduce poverty and inequality to failures of technological advancement. Developmentalism is not only antipolitical in its refusal to analyze the role of exploitative geopolitical power relations in generating such conditions; it is "nonpolitical" and "non-ideological" in that it perceives development as an "omni-historical reality." Althusser suggested of ideology in general "that it is endowed with a struc-ture and a functioning such as to make it a non-historical reality, i.e. an *omni-historical* reality, in the sense in which that structure and functioning are immutable, present in the same form throughout what we can call history" (Althusser 161). It is precisely in this Althusserian sense of ideology that developmentalism takes on an apparently nonideological character. The discourse of development renders development an immutable fact, a value-neutral process taking place throughout history. Development repre-sents itself as an imperative prior to and beyond ideologies of capitalism or Marxism. Hence it is not surprising that although there have been extensive critiques of particular development models, policies, or projects—by depen-dency, unequal exchange, and world systems theorists—few, if any, neo-Marxist critics have questioned the imperative *to develop*. Quite the contrary, most of these critical endeavors have sought an alternative development—a diversified, independent development within equal terms of trade—and not the alternative *to* development for which Escobar and Ferguson, among other recent critics, have called.

To address both the call by neo-Marxists for a model of alternative de-velopment and the call by post-Marxists for an alternative to development, this chapter offers a case study of Sandinista agricultural policy. The Sandi-nista National Liberation Front explicitly attempted to forge a revolutionary approach to development in Nicaragua. While the Sandinista case demon-strates the seductive power that the imperative to develop has had on the Left, it also clearly demonstrates the material limits prohibiting countries from simply stepping outside the paradigm of development.

The FSLN came to power in 1979 after two years of general insurrection in Nicaragua. Although party origins date back to the foquista guerrilla movements of the 1960s, the party that came to power in 1979 corresponded to the "second generation" of armed movements in Latin America. The FSLN of the late 1970s had successfully brought together the different ideological tendencies that engaged in armed struggle in Nicaragua, divisions similar to those that had destroyed armed struggles in other countries. The party had subsequently abandoned foquismo for a policy of national alliance with members of the oligarchy, the bourgeoisie, the press, and various parties. Most important, the FSLN had successfully coordinated its efforts against the dictatorship with the efforts of mass-based social movements: the liberation church, the women's movement, the student movement, syndicalists, and peasant organizations. The Sandinistas—like the FMLN in El Salvador, the URNG in Guatemala, and the M-19 in Colombia—accomplished something the guerrilla movements of the 1960s had been unable to do: they moved, theoretically and practically, beyond a vanguardism that saw the party as creating a mass movement and adopted a vanguardism that saw the party in a supporting or coordinating role for the mass movement.[3]

Once in power, the Sandinistas were committed to restructuring Nicaragua's dependent economy for the benefit of the country's poor majority and to promoting the interests of the mass movement that had brought them to power. The conditions of Nicaragua's insertion into the global market, however, placed certain structural constraints on Sandinista choices in agricultural policy. The devastating U.S. war against the Sandinistas stands as testimony to the ferocity with which these constraints are enforced. But not every choice made by the Sandinistas was predetermined by market, fiscal, and geopolitical constraints. Key decisions in agriculture corresponded to the Sandinistas' faith in a Marxist-Leninist teleology of progress, in a developmentalist model of history. Indeed, Sandinista agricultural policy was itself a regime of subjection: its intention was to produce a model subject in agriculture, one with a revolutionary consciousness that would benefit the citizen and the nation. But this theoretical revolutionary subjectivity did not emerge from the material reality in which the peasants found themselves. Consequently the peasant formation ended up outside a Sandinista vision of revolutionary national development. Even though the peasant was at the center of the revolutionary imagination, the FSLN implemented an agricultural development policy that negatively impacted its peasant base of support in the countryside. By 1985, peasants were filling the ranks of the U.S.-backed counterrevolutionaries, and in 1990 the FSLN lost the presidential and parliamentary elections. How is it that the Sandinista revolutionary movement met with resistance from the very people whom their model of development presumably intended to liberate? Why did the regime of subjection implied in revolutionary agrarian reform policies clash so violently with peasant reality?

What Women Remember

I conducted the research for this study during the three years I lived in Nicaragua, from July 1984 to August 1987, and on two summer research trips in 1988 and 1989. During the three years that I lived in Nicaragua, I was a part-time researcher, writer, and translator at the Institute Historico CentroAmericano (IHCA), a think tank affiliated with the Jesuit-run Central American University in Managua. At that time the IHCA published a monthly academic journal, *Envío*, written in Spanish and distributed primarily to university libraries and solidarity organizations, and a weekly newsletter, *Update*, written in English and distributed primarily to international journalists and U.S. Congress members. In addition to translating *Envío* articles into English, I had a regular "beat" for *Update*. I covered the women's movement (party affiliated and independent), the drafting of Nicaragua's new constitution, agricultural policy, agrarian reform, and peasant mobilizations. Although we published the newsletter without bylines, issues of *Update* written during this period on these topics were generally written by me. As such, I could have written this analysis of the Sandinista regime of subjection from the perspective of women's rights, or from the perspective of the drafting of "revolutionary" national rights (a process that took more than a year and involved extended consultations of almost the entire citizenry). In addition, my experience since then as a cultural studies scholar would have permitted me to examine the question of revolutionary subjection from the perspective of Sandinista cultural policy, or from the perspective of literary production. However, I chose to examine agricultural policy and peasant relations because the success or failure of the revolution was ultimately not determined by women's rights, constitutional guarantees, cultural policies, or literary production under the Sandinistas. Weighty as all of these areas are to any revolutionary endeavor, in the Nicaragua of the 1980s, the revolution's fate was decided by the peasantry. The majority of Nicaragua's population lived in the countryside and were peasants or agricultural laborers. In addition, from the Sandinistas' Marxist-Leninist perspective, the workers and the peasants were *the* primary agents of the Nicaraguan revolution, and the primary goal of the FSLN was to be the catalyst of revolutionary transformation for these peasant and working classes. Peasants were not only one-half of Nicaragua's population but also fully one-half of the Sandinista equation for revolutionary development. They were the agents/objects of the party's revolutionary imagination. Nevertheless, by the mid-1980s, it was the peasants, rather than urbanite feminist leaders, cultural workers, or literati, who were joining the counterrevolutionaries in significant numbers. For all of these reasons, they are the focus of this study.

In conducting my research for *Update* (and consequently for this chapter), I regularly interviewed agricultural policy analysts and technicians in the Ministry of Agriculture (MIDINRA) from several regions in Nicaragua; members of the FSLN-affiliated organization for farmers and ranchers (UNAG); representatives from the FSLN-affiliated agricultural workers' union (ATC); agricultural laborers on state and private farms; beneficiaries of agrarian reform on cooperatives and on private parcels; and small-, medium-, and large-scale private producers who either supported the Sandinistas or actively conspired against them. I also consulted official and unofficial government documents, as well as secondary, background readings. During my research for the institute, I visited dozens of state farms, cooperatives, resettlement communities, private farms, and villages; I also spent extended periods of time on three cooperatives (up to two months on one of these) and on two state farms working with development projects sponsored by U.S. solidarity organizations and sister-city projects.

It is as difficult for me to write up this research as it was to conduct it, although for very different reasons. In the mid-1980s, every visit to a cooperative or state farm was difficult because I never knew if the friends that I had laughed and argued with, played cards and shared lean meals with, would still be alive. Or if they would be dead—tortured and killed by counterrevolutionaries trained and financed by the United States for daring to imagine a different set of power relations, a different distribution of wealth. Today it is difficult to write about this research not because I naively find it a betrayal to criticize the Sandinista vision of development for which so many people died. Rather, it is difficult because of the growing consensus between conservatives and leftists (in the apparent triumph of neoliberalism), in which it is all too easy to blame the failure of socialism to take root in Latin America on the "antidemocratic tendencies" or "dogmatism" of revolutionary groups, or on the structural impossibility of placing controls on markets. To paraphrase Zora Neale Hurston's words from this chapter's epigraph, we forget perhaps because it is too painful to remember. Nevertheless, I choose to remember because I refuse to forget that the blame for the failure of the Sandinista attempt to institute a different model of development lies first and foremost with the U.S. government. The CIA's recruitment and direct support of the counterrevolutionaries caused nearly $5 billion of damage in eight years to a country with a GNP of less than U.S. $800 million in any given year between 1980 and 1990. However, the credit for the Sandinista successes—most notably the improvements to education, nationalized health care, enforcement of child support payments and domestic violence laws, lasting changes in land tenure, and, of course, the institutionalization of representative democracy—belongs foremost to the revolutionary spirit of the Nicaraguan people, and also to the courageous vision of thousands of FSLN members. And so I write this chapter because I believe in the possibility of these successes and not in the inevitability of failure.

The Legacy of Dependency: Establishing an Agricultural State Sector, 1979–1981

On 20 July 1979, one day after the triumph of the revolution, the new government nationalized the country's entire banking system, as well as the property belonging to Somoza and his associates. The expropriation of Somocista property brought 20 percent of Nicaragua's arable land under state control. From these expropriated lands, the new government created the Area of People's Property (APP), or state farms, to be administered by MIDINRA.[4] The Sandinistas envisioned state farms as the most direct path to satisfying the interests of the majority of the peasants.

Before proceeding, it is necessary to clarify which sectors of the peasantry I will focus on, since agricultural policy clearly affected different sectors of the peasantry differently. During the decade of Sandinista government, the peasantry as a category represented a broad, heterogeneous, diffuse, and in-flux population in Nicaragua. According to MIDINRA's calculations, Nicaragua had always had a significant percentage of production in the hands of private peasant producers with small- and medium-scale holdings, ranging between fifty to five hundred *manzanas*.[5] Most of these producers held enough land to necessitate hiring workers on a full- or part-time basis, whom they either paid or to whom they rented land in exchange for services. Together these producers, the "bourgeoisie" of the peasantry in Marxist terms, made up 30 percent of Nicaragua's economically active population (EAP) in the countryside. Even though they were not officially defined as "land-poor," members of the peasant bourgeois were nevertheless impacted by Sandinista agricultural policy, as they *were* among the intended beneficiaries of credit, pricing, and distribution policies. While they are not the central focus of this study, I will discuss how agricultural policies affected them in contrast to the land-poor peasants.

But even the category of "land-poor peasantry" demands clarification. Carlos Vilas, a political economist who worked for the Ministry of Planning (MIPLAN) in Nicaragua from 1980 to 1984, helps us understand the complexity of this category in his book *The Sandinista Revolution*. Vilas estimated that by the end of the 1970s, half a million Nicaraguans worked in agricultural production. Of these, roughly 50,000 were agricultural proletarians, that is, agricultural laborers with permanent employment. Another 75,000 were what he termed the itinerant proletarians, or laborers without permanent employment who changed jobs every three to four months. These "itinerant proletarians," however, were the recently dispossessed peasantry. They were peasants who had recently become landless. They had been forced off their land during the post–World War II cotton and cattle booms but had not been absorbed into permanent labor positions.[6] However, by the end of the 1970s there still remained 165,000 *minifundistas*—peasants with ten manzanas of land or less—who sold their labor during harvest seasons because their holdings were not sufficient for meeting their needs for the entire year. Vilas identifies these minifundistas as the semiproletariat (Vilas 63–69). Together with the permanent proletariat, the itinerant proletariat and the minifundistas made up 68 percent of the rural EAP in Nicaragua.

Vilas's schematization of the rural population illustrates the level of stratification that existed among the poorest of the rural EAP. It also betrays the Second World developmental imperative shared by the administrators at MIPLAN who viewed these sectors of the peasantry as a social formation in transition.[7] Vilas's purpose was to show that the proletarianization in Nicaragua's countryside remained "incomplete" in a dependent agro-export economy. By defining the process as incomplete—that is, in need of completion—Vilas defines sectors of the rural population as "problems" with calculable parameters. However, the peasants in these sectors constitute "incomplete" social formations only insofar as proletarianization constitutes *the* natural developmental outcome for MIPLAN. At the level of consciousness, or even of self-identification, such a transformation had not even begun to transpire. After all, less than a generation separated many of the itinerant proletariat and semiproletariat from viable land tenure. Invariably, when I interviewed minifundistas, itinerant laborers, and even most members of the permanent proletariat, they continued to identify themselves as *campesinos*—as peasants. They identified as such not out of ignorance of their "true" economic position but rather because they recognized that their *dual* positionality, as subsistence farmers and agricultural laborers, facilitated the extraction of higher rates of surplus from them and increased profit for the agro-export economy. While the members of all three of these categories had a definite interest in improved labor conditions, their future aspirations were actually tied to a return to a prior, perhaps even mythical, autonomy as *campeches* (*campache* is slang in Spanish for *campesino,* which means peasant/farmer). The minifundistas, the itinerant proletarians, and even many of the permanent proletarians still identified greater access to land as their overriding interest. Together the itinerant proletariat and the minifundistas made up 240,000 people, roughly half of the rural EAP. Their interests and the interests of an agro-export economy were directly at odds, because this economy could neither absorb them as full-time workers nor afford to lose their part-time or seasonal labor. These two groups of peasantry, the minifundistas and the itinerant proletariat, are the central focus of this study in considering the model of revolutionary development put forth by the Sandinistas.

MIDINRA's decision to create state farms rather than redistribute lands suggested that the ministry intended to "complete" the process of proletarianization through increased employment and improved conditions on state farms. They assumed, to some degree correctly, that the workers on these farms would gain not only a sense of ownership over these farms but a proprietary identification with the FSLN's vision of centralized, large-scale, industrialized farming. However, there were never enough jobs. The newly established MIPLAN called for the creation of 50,000 permanent jobs in state agriculture in its 1980 plan for economic reactivation (MIPLAN, *Programa de reactivacion economica* 17). Although this was a significant number of jobs for the new government to generate, it was by no means enough to absorb the 240,000 minifundistas and itinerant proletarians. In fact, it took three years for MIDINRA to attain accurate estimates of these sectors of the peasant population, a delay perhaps symptomatic of the government's persistent and more general misapprehension of the condition of the land-poor peasantry. The measures creating new jobs left 190,000 minifundistas and itinerant proletarians in exactly the same precarious economic conditions as before the revolution. This initial reform did nothing to benefit the majority of minifundistas and itinerant proletarians who worked on these farms only seasonally, if at all.

To the itinerant proletarians and the minifundistas who were not guaranteed full-time employment, this limited agrarian reform appeared as a betrayal by the party that had rallied the peasants to its side with the promise of "land to those who work it" (J. Collins, *What Difference* 45). Pressure for land from the peasantry had increased during the two decades prior to the revolution, given the accelerated dispossession that had taken place with the cotton boom. In one region alone, Leon and Chinandega, peasants launched 240 land takeovers between 1963 and 1973 (Spalding 30). These were just the most evident forms of resistance to the agro-export economy. There is no way to calculate the less spectacular acts of everyday resistance, such as squatting and production sabotage that went on before the insurrection.[8] But as just one example of more hidden forms of resistance, an agricultural laborer on the state farm La Concepcion in Chinandega told me that many of the workers on this farm, prior to the revolution, had channeled part of the foodstuffs and revenues from their private production to the guerrilla ranks.

This rash of takeovers during the 1960s and 1970s and the pursuant repression by Somoza's National Guard contributed not only cadres to the ranks of the guerrillas but moral legitimacy to the FSLN's cause. And during the two years of insurrection, the permanent workers in coordination with the itinerant proletariat and the minifundistas took over abandoned farms and organized production cooperatives, providing crucial logistical support for the Sandinistas. Nevertheless MIDINRA legalized only a chosen few of the cooperatives that had formed during the insurrection, and less than 1 percent of Somocista lands were turned over to these peasants as cooperatives in this initial phase of agrarian reform. In most cases, once in power, the FSLN used its moral (and sometimes military) authority to disband cooperatives that had formed on the APP lands or on private farms unaffected by the anti-Somocista decree of 20 July 1979 (CAHI, "Agrarian Reform" 2).

Certainly the conditions of development that already existed on the confiscated lands favored the state farm structure. Of the 2,000 farms confiscated, half were larger than 500 manzanas in area and had belonged to the wealthiest clique of large-scale farmers (Ruccio 67). They were immense, technologically sophisticated estates representing millions of dollars worth of investment in highly mechanized production practices that "unified" the landholding. Breaking up these coherent units into smaller parcels would not lead to efficient use of the technology on these estates, and this in turn would lead to a sharp decrease in their productivity. Planners in MIDINRA feared, probably justifiably, that if they distributed land to the land-poor peasantry, the new recipients of land would stop tending to export production altogether and begin planting basic grains and domestic foodstuffs (J. Collins, *What Difference* 60). Nicaragua in 1979 was a model of the first stage of dependent capitalist development in the periphery: exporting primary goods to the center while importing most manufactured goods. Trade acted as a substitute for production, with Nicaragua depending entirely on the export of a few primary products (coffee, cotton, beef, sugar) to generate foreign exchange for purchasing almost all capital goods and inputs necessary in the agricultural sector *and* the nascent industrial sector (Fitzgerald 1).[9] Thus, maintaining the agro-export sector was essential to the basic reproduction of the national economy, even though this ironically entailed maintaining an inexpensive seasonal labor force to ensure margins of profitability in a world market.

The technological sophistication of these farms and the policy of proletarianization of these land-poor peasant classes dovetailed with the FSLN's vision of state vanguardism in the economy. MIPLAN's 1980 plan established the state as the *eje dynamico* (the dynamic axis) in all economic sectors. Through the direct ownership of some of the means of production, and the nationalization of the financial system and segments of the commercial system, the state would manage the entire economy (MIPLAN, *Programa de reactivacion economica* 13). The state was to become the center for the accumulation of surplus and would thereby direct its redistribution through investments intended to benefit the various classes more equitably. Where the state did not directly own the means of production, it could direct production and accumulation of surplus through the distribution of foreign and domestic credit, controls over wages, and the control of international commerce (Ruccio 76). Where the state could not act as direct employer, the state would service the permanent rural workers on private farms, and the itinerant proletarians and the minifundistas through investment in a social wage—education, health care, child care, credit—rather than through measures involving land distribution.

However, the implementation of the social wage measures often exacerbated the stratification between the permanently employed and the underemployed, land-poor peasantry. The literacy and health brigades of the early 1980s were extensive in their reach. Since these were roving brigades made up of volunteer urban youths, they were able to extend basic literacy, child immunization, prenatal care, and preventive medical information to the most isolated areas in the countryside. Follow-up measures, however, tended to benefit the already privileged state farm worker. Health clinics, schools, and child care centers were constructed first on the state farms and then in outlying villages. Thus the social wage was disproportionately distributed to the most economically stable sector of the rural poor—the permanent proletariat. Although schools, child care centers, and clinics were subsequently constructed in rural villages, itinerant proletarians were by definition a transient population moving from farm to farm, and the minifundistas' tiny plots of land were often located far outside the villages. Also, the precarious economic position of the minifundistas and the itinerant proletarians meant that they were less likely to spare the labor of their children so that they could attend school. Thus access to these services did not have as dramatic an impact on their daily lives as it did on the lives of those living on state farms or in the villages. Most often, those living in the villages were the peasants with small- and medium-sized holdings who could afford to maintain a house in the village as well as on their farms; and after 1983, these centers became the primary targets of counterrevolutionary activity, further limiting the scope of these social wage projects.

The Sandinistas hoped that this first economic plan, which resisted radical redistribution of lands, would calm private-sector fears and maintain the delicate balance of forces in the governing junta. The Sandinistas had come to power thanks to the alliance of classes and nationalist visions that had formed to remove the figureheads of a despotic regime. However, it was clear to the FSLN that propertied classes would not long support a party promoting the rights and welfare of the classes these elites exploited for capital accumulation. Thus contradictions between classes reemerged quickly to affect the broad-based approval the FSLN enjoyed immediately following 19 July. The FSLN initially appealed to national consciousness, foregrounding the principle of unity and insisting that its political and economic platforms for participatory democracy and a mixed economy could incorporate the *patriotic* private producer. Any Sandinista concession to minifundista and itinerant proletarian demands for "democratizing" land tenure at this early stage in the revolution would have been interpreted by the elite classes as an indication of more expropriations to come. Such a possibility would lead to decreased investment or outright liquidation of investment capital by the agro-export sector. And once again, if the minifundistas and itinerant proletarians found themselves in the capacity of reproducing the family through private agricultural production, they would have little reason to sell their family's labor to the private and state sectors during the harvest season.

John Weeks, in "The Mixed Economy in Nicaragua," argues that it was naive of the Sandinistas to expect the private sector to participate in this economic model, since this sector had been stripped of its political power to direct the economy.[10] Owing to the nationalization of financial institutions, government control of exportation and importation, and qualitative increases in permanent workers' rights and wages, the private sector lost its ability to accumulate capital on its own terms: "It is difficult to produce any other example of a country in which private capital remained the dominant form of property, while in the political realm capital had been disenfranchised. . . . The typical outcomes are either a counter-revolution by which propertied interests regain the political power commensurate with their economic importance, or a rapid move by the revolutionary government to confiscation of large-scale property (in part to prevent the former outcome)" (Weeks 49). Weeks goes on to attribute the rapid withdrawal of private capital from large-scale property that followed the revolution to the bourgeoisie's lack of a nationalist identity that would supersede this sector's historical ties to the United States (60). However, Weeks's analysis shows a narrow understanding of affective ties of nationalism. I would argue that the bourgeoisie was committed to a vision of national progress that agreed with liberal, free-market modernization theory and was bound to conflict with a revolutionary model of centrally planned development. The bourgeoisie believed that the country's "development" was best left to a few responsible men, meaning themselves, who could reinvest accumulated capital prudently and according to the laws of a competitive international market. The Sandinistas not only eliminated the competitive market but displaced the bourgeoisie from their function as the agents of economic change. The bourgeoisie saw Somoza's monopolistic control of the economy as a flaw in an otherwise rational and just system. With the correction of this flaw, the bourgeoisie expected a perfected capitalist development to proceed under the direction of private capital. Ultimately the bourgeoisie did not abandon Nicaragua out of a lack of patriotism. They did not abandon Nicaragua at all but rather invested the money they decapitalized from their farms and industry in the counterrevolutionaries.[11]

The landed elites were far more antagonistic to a consolidated state sector in agriculture than they may have been to the redistribution of lands to the itinerant proletarians and minifundistas, even with the reduction of the labor force this redistribution would have entailed. I conducted many interviews with landed elites who are members of the conservative Union of Nicaraguan Agricultural Producers (UPANIC), and at some point during these interviews, the representatives invariably charged that the Sandinistas were "worse than Somoza ever was" because of the state's "monopolistic" control of the agricultural economy. During an interview with me in 1986, Rosendo Diaz, then president of UPANIC, displayed questionable sympathy for the plight of the agricultural proletariat and declared: "Before the revolution, the Sandinistas lured the campesinos with flowery promises that they would own their own land; instead MIDINRA has turned the campesino into a peon of the state, a slave of the state who is going to do whatever the state says, whenever to do it, and by whatever means it dictates." Whether this was rhetorical posturing on the part of the landed elites or an accurate representation of state control is beside the point. These representatives echoed the positions of counterrevolutionary leaders in Washington, in Miami, and in the Nicaraguan countryside. This right-wing critique by these elites and the counterrevolutionaries made political headway among the dissatisfied minifundistas and itinerant proletarians because it asserted, above all else, the autonomy of the peasantry, albeit within the bourgeoisie's framework of private property. In other words, these elites capitalized on the itinerant proletarians' and the minifundistas' continued identification as campesinos. In effect, this right-wing rhetoric positioned the landed elites and the land-poor peasants in a relationship of equivalence vis-à-vis a state that denied an abstracted concept of freedom. These appeals by the elites and counterrevolutionaries spoke to the itinerant proletarians' and the minifundistas' interest in autonomy, which superseded their interests as workers, especially since the FSLN was unable to dramatically improve their status as a proletariat.

Consider the impact such a critique would have even among the laborers with secure permanent employment on state farms in the following situation. With relatively few exceptions, MIDINRA did not allow agricultural workers to cultivate small parcels of land on state farms for their personal consumption, whereas previous owners had allowed the workers to do so. The Sandinistas interpreted this practice by private owners as exploitative and paternalistic (IHCA, "The Nicaraguan Peasantry" 8c). Undoubtedly, it was both. Private owners allowed workers to cultivate unused parcels of land to keep the capital costs of reproducing labor to a minimum. Wage laborers employed on private farms provided some of their own foodstuffs by farming these parcels on their own time. This private production, in effect, functioned as part of their wage, allowing the employer to pay them less. MIDINRA policy makers associated this practice with "precapitalist" forms of labor that hindered the complete proletarianization of the peasantry. However, MIDINRA officials were wrong to expect the agricultural worker to interpret this practice similarly—strictly as a form of precapitalist labor exploitation and paternalism. Instead, what the *terrateniente* (large- or medium-scale landowner) may have interpreted as his own benevolent patronage, the workers interpreted as a hard-earned right ensuring them a minimal level of autonomy, a wage supplement, and an identification with a subject position other than strictly "worker." In the context of soon-to-be chronic inflation and food shortages, permanent workers on state farms experienced the elimination of this practice as a decline in their material condition and an infringement on their rights. Again, from the ministry's teleological perspective, this policy was meant to pull the workers further toward their true positionality. But one of the long-standing claims pressed by the ATC leaders at the local, regional, and national levels was the right of state farm workers to use part of the state farms for individual production of basic grains.

I have emphasized the Sandinistas' efforts to "complete" proletarianization among the permanent workers, the itinerant proletarians, and the minifundistas to underscore their tendencies to redefine these sectors' interests in the state's developmentalist terms. From the FSLN's perspective, the interests of these three groups of peasants and the interests of the nation's development were best served through the combination of their freed labor and the state's capital. While the impetus behind initial agrarian reform policy was to hurry the process of proletarianization, the Sandinistas *did* enact some policies that were intended to reinforce the economic position of small-scale farmers and the minifundista segment of the peasantry as such. Two policies were aimed specifically at making them more effective private producers: a policy for the extension of credit, and a policy for pricing and marketing basic grains and foodstuffs. To a degree, the enactment of these policies recognized the important role these groups could play as private producers in generating capital. However, they also revealed a paternalistic bias on the part of the state that ultimately undermined the position of the minifundistas vis-à-vis the richer segments of the peasantry.

Under Somoza's regime, roughly 30,000 producers with small- and medium-scale holdings received 10 percent of the credit extended to rural areas through private banks. The other 90 percent of rural credit went to landed elites. Under the FSLN, 100,000 minifundistas and small-holding peasant producers received 27 percent of the rural credit extended by the nationalized banking system (Enriquez and Spalding 113). The amount of credit extended by financial institutions increased by 600 percent during the first credit cycle in 1979 to 1980 (Deere and Marchetti 57). Thousands of small-scale farmers and minifundistas who had never had access to credit received loans for the production of basic grains and foodstuffs in the first credit cycle (J. Collins, *What Difference* 56).[12] Success of the credit program for the minifundistas and small-holding peasantry depended on their possession of certain entrepreneurial skills: on their ability to invest loans efficiently—that is, to further rationalize production on their lands—and to repay the loans promptly. These "skills" necessary to enhance production on private parcels translated into a knowledge of more sophisticated modes of agricultural production, a basic level of pre-existing technological production on farms that could be enhanced by this new capital, access to means of transporting the new inputs and goods that must be purchased in the cities and towns—in short, an ability to combine increased capital, technology (capital goods such as irrigation systems, processing plants, or even a tractor), and free labor. Since the small-holding producers could improve the relationship between technology and wage labor with their increased capital, their surplus production increased; however, the majority of the minifundistas' production costs are not in capital goods or wage labor but family labor (Colburn, *Post-revolutionary Nicaragua* 85). Hence investment of capital could not increase absolute or relative surplus production on these lands, and most minifundistas used the funds to satisfy immediate consumption needs. Consequently, credit extension did not lead to the expected rise in production, and the Sandinistas had to forfeit the majority of loans extended to the minifundistas, which led to a growing state deficit. After the first two years, the vast majority of minifundistas dropped out of the credit program, leaving the small-holding private producers to benefit the most.[13]

The rural credit program effectively accelerated the stratification among the lower echelons of Nicaragua's peasantry: "That is, the small-holding 'peasantry' [small-holding producers and minifundistas] was becoming increasingly divided into two groups: at one pole, producers who employed wage labor and had access to additional land by buying or renting from others [smallholders], and, at the other pole, producers who were forced to sell their labor power and rent and/or sell their land to that first group [minifundistas]" (Enriquez and Spalding 73). A de facto effect of MIDINRA's rural credit program was to further proletarianize the minifundistas as they were forced to sell their labor, and in some cases their land, to the small-holding peasantry now able to extend their production due to the heretofore inaccessible credit. For the minifundistas, the credit program was an intervention by the state that led to further dispossession and loss of the autonomy they associated with the ownership of land. The FSLN resisted distributing lands to the land-poor peasants because it did not want to reinforce peasant attachment to private ownership among the minifundistas, or to solidify their identification as peasant farmers rather than as proletarians in the making. Yet their policies strengthened the bourgeois position of the small-holding and medium-holding peasants, to the detriment of the land-poor peasants.

In addition, the FSLN displaced the mercantile class by setting fixed prices for the purchase of certain basic goods from these producers (rice, beans, sugar, milk, eggs, beef) and by monopolizing the purchase and distribution of these goods.[14] These policies corresponded to the FSLN's vanguardist position in directing agricultural development. In accordance with Second World development theory's appraisal of the parasitic role of this class, MIDINRA also wanted to guard the minifundistas and small-scale producers against the exploitative practices of these merchants.[15] As I have said earlier, the minifundistas had historically produced the bulk of the rice and beans consumed by the country. While the prices set by the state for these basic foodstuffs initially responded to production costs (they were increased significantly between 1979 and 1984), these prices were ultimately unable to keep pace with the increase in inflation of rural consumer prices. In effect, price controls became another means of extracting absolute surplus from the minifundistas, who were unable to lower their production costs by a relative increase in productivity, as many of the small-, medium-, and large-scale peasants were able to do.

To enforce its pricing policies and to eliminate the exploitative merchant class, the state also attempted to displace merchants from the buying and selling of these basic foodstuffs by taking over these functions. Not only was the state unable to reach all the minifundistas, dispersed as they were through the countryside, but the state was unable to replace all the services offered to the minifundistas by the merchants. Again, the Sandinistas' paternalistic thinking led to a narrow interpretation of the merchant-minifundista relationship. The relationship between the merchant and the minifundista was clearly exploitative, but each merchant serviced a variety of minifundista needs (mail service, short-term loans, transportation, information on part-time jobs in other areas, legal and medical advice) that no single state agency could replace, even if state agents were able to reach the minifundista (Frenkel 211–12). Small-holding peasants were far less likely to need this variety of services. Often, merchants came from the peasant communities and were not necessarily seen as "outsiders." Most importantly, these merchants offered better prices for their goods than the state provided. Inevitably, a black market for the purchase and sale of basic foodstuffs developed because of the low prices the state paid for the goods.

In 1984 I spent two months on La Virgencita, a cooperative eleven miles north of the city of Esteli. This was one of the few production cooperatives awarded during the first period of reform immediately following the revolution. These workers were given the land because of the commitment they had shown to the FSLN. However, the president of this cooperative regularly lent one of the cooperative's trucks to his cousin, a minifundista who farmed nearby, so that he could travel by night and circumvent the state distribution authorities, taking his production directly to the markets in Esteli. Of course I was left wondering if the cousin might not be marketing some of the cooperative's production as well. Thus, although the merchant-minifundista relationship was ultimately an exploitative one, even those peasants most committed to the revolutionary process—those awarded land early in the process because of their loyalty—recognized that the state in its role as merchant was becoming equally, if not more, exploitative of the minifundista.

Stage Two: Agrarian Reform, 1981–1985

The development policies put forth by MIDINRA in the first two years of the revolution strengthened the economic position of the permanent proletariat and the small-holding peasantry. However, for the vast majority of the itinerant proletarians and the minifundistas, these same policies either had no long-term effect on their economic position or, in fact, placed them in an even more precarious economic position. Thus demand for land from these two groups of peasants continued unabated during the first two years of the revolution. In Masaya, the department in Nicaragua with the largest concentration of minifundistas, thousands of these peasants marched on the regional office of MIDINRA in February 1980. They demanded that no more lands be returned to previous owners and that instead they be redistributed among the peasantry (IHCA, "The Nicaraguan Peasantry" 7c). While demands for land in other regions were not as spectacular, they were chronic. In the name of the itinerant proletarians and the minifundistas, the ATC consistently petitioned regional MIDINRA offices for the expropriation and redistribution of unproductive farmland. No one knew better than the agricultural workers and minifundistas in each area which farmers were nonproductive or actively decapitalizing. This early agitation by the minifundistas and the itinerant proletarians clearly indicated their dissatisfaction with their precarious status as agricultural laborers in the government's new development plans and with the revolutionary government's compromise with the landed elites.

The 1981 agrarian reform law cites as its raison d'être the FSLN's historic duty to restore these peasants' right to live off the land with dignity (Consejo de Estado 186). Much of the literature on the first agrarian reform law describes it as a political response by the Sandinistas to their social base among the dispossessed and land-poor peasantry. This was a partial truth. In the context of the inadequate response of landed elites to incentives, the primary purpose of the law was to enable the state to use force where flattery had failed. As early as 1981, it was clear to the government that this segment of the private sector was not fully reinvesting its profits. MIPLAN's 1981 plan for economic austerity indicates that although profits had recuperated faster than salaries, the private sector, especially in agriculture, was in most cases simply maintaining *postrevolution* production levels (MIPLAN, *Programa economico de austeridad* 121). Where were these profits going? Already there were signs of decapitalization by some producers (J. Collins, *What Difference* 45). While domestic agricultural production—largely in the hands of small- and medium-holding peasants—rebounded, export production lagged behind.[16]

The new law stipulated that landholdings in excess of 500 manzanas along the Pacific coast and 1,000 manzanas in the mountainous regions would be subject to expropriation if these lands were abandoned, lying idle, or underutilized. However, productive properties, regardless of their size, would be left untouched (Consejo de Estado 187). Even after the expropriations of Somocista land, 21.5 percent of land remained in private holdings exceeding 500 manzanas. A full one-fifth of the land, then, remained in the hands of large-scale agro-export producers. This was roughly comparable to the state's holdings.[17] Meanwhile, 165,000 minifundista families continued to live off 2.5 percent of the land (J. Collins, *What Difference* 271). And between 25,000 and 35,000 itinerant proletarians owned no land and had no permanent employment. Although the 1981 law stipulated that newly expropriated lands be handed over to the dispossessed and land-poor peasants, allowing for limited private ownership, it emphasized the need for these peasants to organize themselves into production cooperatives in order to receive the land (Consejo de Estado 189). Therefore, the first agrarian reform law allowed for individual or family ownership of land to occur if the beneficiaries agreed to join some type of cooperative association (i.e., credit and service cooperatives or dead-furrow cooperatives).[18] But even if the peasants were willing to join such cooperatives, priority would be given to peasants who had historical ties to the revolutionary struggle. In effect, the only peasants to receive individual plots of land under this law were those with long-standing claims to party loyalty.

MIDINRA's enforcement of the new law between 1981 and 1983 demonstrated the agency's reluctance to recognize an autonomous peasant social formation to any significant degree when it came to the minifundistas and the itinerant proletarians. Sectors of the FSLN in MIDINRA stubbornly adhered to a Leninist construction of small-scale private property as the petit bourgeois basis for the reproduction of capitalist relations. In Lenin's "Speech on the Agrarian Question," which he delivered to the First All-Russia Congress of Peasant's Deputies on 22 May 1917, he discussed what form agrarian reform should take in Russia. Though he called for the expropriation of landed estates and for improving rural conditions for poor peasants, he nevertheless insisted that expropriated estates were the property of the entire nation and should not be divided into small, private parcels:

> That is why we say that farming on individual plots, even if it is "free labor on free soil," is no way out of the dreadful crisis, it offers no deliverance from the general ruin. A *universal labour service* is necessary, the greatest economy of man-power is necessary, an exceptionally strong and firm authority is necessary, an authority capable of effecting that universal labour service; it cannot be done by officials, it can be done only by the Soviets of Workers', Soldiers', and Peasants' Deputies, because they are the people, they are the masses, because they are of the peasant from top to bottom, can organize labour conscription, can organise that protection of human labour that would not allow the squandering of the peasant's labour, and the transition to common cultivation would, under these circumstances, be carried out gradually and with circumspection. (*Selected Works* 138–39)

From Lenin's perspective, small farms are the equivalent of "squandering of the peasant's labor." And although the "dreadful crisis" he refers to in this passage is the lack of basic foodstuffs in Russia following the devastation of World War I, Lenin has just previously referred to the "crisis" as equally the product of capitalist, private-property relations in agriculture.[19] Thus, in their privileging of cooperativization (with the APP, the equivalent of a "universal labour service") during this second stage, the FSLN adhered to a Second World development orthodoxy, in that the party leadership believed a small-holding peasantry would actually obstruct the possibility for *any* kind of development to unfold in Nicaragua, let alone the Sandinistas' alternative model. In holding this position, the party's analysis was in line with, for example, Robert Brenner's account of why there were historical variations in the speed and force with which capitalism took hold in Europe. According to Brenner, a noted Marxist scholar of development and imperialism, agrarian capitalism, and subsequently the industrial revolution, initially flourished in England but *not* in France because in England lands were concentrated in large estates, whereas in France earlier peasant revolts had successfully produced an independent, small-holding peasantry. Thus, in line with Lenin and Second World development theory, Brenner concludes that the rapid pace of all subsequent development in Britain but not in France hinged on the differences in class structure between the two countries: "This outcome depended, in turn, upon the previous success [in England] of a two-sided process of class development and class conflict: on the one hand the destruction of serfdom; on the other, *the short-circuiting of the emerging predominance of small peasant property*" ("Agrarian Class Structure" 30). If rapid capitalist development depended on the absence of a powerful small-holding peasantry, then there was all the more reason for the Sandinistas to circumvent its formation in Nicaragua because, in accordance with Second World development theory, the FSLN planned to accelerate *past* the later stages of capitalist development into an alternative, mixed-economy model of development. Thus MIDINRA was unwilling to create a new small-holding peasantry out of the minifundistas and the itinerant proletariat because such a peasantry, they believed, would slow down the technological development that could take place on large estates (be these privately, state, or cooperatively owned). They could not imagine an alternative outcome to this developmental narrative and instantiated reform policies equally as rigid as any liberal development discourse might have provided. And yet their credit and social wage policies paradoxically, if unintentionally, *strengthened* the bourgeois class position of the small- and medium-holding peasants at the expense of the minifundistas and itinerant proletarians.

In January 1985, I traveled with a technician from Masaya's local MIDINRA office to visit ten farms owned by minifundistas. In the 1984 elections, the FSLN's poorest show of support had come from this department. Several of the men and women on these farms admitted to not having voted at all in the elections. Most claimed that they did not vote because they lacked time or were "not political." However, in a region that had been a historical base for guerrilla operations during the insurrection, these responses from farmers say something in and of themselves. Others admitted that they did not vote because they did not see the point, and one farmer stated, "If you are standing between a person who is hitting you and another who does nothing to help you, you duck." Of those who said they had voted, most said they had voted for the FSLN. However, one woman I spoke to said candidly, "The Sandinistas want us to give them our sons [referring to military recruitment to fight the war]; they want us to give them our produce [referring to the low prices on goods]. Well, I don't have to give them my vote." This woman used the verb *regalar,* which I have translated as "to give"; however, in Spanish the word *regalar* is used in association with the giving of gifts. Thus the woman was implying that she had given something precious to the Sandinistas and was now tired of giving things away without getting anything in return.

Over the course of three years, MIDINRA expropriated 7 percent of the national arable land from the private sector. Private holdings exceeding 500 manzanas shrunk from 21 percent of the national total to 14 percent. Large-scale agriculture was reduced by 33 percent. The honeymoon between the state and large-scale agro-export producers was over. However, improved relations between the state and the majority of dispossessed and land-poor peasants did not immediately follow. MIDINRA redistributed these lands almost exclusively to peasants willing to form production cooperatives: 33,000 peasant families received land in cooperative form; in the same three years, only 1,000 peasant families received land in the form of individual ownership (IHCA, "The Nicaraguan Peasantry" 11c). From the perspective of the state, cooperatives appeared as a compromise between large-scale agro-export production (state or private) and individual peasant production. From the perspective of the itinerant proletarians and the minifundistas, however, cooperatives meant either land on the state's terms or no land at all.

Cooperatives appeared as an ideal form of production to the Sandinistas because, during these four years, it became increasingly clear that MIDINRA could not absorb any more lands and administer them effectively.[20] Cooperative production, then, could form an adjunct to the APP production. Expropriated properties did not need to be broken up; rather, one or more cooperatives could work as coherent units. As such, they posed less of a threat to export agriculture than individual ownership would have, and they could increase food production by planting basic grains between the seasons for export goods. Furthermore, cooperative ownership, because it concentrated the new land recipients into large units, would also facilitate the extension of technical services by an already overextended MIDINRA. This seemed an ideal way of reinforcing the precarious economic living conditions of the land-poor peasant without reinforcing private property as a social formation.

Carmen Deere contends that cooperativization under the 1981 agrarian reform law was strictly voluntary and that the state did not prioritize it over private ownership of land (Deere 127). This analysis, however, is somewhat misleading. Deere projects a liberal agency onto the minifundistas and the itinerant proletarians that effaces the state's power and the poverty of choices available to these peasants. On the one hand, access to land, technical services, social services, and credit was ensured only to peasants willing to form production cooperatives. On the other hand, as the counterrevolutionaries increased their activities in the northern countryside, these production cooperatives became prime targets of their attacks. Thus, if the minifundistas or the itinerant proletarians chose not to join production cooperatives, they "chose" to continue in their marginal economic position, whereas joining cooperatives meant that they risked death at the hands of the counterrevolutionaries. For Deere to presume that the actions of the land-poor peasants were "voluntary" in this context presupposes an equality of choices that simply did not exist. Such a presupposition is naive indeed, especially when projected onto a revolutionary transition that is negotiating the very issues of equality and freedom within the overdetermined constraints of underdevelopment in the context of a war. Arguably, most sectors of the peasantry had more choices under the Sandinistas than they had ever enjoyed under the Somoza dictatorship (or would have under the neoliberalism of the 1990s), but the "choice" to join a cooperative was not among them.

The Sandinistas *did not* use any physical force in their efforts at cooperativizing the dispossessed and land-poor peasantry.[21] However, the state's role in the minifundistas' and itinerant proletarians' lives was already effectively a coercive one with regard to pricing and purchasing policies. I am not arguing that state-initiated cooperativization among the peasantry could not or should not take place. However, even under optimum conditions, there were likely to be subtle forms of pressure by the state to convince peasants to join cooperatives. After all, unlike the indigenous peasants in Mexico and Guatemala, the minifundistas and itinerant proletarians in the Pacific regions of Nicaragua had no history of communal farming. Thus the transformation of consciousness required by the Sandinistas' regime of subjection under cooperativization would necessarily be a violent and troubled one for the peasantry. It requires that these dispossessed and land-poor peasants reconstruct their concept of community. It asks that they, from an extremely precarious economic position, suspend immediate individual and familial needs not only for the sake of this larger collective community but for the national community that has an investment in the cooperative as a revolutionary experiment and an economic unit of production. It requires the abandonment of a traditional mode of production in favor of a theoretical one. Indeed, it requires someone who very much resembles the "reactive nationalist" of development's regime of subjection: a male who is willing to become a risk taker and advantage seeker, willing to transcend vertical, familial ties for horizontal, collective ties, willing to "choose" to relinquish "wanton" modes of agricultural production for proper ones. Thus, while MIDINRA may not have used force to cooperativize peasants, the high rates of labor absenteeism and changing membership that plagued many cooperatives indicate that not all cooperative members were committed to the cooperatives they presumably "chose" to join.

To emphasize the necessarily long-term and materially bound nature of the transformation to collective consciousness instituted by the Sandinista regime of subjection, I recount an exchange I had once with a cooperativized peasant on a return visit to Nicaragua in 1989, while visiting a coffee cooperative outside of El Cua, Matagalpa. This cooperative had been established six years earlier, in 1983, and this man had been a member since it was founded. Most of the members had a history of loyalty to the party. Yet he told me frankly that owing to the scarcity of rural credit in 1989, cooperative members were reinvesting their profits in the farm *for the first time* during the 1989–1990 crop cycle. These are the profits they received after selling their coffee and paying themselves their regular salaries. I asked him what they had done with the profits all those previous years. He said that they had divided them according to how hard each member worked, and each member spent the profits as he saw fit. What does this reveal? Savvy financing on the part of these cooperative members? (After all, why invest your own profits when the bank will provide low-interest loans?) A fundamental lack of a sense of ownership? (After all, who could say what would be the outcome of the war and if they would still own their lands after it was over?) A failure to prioritize national needs over personal needs (even though these peasants were presumably committed to the revolutionary project)? I can only speculate. Until 1988, this zone was virtually off-limits to foreigners because of the heavy fighting in the area. Perhaps, with the relaxation of the counterrevolutionary war, these cooperative members were now physically and economically secure enough to reinvest their profits in their farms for the first time. Perhaps the state's inability to provide services facilitated a reorientation of a previously paternalistic relation. In either case, ten years after the revolution and six years after agrarian reform bene-fited the cooperative's members, the transformation in consciousness and sense of collective agency that would make this cooperative self-sustaining had not finished taking place.

Despite these crises, Deere states that "the internal organization of the cooperatives is quite democratic" and that "the cooperatives are totally inde-pendent of the Ministry of Agriculture . . . [although] they receive technical assistance from the ministry and credit from the National Development Bank" (128). Once again, this romantic rendition presents the relationship between the state and the peasant as an untroubled exchange between equal partners in an uncontested national development project. In effect, MI-DINRA was only able to extend full technical services to five hundred pri-oritized cooperatives. This was 25 percent of the total number of production cooperatives; 75 percent were disenfranchised from most state services (IHCA, "The Nicaraguan Peasantry" 10c). I would not presume that these disenfranchised cooperatives enjoyed a *greater* degree of internal democracy or choice simply because of their autonomy from the state. However, "tech-nical services" on prioritized cooperatives often boiled down to orders from MIDINRA representatives.

Focusing on the cooperatives that *did* receive technical assistance, let us rethink the context of the state-peasant relationship. The state chose five hundred cooperatives with the intention of modernizing their production, of intensifying their production through the importation of technology (IHCA, "The Nicaraguan Peasantry" 10c). This explicit intention of increasing tech-nical sophistication and industrialization precluded any serious autonomy for the chosen production cooperatives, since the modernizing effort would require more than a little advice and a few loans. The prioritized cooperatives represented a *national* investment of increasingly scarce resources. In effect, these cooperative members, even more than their proletarian counterparts on state farms, were the critical link in a new schema of national develop-ment. They were the agents/objects of revolutionary transformation for the Sandinistas. However, these former minifundistas and agricultural pro-letarians would need planning, managerial, and technical skills that would take *years* to acquire, in the best of circumstances, before they could direct industrialized production. Once again, they would require *proper subjection*. In the discursive terms of Rostow's developmentalism, these peasants must be made ready *to be ready* for cooperativization. Until the peasants acquired these technical skills—implying a *further* transformation in consciousness— a paternalistic relationship on the part of the state as the provider of such skills was only to be expected. In effect, a recurrent problem on cooperatives was the tendency toward state intervention in the cooperatives' internal organization, norms, and decisions (CIERA, "Propuesta" 6).

It is not my intention to present peasants on cooperatives as being completely without agency in their relationship to the state. Rather, the relationship was a dialectical one, fraught with power imbalances that played themselves out in the daily exchange of activity between the peasants and the representatives of MIDINRA. It was this daily tension between the particular interests of the peasants and the universalized interest of MIDINRA technicians in the field that eventually forced a reformulation of the state's overall nationalist vision. For example, in 1986 I visited a group of five prioritized coffee cooperatives an hour outside of the city of Esteli. Three of these neighboring cooperatives had been attacked by counterrevolutionaries a week before, and the counterrevolutionaries had burned down a new coffee processing plant. This was the third in a series of five attacks on these cooperatives that would eventually take place in the span of three years. At one of the two cooperatives that had not been attacked on this particular occasion, I was walking up a hill with one of the zonal MIDINRA's five technical assistants to the cooperatives and a cooperative member. The technical assistant enthusiastically explained to me that this cooperative was part of a national project to replace corn production with potatoes and diversify consumption patterns nationally. Not only would this improve nutrition, but it would also provide a potential new export for generating much- needed foreign exchange, *and* it would replenish the soil. When we reached the top of the hill, he looked down at the cooperative members in the valley who were busy planting, and a look of shock came over his face. "I told you to plant potatoes!" he called out in an agitated voice. Deadpan, the coopera- tive member answered, "Oh? I thought you said corn." (The cooperative member slyly explained to me later that they had taken advantage of the technician's weekend away to advance on the planting.) As quickly as anx- iety had overcome the technician, it left him. He shrugged his shoulders and said, "Oh well, no big difference." The technician, from his perspective of resistance to Nicaragua's history of dependent, monocultural development, registered the peasants' resistance to MIDINRA's modernizing vision and accommodated it. Fortunately, this technician was much more attuned to the discrepancies between the peasant interests and the national interests than his superiors in Managua. He explained to me that he and the other technicians in this area were sensitive to the top-down structure of much of the technical assistance to cooperatives and went to great pains to accommodate the peasants' opinions on production decisions. In other words, technicians in daily contact with cooperative members were flexible in their enforcement of, and expectation for, a theoretical model of revolutionary subjection directed from the central offices of MIDINRA. The next time I visited these cooperatives, this twenty-one-year-old technician named Bayardo had been killed in an attack by the counterrevolutionaries.

Although the cooperativized peasants were not free to set the terms of their own revolutionary subjection, they certainly intervened at all levels of the production process whenever possible. Some co-ops were more democratically run and autonomous than others. The newly trained MIDINRA representatives brought technical expertise to the project, but the peasants, who in many cases had previously worked on the farms they now owned, brought an expertise about the specific farms, work relations, and the local community. We can assume that the peasantry asserted this expertise whenever possible, given their newly empowered status in the years following the revolution. Nevertheless modernization through collectivization privileged state power, and peasant agency must always be read in this context. The peasants' participation in implementing cooperativization could only be the result of a complex negotiation among the state's vision of a national development project, its developmentalist regime of revolutionary subjection, individual MIDINRA representatives, and the heterogeneous national and local visions of the peasantry.

To assess the overall success or failure of the cooperative movement in Nicaragua would be inappropriate. Success or failure, in terms of productivity and the cooperatives' ability to maintain long-term members, varied tremendously. A cooperative's viability depended on a number of factors: location, number of members per manzana, labor discipline, members' identification as owners, the degree of democratic practices within the cooperative, appropriate technical sophistication among members, access to small plots of land on cooperatives for familial production, and, perhaps most importantly, the degree of preexisting group consciousness/collective agency and ideological commitment to the Sandinista nationalist vision (CIERA, "Propuesta" 3–7). In northeast Nicaragua, specifically in the departments of Leon and Chinandega, where favorable conditions predominated, productivity on cotton cooperatives surpassed the levels of their state and private competitors (IHCA, "The Nicaraguan Peasantry" 10c). In the mountainous war zone, cooperatives demonstrating a high degree of group consciousness and ideological commitment to the Sandinistas became prime targets for the counterrevolutionary attacks. In this context, it would be incorrect to interpret their subsequent lack of productivity as "failure." Before the institution of the military draft, cooperatives were also the prime source of recruits for fighting the escalating war against the counterrevolutionaries.[22] Thus, in addition to recruits losing their lives, this defense effort also significantly limited cooperative production. In sum, the overdetermining factor in the fate of *all* the cooperatives was the U.S.-backed counterrevolutionary war. In cases where cooperatives were not directly affected by the aggression—through attacks by the counterrevolutionaries or recruitment by the Sandinista army—they suffered from the overall lack of resources, flexibility, and time caused by the war.

Nonetheless the regime of subjection implied by MIDINRA's cooperative program must be critiqued on its own terms. The cooperative program required a peasant subject who had *already undergone a "revolutionary enlightenment."* It required a peasant who was predisposed to collectivization and who was committed to a vision of modernization, one who placed the needs of national development above the immediate domestic needs of the autonomous family and the community, one who viewed the state as an ally in this development—and, finally, one who was willing to die for this nationalist vision. And so we see that it is not Rostow's "reactive nationalist" required by the Sandinista cooperative vision of agriculture, after all, but the "guiding angel" from Guevara's *Guerrilla Warfare:* the angel "who has fallen into the zone," the flexible, ethical, and highly mobile agent/object of his own development (39). In other words, it required a peasant subject who had already attained the transcendent conviction presupposed by Guevara in his own transformation and repeatedly projected onto the rural subalterns in his diaries. In addition, revolutionary peasant subjection under the Sandinistas required the androgynous tendresse found in Guevara's diaries, as the implied peasant cooperative member was suffused both with love of nation and a willingness to sacrifice for the nation. And yet, as we saw in chapter 3, even among the most committed of revolutionaries, such complete and determinant transformation of consciousness was impossible to sustain, and such revolutionary tendresse inevitably turned into the tyranny of patriarchy.

And so it should not surprise that the beneficiary of cooperativization, its implied agent/object, was almost invariably a male. While there are no state figures on the number of female cooperative members, there were very, very few. Although women worked on cooperatives alongside men, women were "represented" in decision making through their husbands, fathers, or brothers. Women were not listed as members on property titles, nor did they have voting power within the collective. Generally, women who *were* members had been granted membership as a reward for their husbands dying in combat. During the debates and town hall meetings that took place around the drafting of the national constitution in 1985 and 1986, women's representatives from the National Assembly, from cooperatives, from the ATC, and from the FSLN-affiliated national women's organization AMNLAE repeatedly petitioned the party and the National Assembly to make land-ownership a constitutional right for women, but to no avail. During the same visit that I made to the cooperative outside El Cua in 1989, I asked a group of women which party they were planning to vote for in the upcoming national elections. Quickly, one woman said, with feigned indifference, "I'm not voting. Remember, I'm not a member of this cooperative." This was received with affirming laughter and nods from the other women in the group.

Any analysis of cooperativization under the 1981 agrarian reform law must recognize the limited scope of this law. Only 33,000 peasants received land under this reform, and some of these were members of the permanent proletariat who had worked on the private farms before they were expropriated. But even if we assume that all of this land went to the dispossessed or land poor, this figure represents only one-sixth of the minifundista and itinerant proletariat population who were in need.[23] After five years of revolution, only 7 percent of the nation's arable land had been redistributed to these peasants, a relatively small amount. The vast majority of this population failed to benefit from the 1981 agrarian reform law. In certain cases, land reform created class stratification among the peasantry, in that those benefiting from these reforms, especially on export-oriented cooperatives, would hire the remaining disenfranchised peasants as seasonal and part-time labor (CIERA, "Propuesta" 6). In part, the slow pace of redistribution was due to the minifundistas' and itinerant proletarians' resistance to cooperatives, but it also reflected the Sandinistas' contradictory reluctance to (1) alienate the private sector, or (2) recognize the potential that small, private holdings might offer not only in terms of economic development but also in terms of political support for the revolutionary process. With the bulk of production still in the hands of medium- and large-scale private production or the state, the FSLN moved too cautiously in their redistribution efforts.

Landownership and National Identity, 1985–1986

On my first visit to the office of MIDINRA's Center for the Study and Investigation of Agrarian Reform (CIERA) in January 1985, an investigator, Freddy Quesada, explained to me that the standard of living for the minifundista and itinerant proletarian had been drastically reduced over the previous three years. During our conversation, a jeep pulled up outside the window, and a man dressed in army fatigues and a white T-shirt got out and entered the office, interrupting our conversation with the agitated pronouncement "Freddy, the peasants in Boaco and Chontales are becoming counterrevolutionaries." He had just returned from a two-week investigation for CIERA of Nicaragua's central mountainous region, comprising the departments of Boaco and Chontales. Freddy Quesada was not terribly surprised. He answered, "¡Se puede jugar con la limozna, pero no con el santo!" [You can fool around with the alms, but not with the saint!]. I asked him to explain what he meant by this, and he responded that the FSLN could afford to make mistakes in policy that affected the urban populations because it was unlikely that they would move to the mountains and join the counterrevolutionaries; however, the dissatisfied sectors of the peasantry were more likely to join, and they formed a more critical proportion of the country's population. Quesada's observation reveals that early in the revolutionary process, some members of the lower echelons *within* MIDINRA were well aware of the flaws in agricultural and agrarian reform policy. Unfortunately, it took some time for MIDINRA's investigators in the field to convey the severity of the situation in the countryside to Managua policy makers.

As stated earlier, pricing and marketing policies intended to benefit the minifundistas and small-holding peasants had failed because of unforeseen difficulties in their implementation. By 1985, the negative impact of these policies on this sector of the peasantry was severe. A comparison of prices for rural and manufactured goods best illustrates the degree of this crisis. While official producer prices for rural goods (rice, beans, corn) had increased sevenfold since 1978, the price of a pair of rubber boots had increased 28 times, and the price of a pair of pants had increased 140 times (Conroy 211). One reason for the disparity in prices was the lack of domestic industry and the scarcity of foreign exchange. Most of the products used by the minifundistas (fertilizers, machetes, wire fencing, rubber boots) were not domestically produced and had to be imported. Thus, with the allocation of scarce foreign exchange to agro-export production and to long-term, capital-intensive state agro-industry, there was little left for importation or subsidization of the goods necessary for basic food production, the domain of the minifundista and the small-holding peasant (J. Collins, *What Difference* 185, 201). Consequently, the costs of these goods skyrocketed, making it impossible to meet production costs without resorting to the black market.

There is another reason for the unequal terms of trade between the countryside and the city. The majority of the original FSLN leadership was forged in the urban underground, from student activists attending the universities along the Pacific coast. Thus their analysis emerged from the perspective of the popular urban classes who had provided crucial support for the revolution and had suffered the worst effects of Somocista repression. The Sandinistas were rightly concerned with immediately improving the purchasing power of these classes; however, they did so by artificially suppressing prices of domestic foodstuffs. This policy dovetailed with the classical development dictate that the exploitation of peasant production facilitates urban industrialization. To maintain low wages in the cities around primary industrialization projects *and* the popular support from the urban population, the FSLN subsidized food costs. However, since the Sandinistas were not inclined to resort to violence as a means of coercion, they were unable to force the minifundistas to stay on their land or keep the itinerant proletarians in the countryside. The dispossessed and land-poor peasants flocked to the cities, where they could buy staples for less than it cost to produce them, benefit from extended urban state services, and enjoy the large profit margins of petty trading (Utting 134–35). The impact of migration on basic grains production was palpable. Whereas in 1981 production of beans, rice, and corn was on the rise, by mid-1984 production of these crops was on the steady decline again (CIERA, *Cifras* 89, 91, 93).

The increase of counterrevolutionary activity in the countryside contributed to migration and decline in productivity; however, agrarian reform, pricing, and marketing policies contributed to the rise in counterrevolutionary activity. Peasants migrating to the cities were not the immediate concern, although it appeared as such to the urbanite. Of greater consequence were those peasants who were not migrating and were thus unable to reproduce themselves from their labor. Where did they go? Estimates on the number of armed counterrevolutionaries operating inside the country at this time fluctuated between 6,000 and 10,000, depending on whether the source was the FSLN or the U.S. Embassy. However, after the war ended, estimates on the number of counterrevolutionaries and their families in

Costa Rica and Honduras in need of relocation ranged from 28,000 to 40,000. Even in 1985 it had become obvious to all but the most idealistic that this was no longer strictly a mercenary force. These counterrevolutionaries were mostly of Nicaraguan peasant extraction. While this is a fraction of the rural EAP, counterrevolutionary operations in the countryside required the tacit complicity of many more. It is impossible to assess the degree of the minifundistas' and itinerant proletarians' political commitment to counterrevolutionary ideology—to distinguish coercion and need from fervor. Nevertheless, they were there in numbers. Leon Trotsky, writing about the transition period in the Soviet Union, once declared: "politically, the civil war is the struggle between the proletariat in opposition to the counterrevolutionaries for the conquest of the peasantry" (CIERA, *Cifras* cover sheet). Such a war was taking place in Nicaragua.

MIDINRA's *Work Plan for 1985* reveals the sudden and strategic changes in agrarian reform policy that took place in that year. Official projections for land redistribution for 1985, made in 1984, show that the ministry intended to continue agrarian reform at the previous sleepy pace. It proposed that 2 percent of the nation's arable land be expropriated from large-scale production; of this 2 percent, 110,000 manzanas would go directly into cooperative production, benefiting 4,000 peasant families, while 10,000 manzanas would go to 400 peasant families as private property. The state sector, which had dropped down to 19 percent in 1984, would remain constant (CAHI, "Agrarian Reform" 4). The projections are worth noting as a comparison with the pattern of distribution that actually came to pass. The FSLN faced deteriorating support from the minifundistas and the itinerant proletariat nationwide. In the war zones, this deterioration registered as counterrevolutionary activity. Along the Pacific coast, especially in Masaya, it registered as political apathy (CAHI, "Masaya Peasants" 3).[24] The war forced the FSLN's hand: maintain a contradictory alliance with the agricultural bourgeoisie and a commitment to cooperativization and lose the countryside, or abandon the bourgeoisie agro-export production, and previous positions on the minifundistas' and itinerant proletarians' preference for individual ownership, in favor of food production and the hope of winning back these sectors. The fact is, however, given the country's economic conditions, the FSLN had no "choice." The war effort required a subsistence economy.

Jaime Wheelock, the director of MIDINRA, announced in June 1985 that emergency expropriations would take place in Masaya and that expropriated lands would be redistributed in individual holdings (CAHI, "Masaya Peasants" 1). Of the 108,000 manzanas actually distributed in that year, 47,000 were given in private holdings to 6,500 dispossessed or land-poor peasant families. The remaining 61,000 manzanas were distributed to 5,000 peasants in cooperative holdings. While the balance of land still favored the cooperative sector, a change in policy was evident. In January 1986, the legislature passed a revised agrarian reform law. The new law allowed MIDINRA to expropriate idle or abandoned holdings of under 500 manzanas on the Pacific coast, of under 1,000 manzanas in the mountainous regions. This did away with the protection of nonproductive medium-holding producers under the 1981 law (CAHI, "Reactions to Agrarian Reform" 1–2).

During the next three years, significant reductions in landholdings occurred, not only in the private sector but in the APP as well.[25] The state no longer had the resources to subsidize inefficient production in any sector. Thirty-three thousand peasants received 550,000 manzanas of these lands. While these overall figures are comparable to the figures from 1981 to 1984, the distribution patterns were radically altered. Sixteen thousand minifundistas and itinerant proletarians received land in cooperative holdings, while 17,000 of these peasants received land in individual holdings. By the end of 1988, roughly 80,000 peasants had benefited from agrarian reform, capturing 16.5 percent of the total national arable land.

The Sandinistas defeated the counterrevolutionaries militarily in 1989. However, in February 1990 the Sandinistas lost the national elections for the presidency and the legislature to the U.S.-backed conservative coalition, the Union of National Opposition (UNO). A pious perspective, exploiting the benefits of hindsight, would admonish the FSLN for doing too little, too late. Certainly, the arrogant delay in responding to the dispossessed and land-poor peasantry's interests undermined the Sandinistas' support among a crucial rural base. This contributed to the decline in food production, which in turn led to a decline in support from an urban base. This negligence on the part of the FSLN had disastrous implications that cannot be ignored. However, the narrative I have recounted here is itself partial. To focus on the Sandinistas' seduction by the paradigm of development in their approach to the peasantry, I have excluded the multifaceted destruction by the U.S.-backed war and minimized the dead to marginal references in the chapter. Rather than pious observations, therefore, I will offer more useful ones.

For the Prisoners of Hope

Regardless of the tarnished, strategic motivations behind the 1985 change in agrarian reform policy, this change registered a qualitative transformation in consciousness on the part of the leadership of FSLN, from MIDINRA policy makers in Managua to the technicians in the field. The changes in policy were complicit with military considerations; nevertheless, a fundamental redefinition of the FSLN's national project took place within the span of six years. Given the uneven productivity on APP and cooperative holdings, the Sandinistas were forced to recognize that the most dynamic production of surplus would come from small, private holdings in the hands of the peasantry. Thus they took a risk in radically redefining their understanding of the minifundista and itinerant proletariat economic formation. Arguably, the dispossessed and land-poor peasantry's interest in private plots of land *was* in tune with a hegemonic and individualistic consciousness privileging private property that predated the revolution. The Sandinistas were adamantly opposed to abetting this "petit bourgeois" consciousness by giving away land in private parcels. Paradoxically, because of the need to maintain agro-export production, the Sandinistas reinforced this bourgeois positionality in the other sectors of the rural population—the medium- and small-holding peasants—with their generous incentive packages. This segment of the rural population benefited enormously during the Sandinista years, whether or not they politically supported the Sandinistas. Unlike the terratenientes, these medium- and small-scale producers did not liquidate the capital invested in their farms. They simply were not wealthy enough to move to Miami and reproduce their same standard of living there. Unlike the minifundistas, they were in a position to benefit from agricultural incentives and to at least withstand the harmful impact of some policies. By 1986, however, the FSLN fell back from its attempt to impose from above an ideal consciousness on the minifundistas and the itinerant proletarians through the cooperative program or state farms. In effect, cooperativization could not bring about revolutionary consciousness because its successful implementation necessitated that a commitment to the revolution, to a particular vision of modernization, and to the national community be in place *before* the cooperative was even formed, as discussed previously. Until this 1986 sea change in agrarian reform policy, the minifundistas and the itinerant proletarians had been judged according to a regime of subjection that read these peasants as a "prerevolutionary" moment of consciousness in a double sense. As a social formation they were considered to be at a *prior stage* of development to the higher formation of collective agency implicit in the cooperatives and state farms. Yet, like Guevara and Payeras before them, the Sandinistas simultaneously projected an organic *predisposition* to revolutionary consciousness and agency onto the land-poor peasants. It was then the role of the party, like guardian angels, to elicit this consciousness from them through MIDINRA's enlightened agricultural policy, a consciousness that, after all, corresponded to a "natural" course of evolution for these agents/objects anyway.

In the end, the FSLN stopped assuming this paternalistic role and did decide to focus on strengthening the minifundistas and itinerant proletariat as private producers in the hopes that these sectors would be able to respond to a call for revolutionary transformation from a more secure economic position. In a 1986 diagnosis of the Nicaraguan cooperative movement, CIERA concluded, "The distribution of land in individual holdings could be preferable for various reasons, in certain situations. Redistribution in this form does not signify an abandonment of the cooperative movement, but rather provides a solid base for future cooperative development" (CIERA, "Propuesta" 4). As this passage suggests, of the 17,000 peasant subalterns awarded lands in individual holdings under the third agrarian reform law (1986), 10,000 of them joined some form of cooperative association: either credit and service cooperatives, or work cooperatives, or dead-furrow cooperatives. This reveals the dialectical nature of the transformation of consciousness that took place. The proclivity toward cooperative associations demonstrated by these producers would not necessarily have been as dramatic without the predominance of the cooperative ideology for the previous four years.

In light of these transformations, how do we explain the Sandinista electoral defeat? Behind agrarian reform policies lay the supposition that ownership of land (in any form) would lead to an identification of the dispossessed and land-poor peasants with the nationalist vision of those implementing the reform. The peasant ownership of land was mediated by the nationalist project from the Sandinista perspective. That is to say, the FSLN assumed that the acceptance of land would implicate the peasant in a model of development predicated on the transformation—"transcendence" —of his or her subject position. However, these sectors of the rural population were never brought into the decision-making process over this development plan because of the FSLN's basic distrust of the peasant formations. For the first six to seven years of the revolution, the Sandinista national development project was devoutly modernizing, to pull the land-poor peasantry into large-scale agro-industry—which may have been progressive in a global context as a response to dependent development, but was regressive in the local context. The minifundistas, the itinerant proletarians, and even the cooperativized sectors of the peasantry suffered the negative impacts of

Sandinista production policies for many years under this nationalist vision. The increase in land turnovers to private farmers was not accompanied by a parallel increase in participation in development decision making. Receiving land from the government implicated the land-poor peasant in a vision of development, but it did so without granting the peasant any say in the development project. Therefore, when I interviewed peasants who had received private parcels of land after 1987, they were hardly filled with a sense of gratitude. Most were guarded, if not openly hostile, in their attitude toward MIDINRA and the party. There was a common assumption among those I interviewed that they had won the land from a recalcitrant state, rather than through "their" revolutionary government, and they felt an uncertainty about their future relationship to the Sandinistas.

It seems clear that ownership of land was not enough to ensure identification with the FSLN, even on the cooperatives. Meanwhile the counterrevolution appealed to conservative elements of peasant consciousness with its emphasis on the church, respect for private property, and, most importantly, autonomy for the producers; in other words, "no more interventionist state policies that end up hurting more than helping the peasant." This held sway not only with the minifundistas and the itinerant proletarians, who were in the most precarious economic position, but with members of cooperatives, those who presumably benefited the most from the revolutionary process as the earliest recipients of lands and services. When I visited El Cua, Matagalpa, in the summer of 1989, I interviewed a local UNAG representative and asked him if production on the cooperatives had improved significantly now that the war had ended in that area. "Production is much better," he replied, "now that they [cooperative members] are sleeping at night." I had lived in Nicaragua long enough to know what this meant. "Counterrevolutionaries on *production cooperatives?*" I asked. Amused by my naïveté, he pulled out a list of the twenty-five local cooperatives and pointed to the ten or twelve that had had members in the counterrevolutionary forces.

In 1979 Sandinista policy makers correctly assessed Nicaragua's economy as an export-orientated, dependent economy. In the FSLN's attempt to remedy this situation, to practice revolutionary socialist development in Nicaragua, we find an implied regime of revolutionary subjection that shared many characteristics with development discourse's model for human transformation. MIDINRA and the FSLN viewed the peasant formation as a precursor to higher levels of political, economic, and social consciousness. Rather than accept these sectors of the peasantry as historically given social formations and basing policy accordingly, the Sandinistas viewed the minifundista and itinerant proletarian formations, if not as "backwards," then certainly as precursors to the preferred model of economic development. In the Sandinista imaginary of revolutionary development, the peasant subalterns existed in a mythological past tense or future tense, but not in the "real," material sense of the present. Given this, the Sandinistas wrongly assessed the desires and interests of these peasant classes and extended the peasantry two options: cooperativization or proletarianization. These peasants, for the most part, lacked either the interest or the possibility to choose either.

Partha Chatterjee has shed some light on the reason for the Sandinistas' assumptions about development and the peasantry. In *Nationalist Thought and the Colonial World: A Derivative Discourse?* Chatterjee considers the formation of twentieth-century Third World nationalist thought as an explicit response to the division of the world into "developed" and "underdeveloped" regions. In Chatterjee's analysis, the term "underdevelopment" diagnoses more than an economic condition; it implicitly refers to the epistemic condition of a country, as well. Because the ideology of development colonizes at the level of representation as well as the level of policy, the effects of underdevelopment are not only material but also social and psychological. Thus various classes in these countries rally nationalism(s) to remedy their prescribed psychosocial and economic condition of "underdevelopment." Through his analysis of India's struggle for national independence, Chatterjee identifies two prominent strands of Third World nationalisms mobilized by Third World peoples to subvert the developed/underdeveloped dichotomy. Chatterjee stresses that the two types of nationalism often occur simultaneously, acting at times in concert and at other times antagonistically. *Progressive* bourgeois nationalism, represented in India by Nehru, is eager to displace foreign economic interests but is committed to the project of modernization and asserts the country's ability to "achieve" development in Western terms. *Conservative* mass-based nationalism, represented in India by Gandhi, is eager to displace exploitative imperialist elements and their internal allies but resists modernization and rejects Western development models to greater or lesser degrees. While this abbreviated discussion may oversimplify Chatterjee's position on Third World nationalisms, I want to illustrate how he brings out the divisions and tensions in Third World nationalisms so often represented in the West as uniform. From Chatterjee's perspective, capitalists and Marxists often share a commitment to a particular mode of development that leads them to similar conclusions and political collusion, though these two groups of nationalists are, in the final analysis, ideologically opposed. For example, capitalists are likely to see recalcitrant mass-based or popular formations, such as the dispossessed or land-poor peasantry, as "backward elements," while Marxists may view them as "precapitalist," or, as in the case of the Sandinistas, as "prerevolutionary," representing an "incomplete" process of proletarianization (Chatterjee preface). It then becomes the mission of classical development theory and socialist revolutionary development to complete this process and bring these elements into productive history by effecting a transformation of consciousness from the top down.

The case of the Sandinista nationalist project as exemplified by agricultural policy fits within Chatterjee's analysis of Third World nationalisms. While committed to a mass-based liberation movement on the one hand, the FSLN was also committed to a large-scale industrialized agro-export economy as the means of overcoming Nicaragua's economic dependence on the United States. These two visions for the nation—mass-based liberation and further industrialization—did not always coincide. Chatterjee's model of heterogeneous and contradictory nationalist visions occurring in the same geographic space usefully frames the tensions the Sandinistas encountered in their model of revolutionary development in agriculture. In their conceptualization and implementation of agricultural policy, the Sandinistas encountered resistance not only from the landed elites but often from the social group they intended to benefit: the land-poor peasantry. Chatterjee's theorization extracts us from the ideological gridlock in which capitalist development and revolutionary socialist development are viewed as diametrically opposed phenomena, allowing us to locate the complicity between the two in their commitment to remarkably similar regimes of subjection. In his analysis of India, Chatterjee also helps us to understand how the Sandinistas, as progressive nationalists with obvious Marxist-Leninist theoretical bases, could have enjoyed so much mass-based support among the peasantry at the beginning of the revolution and have lost this support by as early as 1985. The Sandinistas' resistance to a significant redistribution of land among the peasant classes was due to their belief in a classic developmental paradigm. The FSLN identified the itinerant proletariat and minifundista formations with preproletariat or precollective consciousness and interpreted their desires for land as petit bourgeois aspirations toward private property. The Sandinistas hoped to leapfrog these formations through an acceleration of proletarianization on state farms or collectivization on cooperatives. Had the Sandinistas been truer to their materialist training in their analysis, then perhaps they would have resisted grafting this ideologically determined development narrative onto peasant consciousness and instead based their analysis on the peasants as constituting part of the present tense of the nation.

In the interest of the next revolutionary attempt at improving the quality of life of rural communities, I believe it necessary to critique the paternalistic and narrowly modernistic attitude toward the peasantry so often assumed by revolutionary states under the guise of benevolent efforts toward the development of the peasants into productive members of a nation. This benevolent development can prove deadly to everyone involved. James C. Scott, who studies everyday forms of resistance among the peasantry, has suggested for both conventional and socialist development schemes that "the radical solution [to development] . . . raises as many problems as it solves. Only revolutionary victory and the structural change it brings, they argue, can engender true participation and economic justice. Here the history of socialist revolutions is not encouraging. In most cases such revolutions have brought to power regimes that are, if anything, more successful in extracting resources from their subjects and regimenting their lives" ("Everyday" 3–4). And furthermore:

> Under state socialism . . . all the vital decisions about commodity prices, the prices of agricultural inputs, credit, cropping patterns, and—under collectivization—the working day and the wage, are direct matters of state policy. Conflicts that might have been seen as private sector matters, with the state not directly implicated, become, under state socialism, direct clashes with the state. The peasant meets the state as employer, buyer, supplier, moneylender, foreman, paymaster, and tax collector. . . . Though it may occasionally improve his or her welfare, the aim of state socialism is invariably to reduce the autonomy of a strata previously classified as *petite bourgeoisie*. The loss of autonomy by itself has been a source of ferocious resistance. ("Everyday" 15)

I have tried to document the reasons for, and methods of resistance among, the peasantry to the FSLN's revolutionary development. As Scott suggests, the FSLN's development model intervened in every aspect of the minifundistas' and itinerant proletarians' lives, without ever granting these sectors of the peasantry the political means for negotiating the terms of this intervention. The land-poor peasantry fell out of the revolutionary government's corporativist loop. Representatives of the pro-Sandinista UNAG saw their job as that of defending the rights of the medium- and small-scale producer, and given how much more powerful these sectors are today than in 1979, they did so quite successfully. The Sandinista ATC, while more sympathetic with the plight of the land-poor peasants, was primarily concerned with labor conditions on state and private farms. In ten years the Sandinistas never established an equivalent organization to represent the rights and interests of the minifundistas and the itinerant proletarians within the party.[26] Consequently the dispossessed and land-poor peasants had no way of lobbying the Sandinistas from the inside. Of course, this oversight was symptomatic of the party's fundamental disbelief in the consciousness of these two sectors as a viable or rational form of revolutionary consciousness.

The Sandinistas were working with idealized revolutionary subjects in agriculture. There was "the patriotic private producer," "the state farm worker," and "the cooperative member." The Sandinistas believed that the state, in one way or another, could successfully direct all these idealized citizen-subjects toward technified, rationalized production units. The dispossessed and land-poor peasants were outside or prior to this evolutionary chain of rationalized and enlightened consciousness. Nothing illustrates this better than the Sandinistas' failure to create a political organization to directly represent peasant interests to the party. The Sandinistas believed that land in the hands of the land-poor peasants would lead to irrational production. They believed the peasantry would revert to production for consumption with little or no surplus, and this would lead to a precipitous drop in the production of export crops. Ultimately they feared that this type of production would escape the control of the state and their national plan of modernization. I am not suggesting that the Sandinistas should have abandoned all efforts at production for export and modernization in favor of some utopian pastoral vision. However, the Sandinistas could have negotiated between their own progressive vanguardist nationalist vision and the peasants' "conservative," mass-based—but not necessarily antirevolutionary—nationalist vision of economic development. If the Sandinistas had not considered the peasant formation as regressive, they might have been able to direct political and economic resources toward incorporating this level of peasant production into a revolutionary vision of national development early on in the process. Perhaps then the startling revolutionary vision of the Sandinistas that emerged in 1979 would have been more viable.

Part III

5

Reiterations of the Revolutionary "I": Menchú

and the Performance of Subaltern *Conciencia*

What is at stake in constructing the function of representation in the testimonio may be nothing less than reestablishing the parameters of democracy's function within Latin American society at large and of suggesting, perhaps, that representation—at least in the impure, post-modern sense of the term . . . need not be an alienating marker of the distance to be traversed in the struggle for emancipation, but rather the ineluctable form that all emancipatory practices must take.
—Santiago Colás, "What's Wrong with Representation?"

The temporal paradox of the subject is such that, of necessity, we must lose the perspective of a subject already formed in order to account for our own becoming. That becoming is no simple or continuous affair, but an uneasy practice of repetition and its risks, compelled yet incomplete, wavering on the horizon of social being.
—Judith Butler, *The Psychic Life of Power*

Colás's estimation of the importance of representation in testimonial literature is central to this book's project, to interrogate revolutionary regimes of subjection in an effort to understand why post–World War II revolutionary movements and leaders misrepresented the constituencies they sought to emancipate. Colás suggests that understanding how representation functions in the literary genre of testimonio can elucidate how political representation might function in an emancipatory project beyond the defeated revolutionary politics of the late twentieth century, and certainly beyond the current parameters of liberal democracy and neoliberal economics. In the first two parts of this book, I have considered how political and figural representations of the subaltern were coterminous endeavors in post–World War II revolutionary projects that imagined the emancipatory transformation not only of national economies and cultures but also of subaltern subjectivities and consciousness. The third part of this book considers how subaltern subjects, swept up in the misperceptions of these emancipatory movements, nevertheless seek to rewrite these representations of themselves from *within* a revolutionary project.

In chapter 4, I interpreted the Sandinistas' misapprehension of peasant desire in their attempt to represent subaltern interests in agricultural policy. I argued their failure in this regard was a consequence of the party's attempt to institute a teleological regime of subjection through agrarian reform that was predicated on the transcendence of peasant specificity, interpreted by the Sandinista party as premodern. In chapter 3, I analyzed the revolutionary autobiographies of Ernesto "Che" Guevara and Mario Payeras, suggesting that the racial residue of colonialist desire underwrites these protagonists' self-representation and, more significantly, their representation of the rural subalterns who were the horizon of their revolutionary activity. Acting out of their own sense of compromised masculinity, these revolutionary icons often feminized and primitivized the peasant or indigenous subaltern in their representation of the requirements for transformation, consciousness, and agency. Together, in their political and literary efforts to represent subaltern subjects, these post–World War II revolutionaries paradoxically adhered to the developmentalist model of normative subjectivity and national sovereignty put forth by institutions such as the World Bank, the IMF, and USAID in the service of the Cold War. Through her testimonio, Rigoberta Menchú wrests the (Western) terms of literary and political representation from these revolutionaries, precisely in the hopes of refiguring what Colás calls "the ineluctable form that all emancipatory practices must take." Her testimonio, I argue, is a performative intervention into the theorization of revolutionary subjectivity in the Americas—an intervention which at once challenges revolutionary developmentalism and risks activating an ethnonationalist developmentalism of its own.

"Wavering on the Horizon of Social Being"

In this chapter, I place Menchú's text within the "extraliterary" context that produced it, for the richness of this context has often been reduced to questions of literary protocol by earlier critics who theorize the genre of testimonio within the fields of American studies and Latin American studies.[1] The term "extraliterary" is borrowed from Alberto Moreiras's "The Aura of Testimonio." Moreiras uses the term as a marker for the "real," or that which marks the "referential limits of the literary": "I am not suggesting that testimonio can exist outside the literary; only that the specificity of testimonio, and its particular position in the current cultural configuration,

depend on an extraliterary stance or moment, which we could also understand as a moment of arrest of all symbolization in a direct appeal to the non-
exemplary, but still singular, pain beyond any possibility of representation.
Testimonio is testimonio because it suspends the literary at the very same
time that it constitutes itself as a literary act: as literature, it is a liminal event
opening onto a nonrepresentational, drastically indexical order of experience" (195). Extending Moreiras, I suggest that the extraliterary context in
Menchú's text is not only "the pain beyond any possibility of representation"
but also the theater of Realpolitik, a theater in which Menchú actively participates, in part through her performance of testimonial acts. Moreiras insists
that testimonio will always exceed literary representation, that it will exceed
generic and disciplinary concerns. I place Menchú's text within the context
of a historically particular emancipatory project to illustrate one such moment of its excess as testimonial literature. Thus I will not put Menchú in
dialogue with Franz Boas, Toni Morrison, or the *boom*-writers, as testimonio
critics before me have done. Rather, I will put Menchú in dialogue with
revolutionaries such as Mario Payeras and Ricardo Ramirez (nom de guerre
Rolando Moran), leaders of the Ejercito Guerrillero de los Pobres (Guerrilla
Army of the Poor—EGP) and her comrades in arms. Menchú's text responds
to the EGP's theorization of the indigenous people's revolutionary *conciencia,* especially their portrayal of the guerrilla as the agent actualizing the
revolutionary potential of indigenous peasant subalterns.

David Stoll, in his sardonically titled *Rigoberta Menchú and the Story of All
Poor Guatemalans,* repeatedly characterizes Menchú as little more than a
mouthpiece for the EGP, as a political patsy who fabricated much of her story
in order to bolster the guerrilla army's image abroad and thereby prolong a
costly war at home (Stoll xiv–xv, 11–12, 39–40, 192–93, 203–4, 246). In
particular, he faults Menchú for subordinating ethnic identity to fabricated
class identity in her narrative. According to Stoll, Menchú's class-based
representation of her community was strictly in keeping with the EGP's
agenda of portraying itself as the defender of an exploited peasant class.[2] In
his rush to portray Menchú as an EGP dupe, Stoll entirely misses the critique of the EGP's estimation of indigenous subaltern agency embedded in
Menchú's text. Far from mimicking the doctrinaire positions of a misguided
guerrilla movement, Menchú challenges Moran's and Payeras's portrayal of
indigenous subaltern conciencia. Rather than sacrifice ethnic identity to
class interests, as Stoll accuses, Menchú's text demonstrates how the revolutionary transformation of conciencia emerges from an indigenous identity
that is produced by colonialism and capitalism, and that is capable of an

integrated class, racial, and gender analysis. However, Menchú does not simply write *against* revolutionary leaders like Moran and Payeras. Rather, she is engaged in a critical reevaluation of their interpretation of revolutionary agency. Menchú retheorizes the subjectivity of the revolutionary agent from an indigenous and gendered position.

Rigoberta Menchú, as the testimonial subject of *Me llamo Rigoberta Menchú y así me nació la conciencia,* answered multiple interpellative hails to revolutionary conciencia, some issued by her comrades, others issued prior to the guerrilla's arrival in the region. She tells us in her autobiography that these hailings even preceded her physical birth. Her testimonio, with its narrative description of multiple moments of consciousness birth, reenacts these scenes of interpellation for the reader. In effect, her testimonio is a multilayer performance of interpellative hailings. In addition to describing various interpellative moments, the act of testifying is itself an *interpellative performance:* the interviewer compels her to confess to the birth of her conciencia as an indigenous subaltern woman, and the very reiterative nature of the confession—her repeated admission of the birth of her conciencia— constitutes her as such a subject. In her testimonio Menchú restages the many scenes of her own subjection to revolutionary conciencia and also performs an interpellative hailing of her own: she stages a *repeated* interpellative call to the (Western) reader to subject herself to revolutionary conciencia as well. In addition to this political call to the general reader, Menchú's testimonio stages an intellectual call for *this* particular reader, calling me into a space for retheorizing revolutionary conciencia.

Thus two underlying questions structure my reading. First, can interpellation ever slip or misfire, exceeding the bounds of normativity? Second, if it can misfire, does the genre of testimonio function as a moment of such slippage, as revolutionary interpellation? Is it what Judith Butler calls an "uneasy practice of repetition and its risks" in this chapter's epigraph, one that hails a subject into a new mode of "wavering on the horizon of social being"? To proceed, it is necessary to enter the temporal paradox suggested in this passage quoted from Butler's *The Psychic Life of Power.* To determine whether interpellation might slip or misfire, we must first begin by determining if testimonio might itself function as revolutionary interpellation. That is, how might testimonio embody interpellative excess? Stating tentatively what is by no means obvious—that Menchú's interpellation exceeded the bounds of normativity—we must lose sight of the apparently fully constituted, resistive subject in order to turn our attention to the means by which we come to "know" this subject, the testimonial form. It behooves us to reexamine testimonio criticism, a body of criticism enthralled by testimonio's novelty as a form of cultural expression, and by its potential for democratic representation.

Autobiographical Desire and the Testimonio Critic

Menchú's as-told-to narrative has repeatedly served as the template for critics defining the conventions of testimonio, as the genre's most *representative* example (Jara and Vidal; Sommer, "Not Just a Personal Story"; Beverley, "The Margin at the Center"; Gugelberger and Kearney; Yúdice; Zimmerman). Georg Gugelberger, in his introduction to the anthology *The Real Thing*, delineates three stages in the development of testimonio criticism over the last two decades, each stage challenging and revising the assumptions of the previous one (4–5). Yet in each stage, Menchú's narrative remains a constant in the critical reevaluation of the genre.[3] The nature of the authorial voice in Menchú's text—who is speaking, for whom is she speaking, and to whom is she speaking—has been the subject of much debate in testimonio criticism and has fundamentally shaped the theory of authorial voice in testimonio in general. It is as if the entire future of the genre hinges on the question of representation in Menchú's text, as if without her text there could be no such thing as testimonial criticism. If, as Colás has suggested, the question of representation is as central to the future of democratic change in the Americas as to the future of the genre of testimonio in the Western academy, it behooves us to consider *why* Menchú's narrative becomes central to the representation of the genre (171). Thus, to arrive at a discussion of how Menchú's testimonio alters the possibilities for interpellation within projects of revolutionary transformation, I address the construction of Menchú's narrative as the quintessential form of the testimonial voice.

In her autobiography, Menchú denounces the genocidal military regime in Guatemala, insisting on the humanity and civility of the victims of this genocide, the Mayan population of the highlands, jungle, and coast. As such, her autobiography seems intended for an international audience capable of extending political and material solidarity. After all, she tells her story in Spanish, rather than in K'iche', to an exiled Venezuelan leftist while visiting Paris on a diplomatic mission. The first wave of testimonio critics certainly presumed this to be the intended audience, characterizing testimonio as a genre of "urgency" meant to elicit solidarity from its readers. In "*Testimonio* and Postmodernism," originally published in 1991, for example, George Yúdice defines *testimonio* as "an authentic narrative, told by a witness who is moved to narrate by the urgency of a situation (e.g., war, oppression, revolution, etc.)." "Emphasizing popular, oral discourse," Yúdice continues, "the witness portrays his or her own experience as an agent (rather than a representative) of a collective memory and identity. Truth is summoned in the cause of denouncing a present situation of exploitation and oppression or in exorcising and setting aright official history" (44). The language of witness, denunciation, summons, and truth, used here by Yúdice to describe testimonio, implies a reader presumed capable of responding, juridically or politically, to the urgency of the situation. Turning his analysis specifically to Menchú's text, Yúdice uses her discussion of her "nahual,"[4] a lifelong companion from the animal world, to theorize the nature of representation within this type of urgent communication: "Representation for Menchú, then, is something quite different from classical political representation or the aesthetic reflective mimesis of nineteenth-century European realist fiction. The nahual, more than a representation, is a means for establishing solidarity" (56). From Menchú's discussion of the function of the nahual in her community, Yúdice deduces that something "more than" representation takes place in testimonial literature, something beyond it—some form of communication more immediately connected to the referent—that approximates or elicits solidarity. Representation in testimonio, then, issues an interpellative hail that is different from the usual call to mimetic identification with the protagonist; instead, testimonial representation issues an interpellative call to form a community of action.

In "The Margin at the Center: On Testimonio," originally published in 1989, John Beverley classifies testimonio as a new form of cultural production emerging from the "popular-democratic subject(s)" contending for power in an era of "transition or potential transition from one mode of production to another" (24).[5] Stated differently, Beverley suggests that new modes of interpellation, engendered by this transition from bourgeois hegemony to a new revolutionary order, are represented in the testimonial genre. This new cultural form connotes a different mode of both authorship and readership. Beverley analyzes both in his discussion of the role of Elizabeth Burgos-Debray, the Venezuelan who interviewed Menchú and edited her oral history into printed form: "Testimonio gives voice in literature to a previously 'voiceless,' anonymous, collective popular-democratic subject, the *pueblo* or 'people,' but in such a way that the intellectual or professional, usually of bourgeois or petty-bourgeois background, is interpolated as being part of, and dependent on, the 'people' without at the same time losing his or her identity as an intellectual. In other words, testimonio is not a form of liberal guilt. It suggests as an appropriate ethical and political response more the possibility of solidarity than charity" (31). Although Beverley begins by specifically addressing the role of that intellectual "of bourgeois or petty-bourgeois background" usually involved in the joint authorship of testimonial literature, his analysis broadens to encompass the "appropriate ethical and political response" of *any* intellectual or professional confronted with a testimonial text as that of "solidarity" rather than "charity." Indeed, even beyond the professional or intellectual, Beverley implies that the readerly relationship established by the testimonial text is one of solidarity. Once again, the interpellative call of testimonio is refigured and refiguring: it is a *collective* hail to the individuated reader, a hail to collective action—"as being part of, and dependent on, the 'people'"—rather than sentimental cathexis. And yet it is interesting to note that while the testimonial voice *is* encompassed by, or absorbed into, the anonymity of the "collective popular-democratic subject," testimonio does not require the same of the intellectual/reader. Thus, while the liberal subject's authorial voice is challenged by the narrative structure of Menchú's testimonio, the same does not pertain for the (liberal) intellectual, readerly subject.[6] As we will see, the critic's own desire to see pure, collective action in testimonio risks reestablishing the very sentimental understanding of the subaltern that Menchú's text works to undermine. For what is at stake in denying testimonial protagonists the liberal, individuated authorial function while preserving the liberal, individuated readerly function for the critic? What is the effect of this erasure of the author function in Menchú's text? Is this testimonial voice completely new to Western letters, as Beverley suggests, and what is at stake in this claim to novelty?

Together, these now influential definitions of testimonio set the early protocols for the genre. First, the narrator of testimonio is of popular extraction (in the Latin American sense of the term *popular*—of the people) and speaks metonymically for a collective memory, identity, or subject. Second, the narrative in testimonio is considered uniquely "true" in comparison with all previous forms of literary representation: it is "authentic"; truth is "summoned" by it. At an earlier point in his essay, Beverley states that "unlike the novel, testimonio promises *by definition* to be primarily concerned with sincerity rather than literariness" (26; italics mine). Third, because of the protagonist's popular extraction and the unmediated nature of representation in her or his testimonio, the authorial function is mitigated, if not erased, in the testimonial voice. Finally, the reader—and particularly the professional intellectual, the critic—is placed in a privileged relation to the testimonial text, as testimonio demands an active/activist participation from its recipient. Testimonio demands, in light of these protocols, what Moreiras has called a "hermeneutics of solidarity" from the critic/reader. Again, from Moreiras's "The Aura of Testimonio," originally published in 1995: "Beverley recognizes that the positional distance between the literary text and the literary critic is different from the radical break separating the testimonial subject and its reader. The testimonial subject, by virtue of its testimonio, makes a claim to the real in reference to which only solidarity or its withholding is possible. The notion of total representativity of the testimonial life, which in fact points to a kind of literary degree zero in the testimonial text, paradoxically organizes the extraliterary dimension of the testimonial experience: solidarity is not a literary response, but that which suspends the literary in the reader's response" (202). A paradox is produced by the first generation of testimonial critics' insistence on the unmediated nature of the testimonial. As Moreiras implies, these critics paradoxically, if not unwittingly, produce their own erasure. The early protocols set by the critics for the genre produce a textual veracity—a "notion of total representativity of the testimonial life," a "literary degree zero"—that, in effect, precludes the task of literary analysis. Solidarity with the extraliterary dimension of testimonial is demanded instead, suspending "the literary in the reader's response."

This early criticism of the genre responds to a particular historical context, one in which U.S.-backed counterinsurgency movements were claiming hundreds of thousands of lives in Central America. The situation in Guatemala was particularly severe, as Guatemala's military dictatorship was engaged in a tactical genocide, a scorched-earth policy intended to eliminate 30 percent of the indigenous population while bringing the remaining 70 percent under the army's control (Bastos and Camus, *Quebrando el silencio* 36; Sanford 40–41).[7] Thus the early testimonial critics were in step with the U.S.-based solidarity movement's attempt to halt U.S. intelligence and military aid to the region. In this context, it is not difficult to understand—indeed, to support—the testimonio critic's own sense of urgency: these texts, particularly Menchú's, were not to be pondered but acted on. Hundreds of thousands of civilians, mostly indigenous peasants, were victims of Guatemala's genocidal regime, and the publicizing of Menchú's experiences with the military and paramilitary death squads played no small part in eliciting the international condemnation of the Guatemalan government.

However, more is at stake in the critical urgency of early testimonial criticism than demanding an end to U.S. imperialist intervention in the region. Moreiras suggests a "hermeneutics of solidarity" is antithetical to testimonio's extraliterary solidarity project, and this hermeneutics inevitably produces its own knowledge effect: "As a consequence of this turning of solidarity into a critical poetics, or a hermeneutics, of solidarity, testimonio criticism reauthorizes itself within the epistemological power/knowledge grid at the expense of that which it originally sought to authorize. Testimonio will then be institutionalized within a strict codification: the canonization of testimonio in the name of a poetics of solidarity is equivalent to its reliteraturization following preassigned tropological and rhetorical registers. Thus, in the hands of testimonio criticism, testimonio loses its extraliterary force, which now becomes merely the empowering mechanism for a recanonized reading strategy" (204). Testimonial criticism quickly comes full circle, according to Moreiras, from emphatically insisting on testimonio's antithetical relationship to institutionalized literary practices, to antithetically creating the protocols—the "tropological and rhetorical registers"—for a "recanoniz[ing] reading strategy." Indeed, this first wave of critical interpretation of the testimonial text is activated by an autobiographical desire—a desire for power/knowledge, as suggested by Moreiras—that exceeds the urgency of the historical context. This underlying autobiographical desire in the interpretation of Menchú's testimonio requires its own critical attention.

Although early testimonial critics were nuanced in the claims they made for the immediacy of the testimonial voice,[8] they nevertheless participated in and perpetuated an intellectual fantasy of presence in their discussion of testimonio. Critical presumptions about the unique and unmediated presence of the collective subaltern in the testimonial text wished away the problem of subaltern political and figural representation.[9] Furthermore, by establishing "sincerity" as the standard of testimonial value rather than "literariness," these critics opened the door for attacks on Menchú's veracity, such as the one launched by Stoll. Because Menchú's narrative deviates from his research, unearthed ten years after her book's publication, Stoll is able to challenge her narrative precisely on the grounds made available by testimonial criticism: he questions her sincerity by imputing secret political motives to the deviations in her text from his questionable "evidence." The fantasy of subaltern presence, the belief in an unmediated text, the standard of sincerity, all led to a hermeneutics that simply—perhaps irresponsibly—failed to account for the multiple factors mediating the gap between referent and sign in Menchú's testimonio, as in others. Thus early analysis of Menchú's narrative failed to consider the effect of terror and torture on the individuated and collective memory Menchú represents. It failed to consider how Menchú's personal response to, and interpretation of, the horrific events transpiring around her influenced her representation: the lingering fear of further persecution, the need to protect those still exposed to state-sponsored violence in Guatemala, her acknowledged political affiliation with the Guatemalan guerrilla movement.[10] Analysis of Menchú's testimonio during this first wave of criticism, I would argue, was primarily concerned with using her text to establish the protocols for a *new* genre requiring a *new* hermeneutics of solidarity, a hermeneutics that paradoxically divested the critic of intellectual responsibility. These critics misheard the complex interpellative hail issued by testimonio to them, as critics, because of their own autobiographical desire for subaltern presence.

The resistance to interpreting the testimonial voice in Menchú as a voice transversed by specific and conflicting traumas, fears, motivations, interests, and conscious and unconscious desires precisely serves to abstract her particularity—the concrete materiality of her situation—into a generic subaltern subject whose voice may then be codified into a recognizable set of criteria for an appropriative critical practice. The elision by critics of the difference between Menchú's authorial "I" and the collective "we" tells us more about the Latin American(ist) intellectual's autobiographical fantasy of a collective Indian experience than it does about Menchú's story. There is a binary at work in the disciplinary practice of testimonial criticism, one that Patricia Seed has designated the "binary of the Requerimiento." As discussed in chapter 3 with reference to Guevara and Payeras, the Spanish Requerimiento presented the indigenous populations of the Americas with the option of complete religious and political subordination to the Spanish Crown or of fighting against the Crown unto death. According to Seed, this dichotomous colonial "choice" imposed on the indigenous populations led to a binary pattern of subalternization in Latin America, one in which the indigenous subaltern would be forever identified either with a state of total abjection or with a state of glorious resistance. This binary of subaltern representation produces among the Latin American Left a "requirement for resistance." The desire for a homogeneous, resistive subaltern subject in testimonio expresses residual desire for the Indian warrior who resisted Spanish colonialism unto death.

Thus, circuitously, we arrive at an explanation of why Menchú's text became emblematic of testimonial literature: it complies with what Seed has called the Latin American Left's "requirement for resistance" in identifying the indigenous as subaltern. Menchú's testimonio is not only the testimonio of an indigenous woman but also the narrative of an indigenous woman who resisted, figuratively, unto death. Three of Menchú's family members—her father, mother, and brother—*are* killed by the Guatemalan military, each subjected to torture, including the repeated rape of her mother, the death of her father in the Spanish embassy fire of 1980, and the kidnapping and public assassination of her fourteen-year-old brother. Her remaining family members—indeed, her entire village—are forced to disperse by the military's continuing persecution. In response to these dire circumstances, Menchú neither submits to relocation in one of the military's model villages nor disappears into the anonymity of the Guatemalan refugee camps in Chiapas, Mexico. Instead, Menchú joins the EGP, goes into political exile, and becomes a crusader for Guatemalan human and civil rights at the United Nations headquarters in Geneva. Menchú's resistance is neither uniform nor unique among the Guatemalan indigenous population, a significant percentage of whom continue to organize actively against the model villages, as well as the army-imposed Patrullas de Autodefensa Civil (Self-Defense Civil Patrols—PACS).[11] As anthropologist Jan Rus suggests, though, "During rural rebellions . . . it is not unusual for neighboring communities and even different factions within the same community to react differently, some participating in the revolt while others with apparently identical characteristics try to remain neutral or even aid the government" ("Introduction" 9). Regardless of these heterogeneous survival strategies of the Maya, not all of which resemble the kind of resistance desired by the testimonio critics, early testimonial criticism universalized Menchú's spectacular resistance when the protocols for the genre insisted on identification between the testimonial voice and the Latin American popular subject.

In his critical introduction to *The Real Thing*, through a discussion of second- and third-wave testimonial criticism, Gugelberger fearlessly and repeatedly describes the autobiographical desires that subtended the first wave of testimonial criticism, including his own: "The desire called testimonio was the desire called Third World literature" (1); "We wanted to have it both ways: from within the system we dreamed about being outside with the subaltern; our words were to reflect the struggles of the oppressed" (2); "While not necessarily making the subaltern 'visible,' testimonio has helped to make ourselves visible to ourselves" (3); and, most pointedly, "Testimonio has been the salvational dream of a declining cultural left in hegemonic countries" (7). To this list, I would like to add another, related Latin American(ist) critical desire. The collapsing of the distance between Menchú's claim of authorial representation and a pure, universal category of "we" betrays a desire for the recognizable indigenous-subaltern-Other. This desire is doubly redemptive, for not only does this recognizable indigenous subaltern, in her/his resistive image, promise to deliver a new revolutionary order; s/he reestablishes the centrality of the First World critical "I," as Gareth Williams has suggested, for it is the testimonial critic who provides the hermeneutics of solidarity for appropriat(iv)e readings of this new revolutionary subject/order.[12] To deny Menchú a mediated and complex autobiographical function—representational distance between sign and referent —I would suggest, is to participate in the developmentalist regime of revolutionary subjection discussed in the previous two chapters. It is to deny her the subjectivity associated with any authorial intervention, a subjectivity inevitably inflected by intentionality, interest, desire, artifice, and the power to manipulate and be manipulated by these factors in representation for politically motivated ends. In other words, Menchú is inevitably interpellated by the authorial function of the Western literary tradition when she is called to witness through representation.

Is the normative hail to authorial function the only interpellative hail operating in or through testimonio, however? I would argue that testimonio criticism to date has inadvertently obfuscated that which it sought to reveal: the novel interpellative functions of testimonio. All three waves of testimonial criticism have demanded that the protagonist of testimonio be either agent or author. The testimonial voice is either the voice of the collective democratic "we" or an individuated "I." Either subaltern presence or bourgeois literary representation takes place inside the text. Either egalitarian cultural exchange or appropriative reading takes place outside the text. Testimonio elicits either extraliterary solidarity or appropriative literary analysis from the critic. Such an either/or structure can certainly be deduced from testimonial literature, but I would like to deviate from the debate over whether agency or representation takes place in testimonial literature. Instead, I would suggest, one must look at agency and representation as completely imbricated with each other. The literary, I would suggest, is the structure of possibility for the interpellation of Menchú and the reader. After all, a readerly response of solidarity is formed *by way* of the literary, through the "artifice" of sincerity performed by Menchú in testimonial representation. Agency emerges by way of the literary, as well, in Menchú's representation of the interpretative ambivalence of interpellation. It is precisely in Menchú's slippage, her performative slide between agent and author, between the "we" and the "I," that we can locate the misfire of normative interpellation and begin to unravel its interpellative excess. Once again, Menchú's revolutionary theory calls me into the space between the "I" and the "we," into a space for thinking about how her theory deviates from the revolutionary paradigm that called her.

The binary structure of reading in testimonio criticism mirrors a larger debate over the very possibility of agency taking place between Marxists and poststructuralists in U.S. and Latin American literary and philosophical disciplines. As Butler suggests:

> Whether power is conceived as prior to the subject or as its instrumental effect, the vacillation between the two temporal modalities of power ("before" and "after" the subject) has marked most of the debates on the subject and the problem of agency. Many conversations on the topic have become mired in whether the subject is the condition or the impasse of agency. Indeed, both quandaries have led many to consider the issue of the subject as an inevitable stumbling block in social theory. Part of this difficulty, I suggest, is that the subject is itself a site of this ambivalence in which the subject emerges both as the *effect* of a prior power and as the *condition of possibility* for a radically conditioned form of agency. A theory of the subject should take into account the full ambivalence of the conditions of its operation. (*The Psychic Life of Power* 14–15)

In this chapter, I attempt to account for the ambivalence in the interpellative operation of power at the site of subjectivity embodied by testimonio. However, I offer one caveat to Butler's analysis of ambivalence in the function of interpellation. Indulging a perhaps unwarranted optimism, I would suggest it is not only a "radically conditioned form of agency" that may emerge from this ambivalence at the site of interpellation but a condition of radical agency, as well. Gugelberger views testimonio criticism as having moved through three stages or phases: from "unconditional affirmation," through a critique of the terms of this affirmation, to a critique of testimonio's institutionalization in the multicultural canon of the United States on the basis of the genre's initial critical acclaim. From our current standpoint, it is perhaps more accurate to characterize the entire period between the publication of Jara and Vidal's 1986 *Testimonio y literatura* and Gugelberger's 1996 *The Real Thing* as one single stage of testimonio criticism. During this initial stage, critics were primarily concerned with theorizing the parameters of the genre, the place of the genre within literary studies in the Americas, and the function of representation within the genre.[13] In the hopes of inaugurating a next stage, one that extends the insightful criticism of this previous stage beyond the binaries of Marxist and poststructuralist readings of Menchú, my reading attends to her performance not at the margins or at the center of hegemony but in her vacillation between these two sites of interpellative power.

The Autobiographical "I" and the Ruse of Authenticity

In her autobiography, Menchú enters into a theoretical dialogue over the contours of revolutionary conciencia that begins in Latin America with Ernesto "Che" Guevara's testimonios in the early 1960s and continues through the diaries of Menchú's immediate testimonial predecessor in Guatemala, Mario Payeras. As one of the original founders of the EGP, Payeras wrote two diaries on his involvement in the armed struggle in Guatemala. The first, *Los dias de la selva*, which I discussed in chapter 3, was published in 1980, just three years before the publication of Menchú's autobiography. Thus, in this chapter, I read Menchú's autobiography as a performative response, staged through literary representation in the theater of Realpolitik, to Payeras's construction of revolutionary conciencia, ethnic subjectivity, and the modern nationhood. Menchú offers a model of revolutionary transformation, an interpretation of ethnic consciousness, a construction of nation, and a vision of development in an international geopolitical context that stands in contrast to that of Payeras and the era of revolutionary movements he represents, an era Menchú embraces but also reformulates. Butler has posed the question of agency thus: "How can it be that the subject, taken to be the condition for and instrument of agency, is at the same time the effect of subordination, understood as the deprivation of agency? If subordination is the condition of possibility for agency, how might agency be thought in opposition to the forces of subordination?" (*The Psychic Life of Power* 10). These are the questions addressed through an analysis of Menchú's text.

As discussed in chapter 3, Guevara and Payeras operate within the representational terms of the Spanish colonial legacy in their revolutionary autobiographies. They represent themselves and the peasant/indigenous subalterns they encounter within the racialized and dichotomous terms of the Requerimiento. Guevara represents the mountains and the jungle that the Cuban guerrillas traverse as chaotic and dangerous, whereas Payeras represents them as a tabula rasa. In either case, the mountains and jungles are not only the scene of their revolutionary transformation but are transformed by them as revolutionaries. They represent themselves as transformative agents who refigure the mountains and jungles of Cuba and Guatemala as the horizons of their revolutionary/religious errand. The native inhabitants of these jungles and mountains, however, are invariably represented as suspended in precapitalist formations, awaiting the arrival of these transformative agents to bring them into epochal revolutionary history by eliciting from them a dormant resistance.

To review, in *Los dias de la selva* Payeras describes the guerrillas' time in the jungle as an era of forgetting followed by an era of invention. First, the jungle swallows whole the signs of civilization, of their previous knowledge —Payeras tells us that the rains and termites of the Petén destroyed the library that they brought with them, including *One Hundred Years of Solitude* (18). The Petén devours Latin America's most famous intellectual—García Márquez—metaphorically displacing Macondo as the quintessential place that time forgot. Once cleansed of their prior bourgeois subjectivity, the guerrillas exist as a kind of primary collective man. Payeras tells us that the guerrillas proceed to enter "an era of great invention" in which they "discover" which plants are edible and which are medicinal, as well as how to tell direction and time in the jungle (48). Thus they settle the jungle that has been the scene of their own conversion into *el nuevo hombre*, the new man. Through all this there is no sign of the indigenous population, of the bearers of precisely the knowledge of the jungle that they are said to acquire or invent on their own, no sign of those who will be the object of their revolutionary errand. Finally, one-third of the way through the book, the guerrillas *do* stumble on a group of indigenous peasants: "We waited a long time, listening to the beating of our hearts. Then we heard the crowing of a cock from the direction of the town. It was the first time in months that we had heard that welcome trumpeting. We all exchanged a glance that held both trepidation and joy in it. *There they were, at last, the poor people of our country; but we were ignorant of what would be their response.* . . . That night we brought together the men of the village, and we explained extensively the reason for our struggle, and we announced simply that we were going to triumph" (28–29; italics mine). Payeras constructs the peasants as passively awaiting the guerrilla force, rather than as protagonists in their own lives. They are the horizon of guerrilla activity: "There they were, at last, the poor people of our country." Payeras displaces his desire onto the peasants when he represents them as "in waiting." It is the guerrilla troop that has been waiting for just such a group of peasants, so that they may announce themselves into being, so that their mission may have meaning. Like Guevara, Payeras repeatedly betrays this autobiographical desire in his representation of peasant consciousness as simultaneously abject and rebellious, as a preconsciousness on the verge of "becoming"—a "becoming" that only the guerrilla can usher into being.

Rigoberta Menchú and her community were indeed some of the indigenous peasants that Payeras and his fellow guerrillas stumbled on in the northern highlands of Guatemala. Like the peasants described in Payeras's narrative, in the early 1960s Menchú's parents and their community of K'iche' Indians had been dispossessed of, or displaced from, lands near a central town in the valley of the department of Quiché. Forced to move into the mountain range, these peasants settled an area they named Chimal, near the region of Ixcán, the scene of the EGP's first organizing and recruiting mission, and also the scene of Payeras's narrative (Burgos, *Me llamo* 22). Unlike the indigenous people in Payeras's account, however, Menchú and her community are not simply awaiting the arrival of the guerrillas to solve or analyze their problems. Menchú tells a story of resistance to Guatemala's dictatorial regime that begins for her and the members of her indigenous community at birth.

Payeras's narrative, I have suggested, frames the spectacle of his personal transformation, as well as his transformative revolutionary power. Menchú undergoes no such spectacle of transformation, however, though the title of her book—*Me llamo Rigoberta Menchú y así me nació la conciencia* —which literally translates as "I am called Rigoberta Menchú and this is how conscience/consciousness was born to me"—portends that we will be privy to just such a conversion. In Menchú's narrative there is no dramatic moment of revelation of her own oppression, nor is there the retroactively constructed moment of innocence such revelatory moments necessarily entail. Unlike Payeras's and Guevara's narratives, which begin with just such scenes of transformation, Menchú's first mention of a transformation of conciencia does not occur until the sixth chapter of the book.

When she was eight years old, she tells us, she decided to start work on the *finca*, the large plantations along the coast where she and her family migrated to each year.[14] She tells us that her mother generally worked as a cook on the fincas, but in her spare moments her mother also cut coffee to earn more money for the family: "So, given this, well, I felt very useless and cowardly about not being able to do anything for my mother, only take care of my little brother. And that/this is when my consciousness was born to me, then. Even though my mother didn't like it very much that I should start working and making my own money, but I did it and I asked to do it more than anything to help her, both economically and in strength" (55). In com parison to those documented by her male counterparts in their guerrilla testimonios, this "birth of conciencia" is represented as fairly incidental. There is no burst of bullets forcing her to choose sides, as in Guevara's narrative, nor is there a superior or transcendent awakening about who is the enemy, as in Payeras's narrative. Instead, even her explicit pronouncement on the birth of her conciencia in this passage, structured as if in answer to a question posed by the interviewer, is undercut by all the subsequent, similar pronouncements she makes as she narrates different moments in her life. Throughout the text, she recounts a repetitive and continual process of conscience/consciousness birth that defies the unilinear, messianic model of revolutionary transformation.[15]

Thus Menchú's representation of attaining "revolutionary conciencia," of being hailed as a potential revolutionary agent, is not of a monumental or deafening call to conversion but of a continuous and reiterative call: conciencia is an understanding that comes for Menchú as a consequence of repeatedly interpreting her life condition. Even before she narrates this first "birth of conciencia" at eight years of age, she lets it slip to the reader that she had grasped the conditions of her life at an even earlier age. When she was a very little girl traveling with her family to the finca, she asked her mother why they had to go there: "And my mother would say: because we have the need to go to the *finca* and when you are big you will understand the need we have. *But I did know*, but I would get bored by everything [on the *finca*]. When I was big, it was no longer strange to me [to have to go to the *finca*]; because little by little a person begins to see/understand the need, and a person begins to see/understand that it must be so and that the problems, the pain, the suffering was not only ours, but rather that all this was an entire people's and we came from all different places" (46; italics mine). Once again her realization of her own exploitation is not epochal but rather is gained repetitively from the mundane experience of living: "Little by little" Menchú comes to identify with her mother's exploitation as a woman, as an indigenous person, and as a peasant laborer through the everyday interconnectedness of these three subject positions. Already, as a child, Menchú does not need Payeras and the EGP to reveal to her the reasons for struggle. Instead Menchú emphatically claims authority over her own experience of exploitation. Thus I would suggest that to convey her political vision, Menchú, like her male counterparts, assumes the position of the authorial liberal subject. She dons the self-reflexive and masterful autobiographical "I" of a Western literary tradition—"But *I* did know"—to assert her ability to interpret, and thereby represent, her own experience.

She claims the right to represent her own experience and the experience of her tribe *away from* Payeras and other urban Ladino revolutionary leaders she later worked with when she insists on her interpretive capabilities as an authorial "I."

How does the ambivalence of interpellation function in these two passages describing Menchú's repetitive call to conciencia? In the specific context of Menchú's call to subalternized subjectivity, conditions of power interpellate her as a racialized and feminized laboring subject on a finca, subordinated to the power of a white *finquero* or his agents, and conditioned by her gender as doubly exploitable laborer: as caregiver and day laborer. Nevertheless, the very repetitive excess of her interpellative call to subordination—her boring, day-to-day, repetitive performance of this subjectivity—provides the context for Menchú to recognize the conditions of her own subjection. In addition, the reiterative performance of this recognition in her testimonio generates Butler's "radically conditioned form of agency," an agency in excess of her subaltern subjection. It is precisely the pretense of agency embodied in the authorized "I" of testimonio—the performative "I" of a reflective, autobiographical subject—that constitutes her as representative of her people, and, in addition, as an indigenous authority over a collective subaltern experience.

In this passage, Menchú tactically generalizes this interpretive capability and birth of conciencia across the entire indigenous community when she switches from the first person singular in "When *I* was big, it was no longer strange to *me*" to the first person plural in "a *person* begins to see/understand . . . that all this was an entire people's and *we* came from all different places." Every indigenous peasant in Guatemala, "from all different places," who has ever worked on a finca may not share the revolutionary conciencia represented here. Once again, though, the effect of this representation—of all the indigenous subalterns sharing a conciencia of their own exploitation and its meaning—is to place her community in the position of authority over their own experience. Menchú's representation of this authority contravenes Payeras's representation of the EGP's first encounter with the Guatemalan indigenous peasantry, a representation in which he claimed this authority for the guerrillas. In Payeras's account, the guerrillas deliver revolutionary conciencia to passive and unwitting indigenous subjects: "we brought together the men of the village, and we explained extensively the reason for our struggle, and we announced simply that we were going to triumph" (29–30). Payeras must import the guerrillas into the Ixcán region to interpret the indigenous peasant's experience with exploitation for her K'iche' community: The guerrillas "explained extensively the reasons for *our* struggle." Menchú not only provides the grounds for a feminist critique of the EGP's revolutionary paradigm through her analysis of her mother's dual exploitation as reproductive laborer and wage laborer, but in her interpellative slip between the "I" and the "we" she generalizes this distinctly feminist revolutionary conciencia born from a recognition of the dual exploitation of women.

In a 1983 interview Menchú gave to the Mexican journal *Fem*, she was asked, "Do you believe, as a peasant woman, participating in all that culture of the Guatemalan people, that your work has *developed more* as a consequence of your participation in the struggle?" (15; italics mine). She answered: "In the first place, I have to acknowledge that in my formation, no one needed to tell me who the poor were and how they lived, because we are poor. Nevertheless, that formation that I had, that rich history, if a person does not interact with other Guatemalans in the same country, a person does not know how to guide that history down a road on which a person looks for alternatives" (15).[16] From the deliberate tone of her response, Menchú understands the question as an attempt to wrest the power of analysis from her, as an indigenous "peasant woman," and place it with an implied leadership of "the struggle" (of the EGP or the URNG) external to the indigenous peasant communities. She "develops" because of her participation, not as a consequence of her own cultural formation. However, Menchú once again halts any such interpretation of her formation by foregrounding her authority over her own experience: "no one needed to tell me who the poor were." And once again, Menchú shifts from the first-person singular to the first-person plural in this passage: "no one needed to tell me who the poor were . . . [because] we are poor." Thus she again insists on this authority not only for herself but for the "we" who are poor. Nevertheless Menchú understands that while this authority over one's experience is in itself a political awareness—a formation—it is not, in itself, sufficient to bring about transformation: "If a person does not . . ." Thus, I would suggest, Menchú recognizes in this passage that authority over one's own experience must necessarily be mediated by interpretation and representation: "rich history" must be "guide[d] . . . down a road," must be made particular sense of, must be reflected on, to produce "alternatives"—coherent representations—to produce revolutionary mediations of this indigenous subaltern authority. Thus in Menchú we find the same claim to authorial voice, to unitary subjectivity, that we found in her testimonial and revolutionary predecessors, Che Guevara and Mario Payeras.

To understand the interpellative functions of this repeated shift from the autobiographical "I" to the tactical "we," let us return to Yúdice: "Emphasiz-ing popular, oral discourse, the witness [of testimonio] portrays his or her own experience as an agent (rather than a representative) of a collective memory and identity" (44). Once again, it is the pretense of authorial agency embodied in the autobiographical "I" that allows Menchú to claim authority over her own experience in the first place. But this "radically conditioned form of agency" generated by the interpellative pretense of subjectivity nev-ertheless exceeds the normative bounds of individuated subjection. Through her oral performance, through her reiterative shift from "I" to "we," she performs agency for her people, performs their ability to experience and interpret their subaltern condition. Indeed, she uses the pretense of the "I" to claim a collective memory of exploitation, to claim a collective authority over it for her community, *by way of representation*. Embedded in the performative agency that hails Menchú is a psychic misfire, for through it she issues an interpellative hail to a collective agency. Thus I would disagree with Yúdice when he insists that the testimonial protagonist is an agent *rather than* a representative, for it is only through her performative representations—her tactical representation of communal conciencia—that Menchú can claim agency for herself and constitute herself as a representative of her people in the theater of Realpolitik: within the EGP's exiled leadership in Mexico, or before the United Nations Human Rights Commission in Geneva. In turn, it is only by way of her representation as individuated agent that the collective agency and identity of her K'iche' community can be recognized.

Menchú recognizes a necessary distance, a necessary gap, between sub-altern authority and revolutionary representation. She also recognizes that the power of transformation lies in the mediation of this gap. She seeks to mediate that gap differently than her revolutionary predecessors, but nev-ertheless within the tradition of revolutionary transformation.[17] She repre-sents herself as within a revolutionary formation, but she is altering the historical tropes of revolutionary representation, as well as its teleological trajectory. For Payeras and Guevara, the indigenous peasant's subaltern condition is rendered as abject subordination, as a premodern stage that must be superseded for transformation to occur. Menchú turns subaltern abjection into a "rich history" in her representation, a cultural and *political* formation that must be included in any future revolutionary subjection. Although her representational tropes are qualitatively different from those of her predecessors, it is not a difference in kind. Hers is still an authorial intervention, vexed by conscious intention and unconscious desire. Thus we must keep in mind that Menchú's authorial performance runs certain risks. From the moment she represents the subaltern in the Western cadence of liberal subjectivity—in the recognizable tropes of authorial agency —she distances herself from subalternity. Furthermore, she runs the risk of having readers read her representation as a celebratory assertion of ethnonationalism, when it is anything but that. This is the constitutive problem of representing subalternity with which Menchú's text grapples. On the one hand, by appropriating a recognizable form of agency, Menchú emerges into singularity, into the autobiographical arena of exceptional experience. She moves away from both the homogenized, racialized tropes for representing the subaltern *and* from unrepresentability that constitutes the subaltern condition in Spivak's terms. On the other hand, Menchú remains committed to representing this subaltern condition. This is the tension animating her text, with all its attendant risks.

Consequently, while Menchú performs this authorial, autobiographical, revolutionary "I," she also repeatedly insists on performing the position of authentic indigenous Other for the Western readerly subject. During the first half of the book, Menchú's personal story—the story of her childhood, her coming-of-age, her integration into the labor force, her family celebrations, her parent's political engagement, their persecution and assassination—sets the stage for detailed descriptions of the major life rituals of her Mayan K'iche' community: those commemorating birth, adolescence, marriage, planting and harvesting, death. Her "own" story stages the spectacle of her culture as "authentic." Menchú moves back and forth between the role of the autobiographical "I" and the role of "indigenous ethnographer," conveying much of her narrative in an anthropological voice of revelation about, or discovery of, the Other.[18] In part, we can attribute this dramatic shift in voice to the mediation of the interviewer/editor.

In her introduction to the book, Burgos-Debray explains that although she was a trained ethnographer, she knew nothing about the Maya-K'iche' culture: "At first I thought this lack of knowledge about Rigoberta's culture would be a disadvantage, but soon it turned into something quite positive. I had to adopt the position of a student. Rigoberta understood immediately; this is why her account of the ceremonies and rituals is so detailed" (Burgos, *Me llamo* 16). Indeed, Menchú's narrative seems to deliver on Burgos-Debray's promise of ethnographic enlightenment about the Maya-K'iche' for the Western readership.[19] As it turns out, though, Menchú's ethnographic enlightenment might not have been so spontaneously forthcoming after all. Although Burgos-Debray states in her introduction that she kept her questions to a minimum during her eight days of interviews with Menchú, asking only for clarification when necessary,[20] in an essay written six-teen years later, Burgos-Debray admits to prompting Menchú to talk about her culture: "Very quickly I realized that Rigoberta Menchú wanted to talk about herself, to go beyond just an account of repression. I therefore opted in favor of delving deeply into her customs, her vision of the world (as much political as religious), and, above all, her identity. Of course, taking the interviews in this direction had much to do with my preoccupations; Rigo-berta's desire to express her personal experiences and issues in my own life coincided" ("The Story of a Testimonio" 55–56). Whether or not Menchú's desire to discuss her culture coincided with Burgos's desire to know about it is impossible to determine; what we do know from the text is that the testimonial protagonist took the prompt, constructing herself for the reader as both native informant and participant-observer of the K'iche' culture. As she passes through the major stages and events of her life, she explains in detail the meaning of each ceremonial act, and the role of each member of the community in these acts.

This provides us with another explanation of why early testimonio critics made claims about the "authenticity" of all testimonios on the basis of Menchú's narrative: they were seduced by the ruse of authenticity in her text. The performance of authenticity in the text is a ruse, I would argue, that on the one hand forms the basis for her political struggle and on the other provides a political critique of her Western readership. This is another mo-ment of excessive interpellation registered in the text, another moment in which Menchú exceeds the bounds of her subjectification as subordinated indigenous subaltern. It is this movement in the text between the authorial, autobiographical "I" and the authentic Other, this oscillation between the reflexive "I" and an anthropological "we," that comes to substantiate her attenuated claim as political representative of her community in the na-tional and international arena.

Menchú performs her "authenticity" by playing on established inter-pellative tropes for the Other in Western discourses: transparency and opacity. Invariably, subsequent to moments of textual revelation about Mayan K'iche' custom, Menchú announces to the reader that there is much she has not told the reader and cannot tell the reader because of the secret and sacred nature of much of her culture (Burgos, *Me llamo* 55, 60, 118, 131, 133, 155, 212, 275, 299). Indeed, Menchú flamboyantly withholds informa-tion from the reader, as Doris Sommer suggests in her articles "Rigoberta's Secrets" (36) and "No Secrets" (142). "It may be useful to notice that the refusal [of knowledge] is performative; it constructs metaleptically the apparent cause of the refusal: our craving to know. Before she denies us the satisfaction of knowing her secrets, we may not be aware of any desire to grasp them" ("Rigoberta's Secrets" 34). On the one hand, these performative secrets create the "craving to know" in the reader, as Sommer suggests: these secrets interpellate the reader, eliciting the desire for ethnography, for discovery about the inscrutable Other. On the other hand, this performative withholding of information also makes what she *does* tell us into *something to be known.* Menchú creates a spectacle out of the cultural knowledge she conveys by framing it with what cannot be known. Her performative refusal to tell only serves to reinforce her position in the text as native informant, for she is endowed with authentic knowledge about the Other through it.

Her narrative, then, first invites the Western reader into readerly appropriation. She appears to say to the reader, "I will tell you so that you will understand." But then she dis-invites the reader from any such identification, insisting on definitive difference—"There are many things you cannot know." On a preliminary reading of the text, its repetitive interplay between revelation and secrecy renders the Other in its most recognizable Western tropes: the quaint transparency of premodern "folk" customs; the dark opacity of exotic conspiracy. In her readings of Menchú's performative secrets, however, Sommer has suggested that this calculated opacity has a double valence: "In fact, any way we read her, we are either intellectually or ethically unfit for Rigoberta's secrets" ("No Secrets" 143). The reader is incapable of knowing, both because of the gulf of cultural "foreignness" between the reader and the narrator and because of the dangers to Menchú and the K'iche' people if the reader should find out.

Sommer does not push her analysis far enough, though. The effect of this doubly valenced opacity is rendered rather benign in her reading: "The calculated result of Rigoberta's gesture for sympathetic readers, paradoxically, is to exclude us from her circle of intimates . . . it produces a particular kind of difference akin to respect. So simple a lesson and so fundamental: it mostly acknowledges that differences exist" ("No Secrets" 143). Sommer ultimately renders the "difference" of Menchú and the K'iche' assimilable through a respectful readerly practice that will simply "acknowledge that differences exist." As Moreiras suggests, "In Sommer's essay . . . silence, identical to itself, and therefore in itself its own end, *has here been made to speak,* and thus also tropologized as that which is beyond the 'impassable' limit" (Moreiras 212; italics mine). Sommer's reduction of silence in the text to a lesson in liberal readerly ethics brings it within the limits of Western ethnographic knowledge. Ultimately Sommer's reading makes it possible to accommodate Menchú's textual "difference" alongside other equally domesticated textual differences on an American studies syllabus, the goal of which is to produce respect.[21]

Menchú's secret is not simply a space that protects her K'iche' community's difference from the acquisitive desire of anthropological reading. In other words, hers is not merely a separatist representational claim. Instead of producing a "difference akin to respect," Menchú's textual interplay between revelation and secrecy creates a difference that is the space for registering a profound critique of colonialism and neocolonialism, of "the truly abject ones." At least according to the lofty goals Western anthropology set for itself at the discipline's inception, ethnography was supposed to operate, on one level, as a critique of Western subjectivity (Marcus and Fisher 20). Menchú's textual interplay between revelation and secrecy accepts the challenge. Having invited the anthropological reader into a relationship with the simultaneously transparent and opaque Other, Menchú instead turns the ethnographic "I" on the Western subject.

What is it that Menchú "lets us know" about K'iche' customs, after all? Very little indeed. What she most consistently reveals about her community's customs are the ways in which her customs provide a reiterative critique of colonization, neocolonial capitalist relations, modernization, consumerism, and revolutionary developmentalism. Menchú answers the interpellative hail of the interviewer to perform the subordinated subject position of abject Indian only to issue another hail from this position: the hail to the Western reader to recognize his or her own subjection to this neocolonial culture.

From early in her narrative, Menchú introduces the element of critique. After having described some of the rituals involved in pregnancy and the birth of a child, she tells the reader:

> What is left is the baptism and the integration of the child into the general community. . . . This is when a talk is given, by the elected male leader, by the elected female leader, by their children, about how they have preserved the customs of our ancestors. At the same time they make a new commitment for the child. That they must continue to teach the child when he is older and that the child must be an example, like the elected leaders. . . . They make a commitment. That the parents have to teach the child . . . this refers mostly to our ancestors—that [the child] must learn to keep all the secrets, that no one can finish off our culture, or our customs. *So, this is something like a critique of all of humanity, and of many of our own people who have lost our customs.* (33; italics mine)

Menchú begins this passage with a quintessential moment of interpellation into Western Christianity. Baptism represents not only the initiation of the child into a "general community" of the faithful but her or his subordination to Christian law. Menchú, as a lay catechist, identifies as Christian, as does her community, she tells us. It is not particularly surprising that K'iche' Maya have syncretically combined elements of an imposed colonial culture with their own to produce a "radically conditioned" form of indigenous agency. However, I would suggest that a misfire takes place within her K'iche' community at this primary interpellative moment, producing the conditions for the interpellation of a radical agency, as well.

An act that should mark K'iche' assimilation (or Ladinization, as Menchú refers to this process) into Western culture serves instead as the occasion for political analysis and critique of this assimilation. Menchú begins by positing baptism as the grounds for identification with Western Christians, her presumed readership. These readers expect a representation of quaint or folkloric baptismal rituals among the Maya that somehow mimic Western Christian rituals, since Menchú functions for this Western readership at this moment as ethnographer. However, we get neither a description of the actual ritual—the anointing of the child, the blessing of the godparents, the presentation of Christian amulets and gifts—nor a description of the subsequent baptismal feast. Instead we get a testimonial reiteration of the "talk" given by the elders of her community. First the elders speak, then the "children" reiterate what their elders have said. The elders, figurative parents of those gathered, perform an interpellative call to "custom," echoed by the community of "children" as a mark of their subordination. The content of this "custom" is neither folkloric rituals nor premodern beliefs, but instead "something like a critique of all humanity." Menchú describes only a partial rejection of traditional Western Christianity, however, for the baptismal ritual itself provides the occasion for the interpellative commemoration of ancestral customs that paradoxically consist of a "critique of all humanity." This will happen throughout her narrative. Once again, embedded within the call to normativity, to Western Christian subjectivity, is a call exceeding its bounds. Whenever Menchú describes a moment of ritual among the Maya that should in some way coincide with Western traditions, such as adolescent confirmation or marriage, it becomes instead a moment for the critique of the colonialist imposition of Western culture or patterns of consumption that perpetuate neocolonialism.

Although in the previous passage Menchú does not give us a substantive account of such criticism, she does a few pages later. As if she were moving down an Althusserian checklist of interpellative moments, Menchú proceeds from the primary scene of religious subordination to the primary scene of secular subordination, schooling. During what appears to be a simple description of education within her community, Menchú adroitly turns the gaze of the ethnographic "I" on the bourgeois liberal subject:

> From the first day it is thought that the child must be the community's [child], and that they cannot be only their parents' [child], and that the community must teach them. Immediately the parents are thinking about the schooling of the child . . . it is as with the bourgeois classes, as soon as the baby is born, they think that that child must be educated, must have a certain standard of living. So, we the indigenous people immediately think that the schooling of the child has to be the community, and that the child has to live the same as the rest [of the community]. And the child's hands are bandaged also precisely so that [the child] will not accumulate things that the rest of the community doesn't have and so that the child learns to distribute the few things s/he has, that his/her hands must be open. The mother is in charge of opening the child's hands. It's a mentality of suffering, of poverty. (36)

Menchú oddly inserts a comparison in her discussion of education in the K'iche' community with the remark "it is as with the bourgeois classes." Again, this provides the ground for an interpellative recognition, as the implied bourgeois reader's interest in educating children is the same as the indigenous community's. Menchú can posit the ground for identification because of the assumed prominence of the liberal social value of education. Menchú's narrative just as quickly withdraws this common ground, for her narrative links the bourgeois classes' interest in education to an interest in accumulation of wealth and in securing a class status, whereas the indigenous community links education to the redistribution of wealth among the community, ensuring economic equality among them all. The effect of Menchú's story is neither to naturalize nor to romanticize this communitarianism. The indigenous child is not born with a predilection to these communitarian values. In fact, the community must use coercion to enforce these values: the child's hands must be bound by the mother so that the child may learn to share and not to hoard things. The visible sign of this communitarianism, the bound hands, also serves to reiterate these values for the community who witnesses it each time a child is born. Always informing this action, Menchú implies, is a critique of the bourgeois society whose primary value is accumulation.

Menchú is also parrying the developmentalism in Payeras's narrative, and his representation of the indigenous people in his revolutionary quest. Payeras describes an early encounter between the indigenous peasantry and his guerrilla group in starkly developmentalist terms. He considers the indigenous peasantry as being locked in a prehistoric moment, in a culture that privileges lineage over class:

> For them, men were not differentiated by their relation to material goods, but rather by their language and customs. With this manner of thinking, the landowners ended up being a separate lineage of men—the ladinos. Never had they [the indigenous peasantry] seen a steam engine or dealt with poor ladinos; since there were regions where only indigenous people lived. . . . Since they knew only a small part of reality, they were lost in the particular and only with difficulty did they understand general concepts. Given this, the war appeared to them as a phenomenon so inexplicable and inconvenient as the typhoid epidemics that had razed the highland villages in the past. (75)

In a rehashing of Talcott Parsons's pattern variables between developed and underdeveloped societies, Payeras characterizes the indigenous peasants as particularistic (language, customs) and ascriptive (lineage) in comparison with the Ladino's universalism (class) and achievement (steam engines) (Long 15–40). In Payeras's representation, the indigenous peasants he encounters understand people only according to their ethnic affiliation. This representation implies these indigenous peoples are consequently incapable of class analysis, of understanding their own class exploitation, of correctly locating the enemy. This lack of economic analysis, this premodern consciousness, he concludes, is the reason for the indigenous people's resistance to the guerrillas.[22]

Although Menchú frequently refers to the importance of ancestral customs to her community, she does not represent communitarianism as a simple continuation of a "prehistoric," pre-Columbian Mayan social formation, or as the refusal to make the ethical "choice" to embrace progress, as Payeras suggests. Rather, in her discussion of education, Menchú describes this communitarianism as a "mentality of suffering, of poverty." Thus redistribution of wealth functions as a strategy for ensuring the survival of the community as a whole in the face of severe poverty and economic exploitation. Once again, interpellation misfires, producing communitarianism in the excess of subordination to capitalist relations of production. Of course, such communitarianism cannot be read strictly in opposition to capitalism, for their communitarianism supplements capital, facilitating the hyper-exploitation of the indigenous subaltern peasantry.[23] Nevertheless this communitarianism produces the space for a collective agency that struggles against the individuated alienation of wage labor. It also produces the space for a critique of accumulation that cannot be equated with an all-out rejection of the bourgeois model of economics based on a "premodern" set of attitudes, for it is at least as much a *contemporary* response to a set of economic relations as it is a cultural tradition.

The effect of Menchú's seemingly anthropological rendering of education in her community is, if not strictly, then in part an analysis of class relations. Although the bourgeoisie and the indigenous people appear to have nothing in common, we cannot assume that the reference to both in this context is insignificant. Instead, the mention of the bourgeois classes serves to implicate them in the lives of the indigenous people, thereby reflecting her understanding of contemporary class relations. The bourgeoisie as a capitalist class and the indigenous people as a class of economically exploited workers are not unrelated formations. The progress of the bourgeois classes, their tendency to maintain their class position—a certain standard of living—is contingent on the continued exploitation of the indigenous peoples. While revealing the Other through ethnographic revelation, Menchú has also revealed the interrelation of the bourgeois subject—the presumed reader—with the indigenous subject laboring in some faraway place. Indeed, I suggest that in this passage Menchú issues an interpellative hail to the reader so that the reader may recognize her or his imbrication in the disembedded social relations of transnational capital.

Contrary to Payeras's representation of the indigenous subaltern's conciencia, Menchú's narrative often recognizes the barriers constructed by colonization between the indigenous people and poor Ladinos. Nevertheless, as the passages about baptism and education in her community demonstrate, when these indigenous people appear most "ethnic" in their moments of practicing their culture, they are often performing the kind of political and economic analysis of which Payeras finds them incapable. In the foregoing passages, as well as in subsequent descriptions of other interpellative rituals, Menchú represents indigenous people linking their ethnic exploitation with their economic exploitation. Thus, rather than casting indigenous people as living a life separate and apart from the modern economic system, she casts them as subject to a dual exploitation within this system. Their collectivism, their understanding of themselves as a "separate lineage of men," as Payeras would describe it, is again cast as a response to their integration into a capitalist mode of production, not as an ignorance of it. As we shall see, rather than being oblivious to the wonders of modernity —such as the steam engine—Menchú's community engages in a limited participation and critique of it.

A Limited Participation

By "limited participation" I do not mean to imply that their participation in a modern capitalist economy is a matter of choice. As Menchú suggests, as a land-poor peasantry dependent on hiring out their labor for most of the year, they are fully integrated into modern relations of capitalist production. Nevertheless, operating in Butler's model of a radically conditioned agency, Menchú represents her community as exerting considerable control over their participation in a capitalist economy. In her representation of this selective participation in, and rejection of, modernization, however, Menchú also articulates a political vision for the future participation in revolutionary transformation by indigenous people. Inevitably, this articulation of a limited participation in modernity as a mode of revolutionary subjection runs the risk of slipping into an uncritical and separatist ethno-nationalism. I would argue this *is not* Menchú's political vision for revolutionary Guatemala; nevertheless her representation of indigenous subjection does leave itself open to such an interpretation.

Menchú begins her description of the marriage ceremony in her K'iche' community by telling the reader that there are four parts to it. Once the woman has accepted the man as her groom, his family comes to officially ask for her hand in marriage, and the two families host a party at the bride-to-be's home. This party is the second marriage ceremony. Once everyone has arrived at this party, the couple kneels and speaks to the community:

> They [the couple] renew a commitment about their indigenous self. They say that we are important. That we all have the duty of multiplying the earth, but at the same time we have the duty of multiplying the customs of our ancestors who were humble. And they make like a little review of the time since Columbus, where they say, "Our parents were violated by the whites, the sinners, the assassins." And that our ancestors were not at fault. Our ancestors died of hunger because they were not paid [for their labor]. We want to kill and be done with the bad examples they [the whites] came to teach us and if this had not come to pass, we would be together, we would all be equal, and our children

would not suffer nor would we only have a bit of land. And this is what they record and it's something of a consciousness raising. Then they make their commitment and they say "We will be mothers and fathers, and we will try to defend the rights of our ancestors until the end and we promise that our ancestors will continue to live with our children and that neither a rich man or a *finquero* can finish off our children." (92)

Importantly, a ceremony that purports to be about the joining of two people has little to do with the actual or generic couple involved. Instead this quintessential moment of heterosexual interpellation provides yet another occasion for an analysis of their own subjection, this time through an analysis of the community's history. Once again, Menchú's process of representation begins with the promise of ethnographic revelation—"They renew a commitment about their *indigenous self*." "The indigenous self," however, is not represented as an internal or independent experience. Rather, indigenous selfhood exists in dialectical relation to a colonial past.

As in Western cultural practice, the marriage moment of heterosexual interpellation carries within it the subordination of sexuality to the purposes of procreation: "we all have a duty of multiplying the earth." Yet again, critical conscience/conscious emerges in the excess of normative subjection, as the couple calls the community to the collective evaluation of their history. Gender relations are also reconfigured in the space created by interpellative misfire, for rather than establishing the bride's subordination to her groom, the bride stands before the community equally empowered to summon forth this critical conciencia. "Multiplying the customs of our ancestors" is linked to "review of the time since Columbus" performed by *both* the bride and the groom. Importantly, it is a review not only of what happened "then," in the initial colonial encounter, but of what happens "now," in the lack of equality between whites and indigenous peoples, in the lack of unity among indigenous people, and in the unjust land tenure system. This suggests that the customs the couple is called on to multiply only acquire meaning in relation to the colonial past and the neocolonial present. Thus colonialism is critiqued on its own terms: the white invaders were "sinners," and the "ways" they brought with them fail to propagate equality, fraternity, or plenty—the promise of liberal democracy. In turn, indigenous people lay an originary claim to such "Western" values—equality, morality, fraternity, plenty—as the ways of their ancestors before the coming of the whites. Menchú represents indigenous women as existing in a condition of gender parity within her community through her description of the marriage ceremony. She also performs the gender parity embodied in critical conciencia as represented in this passage when she reiterates it through the testimonial act. Here is a moment in which Menchú's own description runs the risk of slipping into a celebratory nativism. If we can read her text to be claiming that the Mayas had Western values before the West, then the text runs the risk of effacing subaltern difference precisely by collapsing the distance between Western and indigenous subjection.

Once the couple has finished with its commitment to maintaining the ways of their ancestors, all the elders speak precisely to these ways of their ancestors before the coming of the colonizers:

> It's a whole day in which everyone sits down to talk. They say . . . That our ancestors planted plenty of corn. That no tribe was lacking in corn, not one community and that we were all one [then]. And they start to talk, that we had a king and that the king knew how to distribute all the things that existed among all the people that existed. The cacao is no longer ours—it's the whites, it's the rich peoples. The tobacco. We cannot plant tobacco. Before there was plenty of tobacco for the entire people. Before we were not divided by communities or language. We all understood each other. And who is responsible? The whites are, the ones who came here. . . . Before there were no medicines, no pills. Our medicine was the plants. Our king knew how to cultivate many plants. Before, not even the animals bit us and now they even do that. After, the last part of the ceremony is little sad because, with great feeling, our grandparents remember all this and begin to say how it will be later. They are very worried. Today our sons and daughter cannot live many years. How shall it be later. Today many drive cars. Before our Guatemala was not like this. Everybody traveled by foot, but everyone lived very well. (94–95)

The elders engage in a utopic reconstruction of pre-Columbian society among the Maya. They describe a time when there was plenty of corn, their sacred crop, for everyone. It was an era of a just law, represented by a just king. There was unity among the Mayan tribes, now divided in language and in custom. It was a time before the creation of needs that their system of knowledge could not address. Indeed, it was an era of perfect harmony— even the animals did not bite. This is not a futile nostalgia, although it could easily be read as such. We must remember that the context of this interpellative "talk" is the marriage ceremony; it is delivered in the midst of a particular ceremony with a particular purpose. The elders end explicitly by expressing their concern about how things will be—the "will be" represented in this context by the promise of the couple reproducing the tribe physically and culturally. Whether or not the elders deliver an accurate description of how things were, they express a possibility about how things could be again for their community to the couple who will reproduce this community. Not exactly idle nostalgia or idealized history, for the elders express a political vision directed toward the future of the marriage couple *and* to all the younger members of the community. Like any political vision, this representation of the community's possible futurity contains a critique not only of the external (the white society they live in dialectical relation to) but of the internal, as well (the indigenous community).

Menchú ends this description of what the elders say with a reference to cars, the consummate sign of twentieth-century modernity (in contrast to nineteenth-century modernity, represented by the steam engine): "Today many drive cars. Before . . . Everybody traveled by foot, but everyone lived very well." It would be naive to read this simply as a rejection of technology, in favor of some "return" to an idealized preindustrial state. The problem represented by the cars is not modernization per se but the relations of power that this modernization entails. Before all lived equally well; today only some live well. Thus Guatemala has turned into a country of owners and laboring poor. Importantly, Menchú leaves the referent of "many" driving cars in Guatemala ambiguous. While the reader might assume she means Guatemala's white people, the "many" in this passage also refers back to the indigenous "sons and daughters" of the previous sentence. Thus the car is a metaphor for the class differentiation that is occurring among the indigenous peoples as well as the class differentiation that exists between the whites and Indians in Guatemala.[24] Similarly, in the earlier passage in which the couple speak, the lack of equality they mention refers both to the conditions of inequality between whites and indigenous people and to the conditions of inequality existing within this indigenous community. Thus this interpretation of the lack of equality among the Maya checks the celebratory nativism that echoes in some of her other descriptions, as well as suggesting that ethnic separatism does not resolve problems of inequality and capitalist exploitation.

Menchú's representation of conflict internal to Guatemala's indigenous people further problematizes the "collective we" that the first-stage critics have posited as the true voice behind Menchú's autobiographical "I." Also, this guarded response to modernization could be read by someone like

Payeras as stemming from a folkloric impulse. Instead I would argue that it represents an understanding of the class differentiation and conflicting power relations existing within her indigenous community. Menchú represents this kind of class analysis as intrinsic to ethnic consciousness. Thus the appeal to resist class differentiation among the indigenous people is made on ethnic grounds, by means of the elders' interpellative invocation of an ancestral order.

There are several other examples of this economic differentiation and political division among the indigenous people in Menchú's narrative, many of these involving the *caporales*—the overseers—on the fincas. Menchú tells us that the caporales are almost always indigenous peoples who generally come from the same community as the hired laborers (43). To the indigenous people who travel to the fincas, these caporales are Ladinized indigenous people, men who share the racist attitudes of the landowners they work for (46). The caporales travel from the fincas to their home towns to recruit and transport workers. On the fincas, each caporal is in charge of translating orders for the people from his community and overseeing their work. These caporales play a crucial role in maintaining the system of dual exploitation under which indigenous people work. To maintain the miserable conditions of labor, the plantation system in Guatemala depends on the workers' inability to speak or read Spanish, to know or defend their rights, which are codified in Spanish. Thus the very act of bilingualism on the part of the caporales represents Ladinization, their complicity in a system of exploitation, not because anyone who knows Spanish automatically loses his or her indigenous identity, but because these caporales use their knowledge of Spanish to oppress their fellow indigenous people rather than assist them. Thus the very speech acts performed by the caporales serve an interpellative function. Furthermore, should speech acts fail to subordinate, the caporales are responsible for disciplining the workers if they in any way assert their rights or fail to work. Thus, when Menchú's little brother dies on the finca, the caporal fires the members of the family for missing two days' work and keeps their back wages as payment for burying the boy.

Similarly, many of the soldiers in Guatemala are of indigenous extraction. The terror that these men perpetrate on their own communities has a calculated and interpellative effect beyond the particular victims of terror. For example, when a woman on a finca refuses the advances of the finquero's son, one of the finquero's soldiers hacks the woman to pieces with a machete. Even though the woman was much loved by her community, none of the neighbors come to her aid, although they hear her screams, and afterward none will bury her for fear of repercussions. The fragmentation of the woman's body metonymically stands in for the fragmentation of the indigenous communities that often results as the consequence of the interpellative terror perpetrated by these indigenous middlemen.

Importantly, for Menchú and her community, Ladinos are not only those who are born of mixed heritage, of indigenous and white parentage. Any indigenous person, Menchú repeatedly tells the reader, can become Ladinized to various degrees by abandoning the traditional ways of the ancestors. Given that Menchú most often represents the traditional customs of her ancestors as interpellative "talk" meant to sustain a tradition of critical conciencia, indigenous identity does not conform to classical Western notions of essential identity, either biological or metaphysical. Rather, indigenous identity is a reiterative performance of this conciencia occurring in the excess of normative interpellation. Indigenous identity is sustained and confirmed through repetitive critical practices of everyday life taking place in the misfire of normative interpellation. Thus, while Ladinization marks the success of normative interpellation, it also marks the failure of an indigenous subject to hear the echo of other interpellations in the excess of the hail to assimilation.

While every K'iche' ceremony commemorating everyday life that Menchú describes performs this echo, these alternate interpellations, in the third marriage ceremony, the performance of indigenous identity foregrounds its own constructedness. The staging of this constructedness also stages an ideal resistive subjectivity for this indigenous community, an ideal subjectivity that the members of the community do not necessarily live every day, but rather one that constitutes and maintains the basis for this community's political vision of a transformative future. The third marriage ceremony, I would argue, stages the possibility for a condition of radical agency to emerge from the excesses and misfires of normative interpellation.

The second marriage ceremony commemorates the traditions of their ancestors. Hence everything at this party must be made in the traditional way, by the peasants themselves. Nothing brought to the party can be store-bought, or even made in anything store-bought. At the third ceremony, however, the couple pledges its union, and consequently this ceremony celebrates the *mezcla*, or mixture, that the union represents. This union also provides the community with the opportunity to comment on the mezcla that they inevitably participate in themselves. Thus, while some traditional items are brought to this ceremony, like tortillas and tamales, the guests primarily bring store-bought goods:

And afterward, they show all the modern things. They bring sodas, an eighth of rum that's store-bought, a little bit of bread, eggs, chocolate, coffee. . . . Once again [the elders] present themselves, like the time before, and they begin to give their opinion on everything. For example, if it's "Coca-Cola," our grandparents say, sons and daughters, never teach our children to drink this junk because it is something that tries to end our customs. These are things made by machines and our ancestors never used machines. These *fincas* are what cause us to die young. It's the food of white people and the whites feel rich with these things. Don't let the children drink this junk. This is the content of the ceremony. Then the bread, they say is mixed with egg, flour and egg. So, before our ancestors cultivated wheat. Then the Spanish came and mixed it with egg. It's mixed, it's no longer what our ancestors had. This is white people's food, because the whites are like the bread, they are mixed. . . .

. . . They also talk about the cars, about the bathrooms of the ladinos, about the rich people. It's something like an analysis of the whole situation. They say, for example, even the rich people's bathrooms shine like a new suit, and we, the poor, don't even have a little hole in the ground to go in. And our dishes are not like theirs. And they also say that we do not desire what they have. We have our hands to make our dishes with and we shall not lose them. Even if there are modern things, and even if we have money, we must never buy any of the trash that they have. For example, in our town we do not have a mill [for maize]. This is not for lack of possibility, for their are many *terratenientes* who would have wanted to install a grinder to grind the maize for all the town. But we say no. Little by little they enter with their machines and then they are owners of everything. (97–98)

Once again, this passage captures a moment of political analysis that demonstrates the community's profound understanding of their own integration into capitalist production. Thus Coca-Cola, the fetishized sign of "modern" food and consumption practices, is criticized not only because it is made by machines their ancestors did not use but because it is linked to the fincas. The Coca-Cola, the coffee, the chocolate, the bread, are all processed in factories from the products that are grown on the fincas that hire the members of Menchú's community as laborers. Thus, by buying these products, they are participating in their own exploitation. Also, even if they have money, they must not buy the things that would presumably make their lives "easier." If they do buy these things or allow machines to enter their town, they will progressively lose the skills to live without them—such as the skill to make their own dishes or to grind their own corn—and become more dependent on the system of production and consumption that exploits them. Once again, their poverty, the sign of their exploitation, is linked to the wealth of the rich. The bathrooms of the Guatemalan rich shine while Menchú's people do not even have outhouses. And once again, the bourgeois reader is implicated, as "Coca Cola" and chocolate, so readily available in the First World, are historically derived from the coca and cocoa produced under exploitative and terroristic conditions on fincas all over the Third World. The reader is implicated in the disembedded capitalist social relations crisscrossing the globe, linking the consumption practices of the "modern" reader to the exploitative labor practices subordinating the "pre-modern" indigenous laborer from Guatemala to Peru.

However, something more than this political analysis takes place in the third ceremony. As I suggested earlier, this ceremony hails those commu-nity members present to an ideal resistive indigenous subjectivity, a subjec-tivity that is critical about one's implication in a capitalist chain of produc-tion. This subjectivity will not participate in its own exploitation and will live according to limited needs to ensure the well-being of the entire indigenous community. But the third ceremony stages an *ideal* subjectivity precisely because Menchú's indigenous community does not and cannot live this subjectivity in everyday life. Menchú tells us, for example, that many of the members of her ethnic tribe regularly buy rum for themselves and candy for their children from the finca stores at exploitative prices on credit. She also tells us, however, that she learned to ride the buses to Guatemala City and to speak Spanish in order to better defend the rights of her community. And in this third ceremony, the community purchases and partakes of store-bought goods. Paradoxically, the community participates in modernity through its quintessential sign, consumption, in order to critique it. This paradoxical positionality demonstrates that the ideal indigenous subjectivity posited by the community is neither naive nor absolute. The paradoxical positionality suggested in this third marriage ceremony forms the basis for Menchú's articulation of revolutionary subjectivity.

Menchú occupies Western discourse to defend against its encroachment on her community. To individuate the Other for the Western reader, she assumes the autobiographical "I" and tells us "her" story; and yet, having invited the reader to hear her personal story, she instead tells a more general story about her endangered community. This is not a return to the "I" as the collective "we." Rather, the "I" is a tactical production, a performance irreducible to the "I" that is Rigoberta Menchú beyond the text. Similarly, the "we" in her texts is a tactical production, irreducible to the "we" she at once seeks to represent and refuses to represent. She produces both the "I" and the "we" in her narrative only partially, maintaining the "Other" in the gap between the tactical representation and the lived—just as in the third marriage ceremony her community maintains an ideal resistive subjectivity that is different from the subjectivities they are forced to live. For now, she seeks to preserve the space for the Other *as* Other. There is no other position for the Other in Western discourse, after all; she does not try to get out of this double bind. Instead she gives the reader a representation of the Other that does not exhaust its otherness, that has limits, and these limits ultimately suit her political ends.

What are those political ends? What does she repeatedly tell us, in her anthropological voice of revelation, about this Other we want to know and cannot know? That the Other does not want to know us, her bourgeois Western readership. But even this desire, paradoxically, cannot be fulfilled. She needs the Western reader to know her, in some limited way, to assist her goal of maintaining a space apart from the Western discourse of development in which she already participates. She uses her radically conditioned form of agency in an attempt to preserve the space from which a condition of radical agency might emerge. Again this interpellation into radical agency would occur not outside of hegemonic normativity but in the excesses and misfires of normative interpellation. Thus she learns Spanish to travel around the world and tell "her story," to denounce the genocidal conditions in her country: conditions that are maintained, after all, through the action and inaction of abject actors beyond the borders of Guatemala.[25] Our abjection lies precisely in our failure to recognize our participation in a chain of production and consumption that consumes her community, in the success of our normative interpellation and in our failure to interpret the echoes of alternate interpellations present in the excesses and misfires of normativity. Thus Menchú's story celebrates neither ethno-nationalism nor separatism. Rather, it hails the reader to identify the circuits of exploitation that bind her in social relation with the indigenous subaltern.

Menchú's articulation of revolutionary transformation is not epochal or revelatory. Her story is not a quest for a pure category of revolutionary consciousness. Menchú's vision of revolutionary subjection is not a naive return to a pure category of ethnicity free of contamination. Nor is it a romantic plunge forward into a pure category of a proletariat fully aware of the wonders of a modernization within its control, as Payeras would have it, for such a plunge "forward" would inevitably entail the disappearance of her ethnic specificity. Instead revolutionary conciencia carefully and selectively begins from the present conditions of everyday life. This is where the authority for revolutionary change must come. In her self-representation, Menchú strategically vacillates between the position of autonomous liberal subject and the Other of Western discourse to critique development and modernization from a gendered, classed, and ethnic position, and to critique teleologies of consciousness put forth by her male counterparts that are predicated on an interpellative "transcendence" of her present subject position, that of a K'iche' woman peasant. It is also through this vacillation that Menchú achieves political viability—it is her authorial claim to representation that catapults her into the international arena as the representative of the Mayan people, while her simultaneous refusal to represent the Other maintains critical distance between her authorial "I" and a tentative, tactical "we" whom she seeks to represent in this arena. However, even my use of the word "tactical" harkens back to the tactical maneuvers of her male counterparts and bears the trace of the revolutionary "I" critiqued in chapter 3. Her tactical assertion of the authorial "I" in an attempt to represent the difference of the subaltern "we" necessarily erases difference in the web of autobiographical desire and interest. That is the necessary risk. I interrogate the revolutionary subjection not to dislodge the authorial "I" but to alter the tactics of its deployment, that is, to theorize the "I" with the ethical recognition that it will not—indeed, cannot fully—represent subaltern particularity. Menchú's tactical deployment must necessarily leave itself open not only to the revolutionary Left who accuse her of ethno-separatism, the Pan-Mayan separatist movement in Guatemala who accuse her of failing to articulate a "Mayan" vision, but also to the future subalterns who will challenge her tactics of representation in the hopes of a more inclusive revolutionary imagination.

Thus I return to the many possible interpretations of the title of her autobiography: *Me llamo Rigoberta Menchú y así me nació la conciencia,* "I am named/called Rigoberta Menchú and that/this is how my conscience/consciousness was born to me." The logic of this sentence branches out in many directions. She is named or called—hailed in the act of naming by external agencies—Rigoberta Menchú. Indeed, "Rigoberta" is a Spanish saint's name, given to her by a municipal clerk who refused to recognize her given name, M'in, when her father registered her birth.[26] As such, the name *Rigoberta* reiteratively performs a call to colonized subjectivity. Meanwhile,

Menchú, a K'iche' name, calls her as an indigenous subject who resists colonial subordination. There is a constitutive ambiguity, though, in the possible meanings of the Spanish term *así*, for this term points both backward and forward in time. As *"that* is how my conscience/consciousness was born to me," *así* freezes her interpellation in a past act of hailing. In other words, read as pointing backward in time, *así* would indicate that her interpellation is exhausted in the act of naming her "Rigoberta Menchú," a resistive, but ultimately subordinated, colonized subject. However, *así* also points forward in time, to an interpellation still in process. Read as *"this* is how my consciousness was born to me," *así* suggests that although she has been hailed as a colonized subject, she has yet to tell us how she transformed that subjectivity. More accurately, she has yet to tell us how the transformation of her colonized subjectivity emerged from interpreting and representing the very conditions that she lived as a colonized subject: "my consciousness was born *to* me."

Menchú, in her limited representation of herself and her community, can be said to occupy what Frantz Fanon has called "the zone of occult instability where the people dwell":

> Yes, the first duty of the poet is to see clearly the people he has chosen as the subject of his work of art. He cannot go forward resolutely unless he first realizes *the extent of his estrangement from them.* We have taken everything from the other side; and the other side gives us nothing unless by a thousand detours we swing finally round in their direction, unless by a thousand tricks they manage to draw us toward them, to seduce us, and to imprison us. Taking means in nearly every case being taken: *thus it is not enough to try to free oneself by repeating proclamations and denials. It is not to try to get back to the people in that past out of which they have already emerged; rather we must join them in that fluctuating movement which they are just giving shape to, and which as soon as it has started, will be the signal for everything else to be called in question. Let there be no mistake about it; it is to this zone of occult instability where the people dwell that we must come; and it is there that our souls are crystallized and that our perceptions and our lives are transfused with light.* (227)

In this passage from his essay "On National Culture," Fanon articulates the inherent difficulty in representing a national identity from the position of a subject of colonial rule. The poets, as members of the intelligentsia, are interpellated as subjects by a system of colonial education, of colonial governmentality. These poets have "taken everything from the other side" and have inevitably also "been taken," subordinated by their own subjection. There is no escaping a colonialism that marks the colonized subject in his or her attempts at representing a national identity. Similarly, for Menchú there is no escaping the colonialism that marks her, or the process of modernization in which she already participates, as colonial subject. Hence she is called forth—Rigoberta/Menchú. Hence her community cannot escape the modernization process they participate in, even as they articulate a political futurity. Although Fanon and Menchú have considerable political and cultural differences, they both call attention to a "zone of occult instability" in which people dwell: a site of complex compliance with, and resistance to, colonial authority. This zone, for Menchú as for Fanon, exceeds the possibilities of interpellative representation. Menchú neither looks backward to a state of innocence nor looks forward to a moment of revolutionary redemption. Located in the politics of the present, the zone of occult instability resists transcendent, stable definition and acquires its urgency and contours of representation in the concrete materiality of everyday struggle. It is in such a zone that revolutionary consciousness emerges, between polar abstractions of "I" and "we," between what Spivak has called "elite knowing" and "subaltern being" (*In Other Worlds* 253; see also 268). It is from such a radically conditioned agency that the possibility of radical agency emerges.

6

The Politics of Silence: Development

and Difference in Zapatismo

Hasta que guarden silencio no podemos empesar.
—Comandante David, Oventic, 27 July 1996

Politics is possible because the constitutive impossibility of society can only represent itself
through the production of empty signifiers.
—Ernesto Laclau, *Emancipation(s)*

On the evening of 27 July 1996, five thousand visitors from forty-three
countries gathered under a starry sky in Oventic, Chiapas, invited there by
the Zapatista Army for National Liberation to celebrate the "International
Meeting for Humanity and against Neoliberalism." After traveling half a
day by bus to get there, we gathered in the center of an arena built for the
event. Spirits were high as members of the Italian delegation sang antifas-
cist songs, enclaves of Argentines and Chileans played guitar, and there
were shout-outs and "vivas" all around. By the time Comandante David took
the stage and asked for silence, the crowd's cheers for the EZLN and the
event seemed irrepressible. Although we quieted down considerably to listen, a low but constant buzz of conversation continued among us. This
certainly seemed like silence to us, but Comandante David did not agree. He
asked again for us to be quiet, repeatedly saying, "Hasta que guarden silencio, no podemos empesar" [We cannot begin until you keep silent] and "Hay
que guardar diez minutos de silencio antes de poder empezar" [We have to
be quiet for ten minutes before we can start]. Europeans, Latin Americans,
and U.S. citizens all around grumbled that this seemed unnecessary—even
a bit authoritarian. Eventually, after about fifteen minutes, when we realized
we had no choice, that he was serious, that there might be a point to this, it
happened. We were silent. Completely silent. Not one sigh, not one whisper,
not one chair scraping against the ground.

At first, I could hear—in the silence—people straining not to speak, repressing the urge to hear our own voices. Just when the strain of my interior speech seemed deafening, silence distracted me. Sounds emerged in the darkness of silence: the sound of my own breathing, of a distant humming of electricity, of the hooting of owls around us and the flight of bats above our heads, of the rustling of the wind as it stroked its way through the crowd, of a neighbor shivering—even the stars' shining possessed a quality akin to sound. After a few minutes of this sensual alertness, I noticed color entering the periphery of my vision: The Zapatistas were filing into the bleachers surrounding the central plaza where we, the visitors, were sitting. The bleachers, shrouded in darkness, were almost completely full when I noticed them filing in—men and women wearing embroidered *huipiles* and ponchos, covering their faces with bandannas and masks. I was stunned, because even though we were sitting there being so quiet—perhaps because of the "quiet"—the Zapatistas had been on the move and quieter still. I had not heard hundreds of Zapatistas filling up the seats all around us. It seemed to me that none of us had heard the EZLN as its members surrounded us. While we were distracted by silence, the Zapatistas had added their silence—a silence now reverberating with movement—to our own.

The performative act of silence imposed on our group that evening functioned as a political metaphor: if it was this difficult for me, for us as a group of some five thousand people, to keep silent for ten minutes, what had it been like for the members and supporters of the Zapatistas to keep silent for ten years—one minute for every year? On another level, however, the very content of the silence we experienced that evening is a political metaphor for the fullness *and differentiation* of our own community; more precisely, silence is the condition of possibility for this differentiation and fullness. For it was in human silence that we were able to recognize the musicality of noise, the seemingly infinite possibility of differentiated sound, extending community beyond the territory marked as human. How, then, to read the fullness of this performative silence? "Now," Comandante David spoke, "We can begin." And yet, in retrospect, the silence was the beginning of the political act that followed.

Recent scholarship on subaltern historiography has illuminated the complexity of possible meanings encoded in subaltern silence (Guha, *Dominance without Hegemony*; Guha, "On Some Aspects"; Pandey; Scott, "Everyday Forms of Resistance"). Some theoreticians of subaltern subjectivity, such as Gayatri Chakravorty Spivak, have also addressed the absolute limits of Western knowledge when confronted with subaltern silence and iteration (Spivak, "Can the Subaltern Speak?"). Indeed, as I have argued in chapter 5,

Rigoberta Menchú's performative silence foregrounds precisely those limits to Western knowledge. Menchú repeatedly insists on calling the Western reader's attention to the secrets she withholds in *Me llamó Rigoberta Menchú y así me nació la conciencia*. She does this, I have argued, as part of a political project in which she seeks a strictly limited engagement with a Western audience about her experience as a Guatemalan Indian. Just on the other side of the border of the highlands and the Petén jungle, the scene of Menchú's story, a very different sort of engagement with silence is taking place in the Lacandón jungle between the indigenous people participating in the EZLN and the Western subject. Occurring more than a decade after the publication of Menchú's autobiography, the EZLN's performative silence at the International Meeting in Oventic was a study in contrast. Whereas Menchú's secrets are a stark and purposeful point of dis-identification for the Western reader, the silence invoked by the Zapatistas at Oventic staged multiple identifications for the visiting (mostly Western) outsiders: with the indigenous Zapatistas, with the symbolized Mexican nation, with ourselves and each other, with a vibrant natural world. To begin with, the Zapatistas invited us—required us—to join them in their silence. We were asked to reenact the silence under which the Zapatistas had organized for ten years. We were asked to experience the difficulty of attaining and maintaining silence for even a representative ten minutes. Metonymically, our ten minutes together stood in for the ten years of "silent" Zapatista organizing; however, they also represented another kind of silence, the five hundred years of silence imposed on indigenous peoples of the Americas by subalternizing discourses of the colonial and postcolonial periods. Silence is the mark of alterity, of Indian difference, in subalternizing discourses of conquest, but also the mask for alterity, for in "silence" the Zapatistas experience community and organize resistance. It is important that the silence that evening was not exactly voluntary, as we were mimicking the structural silence imposed on indigenous subalternity in the Americas. Nevertheless, through this performative silence, the EZLN demonstrated to us just how much can be accomplished under its cover.

The Zapatistas, catching us unaware as they encircled us, were also restaging their ten years of organizing in the midst, but outside the awareness, of the rest of Mexico. So then, as visitors, we also symbolized a Mexican nation caught by surprise. We were standing in for those mestizo or Ladinized Mexicans who, prior to 1 January 1994, were oblivious to the plight (and fight) of their indigenous compatriots. And yet, as such, we had also shared in the Zapatistas' silence. The Mexican nation, as represented here through us, shared with the Zapatista Indians ten years of silent suffering under structural adjustment policies and neoliberal mandates. Operating through the visitors' metonymic silence, the Zapatistas were also identifying themselves with the rest of the Mexican nation.

There was yet another identification being staged here, our identification as visitors with each other and with ourselves. For we, the many of us Western and Westernized subjects present, in the habit of thinking about ourselves as freely constituted and purposeful individuals, had also been subjected by neoliberalism. In the "First World," we too had experienced a less violent, but by no means less virulent, structural adjustment in the 1980s and 1990s, disguised by such regionalisms as Reaganism or Thatcherism. And certainly, as leftists and progressives of various stripes and positions, from various "developed" countries, all our criticisms had been equally muted by the triumph of post–Cold War neoliberalism—more effectively, in fact, than criticism in Mexico. This simple reenactment, then, provided the grounds for these multiple identifications—constitutively fleeting and inconclusive—identifications that are central to the Zapatistas' project of wresting national and international terms of political representation for themselves.

The Zapatistas staged these multiple identifications for us by having all of us perform their silence. We had to pass through their silence—to be as silent as an Indian—even to come into identification with our own subjection. But silence, as the quintessential marker of Indian identity in the subalternizing discourses of both North and South America, had been ruptured. The Indian silence enacted here was not the silence of the Indian in modernizing discourses—the silence of an absence, a lack, an incompletion. Neither was it the silence of the Indian in revolutionary developmentalism— the silence of incipient rebels, in waiting for leadership. Nor was it the silence of the Indian in Christian martyrdom—the silence of forbearance in expectation of eternal deliverance. It was a silence filled with noise, with planning, communication, movement, tactics, coercion, frustration, ties, networks, suffering, satisfaction—a silence so filled with activity that it ruptures from within, a truly deafening quiet. In Spivak's terms, from her now-famous introduction to *Selected Subaltern Studies,* the Zapatistas broke apart the semiotic chain from within the terms of the discourse (after all, can you ever really trust a silent Indian?) in an attempt to resignify (to stretch as much as possible) the sign of being an Indian in Latin America before the chain can reconstitute itself into a (slightly) new hegemony.

So now let us return to my earlier, possibly troubling, statement about identifying with our own subjection by passing through identification with the Indian, by being "as silent as an Indian." I want to distinguish this process of identification from the process of identification involved in nation building, where Creole elites—such as those in New Spain—appropriated the identity markers of Indian rebellion to justify Latin American independence movements, and to formulate national cultures different from the culture of empire.[1] I would also like to distinguish it from the various contemporary nostalgic processes of identification in which markers of Indian purity are appropriated by individuals and movements in search of more "natural" states of being. Although inevitably contaminated by both of these kinds of identifications, the identification initiated by the Zapatistas was also different from them. This identification between the visiting outsiders and the indigenous subalterns was not a naive erasure of the difference of these positionalities. When the Zapatistas joined the visitors in this performative silence, they did not take their place among the visitors in the central part of the arena. Or, for that matter, in front of the visitors, on the stage. Instead they encircled us; they filled the bleachers at the margin of the arena. As such, they chose to represent the imbalance in political, economic, and cultural power that sustains the centrality of the Western nonindigenous subject vis-à-vis the indigenous subject. Indeed, as visitors, we participated in this representation, reinforcing our own centrality, since it obviously had not occurred to any of us to sit in the bleachers and leave the middle space for the Zapatistas who might be joining us. On the other hand, the Zapatista call to identify with them, to be "as silent as an Indian," foregrounded the centrality of the "Indian" in our own subject formation. While apparently dramatizing Indian silence, we were, in effect, dramatizing our own silence before neoliberalism. We recognized ourselves as silent, and the silent Indian of our imaginary as a necessary projection in the habit of recognizing ourselves as purposeful and freely constituted individuals.[2]

The act of the Zapatistas encircling the visitors is suggestive of a number of other possible symbolic relationships: that of confinement, engulfment, absorption, protection. These alternate readings of our relative positioning in this shared silence simultaneously suggest force, resistance, commensurability, cooperation, and dependency, all within a context of a materially given imbalance in power. Identification in this case is a complexly structured process, simultaneously conflictual and commensurable, in which differences are only temporarily superseded by the Zapatistas' imposed silence.[3] The differences among the nonindigenous subjects present at the event were also temporarily superseded by our silence. In effect, the many differences existing in the crowd that night were brought into an equivalent relation through the signifier of Zapatista difference—silence. Rather than eliminating differences, silence is the condition of possibility for differences to emerge, but also for a universal identification *in difference* to take place. Silence is the site at which alterity and universality converge.

In Ernesto Laclau's terms, that night in Oventic, the Zapatistas filled the empty signifier of the "fullness of the community" with the sign of their difference (Laclau, *Emancipation[s]*); they brought all of us into a relationship of abstract and temporary parity (exceeding the solidarity of the 1980s) with each other, through our identification with their silence. At this moment, Indian difference comes dangerously close to losing all specificity, as my multiple interpretations of the silence make evident. Each interpretation begins with the specificity of Indian silence only to abstract it into a generalizable silence capable of encompassing all of us present. This is a microcosmic example of the Zapatistas' political project at the national level. The Zapatistas have attempted to become the empty signifier "fullness of the Mexican community" by alternately emphasizing their Indian differences from mestizo nationals and successfully superseding these differences in their bid to shape the contours of a nonbiologized democratic citizenship. As such, the Zapatista model of citizenship poses a serious threat to the terms of mestizo citizenship that have governed Mexico for the last seventy years—not because they insist on their indigenous identity, but precisely because they do not.

Zapatista silence, I suggest, becomes a methodology for interrupting the teleological discourses that have enabled twentieth-century Mexican revolutionary nationalism. It disrupts the deployment of the racial discourse of mestizaje (and its counterpart indigenismo) as a strategy for national identification and unification. The Zapatistas' organized silence also interrupts the deeply related discourse of modernization, a discourse repeatedly promising to deliver the Mexican nation into liberal modernity through development. Instead, the EZLN insists, this modernizing discourse threatens to "develop" the indigenous peasantry right out of existence. These twin discourses have facilitated the emergence of the ideal citizen of a Mexican revolutionary imaginary in the twentieth century: the modern mestizo national. Zapatista silence interrupted this revolutionary imaginary, these twin teleologies of being, on 1 January 1994, and the Zapatistas continue to challenge identification with this ideal—the modern mestizo—by repeatedly and successfully offering alternative processes of identification to disenfranchised Mexicans. In this chapter, then, I analyze the significance of the

Zapatista interruption, on the one hand, and these alternative processes of identification, on the other.

Zapatista silence has broken into twentieth-century discourses of nationalist becoming, and now a new history of the emergence of the Mexican nation can be told by virtue of this subaltern interruption. In the first half of this chapter, I interpret this "new" history of Mexico that the Zapatistas make visible by decoding the subalternizing effect of mestizaje and development. I do not provide an exhaustive history of indigenismo and mestizaje as complementary racial ideologies in Mexico, or an exhaustive history of Mexico's twentieth-century development policies, though I review both of these histories to provide a context for the emergence of the Zapatistas. I revisit these histories in the service of an interpretive analysis of how colonial, postcolonial, and revolutionary regimes of subjection consecutively produced Indian difference as a technique of governmentality. In the second half of the chapter, I interpret selected Zapatista communiqués, and the instances of public democratic practice staged by the Zapatistas over the course of a six-year period (1994–2000). I pay particular attention to the public performance of their negotiations with the government from 1994 to 1996, leading to the signing of the "Accords on Indigenous Rights and Culture." The communiqués, these public performances of democratic practice, and the accords all offer the Mexican people alternative processes of identification, and taken together, they open up the possibility of reconfiguring the meaning of revolution and nation.

Although the EZLN promises to permanently alter the revolutionary imagination in the twenty-first century, I nevertheless believe it is necessary to subject the Zapatista movement to the same critique of developmentalism in revolutionary movements that I have conducted thus far in the book. As much as observers and critics of the EZLN insist on the absolute originality of this movement, it nevertheless stands in genealogical relation to the Central American revolutionary movements, as made evident by the initial Zapatista communiqués and subsequent rhetoric. Critics refuse to acknowledge this genealogical relationship, naively disavowing all that was wrong with the earlier movements. In doing so, these critics forget all that was right with these movements as well, expressing a blind faith in a "new" style of guerrilla politics that, in many ways, is not entirely new. The Mexican revolution of 1910 is *the* paradigmatic revolutionary movement in Latin America. It is the first and longest-lasting revolution of the twentieth century, and the Zapatistas describe themselves as its rightful heirs. As such, it is crucial to a study of revolutionary developmentalism, and to the specific purpose of this chapter—to decipher the developmentalism inherent in the 1910 revolution. Finally, to the degree possible, it is important to examine the Zapatistas' own revisioning of development from their perspective as the first fully indigenous revolutionary movement of the post–World War II period.

I conducted eight months of primary research in Chiapas and in Mexico City over the course of three years (1994–1997). I interviewed representatives of the EZLN, members of pro-Zapatista nongovernmental organizations, PRI officials, leaders of Indianist organizations, members of independent and governmental human rights organizations, and members of the independent and the governmental peace commissions. In addition, I participated as a human rights observer on delegations sent to investigate areas of conflict, and in peace camps established in communities along the border between the Zapatista liberated zones and the Mexican army camps. From these experiences, I learned about many of the tensions that exist among indigenous peasant groups in and around the Zapatista liberated zones, as well as how adroit the government is at exacerbating those tensions to incite violence. Under these difficult circumstances, I was able to conduct a number of interviews in Zapatista-held communities, as well as to engage people in more informal conversations. However, my lack of knowledge of any indigenous language limited my interaction with the base of the Zapatista movement, as well as with supporters of the PRI. My conversations and interviews with people in Zapatista zones were limited to Spanish-speaking men, and to women and men with whom I spoke through a translator. This is an entirely different experience from my research in Nicaragua, where I lived for three consecutive years, worked for a research institution, and spent months at a time in the countryside among peasants who spoke Spanish as a first language, felt relatively free to speak their minds, and came to know me well.

This chapter differs in other ways as well from the previous chapters. Unlike the other revolutionary movements I have analyzed, the Zapatista movement is still going on. This makes the movement an ever-shifting object of study, its analysis messy and indeterminate. One moment the EZLN is an armed guerrilla movement; the next it is a movement for electoral reform and democratic transition. One moment it is a peasant movement for land and resources; the next it is an Indianist movement in pursuit of autonomy and cultural rights. In all of its manifestations, the EZLN has inserted a decisive "Chiapas effect" into the last eight years of Mexican politics (García de León 18). The Zapatista communities are encircled by the Mexican military and are targets of a vicious counterinsurgency campaign waged by paramilitary groups. For all of their media savvy and success, the Zapatistas daily suffer the consequences of this "low-intensity" war and are under no obligation to make themselves more vulnerable by making themselves more accessible.[4] No Zapatista member has published a memoir. No outside observers have spent significant amounts of time among the rank and file of the movement. With the exception of the Accords on Indigenous Rights and Culture, no detailed proposal exists outlining how the EZLN envisions the implementation of revolutionary change taking place. Thus there is no way to ascertain how democratic or feminist the internal workings of the movement may be.

Inventing the "Indian" for Spanish Colonialism

Noted cultural critic and literary scholar José Rabasa has described the project of subaltern studies in Latin America thus: "Less concerned with identifying and studying 'subalterns' as positive entities, the project as I envision it would call for an analysis of the mechanisms that produce subalternity as well as the formulation of political and cultural practices that would end it" (405). Following Rabasa's imperative, in this section and the next I cull the rich historical and anthropological record on colonial violence, Indian exploitation, and racial ideology in Mexico to theorize the production and reproduction of Indian difference in the service of colonial and postcolonial governmentality. I suggest that Indian difference is the effect of a colonial regime of subjection that successfully articulated processes of exploitation with processes of cultural formation. In turn, racial and ethnic differences were reformulated by postcolonial regimes of subjection and techniques of governmentality to structure the modern national identity of nineteenth- and twentieth-century Mexico. An ethnically inflected Zapatista collectivity has been configured as a result of a dialectical relationship between the PRI's policies of indigenismo and economic development and the everyday practices of indigenous members of the EZLN.[5] The PRI's development and indigenist policies together articulate a revolutionary regime of subjection that has created the conditions for the EZLN to emerge. In turn, the EZLN has brought the one-party state to crisis by appropriating Indian difference. It is this recursive relationship between colonial and postcolonial subjection, on one hand, and the Zapatista response, on the other, that I seek to illuminate in this reinterpretation of the historical processes that have produced and reproduced this difference into the present. Once again I caution the reader: the following sections are not meant to provide a complete history of indigenismo, mestizaje, or PRI development policy. Instead I review certain aspects of these histories to provide a context for the emergence of Zapatista subjectivity, consciousness, and agency.

Those characteristics today that seem most authentic to Mesoamerican indigenous culture still bear the imprint of colonial subjection. Take, for example, the formation of the Indian township, thousands of which today dot the landscape from the valley of Oaxaca to the highlands of Guatemala. Each town has its own council of elders as its highest normative authority, its own system of assembly and decision making, its particular religious obligations, rituals, and saints, its unique traditional costume, a central plaza around which social and market life is organized, and each shares a primary indigenous language (Bonfil Batalla 31–37). Indeed, during the first round of negotiations between the Mexican government and the Zapatistas on Indian rights and culture in 1995, the Zapatistas sought communal autonomy rather than regional autonomy in Chiapas, recognizing the township as the basis for Indian identity and for the organization of indigenous life. Yet the Indian town as the organizing unit of indigenous life is the engineered product of Spanish colonial governmentality and economic exploitation (Díaz Polanco, *Indigenous Peoples* 24).

In the sixteenth and seventeenth centuries, the Spanish Crown perfected ways for managing its most valuable asset in the New World: indigenous labor. It established institutions for the subjugation of the indigenous population and for the rationalization of its exploitation. The most pervasive and successful of these institutions was the atomized Indian town, with its set of specific cultural traits. In the first half of the sixteenth century, the Crown's system of the *encomienda* assigned conquistadors individual Indian communities as laborers and servants for their haciendas and mines (Díaz Polanco, *Indigenous Peoples* 29–34).[6] Two plagues in the second half of the sixteenth century severely diminished the indigenous population, precipitating further relocation and concentration of this population. Under the supervision of the clerics, the Crown introduced the systems of *congregaciones* (the forced concentration of dispersed Indian populations) and of *reducciones* (the "voluntary" relocation of entire villages once they converted to Christianity) (52–58). Presumably undertaken for medical and evangelical purposes, these new townships were more effective than the encomiendas in reorganizing indigenous life-worlds for the purposes of ensuring a steady supply of labor that would pay tribute to the Crown. All three systems for appropriating Indian labor relied principally on the re-creation of the pre-Hispanic Indian communities into fragmented townships.[7]

Indian ethnicity was reduced to the level of the town by the colonial regime through a myriad of administrative effects, among them the introduction of a traditional costume for each township as a method of imperial surveillance, the institution of unique religious rituals for each town organized around particular saints' days, the tithing by township for the Crown and Church, and, most importantly, the elimination of supracommunal networks of identification. Indian hierarchies—the form of pre-Hispanic governmentality mediating supracommunal indigenous networks—had their power and jurisdiction reduced as these hierarchies were slowly replaced by elected officials on the local councils. Each council negotiated its interests separately with the Spanish administration, eliminating the need for mediation by supracommunal authorities or the possibility for allegiance among town councils (Díaz Polanco, *Indigenous Peoples* 55).

The communitarianism of village life, then, focused around the town council of elders, which today we identify as a hallmark of various Mesoamerican indigenous cultures, is in fact the by-product of Spanish colonialism's regime of subjection, and its success at dismantling supracommunal levels of organization and identification. Spanish colonialism's regime of subjection universalized Indian identity, as all inhabitants of the Americas were rendered "Indian"—regardless of their heterogeneous cultures and political organizations—in contradistinction to Spaniards. However, colonial policy also parochialized indigenous identities by disarticulating previous cultural, political, and territorial organizations, replacing them with confining local structures of identifications and governance that existed parallel to, though also in the service of, colonial governance. Spanish colonial subjection engineered a lasting Indian difference through this simultaneous process of universalizing and particularizing Indian identity. It reproduced a racialized labor force that spanned two continents, not by applying military force, but by relying on the disciplining power of thousands of atomized "Indian" towns for the production *and containment* of Indian difference. These towns, however, also proliferated ethnic differences among Indians through their fragmentation of identity.[8] Spanish colonialism transformed every aspect of indigenous cultural life and political territoriality through the townships while at the same time (re)producing the grounds for Indian difference at a safe but accessible distance.

Mexicanist historians and anthropologists of indigenous culture who often disagree in their characterizations of pre-Hispanic indigenous culture nevertheless agree that the colonial system, because it so completely restructured indigenous life-worlds, created the "Indian" (Aguirre Beltrán, *Regiones de refugio;* Aguirre Beltrán, *La política indigenista en México;* Varese; Bonfil Batalla; Knight, "Racism, Revolution"; Díaz Polanco, *Indigenous Peoples*). Nevertheless these indigenous communities also produced meaning and value in excess of Spanish techniques of governmentality; they produced a cultural formation that exceeded colonialism's subalternized category of the Indian. This excess, however, neither exists outside of colonialism nor is other to colonialism. Rather, it is from the dialectical relationship between a colonial regime of subjection and the everyday practices of a subjugated population that new and resistant indigenous identities emerged, that new political and cultural indigenous communities coalesced.[9] It is also from this colonial regime of difference that modern national identities emerged in Latin America.

In nineteenth-century Mexico, this Indian difference articulated with the economic and cultural processes of forming a national identity, often in contradictory ways. At the beginning of the nineteenth century, Creole elites claimed the history of Aztec resistance to Spain as their own nationalist origin story, as the historical resistance to Spain that legitimized New Spain's struggle for independence from the Crown (Bonfil Batalla 95). This historical indigenismo, as some scholars have called it, also gave the Mexican insurgency its distinctive popular character—"an agrarian element and an element of 'caste' struggle against Spain" (Díaz Polanco, *Indigenous Peoples* 16). It allowed nationalist elites to fill the content of the emerging nation with a "folk" culture, as they appropriated the Indian religious cult of the Virgen de Tepeyac and translated it into a Creole *guadalupismo* (Bonfil Batalla 95). In other words, indigenismo in the nineteenth-century independence movement provided a regime of subjection for the nationalist elite, and not just the subjugated indigenous population. The appearance of the Virgen de Tepeyac (renamed Guadalupe by these elites) to an Indian named Juan Diego *in* New Spain provided nationalists with legitimization—a Christian blessing—for their cause against Spain in the formation of Mexico. The Virgen de Guadalupe became the patron saint of Mexican independence, and her veneration spread among the Creole class.[10] Creole nationalists were able to appropriate Indian cultural forms as their own precisely because of the colonial regime's reiterative production of Indian difference as an at once universal and particularistic form of subjection.

By maintaining Indian towns as a structure of governance parallel, though subordinate, to Spanish town governance, colonialism's regime of subjection had universalized the difference between Indians and Spaniards. These parallel republics rarefied Indians as the native inhabitants of the Americas and the Spaniards as the Europeans. Indian difference thereby provided Creole nationalists—many of whose very status as mestizo elite defied this rarefied differentiation—with a rich structure of identification in their actions against the Spaniards as foreigners, as European interlopers. The dialectical relationship between particular and universal Indian identity put into play by colonialism allowed the Creole elite to fill the empty signifier of Indian identity with a content they could appropriate precisely because this universalized identity lacked any specific content. On the one hand, the elite filled this empty signifier with the specific content of Aztec resistance and religious mandate. On the other, they were able to overlook the history of particular tribal collaboration with the Spaniards in the overthrow of the Aztec empire, as well as to suture over the evident subordination of particular, living Indians in their ethnic townships to Creole elites in theirs.

By the mid–nineteenth century, however, the Liberal government in independent Mexico had identified Indians, with their communally organized townships and landholdings, as precisely the obstacle to building a modern nation based on the private ownership of land (Bonfil Batalla 104).[11] The Indian became the sign of an absence of modernity or, if you will, the sign of the incompletion of the nation (García Canclini, *Hybrid Cultures*; Bonfil Batalla; Medina).[12] It was the parochial, heterogeneous, and communal aspects of Indian townships that disquieted the liberal reformers. The indigenismo of the republican era, therefore, targeted the Indians, and particularly their townships, as the objects of reform. With the universalization of private property, nationalists intended to transform the particularity of Indian difference into the abstractness of liberal citizenship. Mexico's Lerdo Law of 1856, for example, provided for the disentailment of all corporate property held by the townships, equating these communal properties with the monopolistic estate of the Catholic Church—the largest landholder in Mexico at the time. Both were considered equally backward, colonial institutions. The following year, the Constitution of 1857 did away with all possibilities of communal holdings by recognizing private holdings as the only legal form of tenure. The stated intention of both the Lerdo Law and the Constitutionalists was to create a de-ethnicized small-holding peasantry out of the indigenous rural population for the purposes of national development. In other words, postcolonial governmentality brought about a new regime of subjection for the indigenous population, presumably meant to inculcate in the indigenous peasants liberal notions of individual autonomy and private ownership of property. Instead the breaking up of these corporations only served to dispossess Indian communities and increase Mexican latifundium (large-scale private holding) (Díaz Polanco, *Indigenous Peoples* 75; Durand Alcántara 165–66; Barre 60–61).

Indian towns did not disappear during this period of dispossession and warfare. These towns were preserved as a seasonal labor force for planting and harvesting, or, in many cases, were absorbed by the very latifundios that took over Indian communal lands. The latifundio economy of the mid–nineteenth century necessitated the reproduction of Indians as a source of indentured, racialized labor. In the last quarter of the century, under the dictatorship of Porfirio Diaz (1876–1910), the Porfirian model of development, with its industrialization of rural and urban areas, required the further dispossession of the peasantry for the creation of a reliable labor force in the cities and countryside. Though proletarianization theoretically de-ethnicizes a workforce, the reiterative invocation of the Indian's "natural indolence," by the planters and industrialists alike, reveals a recursive relationship between racialization and the production of a labor force in Mexico.[13] Here again we see the articulation of a postcolonial regime of subjection that conjoined a process of economic exploitation (proletarianization) with a cultural formation (ethnically distinct Indians in their townships) to produce Indian difference anew—this time the slothful Indian, in constant need of labor discipline to ensure the proper functioning of the de-Indianized "modern" nation.

Despite the Porfirian elite's stated desire to assimilate the "antinational" Indian element by force, Indian difference was not absorbed into the universal equality of the liberal Mexican nation in the nineteenth century precisely because of the centrality of Indian difference to the very formation of an abstract national identity. The colonial regime of subjection provided Creole nationalists with the mythical difference that differentiated them from Spaniards in New Spain. After independence was won, however, the regime of difference was reformulated. Indian difference as the negation of the nation paradoxically became the organizing principle for the national elite. "The Indian problem" brought Liberals and Conservatives together in their need to correct it, to address it reiteratively.[14] Perhaps most importantly, the production and reproduction of Indian difference became central for the production and reproduction of an ethnicized proletariat on which to forge a national economy that would finally deliver Mexico into modernity. Even this brief reexamination of Mexico's postcolonial regime of subjection in the nineteenth century demonstrates how, economically and culturally, modern nationalism emerged from, or, more precisely, is articulated with, a colonial regime of difference: the colonial regime of difference is reformulated under liberalism and put in the service of nation building. Time and again, in one form or another, Indian difference summons forth the nation. Revolutionary nationalism in Mexico is similarly summoned forth by the Indian of the subalternizing imagination in the twentieth century.

The Rise of the Revolutionary Mestizo

During and after the 1910 revolution against the Porfirio Diaz dictatorship, the revolutionary elite incorporated Indian difference into their nationalist ideology through a renewed policy of indigenismo.[15] Similar to the role historical indigenismo had played in the struggle for independence, revolutionary indigenismo resuscitated the Indian warrior as the symbol of revolutionary nationalism, as the symbol of the true ancestral rights of the Mexican people. In their confrontation with the Porfirian elite, revolutionaries relied on representations of Indians to authenticate their struggle against elites allied with foreign interests and represented as European interlopers. Revolutionary indigenismo was, in part, a response to the great numbers of Indians who had participated in the revolutionary struggle.[16] But the revolutionary elite also identified Indian difference as a potential threat to the formation of a revolutionary nation. According to Mexicanist historian Alan Knight, the "problem" of Indian difference and the project of nationalism were once again conjoined: "The revolutionaries' discovery of the Indian—of the Indian's capacity for either troublesome sedition or supportive mobilization—was paralleled by their commitment to state and nation-building" (Knight, "Racism, Revolution" 83).[17] At once ancestor to Mexican nationals' rights and devoid of nationalist sentiment, the Indian was paradoxically inside and outside the nation—supportive and seditious—in need of full incorporation, regardless of the fact that thousands of Indians *had* participated in the revolution. The war that took place between 1910 and 1920 destroyed the centralized state and "reduced Mexico to a patchwork of warring factions" (84). Though most of the fighting was among revolutionary elites, these elites, like Liberal and Conservative nationalists of the previous century, nevertheless identified Indian difference as the most powerful threat to the possibility of unifying and homogenizing the nation. In part, elites turned to indigenismo as a strategy in their efforts to create a unified nation out of the chaos of civil war and their own internal divisions. However, indigenismo, as a strategy of unification, also provided a rich rhetorical legitimization for minority rule in Mexico.

Manuel Gamio is considered the intellectual architect of revolutionary indigenismo in Mexico. His book *Forjando Patria* (Forging Nation), published in 1916, was the blueprint for incorporating the Indian in the construction of a national identity in the aftermath of the 1910 revolution.[18] In it Gamio contemplates everything from the sublime to the mundane: from what constitutes "national" fine arts to how to constitute a "national" legislature; from the supremacy of Mexican femininity to the mediocrity of Mexico's coat of arms. In many ways, Gamio lays the foundation for the institutionalization of the revolution, anticipating in these pages the agrarian reform statute of the 1917 Constitution (173), the aesthetic principles of the Mexican mural movement (51–52), and the corporativist politics of the PRI (77). Gamio's ruminations seem to revolve around the central, troubling issue of how to forge one nation out of the two races inhabiting the country—one of Indian descent, the other of European descent. As in the nineteenth century, heterogeneity—racial, ethnic, cultural, and linguistic—is identified as the principal obstacle to forging this nation. Unlike its nineteenth-century counterpart, however, Gamio's indigenismo repeatedly celebrates the Indians' spectacular contributions in realms historical, artistic, cultural, and scientific. He draws the reader's eye to the towering contribution of various Indian tribes, all the while meticulously plotting out their absorption into a future nation built on the greater principle of the "fusion of races, convergence and fusion of cultural manifestations, linguistic unification and economic equilibrium" (183). Members of the 1970s Mexican "critical anthropology" school thoroughly critiqued the numerous policies and institutes built on indigenismo as an integrationism effectively based on de-Indianizing the indigenous population.[19] Thus it behooves us to pause and consider the rhetorical and intellectual force of *Forjando Patria*, published at the apex of revolutionary conflict and debate over the future nation, just one year prior to the promulgation of the 1917 Constitution. In its pages, Indian difference emerges into visibility through the celebratory discourse of Mexican revolutionary nationalism only to disappear again into the "fusion" of mestizaje.

Gamio begins by posing a rhetorical question: "Can eight or ten million individuals of indigenous race, language, and culture . . . harbor the same ideals and aspirations, tend toward identical goals, honor the same patria and treasure the same symbols of nationalism as the six or four million beings of European origin, who inhabit the same territory but speak a distinct language, belong to another race and live and think according to the teachings of a culture . . . that, from any point of view, differs greatly from their own. We believe not . . ." (9).[20] On the previous page, Gamio, the intrepid anthropologist, has already discerned for the reader the three fundamental criteria for constituting a "clear and integrated nation." Taking Germany, Japan, and France as his models, Gamio informs us that a nation depends on the majority of the population sharing (1) an ethnic similarity; (2) a common language; and (3) a set of cultural traits, that is, shared religious, political, moral, and aesthetic values (8). According to these criteria, these two groups, linked by geography but divided by race, language, and culture, are the antithesis of nation.[21] But no sooner does Gamio identify the problem confronting Mexican nationalism as lying in the multiple differences existing *between* these two fundamental groups with his "We believe not" than he displaces this problem onto the heterogeneity existing *among* the indigenous population:

> The indigenous population appears before us [today] as it was during the Conquest, divided into groupings more or less numerous, that do constitute tiny patrias due to their common bond of race, of language and of culture, which in turn, due to their mutual rivalries and reciprocal indifference, facilitated their [own] conquest during the XVI century and caused their cultural stagnation during the Colonial era and in our current time.
>
> The problem, then, is not [how to] avoid an illusory aggression by some ensemble of these groupings, but rather how to channel the powerful energies currently dispersed, drawing their individuals toward the other social group which they have always considered as an enemy, incorporating them, fusing them with [the other "European" group], tending toward, finally, making a coherent and homogenized national race, unified in language and convergent in culture. (10)

Within the space of three paragraphs, the indigenous population of Mexico is transformed from constituting the majority of the Mexican people ("eight or ten million individuals of indigenous race") to constituting a set of petty rival factions responsible for their own conquest ("divided into groupings more or less numerous" with "mutual rivalries"). Gamio dismisses the potential threat posed by the indigenous majority to the minority as "illusionary aggression," but "the problem" of the indigenous population persists. Their stagnation is described as metahistorical, both preceding and proceeding colonization, and seen as entirely a consequence of their distressing heterogeneity. Rhetorically, this indigenous population is transformed for the minority from an equal and numerically superior partner in the future project of the nation into a latent fund of "powerful energies" waiting to be harnessed—channeled—in the service of the nation. Gamio heralds the indigenous population as nationalist agent only to transform them immediately into an entirely passive national resource.

Gamio's formulation of the problem sets the terms of the debate for decades to come. The question is no longer how to mix two equal cultures to forge a third, but rather how to exploit a natural but underused resource. In *Forjando Patria* this is clearly the task of the future revolutionary government, as it is "the revolution that told the Indian to abandon his lethargy and begin to live" (93–94). Surprisingly, though, it is the duty of the *anthropologist* to guide the revolutionaries in this task. The third chapter of his book, "The Direction of Anthropology," is dedicated to determining the field's essential role in the revolution: "It is axiomatic that Anthropology, in its truest, broadest form, should be considered basic knowledge for the discharging of good government, as it is through it that one knows the population that is the primary material for governing and for which you govern. [It is] through the means of Anthropology [that one] distinguishes the abstract nature and the physicality of men, of a people, and deduces the appropriate means for facilitating a normal evolutionary development" (15).

Using the study of the Otomí people as an example of how anthropology may be put in the service of the new revolutionary government, Gamio suggests that the anthropologist establishes a body of knowledge about each indigenous group, ascertaining its "mode of being" and levels of "development."[22] The roles of anthropologist and government functionary become indistinguishable, however, as anthropology becomes a technique of governmentality, a body of knowledge in the service of a revolutionary regime of indigenous subjection. Its purpose is not simply to attain knowledge *about* a population but to create a population *for* governing by diagnosing "needs" on the one hand, and producing governmental duties such as supplying "means" and establishing "observation" on the other. This knowledge production is directly in the service of the nation's political economy, as anthropology's guiding purpose, according to Gamio, is to ascertain "if the capacity for production of the Otomí is normal or abnormal, establishing if this abnormality is motivated by physical incompetence or the result of conscious will" (18). Gamio's anthropologist qua government functionary sifts through the evidence, sorting out the physical from cultural causes for indigenous underproduction, and Indian difference is once again produced ("normal or abnormal") at the articulation of cultural formation ("physical incompetence," "conscious will") with economic exploitation ("capacity for production"). With revolutionary governmentality, Indian difference emerges through a field of knowledge capable of racially codifying the capacity to labor.[23] Indian difference is that fund of "dispersed" energies, of bodies-in-waiting—a capacity for production—to be tapped and transformed into national economy. Indeed, Gamio's discussion of the function of anthropology in government foreshadows the post–World War II developmentalist regime of subjection as evidenced by Rostow, for the anthropologist is precisely engaged in preparing indigenous men to be prepared for development, in making prodigal men ready to be made into productive men. Indian difference also emerges through anthropological knowledge as a capacity for culture in the production of all things "national," as a fund to be tapped in the formation of Mexican identity.

For the remainder of *Forjando Patria*, anthropological knowledge produces just such a cultural fund of Indian difference. Gamio systematically assesses facets of culture in Mexico broadly conceived: fine arts, history, religion, intellectual culture, language, literature, *women*, and work. In each case, he finds the country has yet to arrive fully at an expression of "national" culture. Instead three principal traditions are at work in Mexico: the pre-Hispanic/indigenous, the Spanish/European, and the emergent "intermediate" or "mixed." The Spanish/European tradition is consistently represented as foreign, exotic, inappropriate, at times even perverse (100). Though seen as playing a role in the eventual formation of a national culture, its influence is invariably diminished in comparison with a pre-Hispanic/indigenous tradition repeatedly described in superlative terms (despite his early assessment of pre-Hispanic civilization as stagnant). For example, Gamio criticizes liberal historians to date for their elitist focus on the social classes of European descent. Instead Gamio insists it is the pre-Hispanic/indigenous history that must be documented by historians, as it is "realistic, vigorous, picturesque, allowing us to see . . . how Mexicans lived their lives before the Conquest: original art, an apprenticeship for our aesthetic criteria. Ingenious industry with multiple manifestations. A complex social order, strong and wise" (65). Gamio locates the roots of modern Mexican history in the "vigorous" and "picturesque" "apprenticeship" of pre-Columbian lifeways, as he calls on his contemporary readership—primarily white and mestizo—to identify in their present lives with "how *Mexicans* lived their lives before the Conquest." Gamio retroactively produces this nationalist identification with Indian difference in chapter after chapter.

Indian difference emerges as the capacity for culture because *national* culture must invariably derive from Indian culture in Gamio's indigenismo schema; and yet it is merely the *capacity* for culture because though Indian difference authenticates national culture, indigenous traditions are never enough to constitute national culture in and of themselves. Invariably, only "mixed" or "intermediate" culture may truly constitute a national culture. More precisely, it is only through the intermediate or mixed cultural formations Gamio describes as the third tradition existing in Mexico that we finally arrive at what may be designated a national culture. It is at this juncture, intellectually and historically, that Gamio's foundational text biologizes national citizenship for revolutionary Mexico through the metaphor of mestizaje. Though any white or Indian person should arguably be capable of producing such intermediate cultural forms, this is never the case. Instead only those of mixed race, the mestizos, are capable of producing national culture, for in them "there is the mixture of blood, of ideas, of industries, of virtues and of vices: the mestizo type appears with pristine purity as he constitutes the first harmonious product where the racial characteristics of his origin [exist in] contrast" (66). By conflating blood with ideas, industries, virtues, and vices—the very stuff of culture—Gamio biologizes a cultural metaphor for citizenship in the nation. Only the mestizo is capable of producing a national culture by virtue of his mixed blood, blood that draws him sympathetically toward, though always at a critical remove from, all things Indian and drives him away from all things "foreign." Only the mestizo is capable of national belonging.

Gamio makes this explicit in the chapter entitled "Our Intellectual Culture." The revolution's "deepest roots germinated and germinate still in the indigenous race . . . for this social group has been the most oppressed, and thus, the most disposed to exploding" (93–94). Regardless of this naturalized proclivity toward revolution (germinating indigenous/soil), or perhaps because of it, this population is incapable of actually generating revolution or revolutionary thought, as the Indian "lives four hundred years behind the times," his mental aptitude "vigorous," but his intellectual manifestations "anachronistic and inappropriate" (95). Instead those of "mixed blood" must produce the revolutionary nation from the raw material provided by the Indian, for this mixed-blooded class has been "eternally rebellious, the traditional enemy of the pure-blooded or foreign class, the author and director of the revolts and revolutions, the one that has best understood the just laments of the indigenous class and has taken advantage of its powerful latent energies, which it has always used as a crowbar to contain the oppression of Power" (97). Though the inclination for revolution resides in the Indian class, it is the mestizo who is the revolution's intellectual architect, its "author and director." The mestizo summons forth, through sympathetic "understanding," the liberated nation from the "powerful latent energies" of the Indian masses, indeed by wielding their energies as a "crowbar" against the power of the "pure-blooded or foreign class" (importantly, one and the same). This is not a particularly flattering representation of the intellectual, but one in keeping with the utilitarian metaphorics of Indian representation throughout the book. Just as the Indians' dormant capacity for labor awaits the catalyst of revolutionary government to transform it into national economy, so the Indians' capacity for the culture of revolution requires the catalyst of the "eternally rebellious" mestizo intellectual to transform it into the national culture. Gamio's celebratory indigenismo simultaneously produces Indian difference as the very source of the nation and places Indian difference in liminal relation to the nation, within yet subsumed by the evolutionary logic of mestizaje.

Indians may live *in* the nation—indeed, they are the very precondition *for* the nation—but they will never be *of* the nation unless they undergo a process of admixture themselves, forgoing their Indian identities for this national mestizo ideal. Thus we arrive at the heart of indigenismo as a strategy for minority rule. Gamio instructs the revolutionary elite: "To incorporate the Indian let us not try to 'Europeanize' him all at once; to the contrary, let us 'Indianize' ourselves a bit, to present to him our civilization already diluted with his own, so that he will not find [it] exotic, cruel, bitter, and incomprehensible. Naturally, we should not exaggerate to a ridiculous degree our closeness with the Indian" (96). This quotation demonstrates the central paradox of revolutionary indigenismo as a political imperative. It produces Indian difference in order to finally absorb it: "let us not try to 'Europeanize' him *all at once.*" Indigenismo produces Indian difference as knowledge the revolutionary elite can don lightly—"let us Indianize ourselves *a bit* "—to establish hegemonic control over the indigenous majority: "to present him *our* civilization" diluted only slightly "with his own." Indigenismo, with its celebratory nationalist rhetoric of Indian difference, disguises a political domination that would otherwise appear to the majority population as it actually is: "exotic, cruel, bitter, and incomprehensible." This passage betrays indigenismo's deeply ideological function in the mestizos' regime of revolutionary subjection—to inoculate the modern Mexican nation, to prevent the nation of minority rule from becoming Indianized by the majority. After all, "*we* should not exaggerate to a ridiculous degree *our* closeness with the Indian." Indigenismo facilitates minority rule by placing the ideological onus of racial assimilation squarely with the Indian majority.

Officially—though certainly not effectively—the nineteenth-century republican-era indigenismo sought to de-ethnicize Indian identity through the complete assimilation of the indigenous population, through an eradication of all Indian specificity. Alternately, Gamio believed education and cultural reform could preserve selective positive elements of indigenous culture ("let us Indianize ourselves a bit") while eliminating the negative aspects through mestizaje. Although revolutionary indigenismo may seem more benign than nineteenth-century republican-era indigenismo, it was no less assimilationist, and it was certainly more developmentalist. Mexican revolutionary indigenismo inscribed particular Indian subjectivity within a teleology of becoming more perfect citizens. Nothing testifies more to this developmentalist logic than the paradoxical relationship that exists between indigenismo and mestizaje. Indigenismo glorifies Indian difference as a cultural formation. But it is mestizaje that represents political citizenship in Mexico, as mestizos are the revolution's architects in every sense. Indians may be Mexico's ideal ancestors, but mestizos are Mexico's ideal citizens. Indian difference is an essential precedent for this mestizo nation, but *Indians,* the bearers of difference, are the continuing targets of educational and cultural reform. In the years immediately following the revolution (and the publication of Gamio's influential book), institutes and programs for the education and assimilation of Indians proliferated at national, regional, and local levels.[24] The point, of course, is not to question the intentions of early revolutionary elites who sought to alleviate the oppression suffered by the indigenous class by providing access to education. Rather, it is to underline the fact that such benevolent intentions invariably entailed the violent transformation of indigenous subjects subjected to the teleological imperative of an education that promoted mestizaje as its model of citizenship.[25]

Just as rebellious indigenous identities and communities emerged out of colonial techniques of governmentality, so the Zapatistas emerge from within the terms of revolutionary mestizaje, disrupting this regime of subjection from within its own terms. From indigenismo, mestizaje's constitutive corollary, they appropriate the markers of Indian difference: not only silence, but also the Indian as progenitor of the nation, and the Indian as "a complex social order, strong and wise" (Gamio, *Forjando Patria* 65). However, the Zapatistas also appropriate the terms of the "revolutionary mestizo" as laid out by Gamio: the savvy to wield the masses like a "crowbar" in attaining this freedom. The EZLN's appropriation and reformulation of the discursive terms of mestizaje opens up new processes of identification for revolutionary nationalism, discussed in greater detail later in the chapter. Similarly, the Zapatistas have emerged from *within* revolutionary policies of agrarian reform and agricultural development. The indigenous communities of the Lacandón making up the EZLN were not somehow left out of Mexico's discourse of development, though some critics have argued their exclusion from development as the reason for rebellion. To the contrary, the indigenous peasants making up the EZLN were the targeted "beneficiaries" of development in Chiapas during the administrations of Echeverría and López Portillo in the 1970s and early 1980s, just as the Chiapas indigenous population was the targeted beneficiary of educational and cultural reforms in the 1920s and 1930s (Burbach and Rosset 5–6). Zapatismo is produced by, but also is in excess of, the discourse of Mexican development. In the previous sections, I contextualized the emergence of the EZLN from the macroscopic perspective: first the five-hundred-year view of the production of Indian difference as a result of colonialism's regime of subjection, and then narrowing the scope to the one-hundred-year view of the production of Indian difference as the remainder of subjection under the regime of revolutionary mestizaje. In the following section, I narrow the focus considerably to the last thirty years of economic policy that led directly to the formation of the EZLN, to the discourse of development they emerge from and seek to interrupt. The EZLN wakes the Mexican nation from the dream of development, as Subcomandante Marcos suggests: "I'm willing to take off my mask if Mexican society will take off the mask their craving for foreign pursuits placed [on them] long ago . . . civil society will just now awaken from the long and idle dream 'modernity' imposed on them at the cost of everything and everyone" (20 January 1994).[26]

Cronica de una guerra anunciada

The EZLN's ten-year history of formation in the Lacandón jungle, from 1984 to 1994, unfolds in the aftermath of Mexico's 1982 debt crisis. In response to the debt crisis, Miguel de la Madrid's administration (1982–1988) implemented structural adjustment policies mandated by the World Bank and International Monetary Fund. These policies were later developed into a cohesive neoliberal reform project for the nation under the technocratic vision of the Salinas de Gotarí administration (1988–1994).[27] This project, also known as *salinismo*, consisted of the elimination of trade barriers and production subsidies, the privatization of state enterprises, and the implementation of limited social programs to ameliorate the cost of the transition to the poorest constituencies.[28] Neil Harvey has quipped that for the peasant classes in Chiapas and elsewhere in Mexico, this amounted to "exclusion from markets, abandonment by the state and the political manipulation of limited social spending" (*Rebellion in Chiapas* 6). This is a succinct summary of the effects of a neoliberal policy that helped swell the ranks of the EZLN, as well as rebel groups in other regions. Indeed, Subcomandante Marcos, the principal spokesperson for the EZLN, has stated that the Zapatista ranks grew precipitously between 1988 and 1994 (Montemayor, *Chiapas* 139). Over the last seventy years, however, development policy under the guardianship of the PRI has often shifted course without (in most cases) incurring an armed insurrection (Knight, "Continuidades" 48–49). Economic changes alone cannot explain what occurred in Chiapas. Certainly, Salinas-style neoliberal reforms achieved a paradigm shift from the nationalist development models of import substitution and export-led growth previously followed by the PRI.[29] But beyond its economic scope, this paradigm shift in development policy also required a redefinition of the terms of Mexican citizenship. It brought mestizaje to crisis by terminating the social contract that had existed between the PRI state and the peasantry since the implementation of constitutionally mandated agrarian reform under the Lázaro Cárdenas administration (1936–1940). Once again I caution the reader: the following is by no means a complete historical analysis of industrial and agricultural development policy under the PRI. Rather, it is a discursive analysis of the crisis in the PRI's development policies over the last forty years that led to the demise of mestizaje as a regime of revolutionary subjection.

To fully understand the impact of salinismo on peasant production, we must place it within the larger drama that unfolded in southeastern Chiapas in the 1970s and early 1980s: the boom and bust of the oil economy. As Mexico expanded its oil production for export in the early 1970s, the government borrowed heavily against the future earnings promised by high oil prices. Increased revenues from sales and international loans were invested in further energy development projects, including the construction of two hydroelectric dams on the Grijalva River in Chiapas.[30] The consecutive administrations of Luis Echeverría (1970–1976) and José López Portillo (1976–1982) consistently invested part of the increased revenues in various agricultural development programs directed toward small-scale peasant production as well (Collier 92, 94). This constituted a significant shift in Mexican agricultural policy, which since the 1930s had been characterized by a "divorce between the government's commitment to land redistribution and its productivity objectives" (Burbach and Rosset 4). During the 1930s, under the auspices of Article 27 of the 1917 Constitution, President Lázaro Cárdenas redistributed expropriated latifundios to *ejidos* and communal farms.[31] Agricultural development policy under subsequent administrations, however, clearly favored large-scale private agro-industry in northern Mexico (Burbach and Rosset 4). While Echeverría and López Portillo continued to support agro-industry, they also directed a portion of agricultural investment toward ejidos and communal farms. For indigenous peasants, the combined effect of these new investments in energy development and of this historical shift in agriculture development policy was "the dramatic growth of nonagricultural work and the increasing integration of peasant economies into the national and international markets" (Collier 90).[32]

On one hand, the oil boom brought with it a period of accelerated proletarianization for the indigenous peasants of Chiapas. Mexico's industrial sector expanded from 27 to 38 percent of the gross domestic product (GDP) between 1965 and 1982, while the agricultural sector declined from 14 to 7 percent over the same period. As this industrial sector grew in southeastern Chiapas, workers migrated from their ejidos or communal farms in the highlands and the Lacandón jungle to construction sites along the Grijalva River, or to Tuxtla Gutierrez and San Cristobal de las Casas, service cities that shared the benefits of the energy production boom (Collier 91, 101). On the other hand, "proletarianization" is not precisely the correct term for the process taking place among the state's peasantry. As discussed specifically in the case of Nicaragua in chapter 4, when peasant producers increase their participation in wage work, they neither abandon peasant production nor cease to identify as peasants. According to anthropologist George Collier's extensive research during this period in the highland towns of Zinacantán and Chamula, the majority of the migrant workers from these two towns continued to farm their *milpas,* although the techniques of this farming changed considerably. Migrant laborers were able to continue farming, even though they spent extended periods away from the milpa, by using their wages to invest in labor-saving agricultural inputs they had not used before, such as enhanced seed, pesticides, and fertilizers (Collier 109).[33] The oil boom, then, did not lead unambiguously to the proletarianization of the migrating sectors of the peasantry. Rather, wages generated by the boom paradoxically reinforced peasant affiliations for some by providing these sectors with access to the technologies of the green revolution and modernizing production techniques.

The oil boom revenues reinforced peasant affiliations in another, related way, as well. Echeverría's administration was the only administration to give out land on a significant scale after Cárdenas's initial distribution from 1936 to 1940, and he combined this redistribution with investment in small-scale production, particularly production for export (Knight, "Continuidades" 39; Burbach and Rosset 5).[34] This shift toward export production was planned and supported by the World Bank, which saw Mexico as "a model for its new policy of trying to assist small scale agricultural producers in the third world" (Burbach and Rosset 5). Peasants in Chiapas, as in the rest of Mexico, responded positively to the increased incentives for export production, including credits, subsidies for agricultural inputs, and state absorption of other production costs.[35] Just as agriculture exports began to play a more important role in the national economy, so exports began to play a more important role in the small-holding peasantry's portfolio, as peasants diversified their production to include coffee, meat, and specialty fruits and vegetables. Agricultural production is especially diversified in the Lacandón, the Zapatista base of support, where timber, coffee, and cattle production are as important as corn production. This diversification for export, however, also made the peasants more vulnerable to shifts in international market prices for export goods.

López Portillo's administration followed Echeverría's agricultural policy, increasing credits and subsidies for small-scale agricultural export products, as well. His administration also started the Mexican Food System (SAM) in response to concern over Mexico's increased dependence on foreign imports of basic grains (by 1980, Mexico was importing 25 percent of its corn). This program was designed to improve domestic food production by providing peasants with subsidies for fertilizer and other inputs, credits, and, most importantly, price supports for basic grains (Collier 93–94). This policy of subsidizing agricultural inputs helped to make farming in the Lacandón plausible on a longer-term basis, since fertilizers supplemented the quickly depleted soils of the jungle. Nationally, a government-guaranteed price for corn made it economically feasible for small-scale peasant producers to continue farming this crop though their techniques were not industrialized, and, as such, their production costs not competitive with international corn prices. This crop's continued importance in the peasant's production portfolio is underscored by the fact that in 1991, even after a decade of inflationary debt crisis, "over 2.4 million rural producers . . . cultivated corn during the spring-summer season" (Appendini 145).[36]

The oil boom, then, had multiple interpellative effects on indigenous peasant life all over southeastern Mexico during the 1970s, and especially in Chiapas. The boom drew peasants into an expanded labor and goods market. Migrants' jobs were directly tied to the fluctuating price of petroleum on the international market, while in their traditional economic role, peasants became increasingly dependent on imported agricultural inputs because of changes in production techniques. The boom brought about the overall diversification of agricultural production for a significant portion of the small-holding peasantry in Chiapas, with increased export production again tying peasants into the international market. With its wage work, class differentiation, and increased export income, oil-led development also diversified consumption patterns and "modernized" tastes.[37] It accelerated colonization of the Lacandón jungle, where several energy development projects were located and where increased agricultural investment made farming and ranching viable for small-scale indigenous producers. The oil boom extended the life chances of the indigenous peasant class in Chiapas by allowing its members to augment their household incomes with wages and export earning. Perhaps most importantly, though, the oil boom made possible the price supports that allowed indigenous peasants to continue farming corn. Corn is not only a crop with a great deal of cultural significance for the Indians of southern Mexico; it is also a crop whose production had thoroughly integrated these indigenous producers from Chiapas into the national economy.[38] In all these ways, then, development policies guided by the oil boom were a form of subjection for the indigenous peasants in Chiapas.

When international oil prices fell, precipitating the 1982 debt crisis and shrinking the national budget, the effects were particularly serious for the indigenous peasants in Chiapas who had, in all these ways, been drawn into its economy. The development boom experienced by Chiapas came to an abrupt end, and the labor market contracted, leaving many of the peasants who had been pulled into the market out of work. At the same time, structural adjustment policies that followed the post-boom debt crisis curtailed the subsidies, credits, and price supports that had made domestic and export agricultural production economically viable for hundreds of thousands of peasant families. Once again the peasant's role in the agricultural economy, in basic grain and export production, was cast into serious doubt (Collier 106).

The structural adjustment programs introduced under the administration of Miguel de la Madrid (1982–1988) were nothing short of devastating for the rural sector, and especially the small-holding indigenous peasant producers in Chiapas. Peasant producers in the highlands and in the Lacandón jungle had borrowed money and reoriented production toward coffee and cattle, and to a lesser degree toward soy and sorghum. They had followed the path paved by government incentives and World Bank projects. With a characteristic flip-flop, the World Bank now prescribed the privatization of state-owned industry and the elimination of subsidies in response to Mexico's debt crisis. De la Madrid complied, making huge cutbacks in rural credit programs and coffee assistance programs.[39] In 1989, one year after taking office, Salinas began privatizing INMECAFE and eliminating all its technical assistance programs.[40] In the absence of INMECAFE, marketing and transportation costs were passed on completely to the producers just as credit shrank. This was followed by the 50 percent drop in the international price of coffee in 1989: "With less income and the simultaneous reduction of credit, thousands of growers were unable to invest in their crop. Both productivity and total output in the social sector fell by around 35 percent between 1989 and 1993. On average, small producers suffered a 70 percent drop in income in the same period. Most producers were caught in a cycle of debt and poverty. Unable to repay loans due to the fall in prices and income, they became ineligible for new loans. The accumulation of debts in this sector reached approximately U.S. $270 million by the end of 1993. In these conditions thousands of small growers in Chiapas abandoned production in 1989–93" (Harvey, *Rebellion in Chiapas* 11). The question is, where did they go?[41]

In the new frontier of the free market in rural Mexico, peasants had nowhere to hide. When Salinas de Gotarí included corn and beans, and agrarian reform, in NAFTA negotiations, he signaled the end of ejido- and communal-farm-based agriculture for Mexico. Salinas may have cropped the peasant classes out of his neoliberal snapshot of a modernized Mexico because he saw them as relics of another era, their production techniques backward and inefficient, their communally held lands wastefully under-utilized. Certainly, in comparison with the seemingly endless fields of computerized basic grain production in the central United States, peasant production techniques in Mexico appear outdated, their crops overpriced, their land underdeveloped. But from the point of view of the indigenous peasants of Chiapas who had participated in oil-led growth, for better or worse, they were already fully imbricated in Mexico's modernized economy and culture by the time Salinas stepped in, dressed in his technocratic dream coat, anxious to liberalize trade with the United States and capitalize Mexico's area of comparative advantage: the abundance of cheap wage labor. The PRI had historically and politically maintained a place for a mass-based, small-scale peasantry in the Mexican revolutionary imaginary. Indeed, the peasantry was one of the three fundamental bases of support within the PRI's corporativist structure. Under salinismo, though, these peasants became expendable; their production was viewed as marginal. As such, they must be displaced by commercial agriculture devoted to the production of what Arturo Escobar has called "modern food," "fully commodified and industrially produced food products of remarkable uniformity" (*Encountering Development* 163). The administrations of Echeverría and López Portillo may have seen their investment efforts as an attempt to save the small-scale peasantry, a historical base of support for the 1910 revolution and party, by integrating them into export agriculture. From Salinas's perspective, these administrations only forestalled making an inevitable decision on the fate of small-scale peasant production in a modern economy. Salinas's neoliberal policies in agriculture withdrew the social contract between the state and peasant subjects that had existed since the 1917 Constitution, with its Article 27, and had been renewed under the Echeverría and López Portillo administrations.

In sharp contrast, Salinas revitalized indigenismo policy by increasing funds to indigenist institutions and by bringing Ladino authorities on indigenismo, such as Arturo Warman, into his cabinet. At best, Salinas's pro-indigenismo stance may be read as inconsistent with policies geared toward eliminating the peasantry. At worst, this stance makes evident a historical contradiction in the PRI's policy toward indigenous people, a contradiction that lies at the heart of mestizaje and peasant agrarianism. In the contrast between the revitalizing of indigenismo policy and the shutting down of economic and political options for peasants, the Salinas administration imagined that it was possible to eliminate the peasantry as an economic formation while maintaining indigenous peoples as a cultural formation.[42] However, colonial and postcolonial regimes of subjection, including the PRI's corporativist model of revolutionary mestizaje, have precisely articulated economic processes with cultural formations in the production and reproduction of Indian difference. This is certainly the case in the Lacandón jungle, where a shifting discourse of economic development (through the 1970s, 1980s, and 1990s) articulated with everyday indigenous cultural practices to produce the Zapatistas, a discretely new Indian difference.

Salinismo's contrasting policies reveal that the PRI's corporativist state-client relations have historically been predicated on an artificial division between economic identity and ethnic identity, between political citizenship and cultural citizenship in the nation. This is a relation that the PRI's nationalist imaginary promulgated into being with its separation of agricultural and indigenist policies. Lázaro Cárdenas was a major proponent of indigenismo. Under his administration, numerous cultural and educational institutes for the implementation of indigenismo policy were established throughout the country. His administration organized and hosted the first inter-American indigenist conference, held in Patzcuaro, Michoacan, in 1940. Although he is regarded as one of the greatest advocates of indigenous peoples in Mexican history, he is also responsible for institutionalizing the corporativist model of governing adopted by the PRI party he helped to found (Krauze 446–47, 470–73). This corporativist model effectively excluded the indigenous population from participating in political life *as Indians.*

In the PRI's corporativist model of revolutionary government, the body politic (the corpus) is imagined as being made up of separate limbs, of various constituencies of "popular subjects": industrial workers, peasants, members of popular organizations (i.e., intellectuals, artistic, teachers). Each group participates in a separate patron-client relationship with the PRI party, tying it vertically to the state. These groups are represented as clients before the state by their respective para-state union, all founded during the Cárdenas presidency: for example, the Mexican Workers Confederation (CTM) for workers (founded in 1936); the National Peasants Confederation (CNC) for peasants (founded in 1938); and the National Confederation of Popular Organizations (CNOP) for members of other mass-based groups. For seventy years, these unions, on behalf of their constituencies, negotiated directly and regularly with the PRI state the terms of their members' economic and political inclusion in the country in exchange for electoral support.[43] Immediately following the revolution, indigenous populations were represented as one such client before the revolutionary state, eligible for separate representation. Indeed, Gamio insisted on the importance of separate indigenous representation before the revolutionary government and argued for the importance of indigenous representation in the legislature (75–78).

This representation of the revolutionary nation as a body made up of separate limbs repeatedly thwarts indigenous subjectivity, however, by relegating it to a subordinate role in the processes of identifying with the state. This corporativist model hails the indigenous peasant subaltern not once but twice: once as peasant and once as Indian. But it is the peasant identification that is clearly primary, as the subsuming of the indigenous popular subject within CNOP early in the revolutionary process makes evident. In the political manifestation of the discourse of mestizaje, Indian difference is subsumed within the body politic as a cultural supplement to the peasantry, the class of political subjects worthy of direct representation before the state. It is with peasant subjectivity that the indigenous subalterns are repeatedly called to identify as revolutionary actors. PRI agrarianism performed a subordinating division between economic and ethnic subjectivity.

The agrarian reform statute in the 1917 Mexican constitution, Article 27, extended land rights to landless and land-poor peasants in the form of ejidos and communal farms. It granted separate and discrete ejidos to ethnically identified, clan-based indigenous groups who could establish they had historically formed a community by proving their status as a township dating back to the colonial period. Groups of landless or land-poor peasants who were not so related, or could not document this relation, were granted communal farms. Ejidos granted under this article recognized the centrality of the townships in the production and reproduction of Indian difference, a recognition demanded principally by Zapata and his troops in the original *Plan de Ayala* and the Zapatista Agrarian Law (Womack, *Zapata* 393–411).[44] While rewarding indigenous towns the lands wrongly stripped from them under nineteenth-century liberalism, the ejidos were also a strategic reformulation of a colonial technique of governmentality for the management of Indian difference. On the one hand, the ejidos provided for the continued production and reproduction of the Indian difference, as this difference was necessary in the revolutionary origin story in all the ways discussed earlier in this chapter. On the other hand, the ejidos allowed for the containment of Indian difference when this difference was perceived as threatening to national unity. Though Indians were not contained geographically to their ejidos as they had been to the colonial townships, the ejido structure contained Indian difference in another way, by once again subordinating their ethnic identity as Indians to their economic identity as peasants. It is at this moment that the discourse of mestizaje dovetails with a discourse of development expressed through agrarian policy to produce a revolutionary regime of subjection: The processes of subjection of both discourses conjoin to produce a de-ethnicized peasant polity.

The CNC represented the beneficiaries of agrarian reform as peasant-clients before the state, equal to the worker-client, and the popular-client. The beneficiaries' primary political organization was only interested in pursuing the narrow rights these clients had before the state *as peasants:* the adjudication of further land disputes, the distribution of state resources for the purposes of agricultural production. Any rights these Indian subalterns might have to culturally appropriate education, to official recognition of indigenous language usage, to political representation *as Indians,* were relegated to the series of temporary offices set up under a series of presidencies that were finally formalized as the National Indigenist Institute (INI) in 1948. Indeed, the 1917 agrarian reform statute does not formally recognize the cultural or political rights of Indians as citizens. Thus revolutionary agrarianism contained an inherent contradiction: through agrarian reform, the state simultaneously invoked the *ejidatarios'* Indian identity as the basis of their claim to the land, while requiring the suppression of this difference when claiming the recognition of their economic or political rights as equal citizens before the state.

Although thousands of farm titles were granted under Article 27, benefiting hundreds of thousands of indigenous peasants, Indianist[45] activists have argued that Article 27 was, in fundamental ways, a hindrance to indigenous rights as such (Burguete interview, April 1996; Ruiz interview, April 1997).[46] Recipients of both ejidos and communal farms have economic rights over these farms, but no political rights over these parcels (to self-government, or to the administration of natural resources, for example), and certainly no cultural rights as tribes over their historical domains (to language usage or bicultural education, for example). Agrarian reform, as it took place, precluded the granting of territorial rights over historical domain to associations of indigenous people, rights that may have extended beyond the level of the family or village and would have acknowledged the integrated nature of ethnic and economic identity.[47]

In other words, I would suggest, territorial rights would have recognized a process of identification that privileged indigenous subjectivity, rather than one that privileged disidentification by separating class rights from ethnic ones. Agrarian reform, as it was implemented in Mexico, privileges just such a disidentification. Indeed, agrarian reform performs the division between ethnic and class identity, subordinating ethnic identity to economic identity in the service of the embedded discourses of mestizaje and development that privileged the de-Indianized peasant identity as the modern form of citizen. As I have argued in chapters 2 through 4, post–World War II revolutionary movements often replicated this discursive division between ethnic and economic identity in their pursuit of revolutionary ideals of subjectivity, citizenship, and nation. And yet the historical record examined here, of the articulation of economic processes of exploitation with cultural formations to produce Indian difference, makes evident the impossibility of this division. It is this developmentalist division—a revolutionary mathematics of identity—that the Zapatistas have repeatedly rejected and defied. Salinas's neoliberal policies made manifest the historic contradiction between peasant and indigenous identity within the PRI's corporativist model. The Zapatistas turned this contradiction into a pitched antagonism with their insurrection on 1 January 1994. No sooner had the EZLN started their insurrection, however, than the Mexican people took to the street en masse, demanding a negotiated settlement from the government rather than a military solution. By mid-February, the two sides had agreed to a cease-fire. Having suspended their armed struggle, however, the Zapatistas have successfully maintained this contradiction at the level of antagonism through their communiqués and through the negotiation process.

Death by Development:
"Dolor, pena, muerte, y . . . silencio"

Over the past eight years the Zapatistas have produced two substantial archives. The public record of the negotiation process, including the San Andres Accords on Indigenous Rights and Culture, is an archive offering insight into the reformulation of revolutionary citizenship by the EZLN. Throughout the negotiation process with the government, the Zapatistas have repeatedly expanded the scope of the negotiations to include the rest of the nation. They do so through the strategic public performance of democratic practice, repeatedly calling for and hosting national and international forums, conventions, and delegations on issues of social justice, indigenous rights, and representative democracy. The second archive is composed of the communiqués issued by the EZLN's Clandestine Revolutionary Indigenous Committee—General Command (CCRI), by Subcomandante Marcos, or by Marcos in the name of CCRI. Much has been made of Marcos's impressive literary style and range; however, I will focus on the CCRI's communiqués as a counterpunctual discourse emerging from silence, as expressed in one of their early communiqués: "In the silence we died, living in silence. But in the 'nothing is happening' our steps were walking. With tender care we guarded our fierce word. In silence, we were speaking" (14 April 1994).

The CCRI communiqués mark a transitional moment for the indigenous subaltern in Mexico, documenting an intervention into a Western notion of historical time. This is certainly not the first or the last such intervention by indigenous populations in the Americas, but through the communiqués, the EZLN, like Rigoberta Menchú in her autobiography, takes possession of the written word to write the indigenous subaltern into the historical time of the nation, once again offering us unique insight into the twentieth-century paradigm of revolution in the Americas. I read these archives together for the way in which the Zapatistas successfully occupy both the particularity of Indian identity and the universality of abstract citizenship, alternately manipulating the signifiers of Indian difference and representative democracy, to challenge the developmentalist paradigms of the Mexican Revolution embodied in the contradiction between ethnic and economic identities.

The initial communiqués issued by the EZLN only hint at the indigenous content of their struggle. In their first, the "Declaration from the Lacandón Jungle: Today We Say Enough!" dated 2 January 1994, the reference to the EZLN's indigenous makeup of their troops is indirect, suffused with other identifications:

> To the Mexican people:
> Mexican Brothers [and Sisters]:
> We are the product of 500 years of struggles: first against slavery in the war of Independence against Spain led by the insurgents, then to avoid being absorbed by North American expansionism, then to promulgate our Constitution and eject the French Empire from our soil, then the Porfirian dictatorship denied us the just application of the Reform laws and the people rebelled forming their own leaders, Villa and Zapata emerged, poor men like us . . . (Poniatowska and Monsiváis 33)[48]

In the aftermath of the Pan-American indigenous commemorations of the quincentennial anniversary of the conquest, the "500 years" immediately associates the EZLN with indigenous resistance. And yet the Zapatistas make no mention of the many Indian uprisings that took place prior to Mexico's independence from Spain. Instead they identify themselves with the various struggles establishing the geopolitical contours of the modern Mexican nation: struggles against Spain, against U.S. and French imperialist interventions, against the foreign-allied Porfirian dictatorship. Each of these events looms large in the narrative of national becoming institutionalized after the 1910 revolution in holidays, and in revolutionary art and architecture all over the country commemorating the mestizo protagonists of these events. In this gesture, then, the Zapatistas identify themselves as the "product" of nation-state formation, placing themselves within the historical time of the nation. However, they are also displacing the mestizo icons usually associated with its formation, staking a claim for indigenous peoples as the primary agents in the narrative of the formation of the nation. For each of these struggles is now suffused with indigenous content. Taking a page out of Gamio's own ode to mestizaje, in this passage, the desire for nationhood finds its true origin in the very reference to "500 years," in indigenous struggle that portends the nation from the moment of colonization.[49]

Similarly, the super-sized icons of the Mexican Revolution, Villa and Zapata, are transformed from heroic figures generally represented as mestizos to "poor men like us," denied access to education, decent housing, land, work, health, food, and democracy (33). Thus, in the second paragraph, when the Zapatistas begin with "we are the heirs of the true forgers of our nationalism," they echo Gamio. They allude to Zapata and Villa, but only insofar as these two men have become one with the "true forgers" of nationalism, the EZLN's indigenous ancestors. The communiqué immediately follows with: "*the dispossessed* are millions and we call all our brothers [and sisters] to join [us] on the only road [left] for not dying of hunger before the insatiable ambition of this dictatorship of more than 70 years" (33; italics mine).[50] "Dispossessed" signifies doubly in this sentence: the dispossession of the poor who are "dying of hunger," but also the dispossession of the original inhabitants of the Americas. Using a dichotomy made familiar by the discourse of mestizaje, the Zapatistas identify themselves as the original inhabitants of Mexico, while members of the PRI dictatorship are repeatedly characterized as the interloping foreigners, as a "coterie of traitors," and as *"vendepatrias"* (33). Members of the PRI dictatorship are one and the same as those who opposed the independence leaders Hidalgo, Morelos, and Guerrero; who "sold more than half of our soil to the *foreign* invader"; who "brought a *European* prince to govern us" (referring to Maximilian of Austria); and who, in an utterly ironic reference, "opposed the expropriation of petroleum" (from U.S. capitalists) (33; italics mine). Although the Zapatistas never explicitly refer to themselves as indigenous peoples in this first communiqué, they nevertheless operate from within the discursive terms made available by mestizaje. They appropriate for themselves the representation of Indian difference as the authentication of nationalism and displace the PRI as the true inheritors of the 1910 revolution.

The EZLN's appropriation of Indian difference necessarily redefines it, however. If mestizaje posits Indian difference as an originary moment in the formation of national consciousness to be superseded by mestizo universality, the Zapatistas posit authenticating Indian difference as moving forward through time to encompass and *redeem* the national consciousness of the mestizo. Thus, in the third and last indirect reference to their indigenous identity, the communiqué ends: "The dictators have been waging an undeclared genocidal war against our peoples [nuestros pueblos] since many years ago, thus we ask for your committed participation in supporting this plan for the Mexican people, [a plan] that struggles for *work, land, roof, food, health, education, independence, liberty, democracy, justice and peace*. We declare that we will not stop fighting until we achieve the fulfillment of these basic demands of our people [nuestro pueblo], forming a free and democratic government for our country" (35). The "genocidal" war establishes an indigenous *we* (nuestros pueblos) and a nonindigenous *they*, a mestizo readership from whom the Zapatistas solicit "committed participation." They once again call on their Mexican brothers and sisters to join them in struggle. Surprisingly, though, the readers are not called to participate directly in the struggle against a genocidal war. Instead they are called on to support a "plan for the Mexican people" consisting of eleven points. By the end of the passage there is only one nation: "our people," "our country." Mediating the movement from multiple indigenous and nonindigenous peoples to one nation, from *pueblos* to *pueblo*, then, is this eleven-point plan, each point significant in that it is *already guaranteed* in the 1917 Constitution. Thus the Zapatistas are not articulating a new set of demands for "the Mexican people"; rather, they are reanimating the social contract already established by the 1910 revolution. Importantly, not one of these eleven points appears to address specifically ethnic concerns, yet these are the points invoked by the Zapatistas as the remedy to a genocidal war waged through Salinas's anti-peasant policies. After all, it is the neoliberal policies put in place by his administration that signal the abandonment of this contract. With their own defense of the 1910 revolution and this historic social contract, the Zapatistas displace mestizaje as the discourse mediating the movement from multiple nations to one with their own patriotic discourse. Just as they suffused the geopolitical struggles establishing the Mexican nation with indigenous content, the EZLN suffused the social contract promised by the 1910 revolution with indigenous content through their redemption of it.

Though the EZLN begins and ends this first communiqué with implicit references to indigenous specificity, it is nevertheless significant that they refrain from identifying themselves explicitly as Indians, or identifying their movement as an indigenous one. Instead, sandwiched between these opening and closing references, the communiqué identifies the EZLN with a very different kind of movement: "We have the Mexican people on our side, we have *Patria*, and the tri-colored flag is loved and respected by all our INSURGENT combatants, we use the colors red and black on our uniform, symbols of the working people in their struggles and strikes, our flag bears the letters 'EZLN,' ZAPATISTA NATIONAL LIBERATION ARMY, and with it we will go into battle always" (34). Critics insist on the postmodern nature of the EZLN and on disassociating it from the class-based Central American revolutions in Guatemala, El Salvador, and Nicaragua. However, the EZLN places itself within this genealogy in this first communiqué (Burbach 1994). The love of "Patria," the emphasis on the word "insurgent," the use of the colors red and black, the identification with working peoples, and even the formal structure of their name all associate the EZLN with the Central American revolutions of the 1970s and 1980s.[51] Like the Sandinista National Liberation Front (FSLN) in Nicaragua and the Faribundo Marti National Liberation Front (FMLN) in El Salvador, the EZLN takes its name from an early-twentieth-century figure considered to be the foremost nationalist and revolutionary in their country, and they set out to fulfill this figure's pending mission: national liberation.[52] If the Zapatistas actively place themselves in this genealogy, there is a certain circularity implied in doing so. For if the Zapatistas are the last of the twentieth-century revolutions in the Americas, and specifically of the Central American revolutions, they are mirroring the *first* such revolution by choosing Zapata as their guide. By following in the footsteps of the Central American revolutions, they follow in the footsteps of the 1910 Mexican revolution, the paradigmatic revolution for Latin America in the twentieth century. Faribundo Marti and Augusto C. Sandino, both of whom led major revolutionary movements in their respective countries in the 1930s, were highly influenced by the Mexican revolution. In fact, Sandino, a political exile, lived and worked in Mexico during the 1920s, before returning to Nicaragua to launch his own liberation campaign. Thus, by placing itself in this genealogy, the EZLN claims—reclaims?—the entire century's revolutionary tradition in the Americas for indigenous struggle.

There would appear to be a contradiction, a psychic split, between the indigenous identification implied in the beginning and ending passages of this communiqué, and the class identification implied in this middle passage, devoid as it is of all reference to Indian specificity. But the communiqué as a whole articulates a double refusal of this psychic split between ethnicity and class. The Zapatistas notably refuse to name themselves as an indigenous movement. In both the opening and closing passages, they articulate Indian specificity with the *national* scope of their movement. In the intervening passage, they go even further than this by claiming a revolutionary tradition that at once finds its origins in Mexico and exceeds its national boundaries. Precisely because their identification with this revolutionary paradigm is bracketed by opening and closing references to indigenous specificity, however, I would suggest that they force a reinterpretation of this revolutionary paradigm, as well. By claiming for themselves this anti-imperialist Central American genealogy of national liberation, they reject a revolutionary paradigm that has historically de-ethnicized revolutionary subjectivity in favor of classed-based identity. By bringing the implicit identifications at the beginning, middle, and end of their communiqué together, they attempt to maintain ethnic and class identity in dynamic relation with each other, refusing to privilege either.

On my first research trip to San Cristobal, Chiapas, in April 1994, perplexed about the nature of the EZLN, I asked a member of the Labor Party (PT), Alfonso "Poncho" Carrión, if he considered the EZLN to be an Indianist movement.[53] Carrión insisted the EZLN was not an indigenous movement but an agrarian movement, emphasizing that the first "Declaración" mentioned nothing about racial discrimination. Wavering, though, he added: "Then again, racial discrimination is also because you arrive [someplace] dirty and badly dressed. With the indigenous people [discrimination] happens more because they are the most worst off, always." Carrión attests to how profoundly class is racialized in Mexico. Even if a person is not an Indian, if he or she is poor, dirty, badly dressed, or hardworking, then he or she is rendered an "Indian" in the eyes of government bureaucrats and the bourgeoisie. It also testifies to how race strictly determines class position in Mexico, becoming the "common sense," as all Indians are uniformly always "the most worst off." Carrión continued, once again changing course, "Then again, on the coast [of Chiapas] there are no Indians. In Tapachula, for example, the general economic level of the [nonindigenous] peasants is the same as in the center of the country, and nevertheless they talk of large movements [happening] there since January." Because the Zapatista movement has galvanized the (relatively) wealthier peasant class on the coast, Carrión finds his initial opinion reaffirmed—the Zapatistas cannot be an indigenous movement, since their appeal extends beyond Indians to the wealthier, nonindigenous peasants of Tapachula, among whom "large movements" are taking place.

Carrión's reluctance in labeling the Zapatista movement "indigenous" is symptomatic of the developmentalism inherent in the revolutionary paradigm in Mexico and Central America. He does not believe an ethnically specific movement could have universal appeal, though he himself provides the evidence to the contrary: peasant movements inspired by the Zapatista cause are emerging all over the state. Though Carrión also finds it difficult to disarticulate ethnic from class identity in Mexico, his comments betray a continued belief that ethnic specificity must be superseded by class interests for a revolutionary transformation to take place (and in its wake, modernity). This attitude among the Left in Mexico helps to explain the Zapatistas' own reluctance in asserting their ethnic specificity. Even for sympathizers like Carrión, particularizing the EZLN's struggle would automatically limit its purpose and scope. And yet Carrión provides an analysis of why an ethnically specific movement has universal ramifications in Mexico: if poor, then Indian. Carrión's words lend new insight into the Zapatistas' rhetorical appropriation of Villa and Zapata as "poor men like us." By being "poor men," these two national icons are clearly Indian by association. Indianizing the two most famous heroes of the 1910 revolution necessarily revalues the derogatory phrase "like an Indian," draining it of negative associations and filling it with patriotism, valor, honor, honesty, for all of the poor constituents of the Mexican nation. In practice and in print, the Zapatistas repeatedly thwart the artificial division between ethnic and economic (ergo political) identity institutionalized by revolutionary nationalism through the discourses of mestizaje and development.

On 18 January 1994 CCRI released a half-dozen communiqués, including one dated 6 January. In it, the EZLN "comes out" as an indigenous force to counter government assertions about "foreign elements" having organized the EZLN. Thus, after insisting that neither the FMLN and URNG nor the local Catholic Church played a role in organizing the Zapatistas, CCRI declares most of the EZLN's soldiers and all of its commanders to be indigenous, primarily Chol, Tojolabal, Tzotzil, and Tzeltal. After all, what better way to counter the government's accusation of inauthenticity than by assuming your place as the most authentic Mexicans of all: the original inhabitants of the Americas. Once again, however, the EZLN emphasizes the national importance of their struggle. The communiqué begins with CCRI indicating they have started this war to let the world know about "the miserable conditions in which millions of Mexicans live and die, especially we the indigenous" (72–73). And yet the causes for this poverty are not to be found in the failure of government agricultural policies, in neoliberal economics, or even in the racism institutionalized at every level of Mexican society. Instead, the communiqué explains: "The grave conditions of poverty among our compatriots have one common cause: *the lack of liberty and democracy.* We believe that the authentic respect of liberties and the democratic will of the people are the indispensable prerequisites for bettering the economic and social conditions of the dispossessed of our country. For this reason, just as we hoist the flag for the betterment of living conditions for the Mexican people, we present the demand for liberty and democratic politics" (73; italics mine).

Immediately following the insurrection, political analysts from all points on the ideological spectrum suggested that the Mexican Revolution had never arrived in Chiapas. According to this analysis, economically, Chiapas resembled Central America more than it did the rest of Mexico and thus provided the conditions of extreme wealth and poverty generating rebellion.[54] This line of analysis served the Salinas administration's interest in representing Chiapas as exceptional, and in characterizing the insurrection as a local reaction to these exceptional conditions. By identifying the source of Mexico's problems as its lack of democracy, the EZLN refuses to have the reasons for their struggle reduced to a set of economic indicators, or to place it outside of the Mexican context. Instead they echoed the aspirations of millions of Mexicans frustrated with the PRI dictatorship and circumvented any attempt by the Salinas administration to resolve this problem by simply promising more development aid to Chiapas. After all, the EZLN's insistence on democracy is precisely the result of their experience with PRI development in the 1970s and 1980s. As demonstrated in the previous section, the revolution *did* arrive to the highland and jungle areas of Chiapas, however belatedly. The communities that make up the base of support for the Zapatista forces were not somehow left out of the Mexican development model, or an obstacle to it. Rather, as peasant producers, they were its targeted beneficiaries. The Zapatistas were produced by, within—but also in excess of—the nation-state's discourse of development.

In our initial interview, Carríon ruminated on his experience with the third-tier credit cooperative UU-Pajal Yakactic, one of the first UUs formed in the Lacandón, operating between 1982 and 1989.[55]

> We built economies, but we forgot, or we were incapable of continuing to build a fundamentally political organization. . . . Now it's clear to me that we could not have constructed something different from the static models of development [we were working with] . . . this became obvious when the price of coffee dropped. Pajal had producers in both coffee and corn, but mostly coffee. The coffee producers subsidized the corn producers, and this was a very exciting and interesting stage. But when the coffee prices fell, we were bankrupt. We had bought high and sold low. . . . We did improve people's standard of living considerably. Just as their were problems, there were results. . . .

But for the integral development that we wanted, we learned that you have to be in a position of real power, in other words, in the municipal presidency. Even though these people had economic power, the communities didn't have schools, potable water, enough services. They needed to have double the economic power, and what we needed fundamentally was political power. (Carríon interview)

Once again, Carríon's experience working with the Zapatista base offers fresh insight into the communiqués. When the Zapatistas insist in the 6 January communiqué that "the authentic respect of liberties and the democratic will of the people are the indispensable pre-requisites for bettering the economic and social conditions of the dispossessed of our country," they are speaking from their experience of development without democracy in the Lacandón. The EZLN is also acutely aware of how local "economic and social conditions" in Chiapas, indeed all over Mexico, are traversed by national politics of globalization. Through the expression of "the democratic will of the people," I would suggest, the Zapatistas seek control not only of local development projects but of the national economic and political vision. Salinas's neoliberal reforms wrote the Zapatistas out of the PRI's corporativist script *as peasants*. The Zapatistas, however, write themselves back into the script not as peasants or as Indians but as "the people"—ethnically inflected political subjects seeking authorship not only of their lives but of the terms of their national inscription. They refuse division between the ethnic and the economic, the local and the national, by methodically appropriating Indian difference produced by mestizaje and developmentalism as the very grounds for exclusion from the project of modernity, and then by generalizing this exclusion to include millions of other disenfranchised Mexicans.

This 6 January communiqué puts into play the dialogic relationship between ethnic and economic subjectivity through a complex interplay of voices that sets a pattern for communiqués to come. The body of this communiqué is written in the standard rhetoric of class-based revolution. The CCRI iterates demands, enumerates the just causes for insurrection, authenticates the national origin of troops, tabulates dead and wounded, and puts forth minimal conditions for dialogue with the government in the fairly formal language of negotiation. The communiqué is prefaced with an epigraph, however, written in a very different voice, one that will recur: "Here we are, the dead of always, dying once again, but this time to live" (72).[56] This invocation of "the dead of always" is a recognition of the Zapatistas' positionality as Indians within the terms of national inscription. On one level, the Zapatistas refer to the extreme conditions of marginalization in which they live as poor peasants, conditions that maintain them in a metaphorical state of death. On another level, the Zapatistas tap into the representation of Indian difference as produced by the discourse of mestizaje: indigenous people as the living dead, as the living museum of Mexico's culture, as living relics, as living ancestors of the modern mestizo citizen. Once again, though, they are appropriating these terms for themselves, for "the dead of always" suggests a syncretic identity existing outside of chronological time: they were here/have always been here/are here/will always be here. Naming themselves in this way, the Zapatistas stake a claim in a cyclical identity which refuses a mestizo future in favor of an imminent present. The epigraph of another communiqué released in this batch reinforces this interpretation: "Our voice started walking centuries ago and it shall not be quieted ever again." Their voice and the voices of their ancestors are one and the same, and in future communiqués the EZLN uses "the dead of always" to refer to themselves and their ancestors interchangeably. And yet both of these epigraphs register a transition: their voice shall not be quieted *again;* in dying, they restore life. The appropriation of Christian rhetoric, of the resurrection theme, not only makes evident the influence of liberation theology on the Zapatistas but also registers an entry by the subaltern into Western historical time. What better way to demand an entry into Western history than by appropriating the foundational act of the Gregorian calendar? It is, after all, Christ's death that gives meaning to his birth. The Zapatistas take possession of speech and writing, authorizing themselves through these messianic communiqués.

There is yet another ghostly apparition in this invocation of "the dead of always," for if the Zapatistas enter the historical time of the nation through their communiqués and through their democratic speech, they do so from the position of subjects who were always already there. The PRI severed Indians from political participation in the revolution with the party's exclusion of them from their corporativist model of politics, but now Indians, like a phantom limb, haunt the body politic, reminding it of its nationalist duty. In a communiqué released for the commemoration of International Worker Day, CCRI analyzes the Mexican workers' struggle from this ghostly position: "Mexican workers of the city and the countryside: May your voice walk together with ours. May your cry sound loudly and firmly on this soil. Accept the arm your smallest brothers (*hermanos más pequeños*) extend you. Three forces should unite: the force of the workers, the force of the peasants, the popular force. With these three forces nothing can stop us." The Zapatistas hail the three pillars of corporativist politics: the workers, the peasants, and the popular front. Notably, they nowhere suggest adding the indigenous population as a fourth pillar to this historical triumvirate of revolutionary power. Instead, like a ubiquitous ghost in the machine, they reanimate the body politic that has historically excluded them with their "may," "accept," and "should unite," issued as both blessing and imperative. They haunt the body politic by being everywhere and nowhere at once. In this three-page communiqué, the CCRI never identifies the Zapatistas forces as workers, peasants, or members of the popular front, and yet, as omniscient narrators, they occupy all of these positions: "With these *three* forces nothing can stop *us*." Once again, they extend the terms of indigenous exclusion, referring to the working class as "dying" and as "faceless" ("sin rostro") (230–31).[57] However, the Zapatistas rely on another permutation of mestizaje to produce this identification with the Mexican body politic, because every mestizo bears the imprint of Indian difference, carries the Indian hidden inside. Thus, when Mexican workers, peasants, and popular forces all over the country took to the streets in defense of the Zapatistas with chants of "¡Todos somos indios!" (We are all Indians!), they were recognizing the Indian in themselves. Given Mexico's racial ideology, such an identification with contemporary Indians among mestizos would have been inconceivable before the Zapatistas. Today mestizos are responding to the EZLN's hail, recognizing the Indian in the national imaginary.

For what is arguably the first time in Mexican history, indigenous people are resignifying the meaning of Indian difference at the national level. Until the Zapatista uprising, the signification of Indian difference responded to the exigencies of colonial and postcolonial governmentality. For modern revolutionary Mexico, Indian difference has simultaneously signified "folkloric cultural backdrop" and "abject premodern residual." The Zapatistas have disrupted the semiotic chain of national meaning with their insurrection and with their subsequent antagonistic speech and writing, but they have disrupted it in the only way possible, by occupying the terms of signification made available by it: they persistently write in a folkloric authorial voice, thematizing their own abject state as Indians. In doing so, they stretch the limits of Indian difference to include self-authored Indian experience and specificity. Not all the communiqués are written in this folkloric voice or on this theme. Indeed, many are written in the incendiary rhetoric of revolution, in the reportage of military operations, or in the diplomatic language of negotiation. It is precisely the contrast between these communiqués written in the technical voice of guerrilla operations and those written in the folkloric voice of autoethnographic representation that draws attention to the counterpunctual performativity of the latter. The communiqués written in this counterpunctual folkloric voice are most often addressed to other indigenous groups in Mexico or to the general Mexican population, and they take the form of origin stories, communicating to the outsider the basis of their being and struggle.

The first such "origin story" was written in response to a letter sent to the EZLN by the "500 Years of Indigenous Resistance Council," an organization from the state of Guerrero formed in the late 1980s in preparation for the national indigenous commemoration of the quincentennial. The communiqué was issued on 1 February 1994 and published in the national media. The EZLN begins by formally thanking the council for their strong "words" (sus palabras de ustedes) of support "in the name of all indigenous and nonindigenous Mexicans" (119). The communiqué continues:

> In our hearts there was so much pain (dolor), so great was our death and our misery (pena), brothers [and sisters], that it no longer fit in this world that our grandparents left us to continue to live and fight in. So great was our pain and misery that it no longer fit in the hearts of a few, and it overflowed, and other hearts were filled with pain and misery, and it filled the hearts of the oldest and wisest in our communities, and it filled the hearts of young men and women, all of them brave, and it filled the hearts of the children, even the smallest ones, and it filled the hearts of the animals and plants, it filled the hearts of the rocks as well, and all of our world was filled with pain and misery, and the sun and the wind felt pain and misery, and the earth felt pain and misery. Everything was misery and pain, everything was silence.
> (119)

Immediately we are in a world within a world, the "world that our grandparents left us," referencing the premodern residual in Indian difference. The oral quality of the folkloric voice is communicated in the run-on structure of the second sentence, with its multiple use of "and" and the repetitive structure of each phrase. The prosopopeic rendering of animals, plants, rocks, wind, earth, and light plays with anthropological representations of indigenous people living in harmonious relation with their environment, while simultaneously naturalizing their abjection, their pain and misery. And this pain and misery, pumping through all the hearts of all the people, plants, animals, and elements in their world, transpires in the proverbial silence of the Indian.

Such a reading, leaving all the conventional significations of Indian difference in place, is seductively present in the text; however, the EZLN is also certainly unsettling these significations for "all indigenous and non-indigenous Mexicans." For "everything was silence" is reminiscent of the silence of the clearing at Oventic, with which I began this chapter. The silence described in this communiqué, like the silence performed communally in Oventic, is not the absence of sound but the condition of possibility for registering its fullness, for hearing the musicality of noise. Silence here is the backbeat or counter-time of noise. In the sensuality of silence, inanimate objects are animated, and the Zapatista community hears hearts pumping in the natural world around them. In the sensuality of silence, the Zapatistas hear the fullness of the pain and misery of their communal situation. And as in Oventic, silence is not the silencing of difference but the sensual alertness that allows differences to emerge. Silence is the clearing that makes speech possible, not because it stands in a dichotomous relation to speech, as contentless space, but precisely because it is in the fullness of silence where differences take shape: "In silence, we were speaking." Silence is the noise of democracy. Thus the communiqués written in this voice are not only counterpunctual because they provide a folkloric accent to the communiqués written in the technical voice of guerrilla action; they are counterpunctual because they emerge from the silence existing between the beats of the discourses of mestizaje and developmentalism.

While these communiqués register the musicality existing in the silence, they also make evident the processes of translation and transcription necessary for communicating the content of silence. The communiqué continues:

> Then the pain that united us made us speak, and we recognized that in our words there was truth, we knew that not only misery and pain inhabited our language, we discovered that there was still hope in our breasts. We spoke with ourselves, we looked inside our [collective] self and we saw our history: we saw our greatest ancestors suffer and fight, we saw our grandparents fight, we saw our parents with fury in their hands, and we saw that not everything had been taken away from us, that we had . . . what makes us lift our step above the plants and animals, what places the rocks beneath our feet, and we saw, brothers [and sisters], that DIGNITY was everything we had . . .
>
> And then in our heart there was no longer only misery and pain, fury arrived, courage came to us through the mouths of our oldest

[ancestors] already dead, but alive once again in our dignity which they gave us. And we saw that it was wrong to die of misery and pain, that it was wrong to die without a fight. . . . Then our hands sought liberty and justice, then our hands, empty of hope, were filled with fire with which to voice and cry out our anguish and demands . . . "For all!" our heart cries . . . "For all!" cries our flowing blood, blossoming in the streets of the cities where lies and despoilment rule. (119)

The EZLN's speech translates the silence into language, emerging as it does directly from the pain they register in the silent community existing in the counter-time of mestizaje and development. Pain is translated into hope, misery into dignity, death into futurity. We are still in an anthropological world of oral tradition, where a history of subaltern silence is handed down through parents and grandparents; however, this is not a passive exchange but a creative act of translation. Oral tradition requires actively taking possession of language through speech: "we recognized that in our words there was *truth*." The act of recognizing the truth of their silence in their own words is also an act of re/cognizing the terms of indigenous representation: "we knew that not only misery and pain inhabited *our* language." The EZLN translate their silence into the conventions of folkloric speech to take possession of language as a discursive system—they rewrite the representations of indigenous experience in the twin discourses of mestizaje and development. They rewrite a history of abjection, signified in Indian difference, into a tradition of "fury," "fire," and "fight[ing]," rewriting "misery and pain" into dignity and courage. This "tradition" is passed down *"through the mouths* of our oldest [ancestors] already dead," but also through the act of transcribing their speech into the written word of the communiqués.

In the previous sentence, I placed "tradition" in quotes because auto-ethnographic representation, the act of colonized peoples representing themselves through "partial collaboration with and appropriation of the idioms of the conqueror," does not imply some kind of pure access to the referent, to unmediated Indian experience (Pratt 7–9). Rather, I would suggest that autoethnographic representation involves the active reconstruction of this experience: "We spoke with ourselves, we looked inside our [collective] self and we saw our history." Indian history is not manifest before them. Instead, "speaking with" and "looking at" imply collective investigation by mediating, self-reflective subjects. Representing this reconstructed history also requires its translation into a recognizable idiom for the conquerors. In transcribing the content of their speaking among themselves, the EZLN are actually involved in a double translation. They first reconstruct their grandparents' and parents' experience in silence as a history of never-ending struggle through the idiom of folkloric speech and then translate it once again into the idiom of twentieth-century revolutionary practice. Thus the speech that comes through the mouths of their ancestors is translated into the hands "filled with fire"—armed with the bullet and the pen—and seeking the liberal universals, "liberty and justice." Silence is broken through this translation and transcription. This is not an oral tradition made up of quaint and meaningful stories about Indians' pastoral existence, or even glorious stories of past empires and wars, but one that requires from the EZLN their "blood flowing, blossoming in the streets." Theirs is not a rural world apart, trapped in the folkloric, but a world in sync with—indeed, on a collision course with—the world of "cities where lies and despoilment rule."

The democratic content of silence, the counterpunctual act of speaking their word, and the idiomatic art of translating silence and the spoken word into the idioms of revolutionary practice and representative democracy are all paramount to the EZLN's project. In approximately half of the communiqués issued in the first nine months, for example, the EZLN begin by either invoking the right to "decir nuestra palabra," to speak their word, or thanking an organization or individual for having spoken "su palabra," their words, to the EZLN.[58] In what Subcomandante Marcos has called "the first uprising of the EZLN," the women in the EZLN are said to have demanded "the right to speak our word and have it respected" from their male colleagues in March 1993 (109). And in perhaps their most famous communiqué, "Mandar Obedeciendo," "To Rule by Obeying," their "word" as the translation of silence takes on divine connotations. This communiqué begins in the mythical past tense of the parable: "when the EZLN was just a shadow dragging itself amongst the fog and the darkness of the mountains, when the words justice, liberty and democracy were just that: words." During this mythical past, the "hombres verdaderos," the true or authentic men, spoke to a community through its elders, a community in which "silence had for a long time inhabited [the] house" (175–76).

The communiqué takes the form of a story within a story, as what these "true men" say to this silent community is set off from the rest of the text by quotation marks, but what they say is less a narrative than a treatise on good government. They tell of an earlier time when a previous community was seeking a means of self-government with "reason and will." This previous community followed a simple "path" of executing the will of the majority without disregarding the will of the minority (175). They follow a simple premise of ruling by obeying the heart of the community (176). It is at this juncture, the "true men" explain, that "another word came from far away so that this government could name itself, and that word named our path 'democracy,' but this was a path we had been following since before words could walk" (176). Eventually this community finds itself governed by others who do not follow this same path but instead rule by minority. At this point in the communiqué, the two communities have become one, and the reader realizes the "true men" have told the now silent community's history. The "true men" call on the now silent community to "search for men and women who will rule by obeying, who have strength in their word" (176). The EZLN then drops out of the extended quote, having heeded this call, and the communiqué continues: "The men and women of the EZLN, those without a face, those who walk in the night, those who are the mountains, look for words that other men will understand and they say: . . ." (177). At this point the communiqué radically switches voice, enumerating three demands in great detail: for free and fair elections, for the renunciation of the executive branch, and for the legal participation of nonpartisan groups in the election process.[59] The communiqué then switches voice again, closing with: "This is the word of the EZLN" (177).

Once again tapping into the convention of Indian difference as origin myth, the EZLN lulls the reader into a state of repose through an allegorical storytelling that borrows heavily from the tropes of the Popul Voh. In the first two-thirds of the communiqué, the EZLN speaks the word of its ancestors, "los hombres verdaderos," in the counterpunctual folkloric voice, telling of a utopian community that had representative forms of government long before colonization and independence brought liberal democracy to the Americas. Even when they drop out of the quoted word of the "true men," the EZLN continue in this folkloric voice, describing themselves in the third person as the faceless ones so conjoined with nature, so unmediated that they must search for words others will understand. Their rapid code switching into the vernacular of representative democracy, with their bulleted discussion of the ifs, whens, and hows of the electoral process, reveals the ruse and shocks the reader into a state of attention. Masters of folkloric allegory, the EZLN also show themselves to be masters of idiom of liberal democracy. However, the EZLN have not yet finished demonstrating their translating skills. They end the communiqué by mimicking the Christian convention for closing the gospel, "This is the word of Lord," and thereby infuse their speech with the righteousness of the divine. Their word, their multivoiced call for democracy, is doubly sacred—ordained by their ancestors and by God. Indian specificity is shown to contain all these different voices, and once again, the EZLN moves from the local to the national sphere without leaving the content of the local behind. The signification of Indian "difference" in mestizaje and development is once again disrupted as the idioms of liberal democracy and of Catholic liturgy are claimed as the idioms of the EZLN. Their recoding of the signifier "Indian difference" necessarily affects the content of all the other signifiers on the semiotic chain of national meaning. Patria, flag, community, liberty, Zapata, workers, peasants, corporativism, revolution, and, of course, mestizo are all resignified as the EZLN suffuse the national with indigenous specificity in their effort to resignify the meaning of Indian difference.

In these communiqués, the Zapatistas "speak their word" not only for themselves as Indians but for all Mexican nationals. Though the Zapatistas suggest that their model of democracy has been handed down to them from generation to generation, the specific permutations of "speaking our word" also have a much more recent origin in their experience as migrants to the Lacandón jungle. As I suggested in the previous section, the development of the Lacandón jungle articulated with everyday indigenous cultural practices to produce the Zapatistas, a discretely new form of Indian specificity. Similarly, their form of democracy is generated from the noise of the encounter between indigenous practice and the exigencies of economic development. Colonizing the jungle required a process of identification that departed significantly from the circumscribed, parochial identifications produced by the ejido structure, as well as from the de-ethnicizing identification of peasant agrarianism. The townships, ejidos, and communal farms that took shape in the Lacandón were no longer made up of a single ethnicity, as Tzeltal, Tzotzil, Chol, Tojolabal, and even Mixtec and Zapotec migrants from Oaxaca established multiethnic communities. Interethnic kinship relations developed within the new communities and also between community members from the various new colonies as settlement proceeded (Leyva Solano 207). Clearing the jungle, establishing towns, petitioning the state for land grants as communal farms or ejidos, preparing the conditions for agricultural production, pursuing government services geared toward this production: all these activities required a tremendous amount of organization, of interethnic cooperation, within and between the new colonies.

Among those migrating to the jungle, however, were highland Indians who had organizing experience to match this need: many Indians migrated after decades of involvement in unsuccessful struggles for acquiring new lands in the highlands as *comuneros;* Protestant Indians migrated after expulsion from their communities for refusing to submit to cacique demands for economic participation in Catholic rituals; dispossessed day laborers, after years of organizing for better working conditions on haciendas all over Chiapas, migrated in search of land, as did unemployed workers from the petroleum and hydroelectric projects (Gonzáles Casanova 346). Migration to the jungle also affected gender relations, as colonizing the jungle required that women play new and varied roles in the community. The Catholic Church was especially instrumental in training women to assume more positions of authority in the communities as they began recruiting lay catechists during this period of colonization, improving reading, writing, and orating skills among the women they trained.

The governing structures of these new multiethnic townships are based on principles of participatory democracy, and the town councils in the jungle townships vary in significant ways in makeup and function from the council of elders in the highlands townships. In the highlands, each village has a set of yearlong politico-religious duties that adult males—and only males—from the village take up on a rotating basis. Male members of the community who have discharged all of these duties may then pass onto the council of elders. This council of elders acts as a religious/political guide, regulating all social, political, and economic relationships among the members of the community. This council of elders functions hierarchically, modeled on familial relations between parents and children, with the children rarely disobeying the parents (Bartolomé 364–65). Migrants to the jungle broke with this tradition of gerontocracy, but they also revived indigenous traditions favoring horizontal structures of governance within the communities. They returned to regular town meetings and consensus as the basis for decision making. One Zapatista adviser, Luis Hernández Navarro, has called this insistence on voice, assembly, and consensus "neo-traditionalism" and sees it as a direct result of the struggle against the practice of *caciquismo* that historically propped up the PRI in highland communities ("Cuidadanos iguales" 33). Most notably, this reinvention of tradition by migrants facilitated participation in public community life by women. The migrants call this system of government *el común,* or government by "collective sentiment," as Xóchitl Leyva Solano, a Mexican anthropologist, has translated it.

Leyva worked for many years in the Las Cañadas region of the jungle, in a community made up of Tzeltal and Tojolabal Indians, where she observed the functioning of this type of self-government. El común, or this collective sentiment, emerges out of regularly held communal assemblies, according to Leyva:

> The communal assembly is the *formal* and *real* medium through which the individual members of the locality act, decide, analyze and think; it is the principal medium for making decisions. All men and women over the age of 16 attend, all of them have a voice [in the decision-making process] although in general the youth listen and the more mature men and women take charge of intervening. (208–9)

These assemblies last a minimum of three hours. They are moderated by a "council of authorities" who begin the meeting by presenting an agenda to the assembly. The assembly breaks into four smaller groups for discussion: two composed of women, two of men. These smaller groups then return to the plenary, where each group presents its opinions or solutions to the issues or problems at hand. Accords are thus reached on each point on the agenda for the day, and then a second set of accords are reached establishing the rights and obligations of each member of the community vis-à-vis the first accords. These accords, these agreements, are what constitute the collective sentiment for these communities in the jungle, and it is through this común that control over natural resources is determined and authority over all the town inhabitants exercised (210): "This authority is exercised thanks to the consent of all the inhabitants of the colony. The dominion of the común extends to all spheres of daily life (civic, political, economic, religious, ethical and moral)" (210).

Catholic and Protestant indigenous catechists were key to fostering democratic forms of communication among and across ethnic communities in the jungle through their evangelical work as indigenous catechists (Harvey, *The Chiapas Rebellion* 72–76). These catechists, trained in liberation theology, placed a great deal of emphasis on the "culture of dialogue" and "intercommunicative action," believing that through dialogue, "the written word of the Bible is reinterpreted in the speech of the indigenous people" (Gonzáles Casanova 350). Thus each person's word and the collective word of the común are sacred and cannot be broken. These catechists directly facilitated the culture of dialogue they brought to the communities with their translating skills. The catechists were usually bi- or trilingual. They were often on the town councils of authority, as the members on these councils not only monitored the implementation of the común, but also linked the various communities in the Lacandón jungle together (Leyva Solano 214). A number of these catechists were women, and unlike indigenous communities anywhere else in Chiapas, women in the Lacandón communities were allowed on these town councils. These catechists were instrumental in forming the UES and UUS during the 1980s, and many of them went on to form the leadership of the Zapatistas. Their understanding of the sacred nature of indigenous democratic speech helps to explain the EZLN's belief in the sacredness of their speech.

The noise of the común, where everyone has a right to be heard, mimics the noise of silence, in which all sound is heard. Just as in the clearing in Oventic the performance of silence enacted the fullness of our community, the común enacts the fullness of the Zapatista communities. As in silence, the común is not the elimination of difference but the arena in which differences are vocalized, discussed, and translated into collective sentiment. Neither the silence invoked in the communiqués nor the collective sentiment of the común is natural or intrinsic to pre-Hispanic cultures; rather, both are the materially given by-products of the encounter between indigenous beliefs and practices and (post)colonial techniques of governmentality and discourses of power. In the paradox of this encounter, silence has provided the space for resistance within capitalism, whereas the común has provided the space for alternative democratic practices in an era of neoliberal globalization begging for such alternatives. It is this común, with its secular and sacred permutations, that the Zapatistas have attempted to translate into the idiom of liberal representative democracy. They have attempted to do so both during negotiations with the government of Ernesto Zedillo (1994–2000) and through their performance of democratic practice at the various national and international events they have staged to pressure the government. I now trace the history of the negotiations to analyze the effect of this translation.

One round of negotiations took place between the EZLN and the Salinas administration. After a month and a half of procedural negotiations, during which the government methodically sought to limit the scope of the dialogue to the local arena of indigenous Chiapas, the Salinas administration finally agreed to discuss the EZLN's thirty-four-point agenda. Substantive negotiations between the two sides were held from 27 February to 2 March 1994, in the San Cristobal Cathedral, with Bishop Samuel Ruiz acting as mediator. Only six of the EZLN's thirty-four demands addressed specifically indigenous concerns. The rest reiterated, in much greater detail, the eleven national demands issued in the first "Declaracion from the Lacandón." The government responded, in a limited way, to thirty-two of the EZLN's thirty-four demands, and the Zapatistas took this preliminary accord back to their constituency for discussion and decision making in the común of each community. While the EZLN was consulting its base, Donaldo Colosío, the PRI presidential candidate for the upcoming federal elections, was assassinated on 23 March. On 10 June the EZLN issued a communiqué stating its communities had rejected the government's offer and broke off negotiations with Salinas's lame-duck government.[60]

As the entire country debated over which faction of the PRI might have ordered Colosío's assassination, and as preparations for the first internationally observed federal elections consumed party politicians, the media, and NGOS, the EZLN could easily have slipped off the front page of newspapers, becoming nothing more than a poetic but marginal guerrilla force. Two days after breaking off negotiations, however, the EZLN issued their "Second Declaration from the Lacandón Jungle." It declared: "this revolution will not result in a new class, faction of a class, or group in power but in a 'space' for free and democratic political struggle" (273), once again evoking the space of silence and the común. In the communiqué, the EZLN invited all "honest elements of Civil Society" to a "National Democratic Convention" (CND) in the liberated Zapatista territory to discuss how to guarantee rule by plebiscite, the formation of a transitional government in the event of fraudulent federal elections, and the drafting of a new constitution that would better balance federal, state, and local government (273–76). For the next two months, preparations for the CND regularly made front-page news as the Zapatistas opened a clearing in the jungle near Guadalupe Tepeyac and built an enormous spiral-shaped stadium christened "Aguascalientes."[61] The CND was held from 6 to 9 August, twelve days before the 21 August elections. More than six thousand members of peasant, indigenous, labor, and urban organizations, as well as innumerable members of the Left intelligentsia, attended the CND (Womack, *Rebellion in Chiapas* 48). During opening ceremonies, the EZLN commanders presented a Mexican flag to representatives of "civil society," symbolizing their handing over to the people the responsibility of forging a democratic union.[62]

In the course of discussions about the importance of universal suffrage and electoral transparency, an unexpected consensus for full participation in the federal elections emerged at the CND. A number of people I interviewed after the elections underscored the impact of this consensus in Chiapas. Javier Sanchez, another technical adviser with CNOC, told me, "There were *a lot* of doubts about participating in the election among our membership [because of the history of electoral fraud], but after the convention, our members returned convinced. The indigenous communities in the jungle and in the highlands *did* participate, and they voted for Amado Avendaño" (Sanchez interview). Feminist Blanca Hidalgo, who worked with a local women's NGO, commented, "The CND obliged us to assume our right to be citizens of this country. It pulled feminist discourse into an area it hadn't gone before. People never used to vote because fraud was just assumed, and we certainly didn't think of eliminating fraud as a *feminist issue*, but now indigenous women are defending their right to vote, and even the urbane NGO advisers, like myself, who were abstentionists on principle, are voting" (Hidalgo interview). Thus, while political parties in the Mexican National Congress were negotiating reforms of the electoral law to ensure an accurate voter registry and party observers at voting sites, the EZLN held a parallel National Congress, symbolically producing representative democracy by performing it. By translating the practices of the común into discussion and debate at the CND, they revalued the electoral process for indigenous and nonindigenous citizens, enfranchising new voters.

There was considerable evidence of electoral fraud in Chiapas, and the PRI governor Robledo Rincon was eventually forced to step down. However, national and international observers confirmed that Zedillo, the PRI candidate who replaced Colosío, had won the presidential election without fraud by 50.3 percent. Just a few days after Zedillo's inauguration, the EZLN shifted strategy back to the local arena, reminding the new administration of their nagging presence. On 20 December 1994, the Zapatistas broke through the Mexican military's lines without firing a shot, quietly took over thirty-eight sympathetic municipalities located outside of the liberated zones, and declared them autonomous.[63]

A month and a half later, on 9 February, Zedillo took his revenge by unilaterally breaking the cease-fire and invading liberated communities militarily. Furthermore, government agents arrested alleged Zapatistas in Veracruz and Mexico City and revealed the identity of "Marcos" as Rafael Guillen, humble professor of sociology from Monterrey (Gilbreth 1–2). Once again hundreds of thousands of Mexicans took to the streets denouncing the government's military actions and demanding a peaceful resolution to the conflict in Chiapas. It was during this series of demonstrations in Mexico City's *zocalo,* or central plaza, that demonstrators coined the chants "¡Todos somos indios!" (We are all Indians!) and "¡Todos somos Marcos!" (We are all Marcos!). Zedillo was pressured into a new cease-fire and new negotiations by the demonstrations and by his own National Congress, though he refused to order the retreat of the military forces now occupying dozens of Zapatista communities. Procedural negotiations between the two sides commenced in March at San Andres Larrainzar with a new mediating body, the Commission for Concordance and Peace (COCOPA), made up of congressional representatives from all the parties in the new legislature.

For the following five months, procedural negotiations languished. Between 9 April and 26 July 1995, the two sides formally met six times but were unable to agree on the issues of disarmament and military withdrawal from the conflict zone. More significantly, government representatives steadfastly refused to agree to any negotiations with the EZLN on matters of national dimension. With procedural negotiations at an impasse, the Zapatistas staged their second national civics lesson. On 8 August, the one-year anniversary of the CND, the Zapatistas called on the CND and Allianza Civica (AC), or Civic Alliance, to hold a "Great National Consultation for Peace and Democracy," a nationwide referendum made up of six questions proposed by the EZLN. Though none of these questions was directly about the negotiations, the *consulta* was effectively a referendum on whether or not negotiations should continue, and on what the scope of the negotiations should be.[64]

Over one million Mexican citizens from across the country participated in the consulta, with more than 90 percent of the participants voting to affirm the national scope of the negotiations between the EZLN and the PRI government.[65] According to Marcos, however, the EZLN was not simply interested in people "marking the ballot [with a] YES or NO to each of the six questions, rather, above all, we are interested and our hope lies in the organizational process of this consulta, from its promotion, from its diffusion—what it signifies and how to do it—to the organization to conduct and realize the consulta" (Marcos, "La Consulta" 5). He characterized the consulta as "another mirror in which this society can see itself, a mirror of its own capacity to organize a dialogue with itself," and as "a first step toward new forms of plebiscite, of referendum and interchange of opinions flowing from diverse sectors of civil society" (5). The consulta represented an attempt by the EZLN to have the citizenry *decir su palabra*, "speak their word," at the national level. The aesthetics of the consulta, interpreted here by Marcos, suggest that form mimics content, with the event equal to the result in significance. As in the communiqués, the event—the act of taking possession of language—is the creative act that enables speech. In the case of the consulta, this means taking possession of the language of organizing: reflecting on and interpreting one's own reality, initiating dialogue around this reality, and acting collectively to translate self-reflective dialogue "in which society can see itself" into "the word," nationwide democratic practices.[66] The consulta was a translation of Zapatista revolutionary practice into representative forms of democracy that—though new to Mexican politics—are familiar to Western liberalism, such as plebiscite, referendum.

The symbolism of the event had a very real effect on the negotiation process. In a letter assessing the significance of the consulta, Marcos put it bluntly: "The exhausted San Andres dialogue found new life, not in the will of the government but in the voice of hundreds of thousands of men and women who demanded of the all powerful and his servile bureaucrats to change their attitude at the table" (Marcos, "Mesa Nacional" 2). When the EZLN and government teams met again on 5 September, progress was made for the first time in the procedural negotiations. The government team agreed to the EZLN's agenda, dividing negotiations into four tables: (I) Indigenous Rights and Culture, (II) Democracy and Justice, (III) Economic Development and Welfare, and (IV) Women's Rights.[67] The first two negotiating sessions on Table I took place from 18 to 22 October and from 13 to 18 November.[68]

The Zapatistas expanded public participation in the dialogue even further than the consulta and the CND, however, by calling for a National Indigenous Forum (FNI) to be held in concert with the negotiation process. Negotiations for Table I were divided into six areas of concern: the definition of autonomy and community; the guarantee of justice for indigenous people in state and federal areas of jurisprudence; the rights of indigenous women within national and communal forms of jurisprudence; access to the media; and the promotion and development of indigenous culture. Thus the EZLN invited national Indianist and nonindigenous organizations to participate in a five-day forum divided into six parallel discussion sessions. The forum was held in San Cristobal from 3 to 8 January 1997, two days before the third scheduled round of negotiations on Table I. Organized by the Indianist base from sixteen different states within Mexico, with very little time and resources, the event was yet another historic event precipitated by the Zapatistas but organized by members of civil society (Hernández Navarro, "Cosecha india" 10). Four hundred ninety representatives from 197 organizations attended the forum, of which 236 were Mexican Indians, including Zapotec and Mixtec migrant laborers who returned from the United States to participate in the forum. There were fifty-four indigenous participants from other American countries. The remainder were nonindigenous Mexican citizens (Rojas and Gil Olmos, "Piden una profunda reforma" 1). Though the forum had no official mandate within the negotiations process, the Zapatistas nevertheless presented preliminary accords reached with the government to the corresponding forum sessions for ratification by the participants. Twenty-four members of the EZLN's General Command attended the FNI, and all the legislative members of COCOPA were in attendance as well, having accepted the EZLN's invitation to participate in the forum as observers (Gil Olmos 8).

The forum's stated objective was to "enrich, through ideas adopted by consensus," the proposals and preliminary accords presented by EZLN as the basis for their ongoing negotiations with the government (FNI, "Foro Nacional Indígena"). The forum, however, was far from a rubber stamp of the EZLN's positions. Rather, there was heated debate over a number of issues, and the consensus reached by forum participants often moved beyond or contradicted the positions put forth by the Zapatista delegation.[69] Disagreement among the participants focused primarily on the issue of autonomy: on its juridical reach, and on its ultimate form of governance. Two basic positions emerged over the course of five days of discussion: those who favored regional autonomy and those who favored communal autonomy. The advocates of regional autonomy favored the formation of autonomous municipalities, which would then join together in regional assemblies corresponding to the pluriethnic territoriality of historic tribes. These regional assemblies would equal state assemblies in power and jurisdiction.[70] The advocates of communal autonomy insisted on the legal recognition of the community as the highest form of governance. During a twelve-hour final plenary discussion, no consensus was reached on this issue. The forum's final document stated simply that indigenous peoples had the right to decide on their form of government, be that regional, municipal, or communal autonomy (Rojas and Gil Olmos, "Se requiere un Congreso Nacional" 9; Gil Olmos 8).[71] Although the EZLN's decision to hold the FNI during the middle of its negotiations was clearly a tactical maneuver to pressure the government, it also reflected the Zapatistas' aesthetics of silence and politics of the común.[72]

The forum and its proceedings demonstrate, yet again, the power of the EZLN to summon the citizens of the nation to the project of remaking it. They succeeded in making the most "local" of issues on the negotiating table—indigenous rights and culture—into a national concern by inviting both indigenous *and* nonindigenous organizations to participate in the project of theorizing the formation of a new Mexican state, one capable of encompassing autonomy within it. In the discussions that took place at the forum, indigenous and nonindigenous people searched for ways to combine customary law and Western law, to accommodate rights made available to indigenous citizens under both systems of law in any future project of autonomy. As Father Gonzalo Ituarte,[73] a participant in the FNI, put it, "Autonomy is not a look backward, at traditions that may or may not have existed, but a look at the present and a look forward. The EZLN claims the right to give to the nation and not only to receive from it. The FNI was an opportunity for Indians and mestizos to collectively interpret the kind of nation we desire" (Ituarte interview).

The participants at the FNI were also collectively incorporated into the negotiation process, as the radicality of the positions voiced at the FNI forced concessions from the government's negotiating team. Prior to the forum, the government's position on autonomy had been quite limited: allowing each ethnic community to negotiate the terms of its autonomous government individually with the legislatures of each state, with the federal government then ratifying each individual agreement (Henríquez and Gil Olmos 9). After the FNI, however, the government's position shifted considerably, on this and other issues.

The third and final round of the Table I negotiations took place from 10 through 19 January, during which considerable advances were made, and final accords were reached. In prior negotiating sessions, the government team had insisted on referring to indigenous peoples as "poblados indigenas" rather than "pueblos indigenas" (Moguel 24). The distinction is an important one, for while "poblados indigenas" literally translates into indigenous populations, "poblado" also means town or village, reminiscent of the fragmented colonial township structure. Meanwhile "pueblos indigenas" translates into indigenous peoples, the language used in the Convenio 169 de la OIT. By agreeing to the OIT definition, the government team also recognized indigenous peoples' tie to historical domains and their right to a constitutional guarantee of self-determination (Moguel 24). The San Andres Accords on Indigenous Rights and Culture, as they are officially called, guaranteed state and federal legislative reforms that would (a) establish the autonomy of indigenous communities and peoples, recognizing them as entities with public rights, including the right to form municipalities with an indigenous majority, and for such municipalities to associate freely; (b) protect the integrity of indigenous lands, as specified by indigenous peoples and communities in accordance with the concept of territorial integrity included in the Convenio 169 of the OIT; (c) give preferential privilege to indigenous communities in the granting of concessions for obtaining benefits from natural resources; (d) ensure representation in all legislative bodies, especially the National Congress and state congresses, through redistricting; (e) establish the right of indigenous peoples to elect their own authorities and exercise that authority in accord with their own norms, guaranteeing the equal participation of women; (f) recognize the pluricultural makeup of the nation in all legislative content, so that it may reflect intercultural dialogue, the shared norms for all Mexicans, and respect for the internal normative systems of indigenous peoples; (g) guarantee protection against discrimination on the basis of racial or ethnic origin, language, sex, belief, or social conditions within the Magna Carta; (h) protect all individual guarantees, rights, and freedoms; and (i) guarantee access to media for indigenous peoples so that they may freely exercise and develop their cultures (COCOPA 1996).

The government held fast against recognizing any form of regional autonomy and postponed all discussion of agrarian reform and development (i.e., Salinas's reform of Article 27 from the 1917 Constitution) until Table III. Nevertheless these first accords legally established a national right to autonomous government for indigenous peoples, a right that would require the modification of seven constitutional articles, as well as the modification of the national civil, penal, and electoral codes. The EZLN took these accords back to their communities for ratification and, on 15 February, announced that 96 percent of the members of their communities had approved the accords. They were signed by both teams the next day. This was an auspicious beginning for the negotiating process. In less than five months, the two sides had drafted a detailed and promising accord for Table I.

Negotiations for Table II on Democracy and Justice began almost immediately, but in the following six months, negotiations took a turn for the worse. Though the two sides met repeatedly, no progress was made on the issues of democracy and justice. This time around, the government flatly refused to discuss any national reforms, though the Zapatistas had many such demands on the table. Once again, the Zapatistas turned to the national and international community. In July, they hosted a Forum on the Reform of the Mexican State, resembling the FNI in organization and structure. In August they hosted the International Encounter for Humanity and against Neoliberalism. This time, however, their ability to galvanize the national and international community in these democratic performances had no effect on the Zedillo administration. The Zapatistas suspended negotiations in September, citing the government's unwillingness to negotiate on national issues as a factor.

Why was the Zedillo government unwilling to do so in Table II negotiations when they had been so willing to compromise in Table I negotiations? Why did the Zapatistas' ability to galvanize the Mexican citizenry have no effect on Zedillo's administration this time around? I posed the first question to Adriana López Monjardin, a political scientist and EZLN adviser for Table II, in September 1996. Her response is worth quoting at length. She began by discussing her experience advising the EZLN:

> When the advisers [for Table II] met with the EZLN representatives in our first assembly, we asked them, "So what are your demands?" The Zapatistas answered, "We have no demands, we want to hear what you think." Well, we were a little surprised at first, but it doesn't take much to convince a bunch of intellectuals to talk. So we made many proposals about how we thought democracy could be improved in Mexico. Among all the proposals we made, though, it is no coincidence that the most attractive to the EZLN were those enabling participatory democracy. There were a lot of disagreements among the advisers about how to reform electoral law, but it was clear that the proposals emphasizing direct democracy were the most attractive to the EZLN—plebiscite, referendum, popular initiative. . . . In Mexico the tradition is for the president to initiate laws and the legislature to pass them. Now that there are opposition parties in the Congress, there are more initiatives put forth by the members [of Congress], but this doesn't imply any consultation with their constituency. There is no tradition of consulting your constituency, of lobbying or anything like that. There has never been any relationship of sustenance [with the constituency]. The EZLN was very interested in anything having to do with citizens' action. For example, they were very interested in having the ability to bring charges against officials for violating the Constitution. Right now you can bring civil or criminal charges against officials, but you have no recourse if they violate your constitutional rights—for example, if an official takes away your communal land in order to grant a concession for the exploitation of natural resources. They were very interested in the right to recall an elected official if he [or she] was not discharging his [or her] duty correctly. Participatory democracy is central to the Zapatistas. . . . There lies the utopic dimension of the EZLN—they formulate it as "ruling by obeying," and they want to take this to the national level, they want this as the model for a new relationship between the governed and the governors. In most indigenous communities, you have to earn the right to

hold an office by serving your community in a number of capacities first. To rule by obeying gathers up all these traditions. It's utopic, but they say, "If it is possible for this kind of authority to exist in the communities, then it should exist for the whole country."

When we got to the negotiating table, the government insisted they were in agreement with these issues—with the idea of plebiscite, referendum, recall. Well, the next logical step was to discuss the mechanisms for ensuring these were citizen's initiatives, and not another vehicle for state intervention. You know, rules for who can initiate such measures, how many signatures would be necessary to put a referendum on a ballot, or to require the recall of a state official. The government team absolutely refused to contemplate procedures such as these, which are essential if these things are to become real rights. They said, "Many other actors need to express themselves on these issues before we can proceed with this discussion." Which actors? Who knows. A lot of civil organizations and NGOs participated in the assemblies with the EZLN before negotiations and insisted on these reforms as well.

The Zapatistas and many other indigenous groups are proposing to Mexico a new form of government, one that gathers up all their traditions, one that proposes building a national consensus on issues. This is in direct contradiction with the party system. The party system is based on the idea that there are irreconcilable differences; it is based on antagonism. The Zapatista model recognizes that there are differences but proceeds according to the belief that you can reach consensus as a community, that there is no need for parties. Also you must remember that the party system has brought division to their communities. To participate in even a municipal election, you must belong to a party, and this has introduced artificial divisions and tensions in indigenous communities.[74]

The demands made by the Zapatistas clearly challenged the centralization of power in the one-party system of government that had held sway in Mexico for seventy years. Given the nature of their demands, however, the Zapatistas found few allies among the newly empowered opposition parties in National Congress for continuing Table II negotiations. Indeed, rather than continue negotiations with the Zapatistas, Zedillo initiated negotiations with the opposition parties for the reform of the electoral code. Although the changes to the electoral code made possible the defeat of PRI presidential candidate Francisco Labastida by PAN candidate Vicente Fox in the 2000 elections, they did not limit the power of party politics in any way or augment the channels of participation available to the Mexican constituency. One has to wonder if Zedillo's faction of the PRI was willing to relinquish the party's seventy-year hold on power to an opposition party in order to prevent Indian particularity from translating into the abstract universality of national democratic politics. After all, the reforms suggested by the Zapatistas, though new to Mexico, are present in many other Western democracies. Nevertheless, Zedillo's administration steadfastly refused to resume negotiations on these issues for the remaining five years of his administration. Although the Zapatista reforms and the Zapatistas *did* pose an immediate and direct threat to the PRI's hold on power, I would suggest it was the far more dangerous threat they posed to the discourse of mestizaje that required the permanent breaking off of negotiations.

The EZLN not only tried to translate their Indian specificity into the language of representative democracy within the negotiation process, as López Monjardin suggests, but also successfully translated their Indian particularity into the practice of democracy through the CND, the National Consultation, the FNI, and the Forum for the Reform of the Mexican State. This was their true crime, for in so doing they attempted to build the consensus of the común at the national level, to register the differences in the fullness of the community of silence that is the disenfranchised Mexican populace. The EZLN's successful performance of democratic practice, their successful translation of silence, necessitated the failure of negotiations. Ontologically, the possibility of contemporary Indian particularity informing abstract national universality posed such a unique threat to the myth of the modern Mexican mestizo that Zedillo set about reparticularizing the EZLN into the primitive Indian difference of mestizaje. By breaking off negotiations, Zedillo contained the EZLN to the San Andres Accords, reinscribing Indian difference as "culture." His administration allowed the EZLN a voice in the formulation of the particular rights of indigenous people within these accords, rights that could be construed as "simply" cultural. This was the extent to which his administration was willing to let the EZLN have a say in Mexican politics. When the EZLN attempted to inform the terms of national enfranchisement for indigenous *and* nonindigenous people, his administration shut down the negotiations, redirecting the discussion on national democratic reform to its "proper" forum, negotiations with mestizo legislators and party representatives. The Zedillo administration also sought to reprimitivize the EZLN through the use of counterinsurgency groups in Chiapas. With the support of local PRI officials and with the federal army turning a blind eye to their activities, indigenous counterinsurgency groups, such as Paz and Justicia, organized and swung into action in 1997. In addition to the unprecedented loss of human lives in the Chiapas conflict at the hands of these counterinsurgency groups, their actions gave the conflict an interethnic representation, as the Zedillo administration tried, for the second time in Mexican history, to turn an ethnically inflected class antagonism into a caste war.

Ideologically, the Mexican revolutionary elites of 1910 functioned by invoking the native—the forsaken "folk" nation—as the legitimation for their revolution, and it is through the discourse of mestizaje that the folk became assessable as pure Indian difference, as what gives Mexican national identity its uniqueness. Once the revolution came to pass, however, a European paradigm of nation emerged from behind the mask of Indian difference, as the Spanish variable in the equation of mestizaje was ultimately more valued than its Indian counterpart. From behind the mask of Indian difference emerged the developmentalist paradigm of the revolutionary mestizo, a mestizo who must supersede his glorious Indian past if he is to have access to the promises of modernity in his future. The mask of Indian difference functioned as the quintessential empty signifier within the discourse of revolutionary mestizo nationalism, for while it politically galvanized national identity as the common origin among the population—temporarily providing a mythical fullness of community—it was itself devoid of all particularity. It was a discursive construct which shunned all Indian specificity, preferring instead a content so abstracted as to lose all referential meaning as origin. Indian difference is a signifier unmoored from its presumed referent, the indigenous population of Mexico. The Zapatistas have seized the empty signifier of Indian difference and its function in Mexican culture. From behind their masks, their *pasamontañas* and bandannas, the EZLN calls for a second Mexican revolution to achieve the unfulfilled potential of the 1910 revolution, emphatically and repeatedly placing themselves within the genealogy of this first paradigmatic revolution for Latin America through their communiqués and democratic performances. They make their appeal to the nation from within the discursive terms of the 1910 revolution, even participating in the developmentalism of mestizaje through their autoethnographic choice of representation as the folk origin of the Mexican nation. And yet they also exceed the discursive terms of the revolutionary mestizo nationalism of 1910. The Zapatistas seize the mask of Indian difference in an attempt to fill its "empty" content with Indian specificity, a specificity that is neither pre-Hispanic or postmodern but offers Mexican citizens an alternative modernity. It is an Indian specificity produced within, but also in excess of, the discursive terms of revolutionary mestizo nationalism and developmentalist modernity.

In "Why Do Empty Signifiers Matter to Politics?" Laclau theorizes how empty signifiers function at moments of potential hegemonic transition when various working-class struggles achieve unity in their confrontation with a repressive regime (*Emancipation[s]* 40). He begins with a review of semiotic theory, reminding the reader that the systematicity of a semiotic system always depends on radical exclusion from the system: "the very possibility of signification is the system, and very possibility of the system is the possibility of its limit" (37). As every signifying totality is a system of differences, the signifying system's limit cannot be neutral. It cannot be a limit such as would occur between two signifying terms within the system, but must be antagonistic. The absolute limit of a signifying system, beyond which is radical exclusion, by definition cannot be represented by the signifying terms of the system and exists as pure negativity against which the system defines its totality (37). This is the first empty signifier we come upon in Laclau's essay, the empty signifier of the exclusionary limit. This empty signifier of the exclusionary limit, however, only interests him insofar as it "introduces an essential ambivalence within the system of differences constituted by those limits. On the one hand, each element of the system has an identity only so far as it is different from the others: difference = identity. On the other hand, however, all these differences are equivalent to each other inasmuch as all of them belong to this side of the frontier of exclusion. But, in that case, the identity of each element is constitutively split" (38). It is this constitutively split identity of every signifying term in the system that allows for the empty signifier of the pure being of the system, on this side of the exclusionary limit of pure negativity, to signify itself. Because each element of a signifying system is split ambivalently by difference and equivalence—contains both these possibilities—signifiers are able to "empty themselves of their attachment to particular signifieds" (of their identity as difference) and, in turn, "assume the role of representing the pure being of the system—or rather the system as pure Being" (identity as the equivalence of all the elements of the system) (39). Indian difference, as I have suggested, has historically performed this function of representing the Mexican nation as pure being, as the equivalence of all the elements of the system.

Laclau then uses the logic of the semiotic system as a metaphor to analyze the political terrain at a moment when a repressive regime has increased its repression to such a degree that it becomes "less the instrument of particular differential repressions and will express [instead] pure anti-community, pure evil and negation" (42). Laclau tells us that at such moments, according to Luxemburg, disparate working-class struggles may unite not because of a unity of interests but because they are all equivalent before the repressive regime (41). A community of struggle is created through identification in opposition, through "this equivalential expansion" in which their differences are deferred in their confrontation with the regime. Although this community of struggle is nevertheless punctuated by differential interests, community *will* emerge as "the pure idea of a communitarian fullness which is absent as a result of the presence of the repressive power" (42). Laclau has brought us very close to the function the Zapatistas have played for the idea of "civil society" in Mexico since the time of their uprising. Laclau continues: "The community as such is not a purely differential space of an objective identity but an absent fullness, it cannot have any form of representation of its own, and has to borrow the latter from some entity constituted within the equivalent space—in the same way as gold is a particular use which assumes, as well, the function of representing value in general. This emptying of a particular signifier of its particular, differential signified is, as we saw, what makes possible the emergence of 'empty' signifiers as the signifier of a lack, of an absent totality" (42).

Following Laclau's analysis of the function of empty signifiers in representing the absent fullness of the community, I suggest that the Zapatistas once again mobilize the empty signifier of Indian difference to unite a community of struggle against the PRI dictatorship. After ten years of structural adjustment policies, followed by two years of neoliberal reform, the Zapatistas were able to coalesce the various working-class and leftist struggles in Mexico by mobilizing the empty signifier of Indian difference to represent the fullness of "civil society" in their communiqués and in their repeated performance of democratic participation. When the Zapatistas interrupted Salinas's neoliberal project because it excluded them as Indians, they were successful in generalizing their exclusion as Indian difference. If Indians have traditionally been excluded from the privileges of mestizo citizenship in Mexico, then what the Zapatistas made evident to the general population, through their communiqués and political acts, was that neoliberal reform had turned the entire country into Indians. The popularized chant "todos somos indios" attests to this. The Zapatistas succeeded in making Mexican society aware that they were all Indians before this neoliberal agenda, an agenda that defaulted on the historical promise of inclusion extended by the developmentalist revolutionary nationalism of the PRI. The Zapatistas succeeded in universalizing the alterity traditionally ascribed to Indians.

In mobilizing the empty signifier of Indian difference to unite a community in struggle, however, they also reclaimed this empty signifier discursively for Indian specificity. I am suggesting that the empty signifier is no longer empty. The Zapatistas twice challenge Laclau's antagonistic formulation of hegemonic politics when they fill the "empty" signifier of Indian difference with their own particularity even as they universalize this particularity to represent the fullness of the Mexican community. They fill Indian difference with a specificity—with the aesthetics of silence and the politics of the común—capable of encompassing the abstract national community in struggle and *in difference*. The Zapatistas disrupt the PRI teleology of mestizaje and revolutionary developmentalism by insisting that Indian particularity, finally, openly inform the condition of revolutionary national citizenship, that Indian particularity inform the national forms of democratic representation. In so doing, they offer alternative forms of democratic practice that envision the fulfillment of community not as an empty signifier, as an impossible horizon, but as a community of differences functioning through the building of consensus. If we take the Zapatista challenge seriously, we must take their theorizing of utopia as seriously as we take Laclau's. This challenge cannot be satisfied by the math of liberal pluralism, by the simple addition of a resignified Indian difference onto a long chain of antagonistic equivalences. Rather, we must take seriously the challenge of their politics and aesthetics as presenting modernity with alternative models of representation.

By simultaneously claiming their Indian particularity and the rights of universal citizenship, by insisting that the former inform the latter, the Zapatistas also present us with an alternative modernity. They eschew the antimodernist position of nativist movements because even their particular indigenous forms of democratic representation were produced by modernity and modernization. They eschew the completion of modernity promised yet again by (neo)liberal development because that promise went unfulfilled under the PRI's last modernization scheme. But they also eschew the promise of a more perfect modernity offered by the Central American guerrilla movements of the 1980s because history has taught them—and us—that it does not exist. Instead they are interested in presenting modernity with the gritty task of reevaluation, of presenting modernity with another vision of itself by weaving together the social justice of revolutionary radicalism, the consensus-building practices of their indigenous communities, and the democratic promise of representative liberalism. This is the vision and knowledge not of those excluded from developmentalist modernity but of those who have fully suffered its consequences and have seen its possibilities.

7

Epilogue   Toward an American

"American Studies": Postrevolutionary

Reflections on Malcolm X and

the New Aztlán

This book has offered a genealogy of the regime of subjection under revolutionary movements in Latin America over the course of the last half century. In the interest of further understanding the internal contradictions that led to the demise of these post–World War II revolutionary movements, I have investigated the disturbing resemblance between the discourse of development and the revolutionary imagination in the Americas, suggesting that these two seemingly vying models of futurity paradoxically converge at the site of subjectivity, with each demanding from its agent/object a similar transformation in consciousness and mode of being. The similarity between these vying theories of history lies in their mutual dependence on a teleological and meliorist concept of human development, derived from imperial reason but reformulated through the rhetorics of decolonization, development, and national liberation after World War II. As a consequence of this mutual dependence on reformulated Anglo- and Spanish-colonial legacies of race, First World development discourse and Third World national liberation struggles in Latin America shared a requirement for deracination that was placed on their respective agent/objects. Thus, on the one hand, revolutionary agents such as Ernesto "Che" Guevara, Mario Payeras, and the vanguard leadership of the FSLN represented personal transformations as epochal, revolutionary consciousness as unitary and universal, and collective agency as willful, masterful, and finally masculine. On the other hand, the targets of their revolutionary errand—those feminized objects scheduled for revolutionary transformation by these manly agents—were invariably in need of development: trapped in precapitalist formations, steeped in the false consciousness of ethnic particularity and peasant custom. These agents of early post–World War II revolution proceeded much as one might imagine their bureaucratic counterparts in the development apparatus would have: by locating the "traditional," the "premodern," the "folk" and then subjecting it to reform. Indeed, a developmentalist regime of revolutionary subjection demands of its agent/object a transcendence out of particularity into the presumably universal consciousness of a fully developed, masculinist, deracinated, self-determined and determining proletarian subjectivity.

The agent/objects of this revolutionary errand responded to this regime of subjection with deafening silence. The texts produced by Rigoberta Menchú and the Zapatistas are texts performed in the "silence of the Indian." And yet these texts and their authors insist on retheorizing revolutionary subjection from *within* the revolutionary tradition in Latin America and from *within* development. To wit, while the silence in Menchú's autobiography and in the Zapatista communiqués enacts the impossibility of accessing an authentic "Indian" difference—the impossibility of an authentic subaltern representation—they nonetheless insist on just such representation by appropriating the compromised terms of liberal *and* Marxist subjection and democracy. In other words, these subaltern subjects refuse to vacate their responsibility in formulating a revolutionary alternative for the Americas, one that could include the specificity of both their class oppression and their ethnic particularity. In laying claim to the legacy of the twentieth-century revolutionary movements in the Americas, they claim the liberal, authorial voice necessary for articulating their ethnic specificity *with* their role as transformative agents. In so doing, these subaltern subjects begin a transformation of the conditions of their own subjection, away from the unrepresentability of their subaltern experience toward the terms of Western representation. They are engaged in the tenuous and tentative process of emerging out of subalternity in a Spivakian sense. However, in so doing, they also shift the terms for that transformation away from a teleological development out of particularity and into universality. Instead they insist on locating their particularity, as it already exists (has always existed?), within the terms of a "universal" model of full humanity. Thus although both the Zapatistas and Menchú resort to the ruse of authenticity, of the folk, in laying claim to the Latin American revolutionary tradition, they do so from a distinctly modern positionality. They do not "escape" the developmentalism of modernity; no one does. Rather, they bring an understanding to the revolutionary tradition of precisely how their ethnic specificity is an effect of the development of the productive forces in Latin America. The indigenous subalterns represented in Menchú's autobiography and the Zapatista texts understand themselves as fully imbricated with Latin American modernization.

Consequently there is no authentic consciousness of the Indian to be located through them; there is no "tradition" left to reform them out of, as these traditions were forged in the colonial encounter with imperial reason and modernity. What these subalterns bring to the revolutionary regime of subjection is a profound understanding of how ethnic identity and economic identity are articulated together, of how their particularity is produced out of the presumably universalizing experience of economic development, and vice versa. Rather than reject this constitutive experience with modernization and its subjection out of hand, through a retreat into ethnic separatism, these indigenous subalterns instead assert their place *within* a revolutionary developmentalism. They insist on negotiating the terms of revolutionary subjection in order that the revolutionary imagination in the Americas may incorporate their living and modern difference.

Two sets of questions, then, are generated from this genealogy of revolutionary subjection. First, does this paradigmatic subject of revolution—embodied in the diaries of Guevara and Payeras, and in the agrarian reform policies of the FSLN and the PRI—have a more global reach? Does this paradigmatic revolutionary subject cross the formidable South-North border into the United States? Is s/he truly an "American" subject, forged in the spirit of José Martí's writing? If the answer to these questions is yes, as I believe it is, then does the critique of this paradigmatic revolutionary subject issued by indigenous subalterns *from within revolutionary practice* pertain to the experience of revolutionary subjection in the United States? And if the call to revolutionary subjection is issued from the ethnic and raced positionalities of Chicana/o and black nationalism, is the treatment of subaltern difference necessarily different? Are the regimes of subjection under these two U.S.-based movements for "national" liberation any less developmentalist in their requirement for transformation? The answers to this second set of questions are by no means obvious, but these questions nevertheless demand a response from any serious study of revolutionary subjection in the Americas. Thus I turn my attention in this epilogue to the "early" revolutionary black nationalism of the 1960s as represented in *The Autobiography of Malcolm X*, and to the "late" Chicano revolutionary nationalism in the 1990s as represented in the texts of Tomás Rivera, Gloria Anzaldúa, and, yes, even Richard Rodriguez.

My interest in pursuing this comparison of Latin American revolutionary subjection and U.S. minority revolutionary subjection is multifaceted. On one hand, this interest is generated organically, as the texts speak to each other across the artifice of geographic and disciplinary divides. Malcolm X and Che Guevara speak to each other in the language of anticolonialism and in the interest of independent national development. Similarly, the Zapatistas and queer Chicanas/os such as Anzaldúa and Rodriguez speak in the "common language" of mestizaje, if only to say very different things. Thus I am interested in making the dialogue among all these revolutionary subjects explicit, in "tuning in" to all the reverberations of the sounds of subjection.

On the other hand, my interest in the comparison is also "purely academic." Over the course of the last decade, American studies has called on scholars to move beyond the paradigm of U.S. exceptionalism in the Americas and has insisted on studying U.S. literature and culture in a transnational frame. These programmatic calls have nevertheless failed to produce such a body of transnational scholarship, largely because such scholarship, when it occurs, steers clear of the difficulties and complexities of archival research, ethnography, multilinguality, and multiculturality required by this approach. Often such studies run the risk of turning into intellectual tourism, with U.S. scholars selectively revisiting one or two Latin American intellectual luminaries in study after study. Alternately, these studies move from North to South, presupposing the dominant influence of the imperial center on the neocolonial periphery, resubalternizing the subaltern.

Meanwhile, over the last ten years, Latin American studies has realized that a significant portion of Latin America now lives in the United States. Thus Latin American studies recently "discovered" the Latino, his liminal cultural forms, his racial resistance. While usually the purview of Ethnic studies, Latinas/os in the United States may well be a natural extension for scholars of Central America, Colombia, Mexico, Brazil, et cetera. Nevertheless there is also an ulterior motive behind this newfound *institutional* interest in the U.S. minority subject. All at once, a new constituency has come into focus for an area studies threatened with extinction in the post–Cold War academic politics of the twenty-first century. Indeed, in the case of both U.S. American studies and Latin American studies, the "transnational" and the "Latino" run the risk of being instrumentalized for the purposes of rejuvenating aging fields of inquiry, sagging under the weight of poststructuralist and postcolonial critique.

Thus I pursue this comparison *against* this instrumentalizing institutional effect. This epilogue is an attempt to read from South to North, or rather to read horizontally across the regimes of subjection put forth by revolutionary figures in the United States and in Latin America, not because these modes of subjection are *the same*, but rather because in their difference they nevertheless share paradigms of gender and racial codification and could potentially share a new model of oppositional consciousness. Thus I pursue this comparison in the interest of an American "American studies."

Malcolm X: Angry Prince or Gentle Servant?

Although Ernesto "Che" Guevara and Malcolm X were from different nations, classes, and races, these two men were nevertheless brought together on the terrain of resistance to capitalist relations and to legacies of race. These two revolutionaries were products of their time and were influenced by the theories of neocolonialism in Latin America and of internal colonialism in the United States that were generated from dependency theory. Guevara and the revolutionaries who followed his example directed their revolutionary struggles against U.S. neocolonialism and its local representatives, the comprador classes. However, as I have argued in chapter 3, they also attempted to recuperate an uncompromised masculinity through their armed struggle. Meanwhile Malcolm X's autobiography and speeches offered an unflinching critique of the racism associated with U.S. internal colonialism and, as well, of the internalized racism caused by the "dependent development" of U.S. minorities. These two historic revolutionary figures, then, are brought together not only by a shared anticolonialist understanding of the United States as an imperial power. They are also brought together, across international and disciplinary divides, by their shared desire to break free from the *psychic* dependency of neocolonialism and internal colonialism. Guevara and Malcolm X moved beyond the economic orientation of dependency theory when, in their diaries and autobiography, they theorized just what such psychic freedom might entail— indeed, what it *had* entailed in their own lives at the level of subject formation and consciousness.

Thus I suggest they are brought together not only negatively—against colonialism, capitalism, and racism—but also positively, within developmentalism. The narratives of these revolutionaries—Guevara's diaries and Malcolm X's autobiography—bear a powerful resemblance to each other. Indeed, the representations of revolutionary self-construction in these texts share, perhaps unsurprisingly, a formulaic narrative structure and a similar tropological register. Beyond this resemblance to each other, however, Malcolm X's formulation of revolutionary subjectivity and agency, like Guevara's, bears a remarkable resemblance to the ethical subject of development typified by Rostow. To review, in development discourse, the pivotal moment of entry into modernity is repeatedly figured as a transcendental moment of choice. The underdeveloped subject must make the ethical choice to enter development and thereby history, to leave behind a prodigal life in favor of a productive one, with this prodigal life most often thematized negatively as ethnos—as clan, caste, tribe, or extended family. Meanwhile the developed subject must choose to do the civilized thing, the ethical thing, and assist the underdeveloped subject in achieving this end once he has made his choice. Both choices are posited as transcendental, as life altering and epochal. Thus a powerful discursive dichotomy between premodern forms of consciousness and modern forms of consciousness is put into play by this developmentalist regime of subjection. Fully developed subjectivity, on one side of the binary, is repeatedly metaphorized in masculinist discursive terms privileging unitary, self-determining consciousness and agency; while underdeveloped subjectivity, on the other side of the binary, is metaphorized as emasculated and as bearing the taint of ethnos. In his eulogy, Ossie Davis makes clear on which side of this binary the figure of Malcom X belongs: "Malcolm was our manhood, our living, black manhood! This was his meaning to his people. . . . [He was] a Prince—our own black shining Prince!—who didn't hesitate to die because he loved us so" (Clarke xii). As occurs in Guevara's diary, this discursive chain of signification accompanies the autobiographical representation of Malcolm X's transformation from the degenerate Harlem hustler to Harlem's most revered minister. And again, as in Guevara's diary, *The Autobiography of Malcolm X* repeatedly deploys a discursive binary to describe those saved and those unsaved by revolutionary transformation in the black community. This developmentalist dichotomy has deleterious consequences for the constitution of blackness in the Americas, as we shall see.

The biographical writing on Malcolm X engages in a binarized representation of him, as well. In the literature on Malcolm X, by both those who knew him well and those who knew him at a distance, commentators frequently note the difference between the public and the private Malcolm X. Friends, journalists, and academics all mention that the fiery Malcolm X of public lecture or debate receded into the background in private conversation, and that the kind, polite, "aristocratic" Malcolm X came to the fore. Benjamin Karim, Malcom X's assistant minister and friend, underscores this dichotomous representation: "In his eulogy [Ossie Davis] praised 'our own black shining Prince,' a phrase that for me did not capture the man I knew: the minister, from the Latin word for servant; our counselor, healer, judge, and peacemaker; the teacher at the blackboard with a world in his mind and a piece of chalk in his hand" (Karim 194). Perhaps because of these two different styles of Malcolm X's self-presentation, representations of him span the spectrum from hatemonger to honest denouncer, from angry prince to gentle servant. However, while Ossie Davis's "black shining Prince" and Benjamin Karim's "servant . . . counselor . . . healer" appear to conform to this dichotomous representation of Malcolm X, the "prince" and the "servant" both contribute to the *singular* representation of his life in messianic terms. As Karim's and Davis's statements make evident, for the black community of the 1960s, Malcolm X's revolutionary agency was intimately tied to the possibility of national liberation from U.S. racial subordination. And just as in the case of Che Guevara's iconic status for Latin Americans, Malcolm X's revolutionary agency was, in turn, intimately connected with his performance of masculinity for the U.S. black community: "Malcolm was our manhood, our living, black manhood!"

If Che Guevara and Mario Payeras performed their masculinity within the racial register dictated by the legacy of Spanish colonialism in Latin America, as I argued in chapter 3, then Malcolm X does so within the racial register dictated by the legacy of Anglo-British colonialism in the United States. Houston Baker Jr., in *Blues, Ideology, and Afro-American Literature,* succinctly outlined the "discursive family of statements" that constitute the white, Anglo-American subject of history in the Americas: " 'Religious man,' 'wilderness,' 'migratory errand,' 'increase in store,' and 'New Jerusalem' are . . . [the] essential governing structures of a traditional American history" (19). In *Autobiography,* the representation of Malcolm X appropriates these discursive terms for "whiteness" that accompany the paradigmatic U.S. subject. From the moment of his conversion to Islam in jail, Malcolm X sees himself in a line of prophetic black men sent on a "migratory errand" to lead the chosen black people out of the "wilderness" of American racism into the "New Jerusalem" of free nationhood under Islam. While there are, of course, significant differences between Baker's discursive paradigm and the construction of Malcolm X's subjectivity, it was Malcolm X's appropriation and inversion of this "white man's story" that, I contend, so unnerved members of the white community and thrilled members of the black community. Indeed, his relentless deployment of the tropes of "Americanness" —from his claims to religious mission and revolutionary origins to his no-nonsense, bootstrap, self-reliant representation of the Nation of Islam (NOI) —permanently unsettles that construction.

Guevara and Payeras begin their diaries with scenes of destruction that serve as the narrative (re)births for their revolutionary subjectivity. *Auto-*

biography also begins with a scene of chaos and violence—his earliest memory—that serves as the narrative birth of the revolutionary:

> When my mother was pregnant with me, she told me later, a party of hooded Ku Klux Klan riders galloped up to our home in Omaha Nebraska, one night. Surrounding the house, brandishing their shotguns and rifles, they shouted for my father to come out. My mother went to the front door and opened it. Standing where they could see her pregnant condition, she told them that she was alone with her three small children. . . . The Klansmen shouted threats and warnings at her that we had better get out of town because "the good Christian white people" were not going to stand for my father's "spreading trouble" among the "good" Negroes of Omaha with the "back to Africa" preachings of Marcus Garvey. (1)

In utero, Malcolm X has been baptized by fire into the savage landscape of white Christianity, and into his messianic destiny. Guevara and Payeras arrive in the jungles and mountains of Cuba and Guatemala and proceed to map a wilderness onto them. In his construction, Malcolm X is *born* into the wilderness of white racism simply by being born black. But just as with Guevara and Payeras, so the wilderness portends Malcolm X's coming: the Klansmen have hailed his father to the door—"good Negro" or messianic nationalist? Malcolm X prophetically comes forward, in his mother's womb, answering this call as a preordained revolutionary.

Once again, though, this messianic narrative belies a condition of limited masculinity. When Malcolm is only six, the Black Legionnaires kill his father, Earl Little, making clear the consequences of exceeding the bounds of acceptable black masculinity. This condition of limited masculinity is multiply determined by the discursive, juridical, and material limits placed on the possibility of black male subjectivity in the racist United States of the 1940s and 1950s.[1] As with Guevara and Payeras, then, Malcolm X's transformation into a revolutionary subject is motivated, in part, by a desire for transcendence over this condition of limited masculinity. The murder of his father not only makes these limits viscerally clear but also denies Malcolm *Little* a literal and figurative relationship to the patronymic. In Guevara's diary, dictatorial violence cuts Ernesto Guevara off from his progeny, and this consequently leads *Che* Guevara to "father" the revolutionary collective instead. In the case of Malcolm X, the murder of Earl Little at the hands of white racists not only severs Malcolm Little from his father but symbolically replicates the violence of slavery, which severs an entire race from its ancestry. Thus Earl Little represents an organic, patrilineal tie to a revolutionary consciousness *and* to a prior civilization, an ancestral connection that is generally the strict purview of white citizenship through the myths of (white) founding fathers and (white) immigrant histories. Malcolm Little is severed from the patronymic, but like Che Guevara, Malcolm X reestablishes the mythic patronymic relationship in the narrative through the reconstruction of his father's life in the epic terms of black nationalism. Malcolm X, through his enunciatory act of retelling his father's story, fills the X—symbol of patronymic loss—with precisely an ancestral history of resistance, justice, courage, independence, and self-determination, characteristics generally reserved for the trope of (white) American subjectivity.[2]

In the diaries of Guevara and Payeras, revolutionary transformation required the death of the prior bourgeois subjectivity associated with the accoutrements of civilization. However, these prior subjectivities are never fully elaborated in Guevara's and Payeras's texts, as personal histories are sublated to the "now" of the collective struggle. Prior subject positions are absolutely necessary as the "before" of an epochal transformation in consciousness, but dwelling on early life stories would violate the revolutionary code by privileging the individual bourgeois subject over the collective. For Malcolm X, however, dwelling on his whole life is precisely a way of telling the collective story. Every moment in his life—from birth to his descent into depravity to his jailhouse conversion—is described in *Autobiography* in great detail because, like the "religious man" from Baker's paradigm, every incident in Malcolm X's life is preordained, unique, and yet exemplary of the lives of the members of the "chosen" black nation. Thus, while the opening scene of the narrative christens Malcolm Little with an organic revolutionary consciousness, his father's death temporarily severs Malcolm Little's patronymic relationship to this form of consciousness. This revolutionary consciousness must be reestablished in the course of the narrative. Severed from this ancestry, Malcolm Little has access to two prescribed forms of acceptable "Negro" consciousness in the United States: the "Mascot" and the "Homeboy," as his chapter titles indicate. Malcolm X's analysis of these two subject positions is analogous to Roberto Fernández Retamar's analysis of the Ariel and Caliban positionalities. These dichotomous forms of consciousness are not only sanctioned by white racism (the language of the colonizer), as Retamar insists, but indeed invented and prescribed by it. Retamar concludes his analysis by celebrating the possibility for the subversion of both these categories, which he claims is made evident by Guevara's personal transformation. Malcolm X's story problematizes Retamar's conclusion, however. In *Autobiography* these categories are not simply potential sites for subversion but ultimately sites of a mimicry that are always already surveilled by the state.[3]

As "mascot," Malcolm Little tries hard to be Ariel, only to discover the discursive limitations implicit in this form of mimetic consciousness.[4] While living with his legal guardians, the Swerlins, Malcolm does his chores around the house, gets very high marks in his studies, gets a part-time job, plays basketball on the school team, and even gets elected class president. He believed that this had lifted him out of the category of "nigger" and enfranchised him into American meritocracy through mimicry. Hence when Malcolm's "well-intentioned" English teacher and adviser Mr. Ostrowski asks him what he would like to be, Malcolm unselfconsciously responds that he would like to be a lawyer, even though "Lansing certainly had no Negro lawyers—or doctor either—in those days, to hold up an image I might have aspired to" (36).

White people, like the Swerlins, his teachers, and his neighbors, approved of young Malcolm's mimetic achievements, but only as a respectable but necessarily fraudulent copy of their own achievement. To borrow from Homi Bhabha's "Of Mimicry and Men," I suggest that as representatives of a colonial state, these white people will only authorize young Malcolm's mimetic consciousness if it remains *mimetic,* that is, if it remains a *partial* presence of (white) humanity. However, Malcolm Little, with his high marks and sense of responsibility, comes dangerously close to slipping from partial presence of mimesis into full presence of (white) humanity. Thus when he tells Mr. Ostrowski that he would like to be a lawyer, the teacher as regulatory authority must police young Malcolm's mimicry (just as in Lansing the officers policed his father's) and tell him, "That's no realistic goal for a nigger" (36), reinscribing young Malcolm's identification with "those niggers" who were the consistent targets of white people's derogatory remarks.

After this rude awakening, Malcolm Little abandons his positionality as a mascot for the positionality of "homeboy." For Malcolm X, this turn also marks the beginning of a descent into depravity that ultimately lands him in jail. Malcolm X inscribes this dramatic shift in consciousness as a necessary, indeed *preordained,* precursor to revolutionary consciousness even though it led to degradation: "All praise is due to Allah that I went to Boston when I did. If I hadn't I'd still be a brainwashed black Christian" (38). For Malcolm X, it is all but impossible for a black man to attain true revolutionary consciousness from the representationally feminized position of the mascot. Later in his life, Malcolm X often derided the black leadership of the civil rights movement for precisely this "effeminate" mascot mentality. Better a tough, streetwise hustler than a meek and docile Christian, in his eyes. Better the organic rebellion of Caliban than the sycophancy of Ariel. This was a belief he held firmly from the time he went to Boston until after the end of his tenure with the NOI.

Robin D. G. Kelley, in his essay "The Riddle of the Zoot: Malcolm Little and Black Cultural Politics during World War II," has greatly elucidated the oppositional content of Malcolm X's homeboy days by contextualizing his zoot suit, lindy hopping, and hustling during this period within the black working-class youth culture of the day. However, Kelley assumes that Malcolm X, in his retelling of the story, either dismisses the resistive knowledge encoded in these oppositional signifiers or is simply unaware of their truly radical character. "As Malcolm tells the story, this period in his life was, *if anything*, a fascinating but destructive *detour* on the road to self-consciousness and political enlightenment. . . . Malcolm had reached a period of his life when opposition could be conceived only as uncompromising and unambiguous" (156–57). However, I would disagree that Malcolm X regarded any part of his life, especially *this* part, as a "detour." For a religious man whose life is prescribed by Allah, there are no detours. Again, *Autobiography* messianically reconstructs every event, every turn of Minister Malcolm's life as charged with significance, as leading or contributing to his revolutionary Islamic awakening. And this is not the reductive significance of a negative consciousness against which to measure the transformation. Malcolm X does understand that the consequences of this period were self-destructive, but he never underestimates the latent revolutionary content of his homeboy consciousness.

Rather than forget the resistance of the hustler, the homeboy, the hipster, their resistance constituted the *revolutionary horizon* of Malcolm X's religious errand, just as the peasants of Guatemala and Cuba constituted the revolutionary horizon of Payeras's and Guevara's guerrilla errand. After all, it was among these people, more than any other class of blacks, that Minister Malcolm regularly "went fishing" for converts to the NOI. In *Autobiography* the inherent rebellion of these black subjects, like their peasant counterparts for Guevara and Payeras, functions as a preconsciousness to revolutionary transformation. While the inherent resistance ascribed to these disaffected black youths resembles the organic resistance ascribed to the peasant classes by Guevara and Payeras, there is also a difference. Payeras and Guevara naturalize peasant consciousness in a way that Malcolm X never completely does with black consciousness. For Malcolm X, who is of the "ghetto," this resistive consciousness is an *acquired* knowledge for survival that is the counterpart to racist white knowledge. This unhoned, resistive knowledge operates as a preconsciousness that holds the potential for transformation into revolutionary collectivity under Islam and Malcolm X's guidance: "Many times since, I have thought about it, and, what it really meant. In one sense, we were huddled in there [the hustler's society], bonded together in seeking security and warmth and comfort from each other, and we didn't know it. All of us—who could have probed space, or cured cancer or built industries" (90). Thus within the degenerate community of hustlers lies an organic resistive knowledge, as well as an organic collectivity of a brotherhood "bonded together," albeit through criminality, to be tapped by the N O I for the greater good of curing cancer or building industries for the larger black community.

Just as peasant consciousness in Guevara's diary functions as the site of displacement for Guevara's anxiety over his own transformation, so too does resistive black consciousness reiteratively return as the site of anxiety in Malcolm X's *Autobiography*. As Kelley suggests, and I would agree, Malcolm X's retelling of his teenage years should be read "as a literary construction, a cliché that obscures more than it reveals." However, it is not the latent revolutionary content of these years that is obscured as Kelley presumes, because such revolutionary content is de rigueur in *Autobiography*'s messianic reconstruction of Malcolm X's life as revolutionary. Rather, what is obscured, what constantly resurfaces only to disappear under the disciplining eye of Minister Malcolm's interpretation, is the sheer pleasure of those days. Indeed, the tension between Minister Malcolm disciplining "Harlem Red" (his nickname during his hustling days) into the appropriate subject for revolutionary transformation and Malcolm X appreciating this period as something pleasurably more than just preparation for transformation animates the entire "Homeboy" section of the autobiography. Thus Malcolm X is not Kelley's "uncompromising and unambiguous" political animal in his reading of his own past. Rather, he is full of anxiety and ambivalence about the place of pleasure in black oppositional consciousness.

To catch Malcolm X in the act of repressing the unmistakable element of pleasure associated with the "prerevolutionary consciousness" of the homeboy hustler, let us turn to the epilogue of the book, the one section of *Autobiography* that never passed his censoring eye. In his epilogue, Alex Haley tells the reader that Malcolm X's mood during the retelling of his childhood ranged "from somber to grim," but when he reached his move to Boston in the narration:

Malcolm X began to laugh about how "square" he had been in the ghetto streets. "Why, I'm telling you things I haven't thought about since then!" he would exclaim. Then it was during recalling the early Harlem days that Malcolm X really got carried away. One night, suddenly, wildly, he jumped up from his chair and, incredibly, the fearsome black demagogue was scat-singing and popping his fingers, "re-bop-de-bop-blap-blam—" and then grabbing a vertical pipe with one hand (as a girl partner) he went jubilantly lindy-hopping around, his coattail and the long legs and the big feet flying as they had in those Harlem days. And then almost as suddenly, Malcolm X caught himself and sat back down, and for the rest of that session he was decidedly grumpy. (391)

The energy and jubilance of this "scat-singing" and "finger-popping" recursively returns in his dazzling descriptions of this period in his life: from his first awestruck visits to the black sections of Boston and Harlem to the elegant fit of his zoot, from the staying power of his lindying to the grandeur of his hustle, Malcolm X's descriptions are exuberant. And always the "decidedly grumpy" spin doctor steps in to make sure that the reader does not get as carried away as the narrator. For example, he describes Harlem with clear race pride as a "technicolor bazaar" with palatial ballrooms, wailing music, and "fever-heat" dancing, with bars full of sharply dressed sophisticates and musical celebrities (many of whom, he never fails to mention, became his good friends) (74). Malcolm X sums up: "That night *I was mesmerized*. This world was where I belonged. On that night I had started on my way to becoming a Harlemite." Then, immediately, Minister Malcolm steps in with "I was going to become one of the most depraved parasitical hustlers among New York's eight million people—four million of whom work, and the other four million of whom live off of them" (75).

Repeatedly, Malcolm X's description of this world, of himself, his hustling, and his associates, builds to a captivating crescendo of wit, grace, sophistication, and musicality. Then, as if catching himself, Minister Malcolm silences the orchestra with the material reality of racism and poverty. While this is used, of course, as rhetorical technique to drive home his political message, there is also always something more in these descriptions.[5] I ask, then, of Malcolm X as homeboy, as Detroit Red, as Harlem Red, what is this *something more* that must be obscured? What is the source of this ambivalent pleasure, this jubilance that must be repressed by the "fearsome black demagogue," as Haley puts it? What does the "decidedly grumpy"

Malcolm X fear he has revealed through these descriptions of Boston and Harlem, through the expression of scat-singing pleasure over these colorful days? What is the danger Malcolm X senses, and that the minister still admires, in the world he simultaneously leaves behind and carries with him?

If the civilizing discourse of the racist state encodes the "mascot" as the partial presence of (white) humanity, then the "homeboy," with his music, his lindying, and his hustling, is encoded as the excess of that presence.[6] Hence Malcolm X's ambivalence over the interpretation of his homeboy days reflects an appreciation of the inherent contradiction of colonial appropriation. On the one hand, white people, including Red's girlfriend Sophia, want to get close to and participate in precisely this "excess of humanity."[7] At the same time, this excess is also precisely what the state must discipline. Malcolm X tells us that the judge in effect sentences Shorty and him to long prison terms for sleeping with white girls, the sign of their sexual excess, of their inappropriate sexuality, rather than for the burglaries they committed (150). Bhabha suggests in his discussion of mimicry that, as a strategy for colonial appropriation, it ensures its own failure: "The success of colonial appropriation depends on the proliferation of inappropriate objects that ensure its strategic failure, so that mimicry is at once resemblance and menace" ("Of Mimicry" 127). The civilizing discourse of the state calls on the other to mimic the colonizer but guarantees its inappropriateness because mimicry always "*repeats* rather than *re-presents*" (128). Malcolm X is aware that this "proliferation of inappropriate objects," the "excess" of the hustler's life, in the logic of mimicry constitutes a "menace" that summons, indeed sanctions, the discipline and the authority of the state.[8] And thus, I would suggest, Malcolm X resists simply celebrating this "excess" not only because of the moral code of Islam, or because of an uncompromising political consciousness, but out of an understanding of the logic of colonial appropriation.

Malcolm X as minister of the NOI disrupts this colonial logic by appropriating the disciplining function of the state in the service of black nationalism. As a member of the NOI, with its authoritarian organization, its origin story, and its explicit sexual boundaries, Malcolm X disciplines this excess through an appropriation of the tropic confluence between Anglo-American subjectivity and full masculinity. His mimicry turns to mockery in the eyes of white America precisely because, as a member of the NOI, Malcolm X successfully moves from partial or excess presence to a subjectivity encoded as virtual essence of (white) humanity. Three moments of this disciplining function in Malcolm X's life demonstrate this move from mimicry to mockery and elucidate the importance of his mission for African American and white America.

Disciplining the Other and White Anxiety

In the previous section on Guevara and Payeras, I suggested that the whole guerrilla experience served as the trope for fantasmatic recuperation of full masculinity. In *Autobiography*, words and a certain mode of speech serve this tropic function: "Bimbi was the first Negro convict I'd known who didn't respond to 'What'cha know, Daddy?' . . . we would sit around, perhaps fifteen of us, and listen to Bimbi. Normally, white prisoners wouldn't think of listening to Negro prisoners' opinions on anything, but guards, even, would wander over close to hear Bimbi on any subject. . . . What fascinated me with him most of all was that he was the first man I had ever seen *command total respect . . . with his words*" (153–54; italics mine). Bimbi commands respect from blacks *and* whites through a mode of speech that is pointedly *not* the vernacular of the hustler. Rather, Bimbi speaks in a language that lays claim to cataloged encyclopedic knowledge—historical, scientific, and literary. It is Bimbi's deployment of this knowing language that first inspires Malcolm X to take a correspondence course in English and then in Latin. Once Malcolm X converts to Islam, under the tutelage of his brother and Elijah Mohammed, he proceeds to obsessively absorb this cataloged knowledge himself, first by copying the dictionary and then by reading the entire prison library. As with Menchú, this mastery of the colonizer's mode of speech provides Malcolm X with subjection and authority on a personal level, as well. It is through the deployment of the power of words that Malcolm X reconstructs his personal patronymic at the beginning of the *Autobiography*. Malcolm X refuses the racist stereotyping that might label Earl Little as derelict father, and instead inserts his father and himself into the historical continuity of black nationalism through a performative act of knowledgeable speech. Minister Malcolm X learns to speak with the authority of God and history, albeit a Muslim God and an anticolonialist history. The fiery minister in the pulpit and the gentle teacher in the classroom merge in the singular function of these very different performative speech acts, which redeem an Afrocentric history for himself and for black Americans. Malcolm X then proceeds to reclaim the future by disciplining sexual boundaries in the service of the black nation.

What most impresses Malcolm X about the NOI once he has been released from prison is the responsibility it brings to bear on his brother Wilfred and the order it brings to the home: "This Muslim home's atmosphere sent me often to my knees to praise Allah. . . . There was none of the morning confusion that exists in most homes. Wilfred, the father, the family protector and provider, was the first to rise. 'The father prepares the way for his family,' he said. He, then I performed the morning ablutions. Next came Wilfred's wife Ruth, and then their children, so that orderliness prevailed in the use of the bathroom" (193). Wilfred then prepares the prayer rug on which the family, once purified, kneels together in prayer, facing East "in unity with the rest of our 725 million brothers and sisters in the entire Muslim world" (194). This daily ritualized performance of the prayer establishes order in the household. This is not just the order of a morning routine and who gets to use the bathroom first. Rather, through this prayer ritual, gender categories are also performed, ritualized, and hierarchized. This description of Muslim prayer tells us far less about the performance of gender categories in the heterogeneous "Muslim world" than it tells us about the status of these categories and the romanticized nuclear family in the United States of the 1950s and 1960s. Malcolm X's recuperation of a normatively gendered and hierarchized family comes precisely at a moment when the myth of the white nuclear family is being challenged by the 1960s counterculture, and particularly by the counterculture of white youth. Malcolm X sees the recuperation of this normative construction of the family unit as essential for the survival and advancement of blacks in the ghettos of the United States. The recuperation of the family as a model for black nationalist projects has now been soundly critiqued by African American feminists and queer theorists.[9] The legitimacy of this criticism notwithstanding, recuperating the nuclear family has the radical effect of inverting the logic of colonial mimicry. The construction of this family unit within the NOI, and Malcolm X's propagation of this family unit in the entire black community through his preaching, coincides with a growing anxiety among white Americans over the erosion of the family perceived as the foundation of the white nation. Indeed, the NOI's success in propagating this idea of family contributes to this anxiety. Suddenly Muslim black families appear to participate in this gendered, structured, and orderly family with greater success than all other families, black or white. Black Muslims have the myth of the nuclear American family, "only more so."[10] This rationalized and disciplined unit of economic and ideological reproduction is no longer essentially white.

Finally, Minister Malcolm disciplines the hustling society into the industrious society. This was at the heart of the redemptive ministry of Malcolm X and the NOI. Malcolm X, as a member of the NOI, achieves the independence and self-reliance for the black man that his father desired. At various points in *Autobiography*, Malcolm X tells the reader that the NOI had its own newspaper, banking system, farms, processing plants, trucking business, chain of stores, and restaurants. As I have discussed in chapter 2, during the post–War World II politics of the 1950s, 1960s, and 1970s, the U.S. government was the major proponent of such self-sustained, diversified development paradigms in the decolonizing Third World countries. As I argued, this developmentalist paradigm—with the founding of the World Bank, the International Monetary Fund, and the proliferation of development projects —emerged as a method for maintaining colonial surveillance, political influence, and economic control over countries on the verge of national independence. As a refiguration of the logic of colonial appropriation, development held the promise of equal citizenship in the fraternal order of First World nations. Precisely as the First World, led by the United States, was busy propagating development paradigms all over the globe, the black brothers and sisters of the NOI were busy at home creating a modernized Muslim nation within a nation.

The NOI, in establishing this economic organization, adhered to the regime of subjection put forth by development discourse. As typified by Rostow, modernization hinges primarily on choice, on a community making the ethical choice of taking money out of the hands of those spending it on "prodigal living" and transferring it into the hands of those who will amass and invest it as capital (Rostow 24). The NOI, with its strict moral code, does precisely this. Money previously spent by converts on entertainment is centralized through donations to the mosques and funneled by the ministers, who function as an executive board, into Muslim businesses. Profits are "plowed back" into related businesses, jobs for Muslim brothers and sisters are created, wages grow, demand increases, the economy diversifies. Although Minister Malcolm saw his role as primarily spiritual, he played no small part in the NOI's economic efforts. He provided the converts. He fished for converts not only among the working blacks but among those doing the most profligate spending: drug addicts, hustlers, and prostitutes. Malcolm X disciplined the "prodigal" into the industrious, thereby appropriating the terms of the emerging post–World War II discourse of development. The NOI thus becomes a textbook case of the modern nation and demands equal standing with another modern nation, the United States.[11]

As chief minister of the NOI, Malcolm X successfully recuperates the discursive terms of full masculinity for himself: mastery of language, the myth of family—both nuclear and national—with a clearly demarcated role for himself as both father and minister, the industry and self-reliance of the U.S. founding fathers. Through the apparent recuperation of these terms, Malcolm X attains the fantasy of coherence that Judith Butler suggests is at the center of *all* identity formation, and that I suggest motivates Malcolm X's quest for revolutionary subjection:

> According to the understanding of identification as an enacted fantasy or incorporation, however, it is clear that coherence is desired, wished for, idealized, and that this idealization is an effect of a corporeal signification. In other words, acts, gestures, and desire produce the effect of an internal core or substance, but produce this *on the surface* of the body, through the play of signifying absences that suggest, but never reveal, the organizing principle of identity as a cause. Such acts, gestures, enactments, generally construed, are *performative* in the sense that the essence or identity that they otherwise purport to express are *fabrications* manufactured and sustained through corporeal signs and other discursive means. (Butler, *Gender Trouble* 136)

Through his "corporeal signs," his words, acts, gestures, and desire, Malcolm X performs coherence, that "organizing principle of identity as a cause." He successfully performs Baker's tropic Anglo-American subjectivity, but as a black Muslim, he does so as an "inappropriate" subject. In his performance of this subjectivity, full masculinity necessarily appears as hyper-masculinity precisely because it is performed in such an "inappropriate" subject, and consequently Malcolm X's masculinity is perceived as caricature by white America. Nevertheless, when Malcolm X brings discipline to bear on this "hyper-masculinity," when he successfully usurps the disciplining function of the white state, he achieves the appearance of coherence; he successfully achieves the fabrication of essence. He thereby destroys, for the white community, the boundary between the white, Christian subject and the black, Muslim other. Butler suggests: "What constitutes through division the 'inner' and 'outer' worlds of the subject is a border and boundary tenuously maintained for the purposes of social regulation and control" (134). Malcolm X, as inappropriate subject laying claim to this inner world of the (white) tropic Anglo-American subject, erases this tenuous and tenacious border of social control. Thus he threatens the social regulation of the segregated United States of the 1950s and 1960s not by armed insurrection, or even by the peaceful means of nonviolence, but simply by the enactment of a disciplined American masculinity, by the appearance of being. This performance is a parody, a mockery, not because Malcolm X is parodic, but because Malcolm X in his recuperation of full masculinity as tropic Anglo-American subject reveals to white men that they lack an original claim to this masculinity, to this "internal core." Malcolm X reveals that there is no (white) essence to this tropic American subjectivity, that the essence of this subjectivity is a *fabrication* he can successfully represent. Therein lies the violation, the "violence," of Malcolm X, a gentle man who was never personally associated with physical violence. At the time of his death, all he had on his person in the way of defense was a pen that sprayed Mace. But Malcolm X does violence to a discursive term.[12]

Malcolm X's performance of full masculinity, disciplined by ritualized gender categories, a strict Muslim moral code, and a puritanical ethic of industry, does violence to the category of whiteness, to the purity of category. Nevertheless Malcolm X, in his political performance as ideologue, professes the inviolability and purity of categories such as white/black, male/female, "field Negro"/"house Negro," at least for his tenure as minister for the NOI. So that even while Malcolm X's "inappropriate" performance of the tropic Anglo-American subjectivity violates the racial imperative behind the categories of gender and nation, it nevertheless substantiates the categories themselves. Thus the category of the feminine in *Autobiography* is invariably deceptive, weak, and in need of strict policing so that women may better serve the nation run by men.[13] This is the double bind of the performance, that even when the performance of such categories by inappropriate subjects reveals the artifice of such categories, these categories as artifice are necessarily maintained by the performance. I am not suggesting the existence of pure categories outside of those discursively given by cultural systems. Rather, I am trying to locate in Malcolm X's performance of a tropic (male) Anglo-American subject the grounds for exclusion in Malcolm X's construction of a modern black nation.

Cornel West has suggested that Malcolm X's black nationalism was based on a fear of cultural hybridity: "Malcolm X . . . seems to have had almost no intellectual interest in dealing with what is distinctive about the Black Church and Black music: *their cultural hybrid character in which the complex mixture of African, European, and Amerindian elements are constitutive of something that is new and Black in the modern world.* Like most Black nationalists, Malcolm X feared the culturally hybrid character of Black life. This fear resulted in the dependence on Manichean (black-and-white or male/female) channels for the direction of Black rage—forms characterized by charismatic leaders, patriarchal structures, and dogmatic pronouncements" (54). Thus while Malcolm X was exemplary of a cultural hybridity—precisely through his deployment of paradigmatic white U.S. subjectivity as a black man—his fear of this hybridity, his recursive fear of his own pleasurable past, contains an impulse toward exclusion. This exclusion is the exclusion not only of whites but also of blacks who refused to accept the patriarchal teleology of consciousness implicit in the developmentalist trope of the Anglo-American subject that Malcolm X appropriated. This included not only the "house Negro" leaders of the civil rights movement but any blacks for whom this cultural hybridity was not just a pleasurable point of identification but also a means for resisting racial subordination.[14] Malcolm X's break with the NOI led him away from a dogmatic insistence on racial and cultural separation. Perhaps, if he had lived longer, this break might have led him closer to a politically viable understanding of the fact of cultural hybridity that is far more evident today than it may have been in the 1960s.

Nevertheless, I do not intend to end with a trite celebration of cultural hybridity, for if the era of Zapatismo has taught us anything at all, it has taught us that hybridity, as a model of oppositional consciousness, does not in and of itself constitute liberation, nor does it invariably escape the exclusionary developmentalism present in revolutionary nationalisms and their regimes of subjection. The Zapatistas' critique of the much-vaunted category of mestizaje demonstrates that certain concepts of hybridity, no matter how theoretically popular, may subtly reinscribe a developmental impetus as well. And so I turn my attention to the postnationalist, postrevolutionary articulation of mestizaje in the contemporary writings of Chicanas/os.

Ticket to the New Aztlán

As in the case of the black nationalism of the Black Power movement, the Chicano nationalism of the late 1960s and early 1970s was heavily influenced by the theory of internal colonialism. According to this theoretical model, just as U.S. capitalism had a vested interest in maintaining the economies of Latin America and the Third World in conditions of underdevelopment and dependent development, so too did it have an interest in maintaining U.S. minority populations in conditions of underdevelopment and dependency. Furthermore, just as U.S. neocolonialism used any means necessary to maintain Third World countries in this subjugated position, so too did U.S. *internal colonialism* use any means necessary to maintain its minority populations in subjugation. Thus, while the Black Belt extending from southern agriculture land to the northeastern industrial corridor was the geographic site of the black internal colony, the former Mexican territory in the Southwest was the site of the Chicano internal colony. However, unlike black nationalism, Chicano nationalism was able to make a prior proprietary claim on the Southwest. Working under the premise of this model of internal colonialism, Chicanas/os appropriated the Mexican discourse of mestizaje by claiming Aztlán as an indigenous nation historically anterior to the founding of the United States. Indeed, it is the concept of mestizaje that enabled Chicanas/os to claim a biological tie to this Aztec origin story and to place it in the U.S. Southwest. Mestizaje lent a moral and historical legitimacy to claims for economic and civil rights by constituting Aztlán as a space outside the U.S. nation, prior to the U.S. nation, from which to launch a critique of a hegemonic and racist regime of subjection (Padilla). Aztlán-based Chicano nationalism has been eloquently and exhaustively critiqued by Chicana feminists and Chicana/o poststructuralist and queer scholars, and thus I will not rehash these arguments here. Instead I would like to refocus our attention on the residual effect of this era of Chicano nationalism: the continued use of mestizaje as a trope for Chicana/o identity and the presumed access to indigenous subjectivity that this biologized trope offers us. Although the deployment of mestizaje in the Southwest is different from its historical deployment in Mexico, when Chicana/o intellectuals and artists appropriate the tropes of mestizaje and indigenismo for the purposes of identity formation, we are nevertheless operating within the racial ideology from which these tropes are borrowed. We must take seriously, then, the Zapatista movement's critique of mestizaje and indigenismo as a singular racial ideology that incorporates the figure of the Indian in the consolidation of a nationalist identity in order to effectively exclude him. Thus, in our Chicana/o reappropriation of the biologized terms of mestizaje and indigenismo, we are also always recuperating the Indian as an ancestral past rather than recognizing contemporary Indians as coinhabitants not only of this continent abstractly conceived but of the neighborhoods and streets of hundreds of U.S. cities and towns. I would like to suggest that mestizaje is incapable of suturing together the heterogeneous positionalities of "Mexican," "Indian," and "Chicana/o" that coexist in the United States, or, more importantly, of offering effective *political* subjectivity to those represented by these positionalities. Why, in other words, do Chicanos in Austin dance to *tejano* music in one bar, mestizo

Mexican migrants in another, and indigenous Mexican migrants in none at all? In mestizaje, we are reduced to searching for signs of our indigenous past and, more significantly, for a collective political future in some inherent tie to the land—in our "cosmic green thumb," as Guillermo Gómez-Peña, the border *brujo*, has so ironically put it. To recognize this process is not to deny our indigenous ancestry; rather, to recognize this is to refuse to reduce indigenous subjectivity, and indeed Mexican mestizo identity, to biologistic representation that, in discursive and political terms, always already places indigenous peoples under erasure.

The question before us, then, is if postnationalist intellectuals such as Gloria Anzaldúa and Richard Rodriguez are able to recuperate a more sophisticated concept of mestizaje: one that might possibly extend political enfranchisement or literary representation to the broad range of subject positions implied by a common Mexican heritage. In the opening pages of *Borderlands/La Frontera*, Anzaldúa movingly represents *la frontera*, the borderlands, in a way that indeed promises us a new paradigm of mestizaje: "The U.S.–Mexican border *es una herida abierta* where the Third World grates against the first and bleeds. And before a scab forms it hemorrhages again, the lifeblood of two worlds merging to form a third country—a border culture. Borders are set up to define the safe and the unsafe, to distinguish *us* from *them*. A border is a dividing line, a narrow strip along a steep edge. A borderland is a vague and undetermined place created by the emotional residue of an unnatural boundary. It is in a constant state of transition" (3). The border is *the* quintessential site of mestizaje, of the untidy mixture of "lifeblood." In this first image of the borderland, Anzaldúa unsettles the conventional usage of mestizaje by restaging the brutality of the initial colonial encounter between Spaniard and Indian in the neocolonial encounter between the First World and Third World. This encounter, this mixture, "es una herida abierta"—an open wound, a wound that refuses to heal because the violence of the initial encounter continues, metamorphosing into new instances of wounding. The traditional Mexican usage of mestizaje sutures over the violence of the colonial encounter with the developmentalist logic implicit in it as a third term—the Indian and the Spaniard evolve into the mestizo.[15] Anzaldúa interrupts the teleological drive in mestizaje, however, with her image of the wound that has not healed: when the "lifeblood[s]" of these "two worlds" merge in the borderlands, they hemorrhage. Anzaldúa's "third country," her border culture, is not a neat and tidy end of history but a "constant state of transition."

In this passage, Anzaldúa's borderland promises to unsettle the conventional usage of mestizaje for Chicanos, as well. For if Anzaldúa's borderland undoes the artificial duality of a border, of the "us" and "them," it does so in the service of recognizing the material violence of such artificial constructs. Thus, at this point in the text, Anzaldúa could proceed to resituate the Chicana/o as mestizo, the Mexican as mestizo, and the Indian as Mexican within a transnational frame that would address the unequal power relations among such positionalities. In other words, whereas the mestizaje of Aztlán in the 1970s allied Mexicanos and Chicanos through a common past—through a dead indigenous ancestry—the mestizaje of Anzaldúa's borderlands could disrupt such assumption and place each of these positionalities in that uneasy and "constant state of transition" within a capitalist world system that depends on national, cultural, and racial differentiation for the reproduction of its productive forces.

Instead of taking up her own provocative challenge to do this, however, Anzaldúa quickly slips back into the conventional usage of mestizaje, constructing Chicanas/os in the borderlands as the "us" against the Anglo "them." In other words, she once again rallies mestizaje to access an indigenous ancestry that legitimates a prior claim to the Southwest for Chicanas and Chicanos: "The oldest evidence of humankind in the United States— the Chicanos' ancient Indian ancestors—was found in Texas and has been dated 35000 B.C." (4). Ignoring the contemporary Native American inhabitants of the Southwest and their very different mytho-genealogies, Anzaldúa predictably claims this "oldest evidence of humankind" for Chicanas/os as evidence of the occupation of the Southwest by the indigenous ancestors of the Aztecs. Consequently, one page and a few thousand years later, when the settlement of the Southwest by the Spaniards occurs in her book, she continues: "Our Spanish, Indian and mestizo ancestors explored and settled parts of the U.S. Southwest as early as the sixteenth century. For every gold hungry conquistador and soul hungry missionary who came north from Mexico, ten or twenty Indians and mestizos went along as porters or in other capacities. For the Indians, this constituted a return to the place of origin, Aztlán, thus making Chicanos originally and secondarily indigenous to the Southwest" (5).

Let us trace the circuitous route by which mestizaje makes Chicanas/os "originally and secondarily indigenous to the Southwest." According to Anzaldúa, Chicanas/os are originally indigenous to the area because of our biological tie to the first Indians who inhabited it some 37,000 years ago (her date), the mythical Indian tribe that traveled from Aztlán in the U.S. Southwest to Mexico City and subsequently formed the Aztec empire. And we are secondarily indigenous through our "return" to this homeland with the Spaniards as Indians and mestizos. As in Payeras's jungle diary, when he reads the guerrilla as following in the tracks of the "great migrations" of his Mayan ancestors, mestizaje is once again deployed to produce a biological tie with pre-Aztec Indians rather than a political tie with contemporary U.S. Native Americans or Mexican Indians. Consequently, in this system of representation, indigenous subjectivity is once again put under erasure. The condition of possibility for Chicana/o nostalgia over our indigenous subjectivity made evident in this passage is the rarefaction of indigenous peoples as past.

Of course, this is mestizaje with a feminist, queer twist. In an important contradistinction to earlier Chicano deployments of mestizaje, Anzaldúa draws from the female deities in the Aztec pantheon to explain a variety of Chicana-mestiza customs, to explain patriarchy in Chicano culture, and to explain Chicana sexuality. Thus, throughout the book, Anzaldúa links Chicana artistic creativity to Coatlique, the goddess of fertility; Chicana sexual expression or freedom to Tlazolteyotl, a goddess of the underworld; and Chicana mourning or sorrow over oppression in all its guises with Cihuocowatl, goddess of war. To access our mestiza consciousness as Chicanas, we must open ourselves up to the connections in our everyday lives with this pantheon of female deities, to our psychobiological links with the matriarchal Aztec culture of some five hundred years ago: "The new *mestiza* copes by developing a tolerance for contradictions, a tolerance for ambiguity. She learns to be an Indian in Mexican culture, to be Mexican from an Anglo point of view. She juggles cultures. She has a plural personality, she operates in a pluralistic mode" (79). Anzaldúa is certainly correct when she suggests that in her model of mestiza consciousness one "learns to be an Indian in Mexican culture" because in Anzaldúa's model we are right back where we started under the PRI's state-sponsored mestizaje and indigenismo. What Anzaldúa does not recognize—indeed, cannot recognize from her privileged position as First World minority rather than Third World subaltern—is that her very focus on the Aztec female deities is an effect of the PRI's statist policies to resuscitate, through state-funded documentation, this particular, defunct Mexican Indian culture and history to the exclusion of dozens of living indigenous cultures. When she resuscitates this particular representation of indigenous subjectivity to be incorporated into contemporary mestiza consciousness, she too does so to the exclusion and, indeed, erasure of contemporary indigenous subjectivity and practices on both sides of the border.

Turning now to Richard Rodriguez, despite his woeful misinterpretation of contemporary Mexican politics and culture, he reinterprets the tropes of mestizaje and indigenismo in some provocative ways for Chicanos and Mexicans. He begins his chapter "India" in *Days of Obligation:*

> I used to stare at the Indian in the mirror. The wide nostrils, the thick lips. . . . Such a long face—such a long nose—sculpted by indifferent, blunt thumbs, and of such common clay. No one in my family had a face as dark or as Indian as mine. My face could not portray the ambition I brought to it. What could the United States of America say to me? I remember reading . . . the Kerner Report in the sixties: two Americas, one white, one Black—the prophecy of an eclipse too simple to account for the complexity of my face.
>
> *Mestizo* in Mexican Spanish means mixed, confused. Clotted with Indian, thinned by Spanish spume.
>
> What could Mexico say to me?
>
> Mexican philosophers powwow in their tony journals about Indian "fatalism" and "Whither Mexico?" *El fatalismo del indio* is an important Mexican philosophical theme; the phrase is trusted to conjure the quality of Indian passivity as well as to initiate debate about Mexico's reluctant progress toward modernization. Mexicans imagine their Indian part as deadweight, stunned by modernity; so overwhelmed by the loss of what is genuine to him—his language, his religion—that he sits weeping like a medieval lady at the crossroads; or else he resorts to occult powers and superstitions, choosing to consort with death because the purpose of the world has passed him by. (1–2)

In this passage, Rodriguez eloquently captures the failure of literary and political representations of race in the United States and Mexico to capture the complexities of a face. The hegemonic black/white paradigm of race relations in the United States precludes the recognition—much less the reward—of a face like his, so he turns to Mexico. But Mexico has nothing to offer his ambition, either. If black/white relations in this country eclipse the complexities of his mestizaje, Mexican philosophical ruminations on mestizo identity deny him and his Indian features any futurity. The Indian in mestizaje is dead weight, modernity incomprehensible to him. Indeed, Mexican scholars and philosophers since Manuel Gamio have repeatedly shackled the Indian and his lack of futurity with the responsibility for the failure of a system that was predicated on his erasure to begin with.

In this first passage, Rodriguez synopsizes the history of Indian representation in mestizo Mexico: in mestizaje, the Indian is feminized and prehistoric as a "medieval lady" (indeed, she gives birth to the mestizo race only to disappear with Malinche from the script of history), passive and resigned in his "weeping," incomplete in his loss of truth (symbolized by his language and religion). Alternately, like the precapitalist indigenous and peasant formations in Payeras and Guevara, he is treacherous in his fraternizing with the devil through the occult, but nevertheless impotent in his rebellion as he is always already consorting with death. Ultimately Anzaldúa finds nothing but a celebratory hybridity in the concept of mestizaje, but Rodriguez recognizes and reveals mestizaje as the repressive regime of subjection that it is for the indigenous peoples of Latin America. For the remainder of the chapter, Rodriguez resists traditional representations of mestizaje precisely because any futurity that incorporates the reality of his face depends on it. Instead Rodriguez inverts the power relations implicit in mestizaje by insisting that the mestizo is not the evidence of the triumph of the Spanish colonizer over the colonized Indian but the evidence of the triumph of the colonizing Indian over the colonized Spaniard.

Rodriguez begins this inversion with a rejection of the construction of Malinche, the representational birthplace of mestizaje, as either the victim of a Spanish rape or the betrayer of her indigenous past. She is instead the curious seductress of Spain, with all of the agency that postmodern feminism has restored to the power of seduction:

> Because Marina was the seducer of Spain, she challenges the boast Europe has always told about India.
>
> I assure you that Mexico has an Indian point of view as well, a female point of view:
>
> *I opened my little eye and the Spaniard disappeared.*
>
> *Imagine a dark pool; the Spaniard dissolved; the surface triumphantly smooth.*
>
> *My eye!*
>
> *The spectacle of the Spaniard on the horizon, vainglorious, the shiny surfaces, clanks of metal; the horses, the muskets, the jingling bits.*
>
> *Cannot you imagine me curious? Didn't I draw near?*
>
> European vocabularies do not have a silence rich enough to describe the force within Indian contemplation. (22)

The "boast" that Europe tells itself is, of course, that the Spaniards discovered the Indians. Instead Marina casts her gaze on the Spaniard and discovers him. Just as millions of Indians "disappeared" from disease on "discovery," the Spaniard immediately disappears within the gaze of discovery. The complexity of his subjectivity—his heritage, his culture, his history—is immediately dissolved into the dark pool of a mestizaje that swallows him and is "triumphantly smooth" afterward, leaving no trace. Marina is unconcerned with the depth of the Spaniard; what she is enamored of is the surface; what she is after in her seduction are the jingly trinkets. The Spaniard is the spectacle here, not the Indian. And yet this is not a simple anticolonialist inversion of the identity terms. It is more complicated than an inversion, as Malinche is only accessible to us through her Spanish given name, Marina—through the language of the colonizer.

Nevertheless the Indian does not simply return the gaze: the Indian *is* the gaze. And while the European hears the silence as a vanquished enemy, the silence, like the silence in Zapatismo, is not an absence but a presence filled with centered and active contemplation: "The Indian stands in the same relationship to modernity as [Marina] did to Spain—willing to marry, to breed, to disappear in order to ensure her inclusion in time; refusing to absent herself from the future. The Indian has chosen to survive, to consort with the living, to live in the city, to crawl on her hands and knees, if need be, to Mexico City or L.A." (24). The weapons available to the Indian in the colonial and postcolonial regimes of subjection have been the "weapons of the weak": to remain visible, you disappear; to survive, you crawl; to win, you breed (Scott, *Weapons*). Modern Indians find agency in the only way possible, through resistive adaptation (Mintz, *Caribbean Transformations, Sweetness and Power*). And by making assiduous use of the weapons of the weak, the Mexican Indian not only survived in mestizaje but eventually consumed his other, the Spaniard, the European:

> Look once more at the city from La Malinche's point of view. Mexico is littered with the shells and skulls of Spain, cathedrals, poems, and the limbs of orange trees. But everywhere you look in this great museum of Spain you see living Indians.
>
> Where are the *conquistadores?*
>
> Postcolonial Europe expresses pity or guilt behind its sleeve, pities the Indian the loss of her gods or her tongue. But let the Indian speak for herself. Spanish is now an Indian language. Mexico has captured Spanish. (R. Rodriguez, *Days of Obligation* 23–24)

The mestizo is now an Indian. The Spaniard is the museum. Through mestizaje, a thoroughly modern Indian has cannibalized the Spanish markers of identity. The Indian has absorbed the European terms of subjectivity, and consequently these terms are turned into indigenous markers of identity from the inside out. The European is silent; the Indian is speaking.

Rodriguez's reworking of the representational tropes of mestizaje and indigenismo for Chicana/o subject formation is perhaps the most fruitful to date. It refuses the erasure of the Indian by putting the Spaniard under erasure instead—by insisting on the Indian as the primary term in the trope of mestizaje. He recognizes not only the Indian presence in the contemporary world but the Indian as the primary agent of modern Mexican history. However, Rodriguez also ends up at a biological representation of indigenism—one that is exciting and new but has its own set of limits. Ultimately for Rodriguez, the signs of indigenous identity *are* reducible to the surface signifiers of facial features, to genetics: the "beak nose," the dark skin, the almond eyes. And the only avenue to political agency for the modern-day Indian is the avenue of this newly configured domain of mestizaje. While Rodriguez's mestizaje radically reconstructs power relations between the colonizer and the colonized, it nevertheless requires the Indian to give up his or her language, religious practices, and other forms of cultural and social organization.

In other words, Spanish is not an Indian language precisely because most Indians living in Mexico and the rest of Latin America do not speak Spanish as a first language. And for a further understanding of the underlying biologism in both Anzaldúa's and Rodriguez's representation of tropes of indigenism and mestizaje, we need to return to Menchú's and the Zapatistas' insistence that indigenous identity is not reducible to biology. Any person born an Indian, with all the genetic Indian features, can become Ladinized by refusing to practice his or her indigenous identity in the hopes of accessing the limited amount of power made available to poor mestizos. Indigenous identity, for Menchú and the Zapatistas, depends not simply on biology but on the rigorous practice of the thoroughly modern cultural, linguistic, social, religious, and political forms that constitute one as indigenous. And these are not forms that exist in a kind of pastiche grab bag of Indian spiritual paraphernalia, as they seem to exist for Anzaldúa. Ultimately, Anzaldúa's model of representation reproduces liberal developmental models of choice that privilege her position as a U.S. Chicana: she goes through her backpack and decides what to keep and what to throw out, choosing to keep signs of indigenous identity as ornamentation and spiritual revival. But what of the living Indian who refuses mestizaje as an avenue to political and literary representation? What of the *indígena* who demands new representational models that include her among the living? Menchú's and the Zapatistas' texts offer nonbiological forms of culture that are not only shared among a practicing community of indigenous people but hold the possibility of an alternative model of democratic practices for revolutionary subjection. Thus the Zapatista movement appropriates liberal constitutional discourse, but they appropriate it precisely in the hopes of constructing a space for legitimating themselves as multilingual, multi-cultural citizens of the body politic. In other words, these indigenous populations appropriate the Spanish of the mestizo to insist on their inclusion in the body politic not as mestizo but as radically other: as coterminously national citizen and Indian.

In contrast to Anzaldúa and Rodriguez, Tomás Rivera's . . . *y no se lo trago la tierra* offers nonbiological coordinates for revolutionary subjection. And as in the Zapatista communiqués, the coordinates of this subjection lie in the generative place of silence. Rivera's autobiographical fiction employs many of the same literary techniques as the Zapatistas employ in their communiqués. The strategic use of the folkloric voice, the place of silence and language in the formation of community, and the role of intellectuality in Rivera's *tierra* and in the communiqués mirror each other across the span of forty-odd years. (Although I provide the English translation from the bilingual edition of *tierra*, I will be analyzing the original Spanish because the English translation is inaccurate):

> Siempre empezaba todo cuando oía que alguien le llamaba por su nombre pero cuando volteaba la cabeza a ver quién era el que le llamaba, daba una vuelta entera y quedaba donde mismo. Por eso nunca podía acertar ni quién le llamaba ni por qué, y luego hasta se le olvidaba el nombre que le habian llamado. Pero sabía que él era a quien llamaban.
>
> Una vez se detuvo antes de dar la vuelta entera y le entró miedo. Se dio cuenta de que él mismo se había llamado. Y así empezó el año perdido. (7)
>
> [It always began when he would hear someone calling him by his name but when he turned his head to see who was calling, he would make a complete turn and there he would end up—in the same place. This was why he could never discover who was calling him nor why. And then he even forgot the name he had been called.
>
> One time he stopped at mid-turn and fear suddenly set in. He realized that he had called himself. And thus the lost year began.] (83)

On first reading, this scene appears to be a textbook case of Althusserian interpellation. The boy does not know who calls him or why—he even forgets the name he is being called—nevertheless he is certain it is he who is being called. An omniscient voice hails the boy into Subjectivity, with a capital *S*, at once anonymous and universal, and the boy responds appropriately: he turns around. In the necessary extension of this Althusserian interpellation, the boy, evidently, is calling himself: he has internalized the disciplining voice of ideology. And yet the moment of recognizing that he is calling himself is also the moment of an interpellative misfire: "Se dio cuenta de que siempre pensabe que pensaba." He becomes aware of the fact that he "always thought that he thought." It is as if the boy becomes aware of liberal development's imperative that men *must be prepared to be prepared* to become exploited laborers. The protagonist in *tierra* recognizes the workings of ideology through him when he recognizes that he only thinks that he is thinking. As with Menchú's experience working on the finca, interpellation slips, and a "radically conditioned agency," in Judith Butler's terms, begins to take shape.

The rest of the autobiographical novel makes evident why this interpellative misfire is almost a necessary condition of his own subaltern subjection. The boy is being hailed not into the pretense of agency, as suggested in development discourse, but into its exact opposite, into the condition of the muted object, or, to borrow a phrase from African American scholarship, of the commodity that speaks. As Ramón Saldívar argues in his definitive chapter on *tierra* in his book *Chicano Narrative*, the boy in this first scene becomes the chronotopic point of organization for this fragmented postmodern narrative, with each memory of his lost year metonymically representing the collectivity of south Texas migrants. Thus, in the twelve vignettes that ensue, the members of this community are collectively hailed to the positions of religiously ordained subservience, of patriotic fodder for war, of flea-ridden beasts of burden, of psychosis bereft of speech. The extremely exploitative terms of their interpellative subjection suggest interpellation must misfire, if any form of conditional agency, other than criminal agency, is to take shape. The community's interpellation into complete abjection culminates in the penultimate vignette, "Cuando lleguemos." It is this vignette, with the paragraph that follows it, that most closely parallels the Zapatista speech acts.

In "Cuando lleguemos," the members of the migrant laborer community are crammed into the back of a truck, all standing, like cattle, literalizing their positionality as commodities being driven to market. Like the Zapatistas reduced to the level of animals, plants, and rocks, the migrants in the back of the cattle truck have been reduced to muted objects. The migrant workers do not speak to each other; there is no *cotorreo* here. There is resounding silence in the back of the cattle truck, and yet again, this silence is not contentless. As we hear the self-reflective internal monologues of various migrants, the communal experience of misery and pain they share for fourteen uninterrupted hours in the back of the truck is made evident to the reader. However, again, not only pain and misery transpire in the silence: one man, in existential reverie, marks the beauty of the stars above; another finds endless humor in the expression of the man's face who took his order for fifty-four hamburgers; a woman contemplates how much she loves her husband. And once again, the silence in the back of the truck represents the possibility of radical democracy. Silence is the condition of possibility for differences to emerge as each person thinks his or her own thoughts, as in the Spanish adage "cada cabeza es un mundo." Although these thoughts in the silence make evident the mutuality of their suffering, a communal consciousness of their material condition cannot emerge as long as the migrants' expectations of what they will do when they arrive remain isolated in the individuation of internal monologue. As Saldívar points out in his analysis of the novel, "Read dialectically . . . with the recognition that, as one voice puts it, 'es la misma cosa llegar que partir,' the phrase carries quite another valence: when we arrive we are no better off than we were when we departed. At this point we are at a protopolitical level, one step away from the recognition that the cycle of arriving and departing is itself part of the coercive system for guaranteeing the availability of cheap and plentiful labor" (88).

Rivera's tierra suggests that this "protopolitical consciousness" emerges from the democratic silence of each person's thoughts into the fullness of democratic community, into class *for* itself:

> Los grillos empezaron a dejar de chirriar poco a poco. Parecía como que se estaban cansando y el amanecer también empezó a verificar los objetos con mucho cuidado y lentamente como para que no se diera cuenta nadie de lo que estaba pasando. La gente se volvía gente. Empezaron a bajar de la troca y se amontonaron alrededor y empezaron a platicar de lo que harían cuando llegaran. (69)
> [Little by little the crickets ceased their chirping. It seemed as though they were becoming tired and the dawn gradually affirmed the presence of objects, ever so carefully and very slowly, so that no one would take notice of what was happening. And the people were becoming people. They began getting out of the trailer and they huddled around

and commenced to talk about what they would do when they arrived.]
(146)

Once again, the fullness of silence is communicated: the crickets' chirping tapers off as the sound of dawn, quietly animating presumably inanimate objects, takes their place: "The people are becoming people." Enabling this transformation is the emergence of silence into sound: together, the migrants begin to discuss what they will do when they arrive. Their emergence from their muted status as objects into human identity, as well as their emergence into community, transpires at one and the same moment: at the moment of their collective speech about the possibility of what they might do when they arrive. But this is not just idle chitchat; rather, the paragraph-story that follows this vignette pointedly describes the nature of this collective speech act for the reader:

> Bartolo pasaba por el pueblo por aquello de diciembre cuando tanteaba que la mayor parte de la gente había regresado de los trabajos. Siempre venía vendiendo sus poemas. Se le acababan casi para el primer día porque en los poemas se encontraban los nombres de la gente del pueblo. Y cuando los leía en voz alta era algo emocionante y serio. Recuerdo que una vez le dijo a la raza que leyeran los poemas en voz alta porque la voz era la semilla del amor en la oscuridad. (71)
> [Bartolo passed through town every December when he knew that most of the people had returned from work up north. He always came by selling his poems. By the end of the first day, they were almost sold out because the names of the people of the town appeared in the poems. And when he read them aloud it was something emotional and serious. I recall that one time he told the people to read the poems out loud because the spoken word was the seed of love in the darkness.] (147)

Through poetic speech, the subaltern is inserted into historical narration. This poetic speech is the language of subaltern silence. It is the inaudible language at the site of interpellative misfire: the language of the racialized commodity that redefines the meaning of silence as a rebellious reading of his or her own positionality. It is an act of self-love in obscurity. It is the new language of the revolutionary imagination in the Americas.

1. Introduction

1 Homi Bhabha and Partha Chatterjee have each, respectively, elaborated models of colonial mimesis and colonial derivation. In "Sly Civility" and "Of Mimicry and Men," for example, Bhabha argues that the British colonial administration incites mimetic desire in its colonized subjects. The foregone conclusion is that this mimetic desire will be doomed to failure, precisely because mimesis is predicated on repetition with a difference. However, for Bhabha, mimetic acts by colonized subjects inevitably produce, in this difference, a parodic under-standing of colonial civility, exposing it to critique. Similarly, Chatterjee argues that although nationalisms in the colonial world are derivative of European nationalism, this relationship of derivation necessarily produces significant dif-ferences between First World and Third World nationalisms. More importantly for Chatterjee, it produces differences among Third World nationalisms. The relationship of derivation pluralizes the concept of nationalism, such that the historical significance of each variation is greater than the significance of the originary form. Thus Chatterjee focuses his analysis on the Indian case, elab-orating on the difference between bourgeois and popular nationalisms. Chatter-jee's model of derivation will be discussed in detail in chapter 3. My point here is simply to stress that neither of these models provides an adequate account of the relationship between development and revolution. Both models are uni-directional, focused exclusively on how the periphery reworks discursive terms dictated from the center. Instead I suggest that the relationship between de-velopment and revolution is dialogical, predicated on exchanges between the periphery and the center. Thus the articulation of revolution in the periphery repeatedly calls forth articulations of development from the center. Likewise, the discursive terms of development summon those of the revolutionary imagi-nation. Mimesis and derivation exist on both sides of the equation, as either term dialectically constitutes the other.

2 I borrow the term *flash point* from David Kazanjian's work on constitutive flash points in the American history of racial formation. He defines the flash point as a productive historical juncture that, in its episodic occurrence, congeals par-ticular discursive terms for the critic: " 'Flashpoint' in this sense refers to the

process by which someone or something emerges or bursts into action or being, not out of nothing but transformed from one form to another; *and,* it refers to the powerful effects of that emergence or transformation" (Kazanjian 33). For my purposes, the subject of development "bursts into action or being" out of the chaotic post–World War II Cold War historical conjuncture. Rather than emerging "out of nothing," this model of subjectivity emerges out of, and simultaneously transforms, the discursive terms of the prior colonial conjuncture. My project traces the "powerful effects" the emergence of this developmentalist subjectivity had on revolutionary movements in the Americas.

3 It is not my intention to exclude the Haitian revolution of 1787 as a paradigmatic revolution in the Americas. Rather, my limited knowledge of Caribbean history in general, and of Haiti in particular, precludes my tracing the possible influence of the Haitian revolution on the twentieth-century revolutionary movements I consider in this book. Nevertheless, I look forward to Caribbean scholars correcting my limited vision in any response my analysis might incur.

2. Development and Revolution

1 As Larrain points out, it was not until the Sixth Congress of the Third International in 1928 that imperialism was declared an obstacle to the development of colonized areas (9). Furthermore, Larrain contends that it is not until the publication of the work of Paul Baran in the 1950s that a Marxist political economist theorized the effects of colonialism on the periphery.

2 Certainly Churchill recognized Roosevelt's proposition of free trade conducted among free peoples as a call for the end of empire: "Mr. President, I think you want to abolish the British empire . . . everything you have said confirms it. But in spite of that, we know you are our only hope. You know that we know it. You know that we know that without America, the British empire cannot hold out" (quoted in George and Sabelli, who in turn cite it from Georges Valence, *Les Maîtres du Monde L Allemagne, États-unis, Japon* [Paris: Flammarion, 1992], 24–26).

3 See, for example, Helen Alfred's *First Steps toward World Economic Peace* and *The Bretton Woods Accord: Why It Is Necessary.* These pamphlets are the published reports of the proceedings of public conferences hosted by the Citizens Conference on International Union in Washington, D.C. In speech after speech from the proceedings of the Bretton Woods Accord Conference, U.S. senators, State and Treasury Department officials, economics professors, and representatives from the agricultural and industrial sectors repeatedly reference the need for dismantling colonial relations, associating free trade with the key to peace and security. For example, the inaugural speech of the conference, delivered by the conference chairman, Louis Heaton Pink, begins: "Bretton Woods should give us courage and hope. The proposed International Monetary Fund and Bank for Reconstruction and Development should serve as the keystone of future

peace and security. These economic bodies, plus an international tariff agency, a lowering of tariffs and the removal of competitive trade barriers, are all essential to a firm foundation for the future. The most important objective to international cooperation is undoubtedly a large volume of trade. . . . If there were a free flow of trade between all commercial nations there would be no reason for major wars. The interchange of goods and ideas, not only eliminates to a very considerable extent the underlying causes of war, but would help materially to increase world-wide production and minimize unemployment" (Alfred, *First Steps* 5).

4 In the hearings of the House Special Committee on Postwar Economic Policy and Planning in 1944, assistant secretary of state Dean Acheson was more direct about the singular interest of the United States in ensuring access to new markets, not bothering to cloak this priority in the humanitarian language of development. He said, "No group which has studied this problem has ever believed that our domestic markets could absorb our entire production under our present system . . . we need those markets [abroad] for the output of the United States . . . we cannot have full employment and prosperity in the United States without the foreign markets" (U.S. Congress 1082–83). Acheson is quite clear on whose peace and prosperity is primarily at stake.

5 Indeed, as Akhil Gupta demonstrates in his *Postcolonial Developments,* even subaltern populations around the globe came to recognize themselves as "underdeveloped" and to refer to themselves as such (39–42).

6 In *Encountering Development,* Arturo Escobar analyzes how development became the "common sense" of an era, and how this discourse re-created the world into "developed," "developing," and "underdeveloped" components. Escobar investigates how the discourse of development reorganized knowledge, creating new fields of vision and systems of speech, "creat[ing] a space in which only certain things could be said [or] even imagined" (39). Combining historical, anthropological, and discursive analysis, Escobar suggests that new techniques in comparative economic indexing were combined with newly minted international "aid" programs to invent the subjects/clients of "development": "the poor," "the hungry," "the peasant," "women," "the environment." Escobar's study provides an excellent genealogy of how these broad categories of subjects were "discovered" by the discourse of development, how each subject/client was elicited by its own particular type of development knowledge/aid in "food," "health," "agriculture," "population control," and "sustainability." However, while Escobar's analysis of the subject populations and knowledge categories produced by development is exhaustive, he does not specifically focus on the (under)developed subjectivity or consciousness implied by development discourse, which it is the focus of my project.

7 Making "underdeveloped" subjects available for capital investment is also the subject of an address delivered by Samuel P. Hayes Jr., the special assistant to the assistant secretary of state for economic affairs, on 26 January 1950. During

this speech in defense of Point Four before the League of Women Voters in Cambridge, Massachusetts, Hayes responded to criticism that the program was underfunded, especially in comparison with funding for the Marshall Plan. He explained the discrepancy in funding thus: "In Europe, the preconditions for economic recovery were, in 1947, already present. The people were healthy, enterprising, literate, and skilled. . . . This [aid] was a kind of blood transfusion from one developed body to another developed but wounded body. Before capital and modern technology can be fully utilized in an underdeveloped one, there is usually a lot of groundwork to be done. The people in that area must be ready to receive technical knowledge and to make efficient use of capital, and the early stages of economic development in many areas must, therefore, be concerned with improvements in basic education, health and sanitation, and food supply" (Hayes 12). The metaphor employed by Hayes, of a "blood transfusion" from one "developed body" to another, again registers this mapping of the discourse of development onto individuated bodies with subjectivities. Thus, by extension, the implicit "underdeveloped" body must "be made ready" to receive transfusions of capital. The Point Four Program was understood by the State Department as working in tandem with national development loans, as aid aimed at remaking human subjectivities in preparation for remaking their national economies in the image of the United States.

8 These loans were supposedly contingent on Latin American countries instituting land and tax reforms, as well as presenting the Kennedy administration with specific development projects. Tying aid disbursement to land reform once again highlights the dialectical relationship between development aid and revolutionary movements in Latin America. The Kennedy administration is compelled to articulate its aid program in the language of revolution, though in practice Latin American countries received aid regardless of whether or not reforms were effectively introduced and enforced. Hence *New York Times* reporter Tad Szulc represents the Alliance for Progress in revolutionary rhetoric: "It must be noted that the Alliance proposes a fundamental and drastic change in centuries-old patterns throughout [the] region" (Szulc 12).

9 Rostow saw communism as an unfortunate by-product of the difficult transition periods between predictable stages of national economic growth. Rostow's pre-Bolshevik Russia, as his prime example, is already well on its way to modernization, with the Russian Revolution portrayed as a violent interruption in that nation's transition from a traditional to a democratic society. He held that it was imperative to accelerate modernization processes all over the Third World, and to ease transition periods with plentiful development aid (Rostow 162–64).

10 My periodization of development theory is borrowed from Colin Leys. In *The Rise and Fall of Development Theory*, Leys suggests, "The first formulations of development theory were the work of economists, all strongly influenced by the ideas of Keynes and the wartime and postwar practices of state intervention in the economy, including the success of the Marshall Plan, which was in many

ways a model for later ideas about 'aid.' They shared the broadly social-democratic ethos of the period, including its commitment to planning and its conviction that economic problems would yield to the actions of benevolent states endowed with sufficient supplies of capital and armed with good economic analysis. . . . By the end of the 1950s, however, the original optimism that this approach would yield rapid results had begun to evaporate, and the limitations of development economics as a theory of development were beginning to be exposed. . . . What was it about these societies that made them unresponsive to the 'positivist orthodoxy' [of development economics]? . . . 'Modernization theory' was an American response to this question" (8–9). For two excellent historical analyses of the genealogy of development theory, see Larrain and Leys.

11 In the preface to the first edition, for example, Rostow indicates that the book was conceived as a response to Marx: "I found Marx's solution to the problem of linking economic and non-economic behaviour—and the solutions of others who had grappled with it—unsatisfactory, without then feeling prepared to offer an alternative" (xvii). Even as Rostow acknowledges his treatise as a direct response to Marx, he shifts the terms of the debate from the structural relationship between capital and labor in Marx's own analysis to an ephemeral terrain of economic and noneconomic behaviors. Unsatisfied with a Marxist history of economic development grounded in the binary of class struggle, Rostow substitutes instead a far more nebulous binary of human behaviors.

12 Instead of analyzing and comparing economic and population indices for specific nations, for example, Rostow promises to analyze growth as the more elusive "progressive diffusion of new technologies" (xii). He admits that this is impossible to do on the basis of statistical data, especially when one is attempting to construct an "elegant international cross comparison . . . for the historical past" (xii). Indeed, Rostow addresses criticism of the book as too sweeping by in turn eschewing "the easy use, in good conscience, of GNP [gross national product] per capita as a measure of economic growth" (xiii).

13 Rostow's men of science in this passage, capable of manipulating and applying knowledge, are symptomatic of the elusive role of intellectual labor in the division of classes. They elude development's bifurcated regime of subjectification precisely because, as intellectual laborers, their positionality in the division of classes is frustratingly ambiguous. As scientists, are they removed from the entire process of subjectification because they traffic in the realm of "truth"? Alternately, are these intellectual laborers aligned with capitalist entrepreneurs, or are they merely capitalists' well-remunerated lackeys? After all, in Rostow's historical recapitulation, scientific knowledge in and of itself is of little use. It is relevant only when an entrepreneurial class applies it to the production process. This is a particularly telling slip, since Rostow himself was an intellectual laborer for the state for so many years.

14 Larrain here appears to echo Lenin in his analysis of the transformation in consciousness that takes place in the shift from previous modes of production

to capitalism. Lenin, in "What the 'Friends of the People' Are," also describes a shift in consciousness taking place in this historical transition: "Never has it been the case, nor is it the case now, that the members of society are aware of the sum total of the social relations in which they live as something definite, integral, as something pervaded by some principle. On the contrary, the mass of people adapt themselves to these relations unconsciously, and are unaware of them as specific historical social relations; so much so, in fact, that the explanation, of instance, of the relations of exchange, under which people have lived for centuries, was discovered only in very recent times" (83–84). And yet Lenin is far more nuanced in his description of consciousness than Larrain. While Lenin acknowledges that certain modes of analysis have been "discovered only in very recent times," it is nonetheless true for Lenin that people are *never* entirely "aware of the sum total of the social relations in which they live," even in the era of capitalism, which has presumably facilitated a greater sophistication in the analysis of "historical social relations." In other words, although the improvement in the productive forces under capitalism has entailed a complementary improvement in systems of analysis, individual consciousness does not automatically follow on the heels of the development of the productive forces for Lenin.

15 James Ferguson's *The Anti-Politics Machine* provides an excellent Foucauldian analysis of the institutionalization of development as a strategy for managing poverty in the African nation of Lesotho. Ferguson traces the ways in which international development agencies and local state bureaucracies invent a "traditional peasant class" in Lesotho and then proceed to spin out plan after plan for the modernization of an agricultural people. Meanwhile these "agricultural people" lost their land to South Africa in the very processes of modernization and colonization in the last century and have functioned as an international proletariat for five generations, providing domestic labor and seasonal labor in the mines for South Africa. Hence these development agencies and local state bureaucracies appear to be "doing something" about poverty, with their projects for improving the productivity of livestock or for the privatization of reduced tribal lands, while remaining resolutely "anti-political" in their ahistorical interpretation of poverty and its possible solutions.

16 As just one example of the boundless scope of McNamara's early optimism and his driving sense of mission, from the 1968 speech: "We in the Bank . . . set out to survey the next five years, to formulate a 'development plan' for each developing nation, and to see what the Bank Group could invest if there were no shortage of funds, and the only limit on our activities was the capacity of our member countries to use our assistance effectively and to repay our loans on the terms on which they were lent" (McNamara 6).

17 In 1973 McNamara referenced the success of the WB in implementing the goals he had set out in 1968, thereby documenting the massive growth of the development apparatus under his tenure: "To achieve the doubled level of our opera-

tions, it was necessary, of course, to strengthen the Bank both organizationally and financially. Worldwide recruitment was increased and the staff was expanded by 120% during the period. We were determined in this effort to broaden its international charter to the maximum degree feasible. In 1968 the staff represented 52 nationalities. It now represents 92. In 1968 the proportion of staff from our developing member countries was 19%. The proportion is now 29%, and continues to grow" (McNamara 236).

18 The dependency school clearly belongs to the tradition for the study of twentieth-century imperialism beginning with Lenin and Luxemburg, and continuing in Western Marxism through Baran and Sweezy. However, to suggest that they do nothing more than transpose Western theories of imperialism onto the study of the contemporary Third World political economy would represent, as Cynthia Hewitt de Alcántara has so aptly stated, the "acceptance of the very kind of 'intellectual colonialism' against which dependency theorists stood" (*Boundaries* 162). Dependency theorists are among the first to read imperialism from the perspective of the periphery. As such, they not only fundamentally reformulate the theory of imperialism but also (along with cultural theorists such as Frantz Fanon and Roberto Fernandez Retamar) lay the groundwork for postcolonial studies today. However, they remain uniquely "of the margins" in Western Marxist discourse. Their collective theories of imperialism were often labeled flawed, unorthodox, or mere "description" by Marxist social scientists from the First World. Meanwhile contemporary scholars in cultural studies dismiss the dependency theorists as deterministic, appropriate their terms, or ignore them all together, even though they were pioneers in the field of interdisciplinary studies. I believe the anxiety they engender in the First World is at least twofold. They addressed a crisis in democratic capitalism after World War II and anticipated the crisis in orthodox socialism in the "Second World." Thus they not only interrupted bourgeois historiography and its narrative of individuation but also interrupted the progressive teleology that some of these Western schools of Marxism share with developmental capitalism.

19 In anthropology, see, for example, Robert Redfield, *The Little Community and Peasant Society and Culture;* and George Foster, *Tzintzuntzan: Mexican Peasants in a Changing World.* In sociology, see J. O. Hertzler, *The Crisis in World Population: A Sociological Examination with Special Reference to the Underdeveloped Areas;* and B. F. Hoselitz, *Sociological Factors in Economic Development.* In political science, see G. Sjoberg, "Folk and 'Feudal' Societies"; P. M. Hauser, "Some Cultural and Personal Characteristics of the Less Developed Areas"; and D. E. Apter, "The Role of Traditionalism in the Political Modernization of Ghana and Uganda."

20 My choice to begin this discussion of dependency theory with Rodolfo Stavenhagen is purposefully unorthodox. Most intellectual historians would not necessarily include Stavenhagen in a discussion of dependency theorists, and certainly Stavenhagen himself might resist such a nomenclature. I begin with him because his early work on the relationship between indigenous rural areas and

urban centers in Mexico clearly articulates an early dependency analysis. Furthermore, André Gunder Frank's work borrows directly from Stavenhagen. In the process of canonization, many theorists working within the paradigm are ignored or forgotten. Indeed, as a German-born U.S. political economist who worked in Chile for an extended period before the U.S.-backed coup, Frank is not considered a "dependency theorist," though he is most famously anthologized as such. But clearly dependency theory, at the hour of its emergence, was a diffuse, heterogeneous, and pervasive mode of analysis in Latin America. As just some examples of its heterogeneity, much debate took place among theorists over the term "underdevelopment" versus the term "dependency"; over the possible meanings of "mode of production" for Latin America; over the possibility of "liberation" from a condition of dependency. In addition, dependency theorists are interdisciplinary not only in the number of disciplines they collectively represent but also in the integration of historical materialism, culture, political economy, and psychology in their individual analysis of the legacy of colonialism. Consequently, my own analysis of the dependency paradigm is necessarily partial and selective. However, I am not interested in a seamless representation of the various dependency positions. Rather, I am primarily interested in their collective challenge to the bourgeois historiography implicit in modernization theories, and their challenge to the concepts of independence, individuation, and nationalism.

21 By "extraeconomic forms of labor exploitation" I am referring to forms of labor exploitation outside the wage labor form. In the case of the latifundium, laborers are tied to the plantation or hacienda not through wages, although they may earn a wage. Rather, they are obliged to work for the plantation or hacienda through extraeconomic forms of coercion (debt peonage, or sharecropping), or they are forced to give part of their harvest to the latifundium owner as payment for patronage.

22 The extraeconomic forms of labor exploitation maintained in the latifundium made it the link between the subsistence indigenous or peasant communities and production for urban centers. These forms of labor exploitation in the periphery allowed for an increased production of surplus and an accelerated accumulation of capital and raw materials in the European and United States centers (where the surplus was transferred), thereby making possible the precipitous industrialization of those centers. The latifundium, indeed, harnessed the "limited production" of previously self-sufficient communities for the full production of global capitalism. The development of underdevelopment is not only coextensive with development of development; underdevelopment in the periphery is a condition of possibility for the center's modern form of development. Frank's insistence that the latifundio was not a precapitalist mode of production but part of the capitalist mode of production sparked much debate among Marxist and neo-Marxist *dependentista* scholars. Ernesto Laclau, in "Feudalism and Capitalism in Latin America," accepts Frank's claim that the

Latin American latifundio has always been "bound by fine threads" to the "dynamic sector[s] of the national economy and, through [them], to the world market," but rejects the claim that it is thus part of a capitalist mode of production (20). Laclau argues convincingly that Frank confuses a commercial relationship between the latifundio and the world market for a mode of production. From a Marxist perspective, the capitalist mode of production is constituted fundamentally by the "free labourer's sale of his labour-power, whose necessary precondition is the loss by the direct producer of ownership of the means of production" (20). Hence the latifundio, regardless of its integration into a larger world system, is a feudalist mode of production because the laborers involved still own their means of production, although they are forced to work for latifundia or to turn over surplus through servile obligations outside the wage labor form. Feudalism allows for the accumulation of capital by a commercial class, since surplus is privately appropriated by someone other than the direct producer. However, the direct producers maintain ownership of the means of production (31). Frank, according to Laclau, operates under the mistaken assumption that feudalism is a closed system, much like modernization theory's assumption that traditional societies are closed, corporate societies. Therefore Frank insists that feudalism is not an appropriate description of the latifundio as a site of international commerce. Instead, Laclau sees feudalism as a dynamic mode of production that is *distinct* from the capitalist mode of production with which it interacts through the world market. I am not interested in settling this debate here, although it is indicative of larger philosophical divisions between Marxists and dependentistas that lead to different political conclusions. For the moment, my interest is to demonstrate that although Laclau disagrees with Frank's construction of the latifundio as capitalist, he nevertheless agrees with the larger issue of "show[ing] the indissoluble unity that exists between the maintenance of feudal backwardness at one extreme and the apparent progress of a bourgeois dynamism at the other" (31). Whether this is neofeudalism or a form of capitalism, the latifundium as the site of "underdevelopment" *does not exist* prior to, or independent of, bourgeois capitalist development.

3. The Authorized Subjects of Revolution

1 To clarify Spivak's use of the word "travestied" in describing the process of appropriation of Kant's imperative by the state, I quote: "The 'travesty' I speak of does not befall the Kantian ethic in its purity as an accident but rather exists within its lineaments as a possible supplement" ("Three Women's Texts" 270). The colonial state's ethical reliance on Kantian philosophy in delineating its "mission" is not a *misapplication* of Kant's categorical imperative. Rather, the terror enforced by the state is already present in Kantian logic. Kantian logic provides for the exclusion of the non-Western from the rational, and hence from humanity, and for the messianic force behind "conversion."

2 The colonial Other is feminized because the European subject in the colonial arena, operating according to Kant's categorical imperative, exists in relation to the quest for scientific knowledge. As Evelyn Fox Keller has argued, the Enlightenment subject's quest for scientific mastery proceeded according to the discursive practice of feminizing nature as its object. This feminization of nature "solidified the polarization of the masculine and the feminine that was central to the formation of early industrial capitalist society" (Keller 20). This quest for scientific mastery arguably fueled colonial imperialism, as colonialism represented the political extension of scientific domination. The discursive practice of colonial politics proceeds, then, by feminizing the "native" Other (and his or her territory) as its object, its resource.

3 Here I am once again borrowing from Homi Bhabha's "not quite/not white" formulation of colonial mimicry ("Of Mimicry" 132), as discussed earlier in chapter 1, note 1, of this volume.

4 In her discussion of the fraught, often antagonistic relationship between intellectuality and revolutionary cultural politics, Franco elaborates the mixed motivations of the Latin American intelligentsia and artists who joined revolutionary struggle: "The guerilla movements drew the intelligentsia and the middle class into their ranks. Jorge Castañeda calculated that 64 percent of those who died as a result of counterinsurgency repression were intellectual workers, many of whom must have been students who wanted to purge themselves of the original sin of being middle-class intellectuals. Indeed, Che Guevara never confused intellectual work with revolutionary struggle and declared that 'there are no artists of great authority who also have great revolutionary authority . . .' Personal experience of the armed struggle was the motor of transformation that created the new man [for Guevara]" (Franco, *Decline and Fall* 88).

5 All translations of *Pasajes de la guerra revolucionaria* are my own. I refer to this diary as *Pasajes* in the remainder of the chapter.

6 According to Mary Alice Waters, Guevara was only the third person to sign up for the mission to overthrow the Batista regime. From her introduction to the English edition of *Pasajes:* "In Mexico City, Castro soon met Ernesto Guevara and signed him up as the third confirmed member of the expedition. Raúl Castro, Fidel's brother, had been the second" (12).

7 At the risk of over-reading, I would suggest that the juxtaposition of the description of Guevara's "deplorable condition" with the interruption of their discussion of their progeny in this passage is also a reflection of the compromised nature of Latin American masculinity in general, within structurally determined relations of neocolonialism. Castro's men are attempting to regain the sovereignty of Cuba, defending the patrimony of the nation from the exploitative relations of U.S. capitalism. However, Batista's men—the lapdogs of Yankee imperialism, if you will—violently punish the men for the improper assertion of this masculinity. The attack thus doubly threatens the guerrillas: it

threatens to cut them off from their patronymic relations with their children, and from their patronymic relationship with the fatherland.

8 This is not my own but Ileana Rodríguez's formulation, which I will discuss in greater detail hereafter (*Women, Guerrillas, and Love* 49–61).

9 When they approach, they find these soldiers celebrating their "victory" over the guerrillas instead. The ne'er-do-well Benítez is the culprit of their first such encounter, having insisted on making contact with the presumed peasants because of his hunger. Seconds before initiating conversation with a soldier outside a hut, Benítez recognizes him as a member of Batista's forces and retreats. Guevara says of their group's escape, "Truly, Benítez and all of us were born anew" (*Pasajes* 10).

10 Indeed, it is quite possible that the discursive resemblance between bourgeois development's regime of subjection and a revolutionary regime of subjection finds its origin in a previously existing narrative of heroic militancy, with its roots in an imperial genealogy of reason. Nevertheless, as the importance of my work lies in examining the contemporary relationship between the two regimes, I leave the valuable investigation of an imperial narrative of heroic militancy to scholars of colonialism.

11 Fernández Retamar's essay points to an early convergence in Anglo and Spanish racialization projects in the Americas. It is my contention that there are, in fact, significant differences in the racialization projects of Anglo- and Spanish American colonization schemes, made most evident in the contrast between the genocidal policy reservations in early U.S. history and the assimilative policy of mestizaje in early Mexican history. Nevertheless, Fernández Retamar's analysis of how key terms in Colón's writings were absorbed by Shakespeare makes it evident that these discrete racialization projects overlapped at times, contaminating each other. Indeed, I suggest the discursive resemblance in the binary terms deployed by both developmental and revolutionary regimes of subjection is, in part, an effect of this generative cross-pollination in Spanish and Anglo colonial racialization projects.

12 The following are the excerpts from the interview I refer to in the text. On nationalism, Payeras concludes: "El nacionalism produce divisiones, el nacionalism no suma, resta." On autonomy: "Yo creo que la autonomía debe ser una autonomía territorial, es decir, no sólo autonomía legal o reconocimiento de la autonomía cultural, sino una autonomía que tenga base materiales." On the place of the indigenous in revolutionary struggle: "Podemos hacer una revolución, pero si la revolución no tiene una política de lucha contra la discriminación y si los mismos indios no participan en la revolución masivamente entonces la discriminación va continuar."

13 All translations are my own.

14 Franco elaborates further on the symbolism of Macondo in the Latin American cultural imaginary: "The always masculine protagonists of the boom novels, in

their attempt to dream up an economically workable society freed from outside control, encounter the specter of the excluded (especially the feminine) as well as the unhappy consequences of identifying the human exclusively with the domination of nature. Yet to transcend these limits would have meant the collapse of the enterprise itself. The final chapters of *One Hundred Years of Solitude* register the breakdown of the male fantasy in dramatic fashion with the invasion of ants, the death of Amaranta 'rsula, and the reduction of the Buendía enterprise to the solitary task of deciphering. Rather than a retreat from a revolutionary project that Gárcia Márquez never seems to have seriously entertained, the novel is the fantasy of a society based on kinship; Macondo aspires to be a 'cold' society—to use Lévi-Strauss's term for societies whose mechanisms are conservationist rather than geared to change. The change that comes from the outside is degeneration" (*Decline and Fall* 8).

15 Indeed, the *Dictionary of Marxist Thought* defines primitive communism as "the collective right to basic resources, the absence of hereditary status or authoritarian rule, and the egalitarian relationships that preceded exploitation and economic stratification in human history" (Bottomore 445).

16 Importantly, Payeras never identifies the villagers as indigenous, nor does he identify them as mestizos or Ladinos. Indeed, it is unlikely that they were mestizos or Ladinos, as it was almost exclusively land-poor, highland Indians who were colonizing the Péten during the period described by Payeras. Payeras *withholds* ethnic affiliation from the reader. This withholding is underscored because, in the next chapter, the guerrillas encounter a second village, where the villagers run away and hide from them. In his description of this encounter, Payeras, in turn, stresses the villagers' indigenous identity:

> Upon knowing of our presence, the inhabitants of the place locked themselves into their houses or hid in the woods. At certain moments, the situation took on dramatic characteristics. Some of our soldiers were forced to run after the stragglers and threaten them to stop. We will never forget those moments. All of a sudden, the guerrillas were left alone in the streets. The few inhabitants of the village who were willing to talk with us barricaded themselves in their dialect, and it was impossible to get information from them. . . . Here we heard for the first time the word *macá*, a terrible term which for us at the time meant something like, *there is none*, taking on a tone of rejection with centuries-old roots. (*Las dias* 34)

For the first group of villagers, their predisposition toward the guerrillas signals precisely their emergence out of their primitive state; hence they resolve into view from the jungle for the guerrillas and for the reader. The second group of villagers, however, *reject* the guerrillas out of centuries-old prejudice, locking them into a prehistoric mindset. In Payeras's representation, this second group of villagers are still so fully ensconced in their own ethnic particularity that they approach barbarism. Hence they disappear into the woods like frightened animals when man approaches; stragglers from the herd must be corralled by threatening soldiers; and their utterances defy meaningful communication or signal misguided hostility.

Thus I would suggest that Payeras withholds the ethnic identification of the first group of villagers because their openness to the guerrillas already signifies an evolution away from a primitive, indigenous particularity. Ethnic identity is literally put under erasure by Payeras's failure to identify them as Indians. However, even if the first group of peasants were not indigenous but Ladino or mestizo, the effect is the same. Ethnic identity is put under erasure in a narrative of development where the particularity of racial consciousness must give way to class consciousness if revolutionary transformation into fully human subjectivity is to occur.

17 In fact, it is the responsibility of the revolutionary movement's leadership to arbitrate in such matters, as Payeras stipulates at the end of the essay: "It is the obligation of the Revolutionary Movement's leadership to investigate and clarify each aspect, to establish the necessary differences between the positive elements and the negative elements, to take advantage of the first and eliminate the second" (88).

4. Irresistible Seduction

1 Of course, this is a reformulation of early classical economists such as David Ricardo, Adam Smith, and Jean-Baptiste Say.

2 For a more extensive critique of the ideology of development as an epistemological strategy, see Escobar, *Power and Visibility*. Also, James Ferguson's *The Anti-Politics Machine* provides an excellent Foucauldian analysis of the institutionalization of development as a strategy for managing poverty in the African nation of Lesotho.

3 See Castañeda.

4 While realistically one-fifth of the nation's arable land might have been more than the newly organized government could effectively administer, MIDINRA had expected more. Sandinista leaders shared the popular belief that Somoza and his associates owned one-half of all the nation's resources. Until October 1979, when investigators finished compiling estimates of Somocista holdings, FSLN leaders in MIDINRA believed that the state possessed 60 percent of the arable land (J. Collins, *What Difference* 39). These estimates showed that the state sector controlled less than 20 percent of the land in cotton and coffee production, and less than 10 percent of the land in livestock production, and only had significant control (40 percent) of the land in sugar and rice production (Colburn, *Post-revolutionary Nicaragua* 42). Clearly, the state sector had considerably less direct control over agricultural production in general, and

export production in particular, than the FSLN had hoped. This miscalculation increased the political clout of an already powerful sector—the landed elites and medium-holding private producers—in the eyes of the FSLN.

5 These relatively wealthy peasants are not the landed elites. Those owning more than 500 manzanas of land—the landed elites or terratenientes—made up only 2 percent of the EAP and held 36.2 percent of the arable land in 1978 (Vilas 66; CIERA, *Cifras and Referencias*). A manzana equals 1.75 acres.

6 Between 1952 and 1978, there was a 14 percent decrease in the number of landholdings consisting of 1 to 99.9 manzanas, as these lands were taken over by agricultural bourgeoisie. The number of minifundistas decreased by half, with the dispossessed either finding permanent employment or, more often, joining the ranks of the underemployed. This peasant displacement took place predominantly along the Pacific coast, in the departments of Chinandega, Leon, Managua, and Masaya, where cotton production flourished (Spalding 19–20).

7 The stratified composition of Nicaragua's rural population resembles Russia's in 1917, and Vilas's schematization likewise resembles Lenin's description of the Russian peasantry in his *Tasks of the Proletariat in Our Revolution:* "At the present moment we cannot say for certain whether a mighty agrarian revolution will develop in the Russian countryside in the near future. We cannot say exactly how profound the class cleavage is among the peasants, which has undoubtedly grown more profound of late as a division into agricultural labourers, wage-workers and poor peasants ('semi-proletarians'), on the one hand, and wealthy and middle peasants (capitalists and petty capitalists), on the other. Such questions will be, and can be decided only by experience" (*Selected Works* 35). Indeed, Lenin's "agricultural labourers, wage-workers and poor peasants" correspond to Vilas's agricultural workers, itinerant proletarians, and minifundistas. Whereas Lenin's vision of "agricultural revolution" was of a Russian countryside made up entirely of large state farms, MIPLAN envisioned a mixed-economy in the countryside. Nonetheless the Sandinista vision and Lenin's vision share an aversion to reinforcing the small-scale freeholding peasantry.

8 Here I am borrowing from James Scott's concept of "everyday resistance" coined in his analysis of local class relations in the Malaysian village of Sedaka (Scott, *Weapons of the Weak*).

9 Adding to the pressure of maintaining the production of foreign exchange were the immediate costs of reconstructing the agricultural and industrial infrastructure. Material destruction caused by the insurrection was estimated at U.S. $400 million. This figure, not including production losses or losses from decapitalization, equaled more than one-half of an average year's export earnings under Somoza (IHCA, "Nicaraguan Peasantry" 6).

10 The state, in fact, provided a cushy incentive package for private producers: 80 to 100 percent financing of working capital for the production of export crops, subsidized inputs, and fixed prices for the purchase of export crops, which were generally declining in value on the world market. Between January 1980 and

August 1981, 52 percent of foreign exchange was redistributed to the private sector for reinvestment (IHCA, "Right of the Poor" 19). Nevertheless, the *state* was now mediating all these transactions, and in effect, large-scale production suffered a decline in political weight vis-à-vis medium- and small-scale agricultural production. For example, under Somoza, large-scale agro-production had received 90 percent of all credit extended; with the democratization of credit under the Sandinistas, large-scale producers were receiving only 29 percent of the credit extended by 1985 (Enriquez and Spalding 114). The increase in credit extended, in cordobas, was artificially maintained through the printing of money, which in turn lead to spiraling inflation. Ironically, guaranteed financing of production costs negatively affected the productivity of state and large-scale production. In an economic crisis, private enterprise will use credit as a means of rationalizing production, forcing unprofitable businesses into liquidations, mergers, or bankruptcies. The state financial institutions never performed this regulatory role because of political considerations; hence nonproductivity escaped reprisals (Weeks 53).

11 Another problem with Weeks's analysis is his failure to differentiate between sectors of the bourgeoisie. His analysis holds true for large-scale producers (with few exceptions), and some medium-scale producers. However, over the course of ten years, medium- and small-holding peasant producers proved to be the most consistently productive, taking full advantage of the benefits extended by the Sandinistas. Even according to Weeks's construction of nationalist identity, these producers prove to be quite "patriotic."

12 For a thorough critique of the Sandinista credit policy see Enriquez and Spalding. Also see Joseph Collins, *What Difference Can a Revolution Make,* chap. 6.

13 By 1985, there were only 66,000 recipients of the rural credit program. Stricter state regulations on credit, fear of indebtedness, inaccessibility of banking facilities, and inability to deal with bank bureaucracy combined to discourage eligible minifundistas—and even many small-holding producers—from attaining loans (Enriquez and Spalding 118).

14 For a thorough critique of the state's pricing policies, see Frenkel 211–13. For a critique of the state's ability to handle the marketing of goods, see Saulniers.

15 Engels described the role of merchants in terms that correspond to the Sandinista assessment. In *The Origin of the Family, Private Property, and the State,* he discusses the emergence of this class: "Now for the first time a class appears which, without in any way participating in production, captures the direction of production as a whole and economically subjugates the producers; which makes itself an indispensable middleman between any two producers and exploits them both. Under the pretext that they save the producers the trouble and risk of exchange, extend the sale of their products to distant markets and are therefore the most useful class of the population, a class of parasites comes into being, 'genuine social ichneumons,' who, as a reward for the actually very insignificant services, skim all the cream off production at home and abroad,

rapidly amass enormous wealth and correspondingly social influence" (214–15).

16 By the 1983–1984 crop cycle, domestic production had surpassed its prerevolutionary average of manzanas planted; in the same crop cycle, the export sector had not yet recuperated its prerevolutionary average (Gibson 39). The 1979–1983 period was the most favorable for production in Nicaragua because the counterrevolutionary war was not yet fully under way. While we cannot attribute the drop in export production exclusively to ill will, it was clear early on that the large-scale agro-exporters were recalcitrant.

17 The only figures that I have been able to find in my research for the evolution of land tenure between 1979 and 1983 are from Joseph Collins, who gives figures for 1980 (*What Difference*, 271). He cites MIDINRA as his source but does not give the name of publication. Collins's figures place state holdings at 18 percent for 1980. Conflicting estimates of state holdings during this period exist in the literature on Nicaragua. However, I will continue to use 20 percent as a rough estimate.

18 A dead-furrow cooperative is a cooperative in which members own a farm collectively but divide the farm into individualized plots separated by dead furrows. This allows them to farm individually but to do some of the work collectively, especially work involving large capital goods such as tractors and irrigation systems.

19 From Lenin's "Speech on Agrarian Question": "The dire need I speak of is precisely this—we cannot continue farming in the old way. If we continue as before on our small isolated farms, albeit as free citizens on free soil, we are still faced with imminent ruin, for the debacle is drawing nearer day by day, hour by hour. Everyone is talking about it; it is a grim fact, due not to the malice of individuals but to the world war of conquest, to capitalism" (*Selected Works* 138). Although the direct referent of the "imminent ruin" Lenin refers to is starvation brought on by the devastation of World War I, the referent is also the referent "capitalism" with which he closes the sentence. From Lenin's perspective there is a direct logical progression from the petit bourgeois relations embodied by "small isolated farms" to the development of capitalism, to the provocation of wars of colonial conquest, to the devastation of productive forces caused by these imperial wars. Thus a small-holding peasantry would not only be incapable of technically achieving the needed food production but also be the first step toward consolidating a bourgeois capitalist order in the countryside.

20 One way of gauging APP productivity is to examine its credit history. Between 1981 and 1984, the APP share of agricultural credit grew from 34 percent to 41 percent, even though the share of land under its control decreased from 20 percent to 19.2 percent in that same period. Meanwhile credit recuperation rates for the APP had reached only 60 percent by 1984 (Enriquez and Spalding 120–21). Continued growth in credit to the APP is partially explained by MIDINRA's continuing investment in capital-intensive, long-term agro-industry. During this

period of regional recession, Nicaragua was the only Central American country with growth in investment (Enriquez and Spalding 138). Several external and internal factors, however, explain the drop in productivity that led to low profits on the APP farms. Nicaragua experienced a general decline in its terms of trade during this period. The country suffered a severe drought in May 1982, affecting production. State farms became the prime targets of the escalating counter-revolutionary war. Finally, state farms experienced a decline in both the number of hours worked and productivity of labor. In some sectors of the agriculture, norms for labor productivity were reduced between 25 and 40 percent. The reduction of labor productivity was not restricted to the working class. Professionals and technicians lacked the expertise to effectively do their jobs (Enriquez and Spalding 77, 137).

21 I exclude the resettled communities in regions I and VI from my discussion of cooperatives because of the extraordinary circumstances surrounding their formation. Although these communities were resettled as cooperatives by force, this was strictly a military decision that affected a very small segment of the rural population and fell outside the purview of MIDINRA and the agrarian reform law.

22 By 1984, the defense effort required between 70,000 and 100,000 people-in-arms, an effort the permanent army alone could not meet (Utting 136). Men and women from cooperatives and state farms were mobilized into battalions to fight the war. If the prospect of possible counterrevolutionary attack did not sufficiently discourage peasants from joining a cooperative, the probability of military recruitment did.

23 In their assessment of the first five years of agrarian reform, the IHCA claims that by the end of 1984, 22 percent, or one-fifth, of the total peasant families had received lands through cooperativization (IHCA, "The Nicaraguan Peasantry" 12c). I believe this is a miscalculation that underestimated demand for land and overestimated Sandinista efficacy in meeting that demand. In these calculations, the IHCA adheres to a rigid definition of peasant identity, maintaining a distinction between the minifundistas as "true peasants" and the dispossessed itinerant proletariat as "true proletariat." However, it is necessary to recognize the itinerant proletariat as dispossessed *peasantry* in order to fully comprehend the inordinate pressure for land.

24 For a complete analysis of the Masaya situation, see IHCA, "The Nicaraguan Peasantry," 51.

25 Between 1984 and 1988, the percentage of national arable land in holdings exceeding 500 manzanas decreased from 13 percent to 6.4 percent; in holdings between 50 and 500 manzanas, from 43 percent to 26.4 percent; in state holdings, from 19 percent to 11.4 percent (CIERA, *Cifras* 39).

26 Ironically, although the Sandinistas shared Lenin's prejudice against a small-holding peasantry, they apparently did not share his view on the importance of political representation for the itinerant proletariat and the minifundistas. In

Tasks of the Proletariat in Our Revolution, Lenin insisted on the importance of ensuring they have separate representation from the agricultural laborers of the more economically secure peasantry: "Without necessarily splitting the Soviets of Peasants Deputies at once, the party of the proletariat must explain the need for organizing separate Soviets of Agricultural Labourers' Deputies and separate Soviets of deputies from the poor (semi-proletarian) peasants, or, at least, for holding regular separate conferences of deputies of *this class status* in the shape of separate groups or parties within the general Soviets of Peasants' Deputies. Otherwise all the honeyed petty-bourgeois talk of the Narodniks regarding the peasants in general will serve as a shield for the deception of the propertyless mass by the wealthy peasants, who are merely a variety of *capitalists*" (*Selected Works* 35).

5. Reiterations of the Revolutionary "I"

1 Of course, I realize that such a "return" to the extraliterary may inevitably become just another reading strategy for canonization, as Moreiras also suggests. Though I do not share the anxiety expressed by some of my colleagues over the inclusion of Menchú's texts on countless syllabi throughout the country, I do believe that one way of combating the incorporative logic of canon formation is to proliferate readings of texts such as Menchú's, readings that are perhaps more difficult to assimilate.

2 Indeed, according to Stoll, Menchú gains international acclaim precisely for this reason, through a powerful Marxist cabal posed to take over the coveted discipline of Ethnic studies: "For Marxists moving into ethnic studies, the Menchú-Burgos collaboration became a classic text because its description of a young woman's political awakening turned indigenous tradition into a platform for class organizing" (*Rigoberta Menchú and the Story* 209). However, Stoll's own narrative is deeply contradictory on this point. Later in the book, he faults Menchú's narrative for foregrounding her indigenous identity, thereby playing on the sympathies of the U.S. solidarity movement: "Mayan Indians have been at the heart of Guatemala's appeal for foreigners. With the women still dressing in traditional garb, it is easy to imagine that Mayan culture is unitary, or would be if it were not for the ravages of colonialism" (236). In his insistent and largely unsubstantiated accusation that Menchú simplified her story to garner solidarity for the guerrilla movement abroad, Stoll simplifies the solidarity movement in the United States. He portrays the solidarity movement's members as loyal advocates of the URNG, instead of the ideologically heterogeneous group of people that we were. As a movement, solidarity's primary goal was to draw attention to the atrocities committed by the Guatemalan army and its paramilitary death squads, and to bring an end to the indirect U.S. military aid flowing to the dictatorship through Israel. In addition, as Norma Chinchilla Stoltz has pointed out, "Powerful as Rigoberta's book and even more, her persona were in

reaching uninitiated audiences, heads of state, and international diplomats, however, *I, Rigoberta Menchú* was hardly the human rights and solidarity movement's 'little red book,'" (33). Stoll repeatedly equivocates on the military's culpability for the genocide in Guatemala. As Victoria Sanford suggests, "Stoll's narrative strategy appears to be to distract attention from the army's culpability for is atrocities—a difficult task given that these range from selective assassinations to such public acts as the firebombing of the Spanish embassy and massacres of 626 villages, acts which finally claimed the lives of more than 200,000 Guatemalans" (39). At one point in his narrative, even Stoll has to admit that the preponderance of the killing was done by these forces, and not the forces of the URNG:

> During this period [the 1980s], army killing became so massive, and so obviously required an emergency response, that it was difficult not to accept other claims made by the guerrillas. If peasants did not support the guerrillas, why would the army kill so many? It also seemed logical that the guerrilla movement grew out of basic peasant needs. All those dead civilians began to certify not just that the Guatemalan army was committing mass murder but other propositions advanced by the guerilla movement. If most of the combatants were indigenous, then the insurgency must have been a popular uprising. It must also have been an inevitable product of oppression triggered exclusively by Guatemala's power structure. (238)

Though Stoll poses these questions rhetorically, he never successfully addresses the issues raised here. Stoll's book is largely an apologia for the Guatemalan military's genocidal policy. He blames the guerrillas for provoking the violence, for somehow they should have known their organizing in the mountains among the peasants would lead to the massive retaliation by the army. Indeed, in Stoll's twisted logic, Rigoberta Menchú is most culpable, for without her testimony, he claims, the URNG would have admitted defeat in the early 1980s and thereby somehow avoided further civilian massacres by the Guatemalan military. Thus, according to this logic, since Menchú's book lent credibility to the guerrillas' cause, it was the primary factor that allowed them to continue the war.

3 Of the twelve essays in Gugelberger's anthology, nine analyze Menchú's text as exemplary of the genre. Of course, as the second- and third-stage essays are in dialogue with the first-stage essays, the return to Menchú is somewhat predetermined. Nevertheless the question of how to interpret authorial representation in Menchú became absolutely fundamental to establishing the parameters of the genre and the genre's political significance and potential, as well as to insisting on the possibility of authentic subaltern representation, a point hotly debated in Western letters, at the time.

4 According to Menchú, each person is born into the community with a "nahual" that is his or her lifelong companion and connection to the natural world: "His

or her nahual is like a shadow. They are going to live parallel lives, and almost always, the nahual is an animal. The child has to dialogue with nature. For us, the nahual is a representative of the earth, a representative of all the animals and a representative of water and the sun" (Burgos, *Me llamo* 39). The identity of the child's nahual is not revealed to the child until s/he becomes a young adult. All translations of Menchú are my own, unless they are within a quote from another critic.

5 Beverley does not specify if he means by this a transition from a capitalist mode of production to a socialist mode of production, but one may assume so. From our present vantage point, Beverley's appraisal of the period may seem ludicrously optimistic, but within the historical context in which he wrote this essay, such a transition did, in fact, seem imminent. At the height of the Central American revolutionary movements in the mid-1980s, it appeared as if the FMLN in El Salvador and the URNG in Guatemala would follow in the victorious footsteps of the FSLN in Nicaragua, establishing a mixed economy (private and state capital investment under strict government supervision) and a popular, participatory democracy. Indeed, plans for a common Central American market based on these political principles were seriously theorized at Nicaraguan research institutes throughout the 1980s. Although the transition to this "new mode of production" never fully took place, new modes of subjectivity and conciencia *did* emerge from these revolutionary efforts at transformation, and as such, these subjects continue to organize against neoliberalism and Christian Democrats in the region. However, it is less clear if distinctly new modes of cultural production emerged, as well. My engagement with Yúdice, Beverley, Gugelberger, and other first-wave critics is, indeed, an attempt to retheorize this new subject and his or her cultural production.

6 For Beverley and other first-wave testimonial critics, the author function in testimonial literature is, for all intents and purposes, eliminated. This is in part because testimonios tend to be jointly authored, as slave narratives were in the eighteenth and nineteenth centuries. And yet this is not the only reason for the erasure of the author function. "There is a great difference between having someone like Rigoberta Menchú tell the story of her people and having it told, however well, by someone like, say, the Nobel Prize–winning Miguel Angel Asturias. Testimonio involves a sort of erasure of the function, and thus also of the textual presence, of the 'author,' which by contrast is so central in all major forms of bourgeois writing since the Renaissance, so much so that our very notions of literature and the literary are bound up with notions of the author, or, at least of an authorial intention" (Beverley, "The Margin at the Center" 29). Similarly, Georg Gugelberger and Michael Kearney, in their introduction to the 1991 *Latin American Perspectives* two-part special issue on testimonio, use Menchú to insist on the difference between the bourgeois author and the testimonial author: "Whereas the Western writer is definitely an author, the 'protagonist' who gives testimony does not conceive of him/herself as extraordinary but

instead as an allegory of the many, the people. This collective identity is particularly revealed in female-gendered testimonials, in the often quoted opening of *I, Rigoberta Menchú:* 'I'd like to stress that it's not my life, it's also the testimony of my people' " (8). In 1992, of course, Menchú joined Asturias's award-winning company, becoming the second Guatemalan in history to receive a Nobel Prize—although for peace rather than literature—and causing some of her detractors, such as Stoll, to accuse her of elitism and insist that there was no difference between Menchú and the Guatemalan intellectual Left. Clearly there is a difference between Asturias's subject position as a dissident member of the oligarchic class in Guatemala and Menchú's as an indigenous peasant woman persecuted by the armed forces defending this oligarchic class. Similarly, there is a difference between the authorial form of the bourgeois novel and the authorial form of testimonio. My point is merely to suggest that such racial and class differences in subject positions will not directly or necessarily manifest themselves as the complete erasure of the authorial function, for the authorial function does not depend on subject position. Indeed, Beverley hedges his own claims: it is "sort of" an erasure, but not quite. For similar interpretations of Menchú and the new genre of testimonio, please see, in this same issue of *Latin American Perspectives,* Lynda Marín, "Speaking Out Together: Testimonials of Latin American Women" (52). See also Claudia Salazar, "Rigoberta's Narrative and the New Practice of Oral History"; and Doris Sommer, " 'Not Just a Personal Story': Women's *Testimonios* and the Plural Self" (109–10).

7 Bastos and Camus, in their book *Quebrando el silencio: Organizaciones del pueblo Maya y sus demandas,* quote an indigenous person describing the period of the scorched-earth policy that was put into effect by General Rios Montt immediately following Ronald Reagan's 1980 inauguration: "The target was the Indian, in that moment persecuted on all sides to see that s/he not be organizing, to see what s/he was doing . . . soon, well, the [military] control came . . . they planted a deep mistrust in the interior of our own population, well, nobody trusted anybody, not even your own family members" (36).

8 For example, Beverley qualifies his stance on the presence of the popular subject in testimonio considerably when he writes, "the presence of a 'real' popular voice in the testimonio is in part at least an illusion. Obviously, we are dealing here, as in any discursive medium, with an effect that has been produced, in the case of testimonio both by the direct narrator—using devices of an oral storytelling tradition—and the compiler who, according to norms of literary form and expression, makes a text out of the material" ("The Margin at the Center" 34). Thus Beverley seems to recognize the mediated nature of any representation, and the doubly mediated nature of testimonio, but he hesitates—it is only "in part" that representation in testimonio is contaminated by distance from the referent. The overwhelming effect of testimonio, in Beverley's critical estimation, is "a sensation of *experiencing the real* and . . . this has determinate effects on the reader that are different from those produced by even the most realist or

'documentary' fiction" ("The Margin at the Center" 34). There is a great invest-ment by these early critics of testimonio to differentiate it from other genres, not just qualitatively, but in kind. Beverley continues, "What has to be under-stood, however, is precisely how *testimonio puts into question* the existing institu-tion of literature as an ideological apparatus of alienation and domination at the same time that it constitutes itself as a new form of literature" ("The Margin at the Center" 35). Yúdice also qualifies his understanding of this "authentic" narrative later in his essay: "I do not claim that testimonial writing suffers no problems of referentiality, but I do point out that it is not so much a representa-tion of a referent (say, the 'people' or Lukács's 'typical man') but a practice involved in the construction of such an entity. That is, testimonial writing is first and foremost an act, a tactic by means of which people engage in the process of self-constitution and survival" (46). Yúdice's estimation of testimonio as a tactic, as a performative act, in the Butlerian sense, is close to my own analysis of Menchú's narrative, and I will return to this aspect of Yúdice's definition of testimonio hereafter. Like Beverley, however, he hesitates in allowing for the possibility of mediation of the subaltern voice in testimonio, barely willing to qualify its immediacy: "I do not claim that testimonial writing suffers *no* prob-lems of referentiality."

9 Gayatri Chakravorty Spivak addresses this effacement of the complex geopoliti-cal role of intellectual interpretation, in the context of a conversation between Michel Foucault and Gilles Deleuze, in her "Can the Subaltern Speak?" These two theorists suggest that the desires and interests of subaltern subjects invari-ably coincide, are fully expressed by these subaltern subjects themselves, and are thus available to the attentive and sympathetic First World intellectual. Please see my chapter 2, footnote 12, for a full discussion of Spivak's response to Foucault's and Deleuze's position.

10 For example, to date, no testimonial criticism on Menchú considers how her narrative is influenced by the conventions of Mayan oral tradition. But precisely such textual analysis is warranted and would explain much, if not all, of the incongruities Stoll finds between Menchú's version of events and the version of events he puts together. Jan Rus, an anthropologist who has lived and worked for more than ten years in the highlands of Chiapas, Mexico, has suggested precisely such an interpretation of narrative voice in Menchú. Rus collaborates with his wife on ethnohistories of the area, as well as with Tzotzil and Tzeltal Maya communities in publishing their histories in their own languages. In his introduction to the *Latin American Perspectives* special issue on the Menchú-Stoll controversy, Rus explains that Mayan oral conventions "include the assumption of a collective or amalgamated identity by the storyteller in order to summarize a whole community's history, the creation of a 'golden past' before exploitation or colonialism, in order to show how bad things have become and to identify the causes of the deterioration, and the simplification of the order of events in order to clarify the story line. To appraise *I, Rigoberta Menchú* fairly, then, the reader

must understand both the context in which it was written and the fact that it is a product of an oral, non-Western tradition" (8). Although Rus does not address the specific issues raised by Stoll, these conventions—the amalgamation of identities to summarize a community history, the glorification of the pre-colonial past, the simplification of events to create a coherent time line—can explain the discrepancies Stoll finds in the details of Menchú's narrative.

11 For a discussion of the ongoing resistance to military control of indigenous life in Guatemala, please see Santiago Bastos and Manuela Camus, *Quebrando el silencio: Organizaciones del pueblo Maya y sus demandas*, particularly chapters 2 and 3; and also their *Abriendo caminos: Las organizaciones Maya desde el Nobel hasta el Acuerdo de derechos indígenas*.

12 According to Gareth Williams, there is another binary structure operating within testimonio criticism, for, according to this hermeneutics of solidarity, in testimonio the cultural production of the subaltern exists in a relationship of parity (of "solidarity") with the cultural production of the testimonio critic. Williams has argued that instead of parity, early testimonio criticism reimposed a center-periphery binary on testimonio. In testimonio criticism, Williams argues, "testimonio comes to be a homogeneous and totalizing resistance to the metropolitan center and to metropolitan discourses of centrality" (233). Indeed, the very insistence on the genre's novelty—critics' refusal to place it within the traditions of the slave narrative, autobiography, or earlier Native American "as-told-to's"—represents the genre as a margin uncontaminated by the metro-politan center or its modern discursive forms. In tandem with the requirement for novelty, the protocols for identifying this new genre produce the homogene-ity suggested by Williams. For example, the criteria of the unmediated presence of the collective subaltern subject in all testimonial voice, on the one hand, homogenizes testimonial voices of different subaltern extraction and, on the other, totalizes the testimonial voice as resistive to the metropolitan center. Williams has called the hermeneutics of solidarity a "fantasy of cultural ex-change" resulting from the critic's tendency to fetishize subaltern particularity: "In short, we act as if Latin American subalternity were not, in the very practice of cultural exchange, inevitably submitted to discursive commodification, as if the object actually realized itself as something other than exchange-value within the space occupied and delineated by U.S. institutional critical practices on Latin America" (234).

13 Though in hindsight we can see that testimonio is neither new to Western letters nor unique in its mode of representation, testimonio had been histor-ically undertheorized until this period of testimonio criticism. (The exception to this general rule of neglect is, of course, the African American slave narrative, which received pronounced critical attention beginning in the early 1970s.) As Elzbieta Sklodowska points out in her essay "Spanish American Testimonial Novel: Some Afterthoughts": "The fact that we, the interpretive community of academic critics, has agreed to 'recognize' testimonio and give it institutional

legitimation is, arguably, one of the most important events of the past two decades in Spanish American literary history. I insist on the word 'recognize,' because the presence of testimonial qualities has been a time-honored trait of Spanish American writing since its inception, and one could easily make a case for viewing it, along with realism, as a perennial mode of Western letters" (84). This is true not only for "Spanish American writing" but for American writing broadly conceived.

14 These fincas are large farms belonging to terratenientes that exist in the lowlands of Guatemala where Menchú, her family, and most members of her K'iche' community travel to seasonally, since their own lands do not produce enough food for them to live. They must travel to these fincas for seven to eight months out of the year to supplement their crop production.

15 This may recall for the reader the differences between conversion narratives of male and female saints. Paul and Augustine experience climactic, discrete revelations, while Teresa de Avila's spiritual connectedness to God is achieved through a concatenation of continual, more "homely" events as she meanders through her own life experience. Just as there is no rarefied moment of innocence for the female saint, there is no dramatic moment of redemption.

16 The translation of this interview is my own.

17 Indeed, later in the interview, she thanks the "thousands of Guatemalans," and especially the mestizos, who added to her formation.

18 In the past two decades, much theoretical work in the field of anthropology on ethnography has challenged the nature of ethnographic revelation and the motives behind such revelation as complicitous with colonialism. See, for example, Talal Asad, ed., *Anthropology and the Colonial Encounter;* and more recently, James Clifford and George E. Marcus, *Writing Culture: The Poetics and Politics of Ethnography*. Despite this recent critical perspective in the theory and practice of ethnography, the motif of revelation remains central to ethnography, although the revelatory "I" has turned occasionally on the observer as well as the observed.

19 For a lengthy discussion of the changing function of ethnography vis-à-vis a Western readership in the nineteenth and twentieth centuries, see Marcus and Fisher, esp. the introduction and chap. 2, "Ethnography and Interpretive Anthropology."

20 "I tried to ask as little possible, indeed, to not ask absolutely anything. When some point remained unclear, I would write it down in my notebook, and I would leave the last session of the day for clarifying these confusing points" (Burgos, *Me llamo* 17).

21 Instead Moreiras suggests that the secret in Menchú's text is at once the space in which the abject in her representation of her subalternity is turned on the reader, and the marker of that which "cannot and should not be absorbed by the literary-representational system": "Menchú's secret in my opinion is at the same time the metonymic displacement of the necessary (re)production of

abjection in Menchú's text, and its most proper cipher. After all, Menchú must produce or reproduce unlivability, in order to be persuasive as testimonio; on the other hand, however, Menchú's word is lucid enough to make of that necessary (re)production of abjection, which gives her a place to speak, the region for a counterclaim where abjection is reversed and passed on to the reader: as far as *we* are concerned, Menchú seems to say, our place will remain uninhabited by you, the truly abject ones."

22 In this passage, Payeras assumes that the indigenous population's resistance to the guerrillas is predicated on a *lack of knowledge*—a lack of knowledge about the larger reality, technology, general concepts, and the guerrillas' cause. I would argue that the opposite is true. The indigenous peasantry resist the guerrillas because the peasants *do* know the effects of Ladino technology in the Guatemalan highlands and jungle, and because they know the likely consequences of a guerrilla insurgency in their regions. After the U.S.-backed coup against the Arbenz government in 1954, there were various attempts to launch insurgencies against the installed dictatorship from the jungle and highlands in the 1960s. Consequently, the guerrilla activity chronicled by Payeras as occurring during the 1970s was not exactly new to the indigenous peasantry. And given the Guatemalan dictatorship's counterinsurgency strategy of razing indigenous villages to eliminate the guerrillas in the 1980s, it is eerily appropriate that Payeras suggest that these populations see the guerrillas, with their transformative mission, as "inconvenient as the typhoid epidemics that had razed the highland villages in the past."

23 In *Against the Romance of Community*, Miranda Joseph analyzes the function of "community" in various scenes where it presumably emerges organically as an extension of identity. Joseph interrogates the concept and function of community in, among other sites, San Francisco-based lesbian and gay theater organizations, international nonprofit organizations, the Christian right in the southern United States, and the National Endowment of the Arts. Similar to Menchú, Joseph challenges the utopian connotations traditionally associated with community by analyzing its supplementary relationship to capitalism. Indeed, Joseph argues communitarianism is not only not "natural," but develops as the necessary counterpart to market relations, fulfilling innumerable privatized needs that are generated through the alienation of labor.

24 It is significant that Menchú chooses cars as the site of this differentiation between indigenous people because of an earlier reference to the ideological function of cars. When she is telling the reader about her first visit to Guatemala city at eight years of age, she says that what most impressed her about the city were the cars: "And when we arrived at the capital, I thought that the cars were animals and that they walked. I couldn't get it out of my head about the cars. . . . When I would see [them], I thought the whole world is crashing into each other and, well, hardly any would crash" (52). Here again cars serve as a metaphor for a potentially catastrophic condition of permanent struggle in Guatemala.

25 In her second book, *Rigoberta: La nieta de los maya*, Menchú further illustrates the complex and contaminated nature of her radically conditioned agency, as well as how such agency creates the space for radical critique: "I always walk around with my computer tucked under my arm. I am Maya and I belong to the Mayan culture and I need a computer because it is at the service of my work, but I am not at the service of my computer. In that moment when a person puts herself at the service of her inventions, certainly they trample life, morality, ethics, dignity" (153). Again, she participates in the consummate sign of modernization, computers, but in a limited way. Or rather, her embrace of modernity is limited by her critical worldview: the refusal to subordinate herself—ethics, morals, dignity—to interpellative processes of modernization. Thus the computer does not mark her alienation from Mayan culture; only a misinterpretation of its function can do so.

26 Menchú's explanation, in her second book, of how she came by the name Rigoberta Menchú is an incredible documentation of interpellative misfiring: "I am called Rigoberta Menchú Tum only since 1979. In reality, my real name, the name of my [maternal] grandmother is M'in. Actually, my nieces and nephews and all of my family calls me M'in. My village knew me as such, as did the town of Uspantán. When I was born, my father didn't have time to register me in the municipality and he let many days go by. When he arrived at the municipal offices, the authorities wouldn't accept the name M'in. They gave him a list of saints and he chose Rigoberta from all those names. I don't know why he chose Rigoberta. It is a very complicated name. In my family, no one could ever pronounce it, especially my mother. She never could say 'Rigoberta.' She always said 'Beta,' or 'Tita.' Anyway, in my house I was always known as M'in. When I turned eighteen, my father had to fight to establish my identity. He went to the municipal offices to look for my birth certificate and he wanted them to give him the birth certificate for his daughter M'in. They answered that they had absolutely no M'in registered. In addition, [my father] insisted that I was born at eight in the morning on January 4, and the [municipal authorities] insisted that no Menchú Tum was born on that day. He had to pay a lot of fines to find a name in which the last names of my father and mother coincided, that was Rigoberta Menchú Tum, born on the 9th of January. Well, they supposed that was me and that is how my legal identity was established. And that is how I was named/called" (114). First let us notice that the municipal authorities replace a matrilineally given name with a Hispanic saint's name. We are told her family, especially her mother, could not pronounce the name, but attempted to adapt it. In the end, her family, village, and town just give up on the name and return to the primary feminist and indigenist interpellative, M'in. Gender parity is foregrounded, as the father pays dearly to search for a last name in which her mother's and father's names coincide. Notably, the establishment of her "legal" identity as Rigoberta coincides with Menchú's assumption of a political persona. Again paradoxically she must accept the legal interpellation in order to

defend against it. She establishes a radically conditioned agency in her bid to formulate a radical one. Thus she has two possible birth dates, the January 4th date, when M'in was born, followed by the January 9th date, when Rigoberta was born. Even the attempt to document her normative interpellation as legal subject misfires.

6. The Politics of Silence

1 A similar appropriation of indigenous identity was involved in the formation of U.S. national culture, though the characteristics attributed to indigenous peoples in the subalternizing discourses of Anglo North America varied substantially from the characteristics attributed to them in the subalternizing discourses of Iberian South America. For a discussion of the differences between the Anglo and Spanish subalternizing discourses during the colonial period, see Patricia Seed's "The Requirement for Resistance: A Critical Comparative History of Contemporary Popular Expectations of Subalternity in the Americas." For a discussion of the U.S. appropriation of indigenous identity in the formation of a national character within the sphere of literature, see David Kazanjian's "Charles Brockden Brown's Biloquial Nation: National Culture in White Settler Colonialism in *Memoirs of Carwin, the Biloquist*." For the appropriation of Indian identity in other spheres of U.S. culture, please see Robert E. Bieder's *Science Encounters the Indian, 1820–1880: The Early Years of American Ethnology;* Alden T. Vaughan, *The Roots of American Racism: Essays on the Colonial Experience;* Elisabeth Tooker, "The United States Constitution and the Iroquois League."

2 By refusing to fill the stage in front of the visitors, the Zapatistas were also rejecting the possibility of an inversion of the hierarchical relation between a simplistically rendered colonizer and colonized, a possibility that many anticolonial struggles embraced in the 1960s and 1970s. The Zapatistas refused the purity such an inversion would have granted them, and in so doing, they also refused the visitors the promise of a vanguard that would deliver us safely from our own responsibility.

3 This would be analogous, in psychoanalytic terms, to heteropathic identification, in which the subject identifies self with the other (excorporative), and contrasting to ideopathic identification, in which the subject identifies the other with its self (incorporative) (Laplanche and Pontalis 205–8, 226–27).

4 I would like to thank all of the people who *did* so generously make themselves available to me in a time of war, especially those who were living in communities surrounded by the Mexican military and under the constant threat of violence. Their courage is inspirational.

5 Aída Hernández Castillo, a Mexican anthropologist who has worked extensively among the contemporary Mames, suggests ethnic identity is "the result of a historical process in which everyday practices and governmental discourses and pol-

icies configure the sense of belonging to a collectivity" (132). According to Hernández Castillo, the Mame, an indigenous people on the southeastern border of Chiapas and Guatemala, have invented and reinvented indigenous "traditions" in response to more than a half century of the PRI's shifting indigenist policies. These collective ethnic identities are forged, then, in dialectical relation with governmentality, through resistance and negotiation with the state. This translation of Hernández Castillo is my own, as will be all subsequent translation of her work, and the work of other historians and anthropologists written in Spanish.

6 Presumably placed under the "guardianship" of the conquistador as a reward for his exploits on behalf of the Crown, these *encomenderos* also performed the service of collecting tribute for the Crown from Indian laborers. Out of concern over the depletion of the indigenous labor supply at the hands of the encomenderos, the Crown reformed the encomíenda at the mid–seventeenth century, introducing labor regulations that constrained the encomenderos from squandering this resource. Technically, the encomíenda was not slavery, as it could not be inherited by the heirs of the encomendero. But this limited life span produced its own justification for abuse, as encomenderos anxiously squeezed every last drop of labor power out of their charges before the encomíenda was vacated. Consequently, the reforms of 1549 sought to regulate the use of indigenous labor, but the Crown's interest was always in preserving their assets in the New World. The prominent Mexican anthropologist Héctor Díaz Polanco has characterized the reform as follows: "Control over the labor force passed to the government from that moment on. *Encomenderos* had to request permission from royal officials to use Indian labor on their own *encomíendas*. Those benefiting from the workers' toil had to pay them whether they belonged to their *encomíenda* or not. Officials more actively intervened in the regulation of tributes and working conditions. All these changes benefited the king, who extended his socioeconomic and political control over the colonial society and increased the number of persons offering him tribute" (*Indigenous Peoples* 43).

7 Díaz Polanco has summarized the effects of this transformation thus: "The shift [from pre-Hispanic communities to colonial townships] consisted of turning the communal nucleus into the *single milieu of Indian ethnicity*, given the elimination of preexisting higher levels of political, socioeconomic, and cultural organization and the reduction of their territoriality. The jurisdiction of the Indian hierarchy (nobles and other members of the town councils) was limited to a narrower and narrower communal world. Each separate nucleus established its own links to Spanish power, without the mediation of any intermediate political structure as the expression of a supracommunal authority" (*Indigenous Peoples* 53; italics mine).

8 With regard to native populations, Spanish colonial practices were quite distinct from those of the United States. U.S. colonial governmentality marginalized the surviving native populations by physically removing them from sight onto reservations, as if their difference were contagious. But under Spanish colonial

rule, Indians towns were everywhere visible, with Spaniards and Indians crossing into each others' townships regularly. Spanish colonialism was also quite different from early British colonialism in India, which until the second half of the eighteenth century governed through a class of client rulers without fundamentally changing indigenous governmental structures.

9 As an example of these resistant identities that emerged from within the regime of colonial difference, I refer the reader to four indigenous religious movements that took place in the highlands of Chiapas between 1708 and 1713, the last of which ended in an organized, armed rebellion by the religious members. The four townships involved in these religious movements were Zinacantan, Santa Marta, Chenalho, and Cancuc. The Virgin purportedly made serial appearances to the Indians in three of these towns over the course of five years, and the indigenous peoples of these towns consecutively formed cults of worship to her. Although Indian leaders insisted they were following standard forms of worship, the local Catholic priests objected to the Indians' rituals and repressed their movements, prosecuting for heresy the Virgin's interlocutors. In the case of Cancuc, the cult leaders claimed that God had spoken with them, proclaimed the king of Spain dead, declared the end of tribute to the Crown and church, and asked that the Indians replace Spanish priests, mayors, and governors with Indian priests, mayors, and governors. The cult raised a multiethnic army from more than thirty towns in the region and proceeded to take over other Indian towns and declare their church the official church. For a full account of this resistive religious movement, see Victoria Reifler Bricker (53–83).

10 Of this phenomenon, Bonfil Batalla writes: "Nevertheless, the cult of the Virgin Of Tepeyac had spread widely, and pilgrims, mostly Indians, came from all directions to the same site at which they had previously venerated Tonantzin. It is a fact . . . that the name Guadalupe was unknown to the majority of the Indian pilgrims who arrived at Tepeyac, even in the middle of the eighteenth century. Even so, the history of the appearance was immediately accepted in New Spain and the cult of the Gudalupana . . . spread rapidly. For the creoles, the indisputable fact was that the Virgin Mary had chosen this land among all others. She had not appeared personally in any other nation, leaving behind her image and requesting a cult in her honor" (Bonfil Batalla 95).

11 In viewing the Indian as obstacle, Liberal and Conservative Mexican elites were in line with other nationalist elites in Latin America, who saw the heterogeneous indigenous population as the primary cause of the failure of their newly founded independent societies to congeal as national cultures.

12 Liberal and Conservative elites came to this conclusion even though, as Florencia Mallon has established, indigenous peasant subalterns participated in the struggles for independence *as nationalists,* expressing republican aspirations and defending Mexican territory from the repeated foreign invasions.

13 Alan Knight, historian of the 1910 revolution and of racial ideology in Mexico, has commented on these nineteenth-century proletarianization efforts: "As in

colonial countries, the 'myth of the lazy native' was invoked—by foreign and Mexican employers—to explain peasant resistance to proletarianization and to justify tough measures to overcome it. The coffee planters of Chiapas deplored the 'natural indolence' of the sierra Indians; a Morelos planter lamented that 'the Indian . . . has many defects as a laborer, being, as he is, lazy, sottish and thieving.' Only by strict discipline, which in Yucatán and elsewhere became virtual slave-driving, could these traits be countered" (Knight, *The Mexican Revolution* 88).

14 The idea of Indian difference even brought some Mexican elite on the Yucatán Peninsula into allegiance with U.S. imperialists in their successful joint effort at turning an ethnically inflected class war in southern Mexico into the Caste War of 1847 (Joseph, "The United States," *Rediscovering the Past;* Reifler Bricker).

15 For an exhaustive analysis of revolutionary indigenismo in twentieth-century Mexico, as well as a thorough comparison of revolutionary indigenismo and its nineteenth-century predecessors, please see Knight, "Racism, Revolution, and *Indigenismo:* Mexico, 1910–1940." Knight addresses the ideological differences among the various revolutionary proponents of indigenismo, its uneven application in the realms of culture and politics, as well as the historical and political factors behind its adoption by the revolutionary elites. I borrow substantially from his discussion of indigenismo in this period in my attempt to sketch a broad historical outline of the creation and perpetuation of Indian difference in the service of governmentality.

16 The most notable examples of this participation were the original Zapatistas, the indigenous peasants from Morelos who, under the direction of Emiliano Zapata, were a central force in deposing the Porfirato. Indeed, the 1917 constitution, with its guarantees of agrarian rights to the peasantry, is a testament to the participation of indigenous subalterns in the processes of revolutionary nation building (Womack, *Zapata*).

17 Unfortunately, Alan Knight loses critical distance from the revolutionaries' perspective on the Indians. Although Knight meticulously documents the prejudicial opinions of the revolutionaries concerning the Indians, he nevertheless uncritically adopts the revolutionaries' position that the indigenous population was lacking in nationalism: "For them [the indigenous population] the nation-state was, at best, a source of fiscal and other demands; they owed it no loyalty (revolutionaries lamented the Indians' blind support of antinational reactionary caudillos like Meixueiro in Oaxaca and Fernández Ruiz in Chiapas)." He then goes on to cite one of the great architects of revolutionary indigenismo, Alfonso Caso, in order to characterize the Indian for the reader: "Mexico's Indians lacked 'the essential sentiment of the citizen, that political solidarity which is the very base on which the principle of nationality rests' " (Caso 110; Knight, "Racism, Revolution" 84). While some Indian groups in Mexico did indeed support antirevolutionary forces, indigenous armed support of the revolution and its principles has also been thoroughly documented (García de León; Womack,

Zapata; Womack, *Rebellion* chap. 5); and even Knight recognizes this support at other points in the article.

18 This book is so closely associated to the revolution of 1910 that Justino Fernandez, in the prologue for the second edition of the book published in 1960, refers to it as "un ideario de la Revolución Mexicana," as the ideology or plan of the Mexican revolution (x). Gamio's program for racial unity is considered so fundamental to building a revolutionary nation that Fernandez insists, "Its [the book's] programs for action have been realized, are being realized or will soon be realized, such that his book could also be titled 'The Revolution in Process'" (ix).

19 See works by Ricardo Pozas, Mercedes Olivera, and Arturo Warman. For a synthesis of this line of critique, see Rosalva Aída Hernández Castillo, "Invención de tradiciones: Encuentros y desencuentros de la población Mame con el indegenismo mexicano."

20 All translations of Gamio's text are my own.

21 One could argue that, by his own criteria, the indigenous population already constituted a nation in themselves. After all, as the majority of the population, the indigenous population belonged to one "race," sharing the set of cultural characteristics Gamio describes with only slight variation across ethnic lines. The distinct indigenous languages also shared common roots as well, much like the Romance languages. Of course, the "unfortunate" implication of drawing such a conclusion, from Gamio's perspective, is that the majority population would be in a position to impose its majority culture as the official national culture.

22 "Once we know, scientifically, the mode of being of the great otomí family and the reasons for their mode of being . . . [we] must determine the actual needs of this great family, ascertain and immediately supply the means for remedy[ing those needs] and establish the scientific observation of their development" (17).

23 In fact, Gamio devotes a subsequent chapter to the detailed comparison of indigenous, mestizo, and white laborers' capacity to labor, the kinds of labor they are capable of, as well as the factors influencing the differences in their levels of productivity. Gamio admits that his conclusions are drawn from purely anecdotal evidence; nevertheless he concludes indigenous workers have a greater capacity for work than those of mixed race or European descent, though indigenous workers are physically smaller, consistently undernourished, and generally unmotivated (*Forjando Patria* 140). Thus Gamio suggests the task before the revolutionary government is twofold. First, the government must isolate the factors contributing to Indians' greater capacity to labor so that these factors may be generalized. Second, it is necessary to improve the conditions under which Indians labor so that, in part, they may produce at an even greater capacity. But also, improvement in labor conditions is essential if a "socialist" solution is to be avoided in favor of an "integral development" (141). Gamio produces Indian difference in productivity in the hopes of reproducing it for

national development, but this process of production and reproduction is necessarily informed by an anxiety over that difference—an anxiety over its potential for sedition. Again, Indian difference must be harnessed for the nation or else be lost to "antinationalist" forces.

24 In 1921 the Federal Education System was founded to "promote . . . *national values* and achieve linguistic homogeneity" through universalization of Spanish (Hernández Castillo 133). In the same year, the Department for the Education and Culture of the Indigenous Race was also founded, and a program of traveling teachers was established under its direction to promote, in addition to literacy in Spanish, the principles of "industry" and "saving" among the indigenous populations throughout rural areas (Pozas Arciniega 248; Durand Alcántara 113). In 1925 the Department of Rural Schools for the Cultural Incorporation of the Indian was created to institutionalize the work of the traveling teachers program by establishing a system of permanent rural schools (Barre 61). In this same year the first National Boarding School for Indians opened as a venue for pursuing advanced education (Durand Alcántara 113). In 1934 the Department for Social Action, Culture, and Indigenous Protection was founded in Chiapas, its primary task to promote Western styles of dress among the Indians of the state (Hernández Castillo 133). In 1936, Lázaro Cárdenas nationalized this department, and in 1937 he created a Department of Indian Education to centralize the many national and regional *indigenista* departments and programs already established under a newly created Secretary of Education.

25 Manuel Gamio and other revolutionary intellectuals of this era transformed the legacy of a colonial regime of racial difference into the twentieth-century discourse of mestizaje through their literary and political production. This discourse of mestizaje provided the primary process of identification for the revolutionary nation, and as such, it had devastating effects on the indigenous population of Mexico. In the 1930 census, one-third of the Mexican population identified as Indian, but today the indigenous population makes up a little over one-tenth of the population (Medina 133; Hernández Navarro, "Cuidadanos iguales" 33). In Chiapas, one of the four states with the largest indigenous populations, the 1910 census recorded the indigenous population as 35 percent of the state's total, but by 1950, this percentage was reduced to 26 percent. This figure has remained fairly constant since then, with the Chapanecan Indians making up 26 percent of the population in 1990, as well (Viquera 282).

This precipitous decline cannot be explained by overall growth or a dramatic increase in interracial marriages. Instead, I would suggest, it reflects the partial success of the discourse of mestizaje as a process of identification—Indians were culturally Ladinized into the national mestizo ideal. Mestizaje's rhetorical force did not diminish over the course of the twentieth century, despite the dramatic growth in Pan-American indigenous organizing in its second half. As Sarah Hilbert has argued in her wonderful article "For Whom the Nation? Internationalization, Zapatismo, and the Struggle over Mexican Modernity,"

President Carlos Salinas de Gotarí (1988–1994) repeatedly relied on the discourse of mestizaje in his pitch to sell Mexico's participation in world trade to his own constituency. In nationalist speeches advocating Mexico's participation in NAFTA, Salinas repeatedly invoked the discourse of mestizaje, citing the Mexican people's "adaptability" and "vitality"—their ability to survive and transform—as evidence of their readiness to fully open the country's border to the world market (Hilbert 127–26). Salinas's use of mestizaje to justify the neoliberal reforms necessary to enter NAFTA is symptomatic of the complicity between the discourse of mestizaje and the discourse of development in producing the Mexican nation and national character as modern, a complicity that becomes particularly evident in the second half of the century, as we shall see hereafter.

26 All translations of the communiqués are my own. In instances where the Zapatistas use the masculine noun form to indicate both men and women, I insert the female form in brackets.

27 IMF structural adjustment mandates in the 1980s forced most Latin American countries to adopt neoliberal economic policies. However, the generation of PRI cadres who came of age in the party with Salinas—those trained at Harvard and Stanford business and economic schools—embraced neoliberalism, without reservation, as the only sound approach to economic development left for Mexico.

28 For an exhaustive analysis of the effects of salinismo on all areas of peasant production, see Harvey, *Rebellion in Chiapas*. For the effects of the oil boom and energy development in the Lacandón jungle on indigenous social relations, see Collier, *Basta!*

29 Critics of development, such as Philip McMichael, conclude, somewhat regretfully, that the shift to neoliberalism has effectively brought about an end to the era of development. From McMichael's (1997) perspective, even if models of development were rife with problems—ranging from technical ones to epistemological ones—the idea of development rested on an accepted notion of the need for economic planning and government intervention; it entailed a consideration of the issues surrounding economic inequalities. Government planning, economic intervention, and consideration of social costs are all anathema to a neoliberal understanding of the proper functioning of the economy.

30 Mexico's economy suffered the same oil syndrome that other oil-led economies suffered during their boom periods. The export boom in oil overvalued the national currency, drawing labor and capital into oil production and related nontradable industries, such as construction, infrastructure, and services.

31 An ejido is a geographically restricted farm that is granted to members of a single indigenous ethnic group that have historically formed a community, such as a village or town. A communal farm is granted to groups of farmers regardless of their ethnic, geographic, or historical ties to each other. In both cases, the land is granted under the presumption that the land will be worked communally by the members of the cooperative. Such communal farming does not generally

take place, even on the ejidos granted to indigenous peoples. Generally, the members are granted individual plots of land within the ejido or communal farm, and they may or may not pool their labor for certain seasonal work (Ruiz interview, April 1996). Ejidos and communal farms are discussed in greater detail later in this essay.

32 The indigenous peasantry has been thoroughly integrated in national and international markets since the conquest and has been "involved" in nonagricultural work since the colonial era, as made evident by the Requerimiento and the encomíenda systems discussed earlier. Nevertheless, in Mexico, the nature of their work and the terms of their integration into national and international markets changed dramatically with the oil boom and the shift in agricultural policy that the boom financed. Forms of economic exploitation once again articulated with cultural formations to redefine Indian identities.

33 This apparently innocuous change in farming techniques had profound effects on indigenous social relations, according to Collier, including the increased class differentiation between families that could afford to send family members to do wage work and those who could not. In Zinacantán and Chamula, Collier found that labor-saving inputs made it no longer necessary for these families to employ the services of poorer indigenous peasants in the community. Some migrants were also able to turn savings into capital for investment in other economic activities, such as trucking or small stores, further differentiating themselves within their communities. As relationships of reciprocity and dependency were displaced by a money economy, the existence of the poorest sectors of the peasantry became more precarious (Collier).

34 During Echeverría's administration, corn imports from the United States actually increased. This increase in corn imports was part of a policy to provide cheap food for the poorest sectors and was not simply meant to compensate for decreased domestic production (Collier 93). Nevertheless, such importing of basic grains invariably contributes to a decrease in domestic production, as peasants find it cheaper to buy corn than to produce it.

35 In 1973, for example, under Echeverría, the responsibilities of the Mexican National Coffee Institute (INMECAFE) expanded from research and technical support to include the organizing, financing, purchasing, and distributing of coffee production by peasant producers organized on ejidos and communal farms (Harvey, *Rebellion in Chiapas* 9). By the end of the 1970s, INMECAFE purchased 44 percent of the domestic coffee supply (9). Not only did INMECAFE extend credit to these small-scale farmers through their second- and third-tier cooperative organizations—Uniones de Ejidos (UES) in the Chiapas highlands and the Union de Uniones (UU) in the Lacandón jungle—but INMECAFE also absorbed a large percentage of the transportation costs.

The increased services in export agriculture provided by the state were not simply the result of a newfound sense of duty to its constituency on the part of the PRI. Rather, these UE organized into third-tier cooperatives (such as the Rural Association for Collective Interests–Union of Unions [ARIC-UU] in the Lacandón jungle) and pressured the government for credit and technical assistance. This pressure was the determining factor in garnering assistance from the government. This form of assistance was, nevertheless, in line with López Portillo's agricultural strategy.

36 Nationwide, corn producers make up 68 percent of the economically active population employed in agricultural production (Barry 103). Ninety percent of this 68 percent are small-holding producers, with five hectares or less in land under cultivation. Nationally, on average, they sell a little less than half of the corn they produce on the domestic market, keeping a little more than half for household consumption (Appendini 145). The statistics for Chiapas show some significant variations. In Chiapas, as of 1990–1992, 91 percent of the ejido members still produced corn, with 61.5 percent of the state's arable lands dedicated to its cultivation. In 1992, fully 67 percent of Chiapas's corn produced was destined for the national market. Only 33 percent went to household consumption (Harvey, *Rebellion in Chiapas* 14–15; Orozco Zuarth 101). These figures indicated that the peasantry in Chiapas was more invested in corn production, and considerably more dependent on the domestic market for the sale of their corn (as well as on the subsidies that facilitated that sale), than their counterparts in other states. The figures also demonstrate that these small-scale corn producers, so often misidentified as "subsistence farmers," are in fact deeply integrated into the national economy.

37 Hence, in the EZLN's second declaration from the Lacandón jungle, the Zapatistas were as quick to demand refrigerators, televisions, and laundry machines as they were to demand health care, education, and justice. They were as interested in urbanizing the Lacandón jungle as in guaranteeing peasants access to land.

38 López Portillo's parallel policies of funding both export and domestic agricultural documents a larger, ongoing debate in Mexico over the value of small-scale peasant production. During the 1970s some Mexican intellectuals, such as Roger Bartra, argued that peasant production in general was inefficient and added nothing to the agricultural development policy of enhancing Mexico's comparative advantage in exports. Others, such as Armando Bartra and Arturo Warman, argued it was essential for Mexico to maintain small-scale peasant production to ensure a domestic food supply and subsidize industrialization (Collier 66–67; Hewitt de Alcántara, *Anthropological Perspectives*). The abundance of revenues from oil made it possible for López Portillo to forestall a decision on peasant production. He was able to use excess revenues to support both large-scale agro-industry for export *and* the small-scale peasant production for export and domestic consumption. In addition, oil-led development projects allowed the consecutive administrations of Echeverría and López Portillo to avoid the redistribution of land in Chiapas by providing two safety valves for

absorbing the increasing landless population. First, wage work in the Gulf Coast oil fields, as well as in the hydroelectric projects that oil production financed, siphoned off the indigenous population from the highlands who could no longer incorporate themselves into the existing, but saturated, communal farms and ejidos. Second, oil revenues financed an agricultural policy geared toward making small-scale peasant production viable on a long-term basis, and this, in turn, fostered the continued colonization of the Lacandón jungle (Collier 91–94, 101). Since the 1950s, the Lacandón jungle had functioned as an agricultural frontier for landless indigenous peasants from all over southeastern Mexico. But in the 1970s, migration from the Chiapas highlands to the jungle increased dramatically (Rus, "The 'Comunidad Revolucionaria Institucional' " 296; Harvey, *The Chiapas Rebellion* 60). PRI agricultural development policy during this period targeted the indigenous peasantry, making small-scale production in the fragile ecosystem of the jungle profitable, though not sustainable.

39 Beginning in 1982, the governmental subsidies that had become a standard of peasant life "decreased on average by 13 percent annually, after having increased by 12.5 percent per year during the 1970s" (Harvey, *Rebellion in Chiapas* 11). By 1987, only 43 percent of the rural social sector (those organized on ejidos and communal farms) was receiving credit. In the Chiapas highlands and jungle— the Zapatistas' two strongholds—only 30 and 38 percent of the rural social sector, respectively, received credit that year (7). On the national level, only 37 percent of the area planted in corn, and 43 percent of the area planted in beans, received credit. These are crops that are almost exclusively farmed by small-scale producers. The shift toward commercial agriculture dominated by large-scale private production—favored by the World Bank and the IMF—was already under way before Salinas was elected. Nationally, by 1990, only 12.7 percent of the rural social sector received credit for planting (7, 11).

The effects of structural adjustment were just as drastic in the area of coffee, with the virtual elimination of INMECAFE as a buyer of peasant coffee. In 1982–1983, INMECAFE's purchasing share of the national coffee supply had been 44 percent. By 1987–1988, it was down to just 9.6 percent (Hernández Navarro, "Nadando con los tiburones" 62; Harvey, *Rebellion in Chiapas* 9).

40 Again, the impact of this measure was particularly felt in Chiapas, where roughly one-third of the rural social sector farms coffee. In the Lacandón jungle alone, there were 17,000 coffee producers, 93 percent of them cultivating under two hectares of land (Hernández Navarro interview, September 1994; Harvey, *Rebellion in Chiapas* 10). Chiapas is the principal coffee-producing state in Mexico, in terms of tonnage, and coffee is the third most important crop for the state, in terms of income generated (Orozco Zuarth 101). The vast majority of coffee producers are small-scale peasants, but the distribution of the land in coffee cultivation resembles a Central American nation more than it resembles other states in Mexico. According to Harvey, with nearly 74,000 coffee growers in the state, "91 percent . . . have less than 5 hectares, while 116 private owners

possess 12 percent of the area under coffee cultivation" (*Rebellion in Chiapas* 10). There are approximately 200,000 ejidatarios and comuneros in the state.

41 Since small-holding peasants invariably farm more than one crop, they could presumably have retreated into the safety of basic grains production, which continued to enjoy price supports throughout de la Madrid's administration. This was due to the consistent pressure put on his administration by the peasant producers themselves. Independent peasant organizations flourished during de la Madrid's administration, and mobilizations for increases in the price paid for corn were frequent and partially successful. These mobilizations by peasants generally occurred at the statewide level. In the 1980s, independent peasant organizations in Chiapas staged demonstrations and takeovers of government facilities in support of corn producers. Though the peasant mobilizations in the 1980s were often met with violence by the state government, and leaders were frequently jailed, Chiapas was one of the few states where these independent associations were able to negotiate increases in price supports and credit for corn producers, as well as support for infrastructural development projects (Hernández Navarro, "Cuidadanos iguales" 33, 35). Nevertheless, price supports for corn failed to keep pace with the inflation. By 1987 the tide began to turn against corn producers when the CNC, unsurprisingly, signed onto the Pact for Stability and Economic Growth (PECE). The PECE was an agreement between various sectors on price and wage freezes intended to control inflation and stabilize the value of the peso. It was somewhat successful in this regard, bringing inflation to around 20 percent by 1991. According to Harvey, however, the agricultural sector bore the brunt of the burden: "The real value of guaranteed maize prices fell behind the rate of increase in input costs. As a result, the proportion of maize producers operating at a loss jumped from 43 percent in 1987 to 65 percent in 1988" (Harvey, *Rebellion in Chiapas* 11).

By 1989 to 1993, the period Harvey refers to as the most critical, Salinas was in office. Price supports for basic grains were phased out early on in his administration, and the tide turned definitively against small-scale basic grain producers. Initially Salinas liberalized all basic grains prices *except* for corn and beans. This was devastating for thousands of small-scale producers who had diversified into soy and sorghum under the administrations of the 1970s and early 1980s on the basis of price supports. Nevertheless it left the purchasing price for the two most important basic grain crops safely subsidized. This arrangement, however, was short lived. Though recognized as "sensitive crops," corn and bean price subsidies were nevertheless included in the NAFTA negotiations. The NAFTA accords provided for a gradual phasing out of price supports for these two crops over the course of fifteen years, effective immediately (Harvey, *Rebellion in Chiapas* 13). Corn is Chiapas's most important crop. As I have already mentioned, over 90 percent of the state's small-holding peasantry is involved in producing corn on more than 60 percent of the state's arable land (Orozco Zuarth 101). As incredulous as PRI politicians may be about indigenous peoples' knowledge of NAFTA, the Zapatistas' citing it as one of the reasons for their insurgency makes perfect sense if we consider that NAFTA turned temporary adjustment policies into international law.

42 I am not implying that indigenous identity is contingent on the ownership of land, or even restricted to rurality. Indeed, indigenous identity exceeds the category of the peasant, just as peasant identity exceeds the category of landownership. With regard to Mexican indigenous identity, Stefano Varese has convincingly argued for an understanding of ethnicity as a historical formation of long duration, a formation that is, in most cases, both anterior and posterior to social class (Varese 154). I would add, however, the impossibility of treating these two sources of identity as separate or independent from each other at this particular moment in the historical formation of indigenous subjectivity in Mexico.

43 As a historical formation, this corporate clientelism was the result of a compromise between the elites and the rural and urban subalterns that had participated in the 1910 revolution, a compromise registering the pressure that was brought to bear on elites in the formation of a postrevolutionary state by these mass participants and their aspirations for inclusion in the national project. See John Womack, *Zapata and the Mexican Revolution,* for a study of the peasant pressure brought to bear on state formation during and after the Mexican revolution.

44 The *Plan de Ayala* calls for the restitution of lands to the "oppressed pueblos" of Morelos in Articles 6, 7, and 8. The Agrarian Law delineates the methods and standards under which such restitution will take place. Neither the *Plan de Ayala* nor the Agrarian Law makes specific reference to *Indians* when demanding restitution of the land for the "pueblos." Nevertheless, Article 6 of the *Plan de Ayala* states that "usurped" lands will be returned to "the pueblos or citizens who have the titles corresponding to those properties"; and Article 1 of the Agrarian Law specifically states that for those despoiled of lands, it is "sufficient that they possess legal titles dated before the year 1856, in order that they enter immediately into possession of their [despoiled] properties" (Womack, *Zapata* 402, 406). This would suggest that both documents are acknowledging the land tenure prior to nineteenth-century liberal reforms of 1857. Though these documents never recognize the "pueblos" or the revolutionaries as Indian, the Zapatistas nonetheless base the legitimacy of their claims for restitution on the corporate forms of land tenure granted to indigenous communities under the Spanish Crown and Church.

45 Many indigenous rights activists in Mexico use the term "indianist" instead of "indigenist" precisely to differentiate their movements from the policies and practices of indigenismo, or indigenism. Indeed, Indianist movements define themselves against the indigenist reform movements of the 1940s, 1950s, and 1960s that sought to integrate indigenous populations through cultural assimilation. For the remainder of this chapter, I will use the term "indianist" to describe contemporary movements for rights by indigenous peoples unless I

am referring to government-sponsored movements, in which case I will use the term "indigenist."

46 Araceli Burgette Cal y Mayor is an Indian rights activist with the Independent Front of Indian People (FIPI). Magarito Ruiz is a Tojolabal Indian, a senator to the Mexican Congress for the state of Chiapas, and also an Indian rights activist with FIPI.

47 Southern indigenous communities who participated in the revolutionary war *did* demand the right to self-government in addition to their land rights; Article 27 represented a partial response to these demands. Indian activists suggest, however, that something akin to autonomy rights early on in the revolution would have fully recognized the complex nature of indigenous identity, including the supracommunal aspects of indigenous identity suppressed by colonial *and* postcolonial governments. Territorial rights to historical domains would have recognized larger indigenous social formations by granting broader political, religious, cultural, and economic control over extensive areas of land (Burguete interview, August 1994; Sarmiento interview). Sergio Sarmiento is a Mexican sociologist with the National Autonomous University in Mexico City (UNAM).

48 "Al pueblo de México:/Hermanos mexicanos: Somos producto de 500 años de luchas: primero contra la esclavitud, en la guerra de Independencia contra España encabezada por los insurgentes, después por evitar ser absorbidos por el expansionismo norteamericano, luego por promulgar nuestra Constitucion y expulsar al Imperio Francés, despues la dictadura porfirista nos negó la aplicación de las leyes de reforma y el pueblo se rebeló formando sus propios líderes, surgieron Villa y Zapata, hombres pobres como nosotros."

49 Indeed, Gamio, in a poetic, two-page introductory chapter to *Forjando Patria,* theorizes the indigenous tribes in the Americas as foreshadowing Latin American nations: "There were small *patrias:* the Aztec, the Maya-Kiché, the Inca . . . which perhaps later would have joined together and fused into the embodiment of great indigenous *patrias,* such as those formed in China and Japan during the same period. It could not be thus. When Columbus arrived with other men, other blood, other ideas, the crucible that was unifying the [indigenous] race was tragically overturned, and the mold in which Nationality was being made and *Patria* was being crystallized broke into bits" (Gamio, *Forjando Patria* 5).

50 "Somos los herederos de los verdaderos forjadores de nuestra nacionalidad, los desposeídos somos millones y llamamos a todos nuestros hermanos a ques se sumen a este llamado como el único camino para no morir de hambre ante la ambición insciable de una dictadura de más de 70 años."

51 Also, though this first communiqué is free of any of the explicit vanguardist rhetoric associated with the Central American movements, the EZLN General Command does order their troops to "advance to the capital of the country, defeating the Mexican federal army, protecting in its liberating advance the civil population," calling on Mexicans to join them in this effort. Thus, although the

Zapatistas later insist they are not interested in taking power over the central government, this initial communiqué certainly suggests political power as a possible goal of the insurrection.

52 The ideological affinity between the EZLN and the Central American liberation movements is further demonstrated in the EZLN's "Revolutionary Laws," first published in the EZLN's official newspaper *El Despertador Mexicana* on 1 December 1993. In both structure and content, these laws bear a deep resemblance to the *Historic Program of the FSLN* (FSLN). Though the EZLN's "Laws" are more detailed and up to date than the FSLN's *Program*—for example, EZLN law permits women to hold land titles and guarantees them reproductive freedom—both stress the importance of national sovereignty, particularly with regard to natural resources, the need for economic independence from foreign interest, the commitment to collective agriculture, and the importance of women's participation in the revolution. A law protecting the rights of indigenous people is glaringly absent, given that there are revolutionary laws covering taxation, women's rights, agriculture rights, urban reform, workers' rights, industry and commerce, social security, and justice.

53 There are almost as many Mexican organizers, advisers, participant anthropologists, sociologists, ethnobotanists, biologists, and so forth working with indigenous peasants in Chiapas as there are Zapatistas in the Lacandón. Those I spoke with who had been working among the Zapatista bases on different governmental and nongovernmental projects professed to having been surprised by the uprising and the existence of the EZLN. Though some of these proclamations may have been necessary dissembling in light of government repression, I believe most were genuine, as many of those interviewed expressed distress at not having noticed. Though she herself worked in the highlands, interviewee Reyna Mogel told me she had a colleague who had sought therapy: "She felt so betrayed! She worked in the jungle with these people for fifteen years, and not one of them told her anything. Thank God that didn't happen to me" (Mogel interview). Alfonso Carrión told me that during his first visit to Zapatista territory for the CND, he shook hands with masked Zapatista leaders who greeted him with "Hey, Poncho, how are you, brother?" Nevertheless Carrión said he did not feel betrayed. Instead, like any lifetime politico, he was preoccupied with analyzing the shortcomings of his own organization, which had obviously failed to address the needs of the constituency he worked among. Though Carrión has worked for two of the most successful cooperatives by all accounts (CNOC and Pajal-Yakactic-UU), he spent the entire interview examining the mistakes made by each of these.

54 Though there are similarities between Central America and Chiapas—geography, climate, crop production, racial demographics, government repression, and oligarchic interests—there are also considerable differences between them, most fundamentally in the area of land tenure. Whereas in Central America oligarchic interests came to own as much as 80 percent of the arable land in

their respective counties prior to the revolutionary movements of the 1970s and 1980s, in Chiapas, by the 1990s, more than one-half of the arable land was in the hands of comuneros and ejidatarios. After decades of struggle with large-scale ranchers and their government cronies, the Zapatista base living in the Lacandón jungle had succeeded in obtaining legal titles to the lands they had cleared. It is also worth noting that Chiapas is not exceptional, as other southern states in Mexico—Guerrero, Hidalgo, Oaxaca—share many of these characteristics.

55 Alfonso Carrión is a member of the Labor Party (PT), and a technical adviser for the National Coordinator of Coffee Growing Organizations (CNOC).

56 "Aqui estamos, nostros, los muertos de siempre, murieron otra vez, pero ahora para vivir."

57 Using a language of Marxism-Leninism mixed with syncretic indigenous Christianity, CCRI tells the Mexican workers that a triple oppression hides behind the "mask" of neoliberalism (230). Mexican workers "die" three times in the "factory of the nation's history": once from poverty because of unjust wages; once at the hands of government-run unions that betray their class interests; and once at the hands of "traitors" selling the country's natural resources on the backs of laborers. Just as the worker dies three deaths in the present, his life is restored three times in the future: once when the value of his labor is justly recognized; once when the worker walks hand and hand with the peasant; and once when the worker embraces "all of the people to march together on a new and better path. Faceless, the worker lives and dies three times" (230). Once again the Zapatistas extend the terms of their own exclusion as Indians, death and facelessness, to the entire working class, as well as the terms of the entire country's possible redemption: "Justice! Liberty! Democracy! These are the three keys to unlock the three chains" (231).

58 See, for example, the following communiqués: "Oferta del PFCRN," 11 January 1994 (78–80); "Requisitos para los Mediadores," 18 January 1994 (82–83); "Reconocimiento al Comisionado," 18 January 1994 (94–95); "Dicen Algunos Miembros del EZLN," 26 January 1994; "Al CEOIC," 6 February 1994 (122–24); "Al Frente Cívico de Mapastepec," 8 February 1994 (131); "A la CNPI," 8 February 1994 (133); "A la CNPA," 8 February 1994 (133–34); A la CONAC-LN," 14 February 1994 (145–47); "El inicio del Díalago," 16 February 1994 (155–56); "A las ONG's," 23 February 1994 (163–68); "Al CEOIC," 17 March 1994 (193–95). After the first National Democratic Convention, held in the Lacandón on 6–9 August 1994, and the national elections, held on 21 August 1994, in which the PRI won by more than 50 percent of the vote, the form of address of the EZLN changes tone. Disappointed by the PRI's victory, the EZLN takes a more recalcitrant tone in their communiqués, beginning most of them simply with "the EZLN declares."

59 Current electoral law in Mexico does not allow independent candidates to run for any level of elected office. To run for any office, from the lowest municipal

office to the office of the presidency, any candidate on the ballot must be a representative of a registered political party.

60 They rejected the government's offer, stating that the terms offered by the government once again reduced the scope of their demands: "The bad government tried to limit the demand for autonomy to the indigenous communities, leaving intact the centralist power scheme that magnifies, to the level of dictatorship, the Federal Executive Branch. The real demand for autonomous municipalities was pushed aside by the government's response [to our demands]" (262).

61 The Zapatistas named their site after the revolutionary convention of 1914 in which Villistas and Zapatistas participated, once again evoking the parallelism between the two movements and reinscribing their struggle as national and historic in scope (Knight, *The Mexican Revolution* 256–63).

62 The event was historic. Sergio Sarmiento, a sociologist whose areas of expertise are twentieth-century Indian and agrarian movements, referred to it as "epochal": "the CND symbolizes, for the first time in [Mexican] history, the Indians summoning the rest of the nation, summoning us, the *ladinos,* to the project of remaking the nation, to form a new constituency together" (Sarmiento interview).

63 Sympathizers in these municipalities took over the municipal offices and restructured town governance according to indigenous practice rather than municipal law. The peso devaluated the next day, and though Zedillo immediately blamed the Zapatista offensive, it became apparent the two events were unrelated as the extent of national fiscal insolvency was revealed.

64 The first question, for example, asked if the participant agreed the sixteen "principle demands of the Mexican people are land, housing, work, food, health, education, culture, information, independence, democracy, liberty, justice, peace, security, battling corruption, defense of the natural environment" (EZLN 34). As these sixteen demands were, in effect, an expanded version of the initial eleven Zapatista demands, an affirmative answer would suggest the Zapatista demands were essentially national demands. An affirmative answer would also have the effect of making the EZLN the participant's representative before the Mexican government. The second question asked if all forces in favor of democratization should form a broad citizen's front. The third asked if the participant believed in the need for fundamental reform to the political process, listing a number of specific reforms to broaden electoral rights. This question was particularly relevant to the stalled negotiation process, as the list of suggested reforms comprised precisely the political issues that government representatives refused to discuss with the EZLN (Monjardin interview). An affirmative answer would once again bolster the EZLN's demand to negotiate the terms of national democratic enfranchisement. The next two questions asked the participant to give his or her opinion on whether or not the EZLN should become a political force. The final question asked if women's full and equal participation in civic life should be guaranteed.

65 Specifically, over 90 percent of the participants voted in favor of questions one, two, three, and six, though participants were divided on questions four and five (Gilbreth 3). The six questions asked in the consulta were:

> 1. Do you agree that the principle demands of the Mexican people are land, housing, work, food, health, education, culture, information, independence, democracy, liberty, justice, peace, security, fighting corruption, and defense of the environment?
> 2. Should the distinct Democratic Forces unite in a broad citizen's front, in social and political opposition, to fight for these 16 principle demands?
> 3. Should we Mexicans initiate a profound political reform that guarantees democracy? (Respect for the vote, a trustworthy voters registry, impartial and autonomous electoral organizations, free citizen's participations, including nonparty and nongovernmental participation, recognizing all the political, national, regional and local forces equally.)
> 4. Should the EZLN convert into a independent, new, political organization?
> 5. Should the EZLN join other organizations, together forming a new political organization?
> 6. Should we guarantee the equal participation and presence of women in all the posts of representation and responsibility in civil and government organizations? (EZLN 34)

66 In a subsequent letter reflecting on the results of the consulta, Marcos characterized the experience thus: "The great lesson, the most important instruction of this Consulta is that we can organize ourselves to speak and to listen, that without the guardianship or permission of anyone we are able to construct the mechanisms for dialogue. The results of the Consulta answer that we can, that there are tens of thousands of human beings willing to work and search for the road to a better world, a world that no one promises us or gives us, a world we can construct as we want it and not as Power wants it to be" (Marcos, "La Consulta" 2).

67 The success of the consulta in pressuring the government to negotiate in good faith was due in no small part to the role played by the AC in organizing it. As the coalition of NGOs that had organized the observations of the presidential and federal elections, the AC gained a tremendous amount of national prestigious for its thorough organization of observers at electoral sites, as well as for their impartial reporting of results across Mexico's states. Thus the AC not only had the organizational structure in place for conducting the EZLN's nationwide referendum but also had the respect of the left, right, and center of Mexican politics. Moreover, Zedillo effectively owed the national and international legitimacy of his presidency to the AC, as it had validated the election results.

68 Exercising a clause in the congressional law governing negotiations allowing each side to invite advisers to the dialogue, the EZLN brought 274 indigenous and nonindigenous "advisers" to the first session, for a total of 308 delegates

(Gilbreth 3). The Zapatistas invited indigenous leaders from national Indianist organizations, such as FIPI and ANIPA; representatives from cooperative organizations in Chiapas, such as Luis Hernández Navarro of CNOC; and a coterie of experts on autonomy in Mexico and Latin America, including Hector Díaz Polanco, who assisted in drafting autonomy laws for Nicaragua and Brazil, and Gustavo Esteva, who formally advised the autonomy movement in the neighboring state of Oaxaca (Hernández Navarro interview, September 1996). (Hernández Navarro is a founding member of CNOC, a journalist, and an EZLN adviser for the negotiations process.) The advisers so outnumbered the actual Zapatista representatives that the government representatives protested, threatening to break off negotiations. Since the congressional law did not stipulate the number of advisers each side could invite, the government representatives had no legal recourse but to retaliate by quickly assembling their own group of old-school *indigenista* experts (Hernández Navarro interview, September 1996). In the end, a total of 496 delegates attended this first session of negotiations (Gilbreth 3). Thus the Zapatistas maximized the space for democratic participation even *within* the negotiation process, once again articulating the particularity of their situation with the national panorama through their political aesthetics of form mirroring content.

69 For example, participants in sessions on jurisprudence and political representation in the government insisted on the need for redistricting municipalities to ensure indigenous majorities capable of electing indigenous representatives to the national Senate. This position directly contradicted the EZLN's long-standing opposition to assuming political office (Rojas and Gil Olmos, "Se requiere un Congreso Nacional" 9). There was also considerable disagreement with the EZLN's position on autonomy, which began with the statement "The indigenous peoples have the right to decide their forms of governance in accordance with customary law and within a framework of unconditional respect for human rights and the rights of minorities" (9). Representatives from other Indianist organizations vociferously objected to the inclusion of the phrase "unconditional respect for human rights" on the grounds of its Western, individualist bias. No resolution was reached on the latter issue, and instead the disagreement was entered into the public document produced by the forum (9). On the former issue, however, a consensus around redistricting was reached, and the Zapatista protocol was amended before ratification in the final plenary session.

70 For a detailed discussion of the Pluriethnic Autonomous Regions (RAPS), please see Araceli Burguete Cal y Mayor, "Regiones Autónomas Pluriétnicas . . . y sin embargo se mueven." Also see my article "Who's the Indian in Aztlán? Rewriting *Mestizaje*, Indianism, and Chicanismo from the Lacandón."

71 The communalists agreed with regionalists on the need for the legal protection to form autonomous municipalities, as well as on the need for the legal protection for municipalities to join together when appropriate; however, they rejected the idea of regional assemblies as untenable in the current political climate, and

as potentially stifling of communal differences in forms of governance among Mexico's fifty-six ethnicities (Burguete interview, April 1996; Morquecho interview). (Gaspar Morquecho is a member of the CONPAZ, a coalition of NGOS based in San Cristobal that formed in January 1994 to advocate the peaceful resolution of the conflict. They have played a pivotal role in organizing the Zapatista events discussed in this chapter.) For an analysis of the history of the two distinct historical trajectories within the indigenous movements that have produced these two basic positions on autonomy, see Julio Moguel, "Diálago en Sacamch'en: Tercera llamada."

72 Comandante David spoke at this plenary, calling it a "festival of the word" precisely because of the contentious discussion taking place. Once again, this reenactment of the común writ large was not the silencing of difference but the venue for publicly discussing differences among indigenous groups (Gil Olmos 8).

73 Father Ituarte is a priest affiliated with the San Cristobal Diocese and with its Human Rights Center Fray Bartolomé de las Casas.

74 The San Andres Accords on Indigenous Rights and Culture would allow indigenous municipalities to dispense with the party system in electing local officials; however, these accords have yet to be implemented, and this right to independent candidacy would not extend to nonindigenous municipalities.

7. Epilogue: Toward an American "American Studies"

1 The lynching of black men in the South during these two decades is the most profound example of how these multiple limits on black masculinity overlap. On 28 August 1955, Emmett Till allegedly "whistled at a white woman." For exceeding the bounds of permissible black male sexual behavior, for transgressing the discursive sexual order, this fourteen-year-old boy was lynched, the material "check" on his masculinity even before he became a "man" in age. As juridical sanction of this policing of black masculinity, an all-white jury acquitted the two white men accused of lynching the boy.

2 Thus it is appropriate to discuss, at this juncture, the infamous biography by Bruce Perry, *Malcolm: The Man Who Changed Black America*. According to Perry, Malcolm X's parents, for all their posturing of black nationalism, lacked race pride. He portrays them as currying favor with local whites while distancing themselves from local blacks. He portrays Malcolm X's father as a do-nothing, a swindler, and a womanizer. Perry tells us that his investigations suggest that the Klan never visited the Littles' home in Omaha, that Earl Little burned down his own house in Lansing to avoid eviction, and that he may have died "attempt[ing] to board the moving streetcar because some irate husband was after him" (12). What "really happened," beside being inaccessible, is far less important than Malcolm X's memory of the events, and the political interest that inflects his reconstruction of events. Malcolm X purposely resists this type of racist stereo-

typing precisely by positing another kind of history. Indeed, the power and the danger of Malcolm X's *Autobiography* lies, in part, in his refusal to accept these categories, this racist inscription of his life, even while he illuminates and explores the contradictions in black consciousness that are the result of this racism.

3   Regardless of these differences between Retamar's Ariel/Caliban and Malcolm X's mascot/homeboy, I will read these categories of subjectivity as homologous in the service of understanding the links between Malcolm X's and Che's quests for revolutionary subjectivity.

4   In my use of "mimetic consciousness," I am borrowing from Homi K. Bhabha's discussion of "colonial mimicry." Bhabha has suggested that "colonial mimicry is the desire for a reformed, recognizable Other, as *a subject of a difference that is almost the same, but not quite*" ("Of Mimicry" 126). Thus mimetic consciousness would imply the effect colonial mimicry had on the colonial subaltern. The colonized subject is hailed by the agents of colonialism to mimesis, incited to imitation. The well-interpellated colonized subject, then, responds to the hail with mimetic consciousness, with the desire for reform into the "recognizable Other."

5   Other examples of this self-censoring are the moments in the text when he richly details his zoots, or their effect: "Off the train, I'd go through that Grand Central Station afternoon rush-hour crowd, and many white people simply stopped in their tracks to watch me pass. The drape and the cut of a zoot suit showed to the best advantage if you were tall—and I was over six feet. My conk was fire red." You can almost sense Malcolm X still smiling over the sheer shock effect he had on those white folks, when he follows with an unconvincing "I was really a clown, but my ignorance made me think I was 'sharp'" (78). Even his description of his first conk, which he uses to poignantly demonstrate the devastating effects of internalized racism and self-hate, contains a certain humorous build up and makes clear the comradeship and genuine affection between him and Shorty. And while I would agree with bell hooks, in her article "Malcolm X: Consumed by Images," that Spike Lee wrongly portrays Malcolm X as paranoid and alone at the end of his film *X*, I would disagree with her assessment that Lee glorifies Malcolm Little's days as Red. Lee successfully captures the sheer beauty and joy of those days conveyed in *Autobiography* even as Malcolm X tries to portray this period as self-deprecating preparation for salvation of his soul.

6   For an example of how black cultural practices in this period were encoded as the excess of humanity, see Norman Mailer's infamous essay "The White Negro."

7   Sophia functions as the ultimate marker of excess in the logic of mimicry. Malcolm X tells us, "To have a white woman who wasn't a known, common whore was—for the average black man at least—a status symbol of the first order" (66–67). Possession of a white woman should mark the black man's

slippage from the "not quite white" male to the "not quite/not white" male if, after all, a white woman is a "status symbol of the first order." However, by accepting Sophia as his girlfriend, Malcolm X participates in the fetishization of black male sexuality as the excess of mimicry because, presumably, Sophia is drawn to him (and white men are threatened by him) because of his sexual excess. Sophia's presence as his girlfriend marks Malcolm X as the sexual excess of the phallus that Sophia—and white men—lack.

8 The sailors' riots against Chicano, black, and Filipino zoot-suiters in Los Angeles in June 1943 were the most blatant demonstration of this disciplining of excess. For four days, sailors and army personnel on leave from local bases systematically rampaged neighborhoods, beating up and undressing zoot-suiters with impunity. Los Angeles police responded by arresting the victims, and local newspapers blamed the zoot-suiters for the violence. Newspaper accounts claimed that the attacks were not racially motivated, insisting that the attacks were against *costumes* and not minorities (Acuña 256–59). Unwittingly, these newspaper accounts were half right, since, for the sailors, stripping the zoot-suiters of their excessive dress functioned symbolically to strip them of their ever-threatening excess sexuality.

9 For a feminist critique of the deployment of a conventional family as model for the African American community, see, for example, Hortense J. Spillers, "Mama's Baby, Papa's Maybe: An American Grammar Book."

10 Malcolm X answered a question from a white audience member at a Militant Labor Forum on 7 January 1965 in the following way: "I'm the man you think you are. And if it doesn't take legislation to make you a man and get your rights recognized, don't even talk that legislative talk to me. No, if we're both human beings we'll both do the same thing. And if you want to know what I'll do, figure out what you'll do. I'll do the same thing—*only more of it*" (Brietman, *Malcolm X Speaks* 197–98). In the end, it is Elijah Muhammad's failure to conform to the highly moralized and gendered category of the patriarch that so deeply troubles Malcolm X, leading him to be perceived as dangerous to the NOI by Muhammad.

11 Malcolm X's attempt to bring charges of human rights violations on behalf of black Americans against the United States in the United Nations precisely threatened the U.S. claim to modernization and its attendant civil discourse. Such charges would inscribe the United States in the "barbarity" of the "underdeveloped" world that it set itself against. Also, if the U.S. government was not even going to treat its own self-reliant Muslim citizens as equal, then certainly it would not treat self-reliant nations as equal.

12 Butler suggests that "gender is . . . [a] performative accomplishment which the mundane social audience, including the actors themselves, come to believe and to perform in the mode of belief" (*Gender Trouble* 141). If Malcolm X, along with white and black audiences, believes in his performance as substance (that is to say, if he is inside rather than outside ideology), he also comes to appreciate the

impact of publicly performing this gender category as a mode of belief. In other words, not only does Malcolm X believe in the "authenticity" of his manhood, but he also, or rather simultaneously, understands how threatening this manhood as a mode of belief is to whites and how enabling it is to blacks. Thus he performs it publicly at every opportunity. Malcolm X's acute understanding of the importance of his performance of full masculinity is recognized by him in his understanding of himself as "bogey-man" in contrast to Martin Luther King Jr. and explains the disjuncture in the different perceptions of Malcolm X that I cited in the passages at the beginning of this section of the chapter.

13 See, for example, Malcolm X's discussion of the "true nature" of men and women (*Autobiography* 226), or his comment about the one woman he trusts, Sister Betty, having tricked him into marrying, "maybe she did get me" (232).

14 West points out that even Malcolm X's oft-quoted distinction between the "house Negro" and the "field Negro" "fails as a persuasive description of the behavior of 'well-to-do' Black folk and 'poor' Black folk. In other words, there are numerous instances of 'field negroes' with 'house negro' mentalities and 'house negroes' with 'field negro' mentalities" (51).

15 It is interesting to consider the representation of the rape/betrayal of Malinche as the displacement of the violence that is sutured over by mestizaje as national origin story. To transcend the differences of the heterogeneous population of Mexico in its formation as a nation-state, it is necessary to place the memory of the violence on Malinche and contain it precisely in her marginality.

Works Cited

Acheson, Dean. *Hearings of the House Special Committee on Postwar Policy and Planning, 78th Congress, 2d session.* Washington, D.C.: U.S. Congressional Records, 1944.

Acuña, Rodolfo. *Occupied America: A History of Chicanos.* New York: HarperCollins, 1988.

Aguirre Beltrán, Gonzalo. *Regiones de refugio: El desarrollo de la comunidad y el proceso dominical en mestizo América.* Ediciones Especiales 46. Mexico City: Instituto Indigenista Interamericano, 1967.

——. *La politica indigenista en México, Tomo II.* Mexico City: INI-SEP, 1981.

Alarcón, Norma. "The Theoretical Subject(s) of *This Bridge Called My Back* and Anglo-American Feminism." In *Making Face, Making Soul/Haciendo Caras,* ed. Gloria Anzaldúa, 356–69. San Francisco: Aunt Lute Foundation Books, 1990.

Alavi, Hamza, and Teodor Shanin, eds. *Introduction to the Sociology of "Developing Societies."* New York: Monthly Review Press, 1982.

Alejos García, José. "Los mayas actuales: Identidad e historia." *América Indígena* 1–2 (1995): 37–62.

Alfred, Helen, ed. *First Steps toward World Economic Peace.* New York: Citizens Conference on International Economic Union, 1943.

——. *The Bretton Woods Accord: Why It Is Necessary.* New York: Citizens Conference on International Economic Union, 1944.

Althusser, Louis. *Lenin and Philosophy.* New York: Monthly Review Press, 1971.

Anzaldúa, Gloria. *Borderlands/La Frontera.* San Francisco: Spinsters/Aunt Lute Press, 1987.

Anzaldúa, Gloria, and Cherríe Moraga, eds. *This Bridge Called My Back.* New York: Kitchen Table, Women of Color Press, 1981.

Apffel-Marglin, Frédérique, and Stephen A. Marglin. *Decolonizing Knowledge: From Development to Dialogue.* Oxford: Clarendon Press, 1996.

Appendini, Kirsten. "Transforming Food Policy over a Decade: The Balance for Mexican Corn Farmers in 1993." In *Economic Restructuring and Rural Subsistence in Mexico: Corn and the Crisis of the 1980s,* ed. Cynthia Hewitt de Alcántara, 145–56. Transformation of Rural Mexico Series 2. San Diego: Center for U.S.–Mexican Studies, UCSD, 1994.

Apter, David E. "The Role of Traditionalism in the Political Modernization of Ghana and Uganda." In *Political Development and Social Change*, ed. Jason Finkle and Richard W. Gable, 65–81. New York: John Wiley and Sons, 1966.

Arbit, Marcelo. *El pensamiento revolucionario del comandante "Che" Guevara: Semenario Científico Internacional, intervenciones y debate*. Buenos Aires: Dialectica, 1989.

Arias, Arturo. "El Movimiento Indígena en Guatemala." In *Los movimientos populares en CentroAmérica*, ed. Daniel Camacho and Rafael Menjívar, 62–119. Mexico City: Siglo Veintiuno, 1985.

Arrighi, Giovanni. *The Long Twentieth Century: Money, Power, and the Origins of Our Times*. London: Verso Press, 1994.

Asad, Talal, ed. *Anthropology and the Colonial Encounter*. New York: Humanities Press, 1973.

Aston, T. H., and C. H. E. Philpin, eds. *The Brenner Debate*. Cambridge: Cambridge University Press, 1985.

Baker, Houston A., Jr. *Blues, Ideology, and Afro-American Literature*. Chicago: University of Chicago Press, 1984.

Baker, Houston, Jr., and Patricia Redmond, eds. *Afro-American Literary Study in the 1990s*. Chicago: University of Chicago Press, 1989.

Baran, Paul A. *Political Economy of Growth*. New York: Prometheus Paperback, 1957.

Barre, Marie-Chantal. *Ideologías indigenistas y movimientos indios*. Mexico, D.F.: Siglo Veintiuno, 1983.

Barry, Tom. *Zapata's Revenge: Free Trade and the Farm Crisis in Mexico*. Boston: South End Press, 1995.

Bartolomé, Miguel Alberto. "Movimientos etnopoliticos y autonomías indígenas en México." *América Indígena* 55, nos. 1–2 (January–June 1995): 361–82.

Bastos, Santiago, and Manuela Camus. *Quebrando el silencio: Organizaciones del Pueblo Maya y sus Demandas (1986–1992)*. Guatemala City: FLASCO, 1992.

———. *Abriendo caminos: Las organizaciones mayas desde el Nobel hasta el Acuerdo de derechos indígenas*. Guatemala City: FLASCO, 1995.

Benjamin, Jessica. "A Desire of One's Own: Psychoanalytic Feminism and Intersubjective Space." In *Feminist Studies/Critical Studies*, ed. Teresa de Lauretis, 78–101. Bloomington: Indiana University Press, 1986.

Bernstein, Henry. *Underdevelopment and Development: The Third World Today*. New York: Penguin, 1973.

Beverley, John. "The Margin at the Center: On Testimonio (Testimonial Narrative)." *Modern Fiction Studies* 35, no. 1 (spring 1985): 11–28.

———. " 'Through All Things Modern': Second Thoughts on Testimonio." *Boundary 2* 18, no. 2 (summer 1991): 1–21.

———. "The Margin at the Center: On Testimonio (Testimonial Narrative)." In *The Real Thing: Testimonial Discourse and Latin America*, ed. Georg M. Gugelberger, 23–41. Durham, N.C.: Duke University Press, 1996.

———. "The Real Thing." In *The Real Thing: Testimonial Discourse and Latin America*, ed. Georg M. Gugelberger, 287–304. Durham, N.C.: Duke University Press, 1996.

Bhabha, Homi. "Of Mimicry and Man: The Ambivalence of Colonial Discourse." *October* 28 (1984): 125–33.

——. "Sly Civility." *October* 34 (1985): 71–80.

Bieder, Robert E. *Science Encounters the Indian, 1820–1880: The Early Years of American Ethnology.* Norman: University of Oklahoma Press, 1986.

Bodenheimer, Susanne J. "The Ideology of Developmentalism: American Political Science's Paradigm-Surrogate for Latin American Studies." *Berkeley Journal of Sociology* 15 (1970): 95–137.

Bonfil Batalla, Guillermo. *México Profundo: Reclaiming a Civilization.* Trans. Phillip A. Dennis. Austin: University of Texas Press, Institute of Latin American Studies, 1996.

Bottomore, Tom, et al., eds. *A Dictionary of Marxist Thought.* Oxford: Basil Blackwell, 1983, 1991.

Brenner, Robert. "The Origins of Capitalist Development: A Critique of Neo-Smithian Marxism." *New Left Review* 104 (July–August 1977): 25–92.

——. "Agrarian Class Structure and Economic Development in Pre-industrial Europe." In *The Brenner Debate,* ed. T. H. Aston and C. H. E. Philpin. Cambridge: Cambridge University Press, 1985.

Brietman, George. *The Last Year of Malcolm X: The Evolution of a Revolutionary.* New York: Merit Publishers, 1967.

——. *Malcolm X Speaks: Selected Speeches and Statements.* New York: Grove Weidenfeld Press, 1990.

Burbach, Roger. "Roots of the Postmodern Rebellion in Chiapas." *New Left Review* 205 (May–June 1994): 113–24.

Burbach, Roger, and Peter Rosset. *Chiapas and the Crisis of Mexican Agriculture.* Policy Brief no. 1. Oakland, Calif.: Institute for Food and Development Policy, 1994.

Burgos, Elizabeth. *Me llamo Rigoberta Menchú y así me nació la conciencia.* Mexico City: Siglo Veintiuno, s.a. de c.v., 1988.

——. "The Story of a Testimonio." *Latin American Perspectives* 26, no. 6 (November 1999): 53–63.

Burguete Cal y Mayor, Araceli. Interview by author, August 1994.

——. Interview by author, February 1995.

——. Interview by author, April 1996.

——. "Regiones Autónomas Pluriétnicas . . . Y sin emargo se mueven; Los Altos de Chiapas: Reconquista y autonomía territorial." *Twentieth International Congress, Latin American Studies Association Convention.* Guadalajara, Mexico, 17–19 April 1997.

Butler, Judith. *Gender Trouble.* New York: Routledge, 1990.

——. *The Psychic Life of Power: Theories in Subjection.* Palo Alto, Calif.: Stanford University Press, 1997.

CAHI (Central American Historical Institute). "Masaya Peasants Prompt Land Expropriations." *Update* 4, no. 23 (1985): 1–4.

——. "Agrarian Reform Undergoes Changes in Nicaragua." *Update* 5, no. 4 (1986): 1–6.

——. "Reactions to Agrarian Reform Modifications in Nicaragua." *Update* 5, no. 20 (1986): 1–4.

Camacho, Daniel, and Rafael Menjívar, eds. *Los movimientos populares en Centro-América*. Mexico City: Siglo Veintiuno, 1985.

Cardoso, Fernando Henrique. "Dependency and Development in Latin America." *New Left Review* 74 (July–August 1972): 83–94.

Cardoso, Fernando Henrique, and Enzo Faletto. *Dependency and Development in Latin America*. Berkeley: University of California Press, 1979.

Carrión, Alfonso. Interview by author, September 1994.

Carson, Clayborne. *In Struggle: SNCC and the Black Awakening of the 1960s*. Cambridge: Harvard University Press, 1981.

——. *Malcolm X: The FBI File*. New York: Carroll and Graf, 1991.

Caso, Alfonso. *La comunidad indígena*. Mexico: Secretaría de Educación Pública, 1981.

Castañeda, Jorge G. *Utopia Unarmed: The Latin American Left after the Cold War*. New York: Vintage Books, 1993.

Castillo Falcato, Norma. *Conferencia teórica sobre el pensamiento del Comandante Ernesto Che Guevara: Memorias*. Havana: Editora Politica, 1990.

Chatterjee, Partha. *National Thought and the Colonial World: A Derivative Discourse?* London: Zed Books, 1986.

Chaturvedi, Vinayak, ed. *Mapping Subaltern Studies and the Postcolonial*. London: Verso, 2000.

Chinchilla Stoltz, Norma. "Of Straw Men and Stereotypes: Why Guatemalan Rocks Don't Talk." *Latin American Perspectives* 26, no. 6 (November 1999): 29–37.

CIERA (Centro de Investigacion y Estudios de la Reforma Agraria). "Estudio de Las Cooperativa de Produccion." Managua, Nicaragua: unpublished mimeograph, 1985.

——. "Propuesta de Trabajo Para un Diagnostico de la Situacion del Movimiento Coperativo." Managua, Nicaragua: unpublished mimeograph, 1986.

——. *Cifras y referencias documentales*. Managua, Nicaragua: CIERA, 1989.

Clark, Steve, ed. *Malcolm X Talks to Young People: Speeches in the U.S., Britain, and Africa*. New York: Pathfinder Press, 1991.

——. *Malcolm X: February 1965, The Last Speeches*. New York: Pathfinder Press, 1992.

Clarke, John Henrik, ed. *Malcolm X: The Man and His Times*. Toronto, Canada: Macmillan, 1969.

Clifford, James, and George E. Marcus. *Writing Culture: The Poetics and Politics of Ethnography*. Berkeley: University of California Press, 1986.

COCOPA (Commission for Agreement and Peacemaking). *San Andres Accords on Indigenous Rights and Culture*. Mexico, 16 February 1996.

Coe, Sue, with Judith Moore and Françoise Mouly. *X: For Malcolm X and All Those Who Have Been Xed Out of the American Dream*. New York: New Press, 1992.

Colás, Santiago. "What's Wrong with Representation? *Testimonio* and Democratic Culture." In *The Real Thing: Testimonial Discourse and Latin America*, ed. Georg M. Gugelberger, 161–71. Durham, N.C.: Duke University Press, 1996.

Colburn, Forrest D. *Post-revolutionary Nicaragua*. Berkeley: University of California Press, 1986.

———, ed. *Everyday Forms of Peasant Resistance*. London: M. E. Sharpe, 1989.

Collier, George, with Elizabeth Lowery Quaratiello. *Basta! Land and the Zapatista Rebellion in Chiapas*. Oakland, Calif.: Institute for Food and Development Policy, 1994.

Collins, Joseph. *What Difference Can a Revolution Make?* New York: Grove Press, 1986.

Collins, Patricia Hill. "The Social Construction of Black Feminist Thought." *Signs: Journal of Women in Culture and Society* 14, no. 4 (1989): 745–73.

———. "Learning to Think for Ourselves." In *Malcolm X: In Our Own Image*, ed. Joe Wood, 59–85. New York: St. Martin's Press, 1992.

Conroy, Michael E., ed. *Nicaragua: Profiles of the Revolutionary Public Sector*. Boulder, Colo.: Westview Press, 1987.

Consejo de Estado. *1979–1984 Principales Leyes Aprobadas Por El Gobierno de Reconstruccion Nacional: Managua*. Nicaragua: Consejo de Estado, 1985.

Davis, Charles T., and Henry Louis Gates Jr., eds. *The Slave's Narrative*. Oxford: Oxford University Press, 1985.

Deere, Carmen D. "Agrarian Reform, Peasant and Rural Production, and the Organization of Production in the Transition to Socialism." In *Transition and Development: Problems of Third World Socialism*, ed. Richard Fagen, Carmen D. Deere, and Jose L. Coraggio, 97–142. New York: Monthly Review Press, 1986.

Deere, Carmen D., and Peter Marchetti. "The Worker-Peasant Alliance in the First Year of the Nicaraguan Agrarian Reform." *Latin American Research Review* 8, no. 2 (spring 1981): 40–73.

Díaz Polanco, Héctor. "Etnicidad y autonomía en el pensamiento de Mario Payeras." In *Los pueblos indígenas y la revolución guatemalteca*, by Mario Payeras, 5–12. Guatemala City: Luna y Sol, 1997.

———. *Indigenous Peoples in Latin America: The Quest for Self-Determination*. Trans. Lucía Rayas. Latin American Perspectives Series, no. 18. Boulder, Colo.: Westview Press, 1997.

Diskin, Martin, ed. *Trouble in Our Backyard: Central America and the United States in the Eighties*. New York: Pantheon Books, 1983.

Durand Alcántara, Carlos. *Derechos indios en México . . . derecho pendientes*. Chapingo, Mexico: Universidad Autónoma Chapingo, 1994.

Ebon, Martin. *Che: The Making of a Legend*. New York: Universe Press, 1969.

Engels, Frederick. *The Origin of the Family, Private Property, and the State*. Selection in *Dynamics of Social Change: A Reader in Marxist Social Science from the Writings of*

Marx, Engels, and Lenin, ed. Howard Selsam, David Goldway, and Harry Martel, 884. New York: International Publishers, 1970.

Enriquez, Laura J., and Rose Spalding. "Banking Systems and Revolutionary Change: The Politics of Agricultural Credit in Nicaragua." In *The Political Economy of Revolutionary Nicaragua,* ed. Rose J. Spalding, 105–25. Boston: Allen and Unwin, 1987.

Escobar, Arturo. "Power and Visibility: The Invention of the Third World." Ph.D. diss., University of California, Berkeley, 1987.

——. "Imagining a Post-development Era? Critical Thought, Development, and Social Movements." *Social Text* 10, nos. 2–3 (1992): 20–56.

——. *Encountering Development: The Making and Unmaking of the Third World.* Princeton, N.J.: Princeton University Press, 1995.

Esteva, Gustavo. "Development." In *The Development Dictionary,* ed. Wolfgang Sachs, 6–25. London: Zed Books, 1992.

EZLN. "Consulta National por la paz y la democracia." *Tiempo Semanal: Que informa y orienta,* no. 2 (21 August 1995): 6.

Fagen, Richard, Carmen D. Deere, and Jose L. Coraggio, eds. *Transition and Development: Problems of Third World Socialism.* New York: Monthly Review Press, 1986.

Fanon, Frantz. *The Wretched of the Earth.* Trans. Constance Farrington. New York: Grove Weidenfeld, 1991.

Feal, Rosemary Geisdorfer. "Spanish American Ethnobiography and the Slave Narrative Tradition: *Biografía de un cimarrón* and *Me llamo Rigoberta Menchú.*" *Modern Language Studies* 20, no. 1 (winter 1990): 100–111.

Ferguson, James. *The Anti-Politics Machine.* Cambridge: Cambridge University Press, 1990.

Fernández, Damián J., ed. *Cuban Studies since the Revolution.* Miami: University of Florida Press, 1992.

Finkle, Jason, and Richard W. Gable, eds. *Political Development and Social Change.* New York: John Wiley and Sons, 1966.

Fisher, Edward F. and R. McKenna Brown. *Maya Cultural Activism in Guatemala.* Austin: University of Texas Press, Institute of Latin American Studies, 1996.

Fitzgerald, Valpy. "National Economy in 1985: Transition in Progress." Managua: unpublished mimeograph, 1985.

FNI. "Foro Nacional Indígena: Programa general de actividades." Trans. San Cristobal. Chiapas: FNI, 1996.

Foster, George. *Tzintzuntzan: Mexican Peasants in a Changing World.* Boston: Little, Brown, 1967.

Franco, Jean. *Critical Passions: Selected Essays.* Ed. Mary Louise Pratt and Kathleen Newman. Durham, N.C.: Duke University Press, 1999.

——. *The Decline and Fall of the Lettered City: Latin America in the Cold War.* Cambridge: Harvard University Press, 2002.

Frank, André Gunder. "The Development of Underdevelopment." *Monthly Review,* September 1966, 17–31.

———. *Latin America: Underdevelopment or Revolution*. New York: Monthly Review Press, 1969.

Frenkel, María Veronica. "The Evolution of Food and Agricultural Policies during Economic Crisis and War." In *Nicaragua: Profiles of the Revolutionary Public Sector,* ed. Michael E. Conroy, 201–36. Boulder, Colo.: Westview Press, 1987.

Fried, Jonathan L., Deborah T. Levenson, and Nancy Pechkenham, eds. *Guatemala in Rebellion: Unfinished History.* New York: Grove Press, 1983.

FSLN. *Programa Histórico del FSLN.* Managua, Nicaragua: Departamento de Propaganda y Educación Política, Colección Viva Sandino, 1984.

Furtado, Celso. *Obstacles to Development in Latin America.* New York: Doubleday, 1970.

———. *O mito do desenvolvimento economico.* Brasil: Paz e Terra, 1974.

Gambino, Ferruccio. "The Transgression of a Laborer: Malcolm X in the Wilderness of America." *Radical History Review* 55 (winter 1993): 7–31.

Gamio, Manuel. *Forjando Patria.* 2d ed. Mexico: Editorial Porrúa, 1960.

———. *El inmigrante Mexicano: La historia de su vida.* México: Universidad Nacional Autónoma de México, 1969.

García Canclini, Néstor. *Resistencia y utopía, tomo dos.* Mexico, D.F.: Ediciones Era, s.a. de c.v., 1985.

———. *Hybrid Cultures: Strategies for Entering and Leaving Modernity.* Trans. Christopher L. Chippari and Silvia L. López. Minneapolis: University of Minnesota Press, 1995.

García de León, Antonio. "Redes de transición, selva de símbolos." In EZLN: Documentos y Comunicados, ed. Carlos Monsiváis, 13–20. Mexico City: Ediciones Era, s.a. de c.v., 1995.

Gates, Henry Louis, Jr., ed. *"Race," Writing, and Difference.* Chicago: University of Chicago Press, 1986.

———. *The Signifying Monkey: A Theory of Afro-American Literary Criticism.* New York: Oxford University Press, 1988.

George, Susan, and Fabrizio Sabelli. *Faith and Credit: The World Bank's Secular Empire.* Boulder, Colo.: Westview Press, 1994.

Ghosh, Pradip, ed. *Technology Policy and Development: A Third World Perspective.* London: Greenwood Press, 1984.

Gibson, Bill. "Structural Overview of the Nicaraguan Economy." In *The Political Economy of Revolutionary Nicaragua,* ed. Rose J. Spalding, 15–41. Boston: Allen and Unwin, 1987.

Gil, José, and Rosa Rojas. "Acuerdan participantes del Foro Indígena programa de siete puntos." *La Jornada* (Mexico City, Mexico), 9 January 1996, 10.

Gil Olmos, José. "EZLN: Inicia un gran movimiento nacional indígena e independiente." *La Jornada* (Mexico City, Mexico), 10 January 1996, 8.

Gilbreth, Chris. *Global Exchange Chiapas Peace Process Timeline.* Trans. San Cristobal. Chiapas: Global Exchange Chiapas, 1997.

Goldman, Peter. *The Death and Life of Malcolm X.* New York: Harper and Row, 1973.

González Casanova, Pablo. "Repensar la revolución." *América Indígena* 55, nos. 1–2 (January–June 1995): 341–60.

Gosen, Gary H. "Rigoberta Menchú and Her Epic Narrative." *Latin American Perspectives* 26, no. 6 (November 1999): 64–69.

Grandin, Greg, and Francisco Goldman. "Bitter Fruit for Rigoberta." *Nation,* 8 February 1999, 25–28.

Guevara, Ernesto "Che." *Episodes of the Cuban Revolutionary War, 1956–1958.* Trans. Victoria Ortiz, with revisions by Michael Taber. Ed. Mary-Alice Waters. New York: Pathfinder Press, 1996.

——. *Guerrilla Warfare.* Lincoln: University of Nebraska Press, 1998. Originally published in English in 1961.

——. *Pasajes de la guerra revolucionaria.* Havana: Editorial de Ciencias Sociales, 1999.

Gugelberger, Georg M. "Introduction: Institutionalization of Transgression: Testimonial Discourse and Beyond." In *The Real Thing: Testimonial Discourse and Latin America,* ed. Georg M. Gugelberger, 1–22. Durham, N.C.: Duke University Press, 1996.

——. "*Stollwerk* or Bulwark? David Meets Goliath and the Continuation of the Testimonio Debate." *Latin American Perspectives* 26, no. 6 (November 1999): 47–52.

——, ed. *The Real Thing: Testimonial Discourse and Latin America.* Durham, N.C.: Duke University Press, 1996.

Gugelberger, Georg M., and Michael Kearney. "Voices for the Voiceless: Testimonial Literature in Latin America." *Latin American Perspectives* 18, no. 3 (summer 1991): 3–14.

Guha, Ranajit. "On Some Aspects of the Historiography of Colonial India." In *Selected Subaltern Studies,* ed. Ranajit Guha and Gayatri Chakravorty Spivak, 37–44. New York: Oxford University Press, 1988.

——. *Dominance without Hegemony: History and Power in Colonial India.* Cambridge: Harvard University Press, 1997.

Guha, Ranajit, and Gayatri Chakravorty Spivak, eds. *Selected Subaltern Studies.* New York: Oxford University Press, 1988.

Gupta, Akhil. *Postcolonial Developments.* Durham, N.C.: Duke University Press, 1988.

Harvey, Neil. *Rebellion in Chiapas: Rural Reforms, Campesino Radicalism, and the Limits to Salinismo.* Transformation of Rural Mexico Series, no. 5, Ejido Reform Research Project. San Diego, Calif.: Center for U.S.–Mexican Studies, University of California, San Diego, 1994.

——. *The Chiapas Rebellion: The Struggle for Land and Democracy.* Durham, N.C.: Duke University Press, 1998.

——. "Redefining Citizenship: Indigenous Movements in Chiapas." Unpublished ms., n.d.

Hauser, Philip M. "Some Cultural and Personal Characteristics of the Less Developed Areas." In *Political Development and Social Change,* ed. Jason Finkle and Richard W. Gable, 54–64. New York: John Wiley and Sons, 1966.

Hayes, Samuel P., Jr. "An Official Interpretation." In *The Point Four Program*, a special issue of *The Reference Shelf* 23, no. 5, ed. Walter M. Daniels, 12–16. New York: Wilson, 1951.

Henríquez, Elío, and José Gil Olmos. "Levará el gobierno as EZLN un *oferta generos* sobre autnonomía." *La Jornada* (Mexico City, Mexico), 10 January 1996, 9.

Hernández Castillo, Rosalva Aída. "Invencion de tradiciones: Encuentros y desencuentros de la población mame con el indienismo mexicano." *América Indígena* 55, nos. 1–2 (January–June 1995): 129–48.

Hernández Navarro, Luis. "Nadando con los tiburones: La experiencia de la Coordinadora Nacional de Organizaciones Cafetaleras." *Cuadernos Agrarios* 7 (1991) (nueva época): 52–75.

———. Interview by author, July 1994.

———. Interview by author, September 1994.

———. Interview by author, September 1996.

———. "Cosecha india." *La Jornada* (Mexico City, Mexico), 10 January 1996, 10.

———. "Cuidadanos iguales, ciudadanos diferentes: La nueva lucha india." *Este Pais*, February 1997, 30–40.

Hertzler, J. O. *The Crisis in World Population: A Sociological Examination with Special Reference to the Underdeveloped Areas*. Lincoln: University of Nebraska Press, 1956.

Hewitt de Alcántara, Cynthia. *Boundaries and Paradigms: The Anthropological Study of Rural Life in Postrevolutionary Mexico*. Leiden Development Studies, no. 4. Leiden: Leiden Development Studies, 1982.

———. *Anthropological Perspectives on Rural Mexico*. London: Routledge and Kegan Paul, 1984.

———, ed. *Economic Restructuring and Rural Subsistence in Mexico: Corn and the Crisis of the 1980s*. Transformation of Rural Mexico Series, no. 2. San Diego: Center for U.S.–Mexican Studies, UCSD, 1994.

Hidalgo, Blanca. Interview by author, July 1994.

Hilbert, Sarah. "For Whom the Nation? Internationalization, Zapatismo, and the Struggle over Mexican Modernity." *Antipode* 29, no. 2 (1997): 115–48.

Hirschman, Albert. *The Strategy of Economic Development*. New Haven, Conn.: Yale University Press, 1958.

Hobson, J. A. *Imperialism: A Study*. Ann Arbor: University of Michigan Press, 1965.

hooks, bell. "Malcom X: Consumed by Images." *Z Magazine* 6, no. 3 (March 1993): 36–39.

Hoselitz, Bert. *Sociological Factors in Economic Development*. Chicago: Free Press, 1960.

———. "Social Stratification and Economic Development." *Journal of International Social Science* (UNESCO) 16, no. 2 (1964). Quoted in Rodolfo Stavenhagen, "Changing Functions of the Community in Underdeveloped Countries," in *Underdevelopment and Development: The Third World Today*, ed. Henry Bernstein (New York: Penguin Books, 1976), 83–95.

IHCA (Instituto Historico CentroAmerico). "The Right of the Poor to Defend Their Revolution." *Envio* 4, no. 36 (1984): 1–33.

——. "The Nicaraguan Peasantry Gives New Direction to Agrarian Reform." *Envio* 4, no. 51 (1985): 1–19.

Ituarte, Gonzalo. Interview by author, April 1996.

Jameson, Fredric. "On Literary and Cultural Import-Substitution in the Third World: The Case of Testimonio." In *The Real Thing: Testimonial Discourse and Latin America,* ed. Georg M. Gugelberger, 172–90. Durham, N.C.: Duke University Press, 1996.

Jara, René, and Hernán Vidal, eds. *Testimonio y literatura.* Society for the Study of Contemporary Hispanic and Lusophone Revolutionary Literatures Monographic Series, no. 3. Minneapolis: Institute for the Study of Ideologies and Literature, 1986.

Joseph, Gilbert M. *Rediscovering the Past at Mexico's Periphery: Essays on the History of Modern Yucatán.* Tuscaloosa: University of Alabama Press, 1986.

——. "The United States, Feuding Elites, and Rural Revolt in Yucatán, 1836–1915." In *Rural Revolt in Mexico: U.S. Intervention and the Domain of Subaltern Politics,* ed. David Nugent, 173–206. Durham, N.C.: Duke University Press, 1988.

Joseph, Gilbert, and Daniel Nugent, eds. *Everyday Forms of State Formation: Revolution and the Negotiation of Rule in Modern Mexico.* Durham, N.C.: Duke University Press, 1994.

Joseph, Miranda. *Against the Romance of Community.* Minneapolis: University of Minnesota Press, 2002.

Karim, Benjamin, with Peter Skutches and David Gallen. *Remembering Malcolm: The Story of Malcolm X from Inside the Muslim Mosque by His Assistant Minister Benjamin Karim.* New York: Carroll and Graf Publishers, 1992.

Kazanjian, David. "Charles Brockden Brown's Biloquial Nation: National Culture in White Settler Colonialism in *Memoirs of Carwin, The Biloquist.*" *American Literature* 73, no. 3 (2001): 459–96.

Keller, Evelyn Fox. *Reflections on Gender and Science.* New Haven, Conn.: Yale University Press, 1985.

Kelley, Robin D. G. "The Riddle of the Zoot: Malcolm Little and Black Cultural Politics during World War II." In *Malcolm X: In Our Own Image,* ed. Joe Wood, 155–82. New York: St. Martin's Press, 1992.

Kennedy, John F. "Text of President's Speech on Alliance for Progress Program." *New York Times,* 14 March 1962, A-18.

Knight, Alan. *The Mexican Revolution.* Vol. 2, *Counter-revolution and Reconstruction.* Lincoln: University of Nebraska Press, 1986.

——. "Racism, Revolution, and *Indigenismo:* Mexico, 1910–1940." In *The Idea of Race in Latin America, 1870–1940,* ed. Richard Graham, 71–113. Austin: University of Texas Press, 1990.

——. "Continuidades históricas en los movimientos socials." In *Paisajes rebeldes: Una larga noche de rebellion indígena,* ed. James Dale Lloyd and Laura Pérez Rosales, 13–52. Mexico City: Universidad Iberoamericana, A.C., 1995.

Krauze, Enrique. *Mexico: Biography of Power, A History of Modern Mexico, 1810–1996.* Trans. Hank Heifetz. New York: HarperPerennial, 1997.

Laclau, Ernesto. "Feudalism and Capitalism in Latin America." *New Left Review* 67 (May–June 1971): 19–38.

——. *Emancipation(s).* London: Verso, 1996.

Laplanche, J., and J.-B. Pontalis. *The Language of Psycho-Analysis.* Trans. Donald Nicholson Smith. New York: W. W. Norton, 1973.

Larrain, Jorge. *Theories of Development: Capitalism, Colonialism, and Dependency.* Cambridge, England: Blackwell Publishers, 1989.

Lenin, V. I. *Selected Works in Three Volumes.* Vol. 2. New York: International Publishers, 1967.

——. "What the 'Friends of the People' Are." Selection in *Dynamics of Social Change: A Reader in Marxist Social Science from the Writings of Marx, Engels, and Lenin,* ed. Howard Selsam, David Goldway, and Harry Martel. New York: International Publishers, 1970.

——. *Imperialism: The Highest Stage of Capitalism.* Moscow: Progress Publishers, 1986.

Leys, Colin. *The Rise and Fall of Development Theory.* London: James Curry, 1996.

Leyva Solano, Xóchitl. "Del cómon al Leviatán (Síntesis de un proceso sociopolítico en el medio rural mexicano)." *América Indígena* 55, nos. 1–2 (January–June 1995): 201–34.

Long, Norman. *An Introduction to the Sociology of Rural Development.* Boulder, Colo.: Westview Press, 1977.

Lott, Davis Newton. *The Presidents Speak: The Inaugural Addresses of the American Presidents from Washington to Clinton.* New York: Henry Holt, 1994.

Lowe, Lisa, and David Lloyd, eds. *The Politics of Culture in the Shadow of Capital.* Durham, N.C.: Duke University Press, 1997.

Lowy, Michael. *The Marxism of Che Guevara: Philosophy, Economics, and Revolutionary Warfare.* New York: Monthly Review Press, 1973.

Luis, William. *Voices from Under: Black Narrative in Latin America and the Caribbean.* London: Greenwood Press, 1984.

Magdoff, Harry. *The Age of Imperialism.* New York: Monthly Review Press, 1969.

——. "Imperialism: A Historical Survey." In *Introduction to the Sociology of "Developing Societies,"* ed. Hamza Alavi and Teodor Shanin, 11–28. New York: Monthly Review Press, 1982.

Malcolm X, with Alex Haley. *The Autobiography of Malcolm X as Told to Alex Haley.* New York: Ballantine Books, 1984.

Mallon, Florencia E. *Peasant and Nation: The Making of Postcolonial Mexico and Peru.* Berkeley: University of California Press, 1995.

Marable, Manning. *Race, Reform, and Rebellion: The Second Reconstruction in Black America, 1945–1982.* London: Macmillan, 1984.

Marcos. "La Consulta: Parte de un dialago nacional." *Tiempo Semanal: Que Informa y Orienta,* no. 2 (21 August 1995): 4.

——. "Mesa nacional de diálogo independiente: *Marcos.*" *La Jornada* (Mexico City, Mexico), 1 October 1995, Perfil: 1.

Marcus, George E., and Michael J. Fisher. *Anthropology as Cultural Critique: An Experimental Moment in the Human Sciences.* Chicago: University of Chicago Press, 1986.

Marín, Lynda. "Speaking Out Together: Testimonials of Latin American Women." *Latin American Perspectives* 18, no. 3 (summer 1991): 51–67.

Marx, Karl. *Pre-capitalist Economic Formations.* In *Dynamics of Social Change: A Reader in Marxist Social Science from the Writings of Marx, Engels, and Lenin,* ed. Howard Selsam, David Goldway, and Harry Martel. New York: International Publishers, 1970.

——. *Early Writings.* Trans. Rodney Livingstone and Gregor Benton. New York: Penguin Books, 1975.

——. "The Future Result of British Rule in India." In *The Marx-Engels Reader,* ed. Robert Tucker, 659–64. New York: W. W. Norton, 1978.

——. *Surveys from Exile.* Ed. D. Fernbach. Harmondsworth: Penguin, 1973. In *Theories of Development: Capitalism, Colonialism, and Dependency,* ed. Jorge Larrain. Cambridge, England: Blackwell Publishers, 1989.

McCaugh, Michael. Interview by author, 1995.

McMichael, Philip. *Development and Social Change: A Global Perspective.* Thousand Oaks, Calif.: Pine Forge Press, 1996.

McNamara, Robert S. *The McNamara Years at the World Bank: Major Policy Addresses of Robert S. McNamara.* Baltimore, Md.: Published for the World Bank by the Johns Hopkins University Press, 1981.

Medina, Andrés. "Los pueblos indios en la trama de la nación: Notas etnográficas." *Revista Mexicana de Sociología,* January 1998, 131–68.

Menchú, Rigoberta. "Entrevista." *Fem: Publicacion Femenista* 8, no. 29 (August–September 1983): 13–16.

——. *Rigoberta: La nieta de los mayas.* With Gianni Minà and Dante Liano. Mexico City: Aguilar, Altea, Taurus, Alfaguara, s.a. de c.v., 1998.

——. "Los que me atacan humillan a las víctimas." *El Pais* (Madrid), 24 January 1999, morning ed., Suplemento Domingo, 6.

——. "Truth-Telling and Memory in Postwar Guatemala: An Interview with Rigoberta Menchú by Jo-Marie Burt and Fred Rosen." *NacLA: Report on the Americas* 32, no. 5 (March–April 1999): 6–8.

Mintz, Sidney W. *Caribbean Transformations.* Chicago: Aldine, 1974.

——. *Sweetness and Power: The Place of Sugar in Modern History.* New York: Viking, 1985.

MIPLAN (Ministerio de Planificacion Nacional, Nicaragua). *Programa de reactivacion economica en beneficio del pueblo.* Managua, Nicaragua: MIPLAN, 1980.

——. *Programa economico de austeridad y eficiencia.* Managua, Nicaragua: MIPLAN, 1981.

Mogel, Reyna. Interview by author, 1994.

Moguel, Julio. "Diálago en Sacamch'en: Tercera llamada." *La Jornada* (Mexico City, Mexico), 23 January 1996, 24.

Monjardin, Adriana Lopéz. Interview by author, September 1996.

Monsiváis, Carlos. EZLN: Documentos y comunicados, 15 de agostos de 1994/29 de septiembre de 1995. Mexico City: Ediciones Era, Colecciónes Problemas de México, 1995.

Montemayor, Carlos. *Chiapas: La rebellion indígena de México.* Benit Juarez, D.F.: Editorial Joaquín mortiz, S.A. de C.V., 1997.

Moreiras, Alberto. "The Aura of Testimonio." In *The Real Thing: Testimonial Discourse and Latin America,* ed. Georg M. Gugelberger, 192–224. Durham, N.C.: Duke University Press, 1996.

Morquecho, Gaspar. Interview by author, May 1996.

Morrison, Toni. "Rootedness: The Ancestor as Foundation." In *Black Women Writers (1950–1980): A Critical Evaluation,* ed. Marie Evans, 339–45. Garden City, N.Y.: Anchor Press/Doubleday, 1984.

Myrdal, G. *Economic Theory and Underdeveloped Regions.* London: Duckworth, 1957.

——. *The Challenge of World Poverty.* London: Allen Lane, 1970.

Nugent, David. *Rural Revolt in Mexico: U.S. Intervention and the Domain of Subaltern Politics.* Durham, N.C.: Duke University Press, 1988.

Orozco Zuarth, Marco A. *Sintesis de Chiapas.* Mexico City: Ediciones y Sistemas Especiales, S.A. de C.V., 1994.

Pacheco, José Emilio, et al., eds. *En torno a la cultura nacional.* Mexico City: Fondo de Cultura Económica, 1982.

Padilla, Genaro. "Myth and Comparative Cultural Nationalism: The Ideological Uses of Aztlán." In *Aztlán: Essays on the Chicano Homeland,* ed. Rodolfo A. Anaya and Francisco A. Lomeli, 111–34. Albuquerque: New Mexico University Press, 1989.

Pandey, Gyanendra. "Voices from the Edge: The Struggle to Write Subaltern Histories." In *Mapping Subaltern Studies and the Postcolonial,* ed. Vinayak Chaturvedi, 281–99. London: Verso Press, 2000.

Payer, C. *The World Bank: A Critical Analysis.* New York: Monthly Review Press, 1983.

Payeras, Mario. *Dias de la selva.* Madrid: Editorial Revolución, 1984.

——. *El trueno en la cuidad: Episodios de la lucha armada urbana de 1981 en Guatemala.* Mexico City: Juan Pablos Editor, 1987.

——. *Los puebos indígenas y la revolución guatemalteca.* Guatemala City: Luna y Sol, 1997.

Perry, Bruce. *Malcolm: The Man Who Changed Black America.* Barrytown, N.Y.: Station Hill Press, 1991.

Pinkney, Alphonso. *Red, Black, and Green: Black Nationalism in the United States.* Cambridge: Cambridge University Press, 1976.

Poniatowska, Elena, and Carlos Monsiváis. EZLN: Documentos y comunicados, 1 de enero–8 de agosto de 1994. Mexico City: Ediciones Era, Colecciónes Problemas de México, 1994.

Pozas Arciniegas, Ricardo. "La proletarización de los indios en la formación econónomica y social de México." *Revista Mexican de Ciencias, Políticas y Sociales* 88 (April–June 1977).

Pratt, Mary Louise. *Imperial Eyes: Travel Writing and Transculturation*. New York: Routledge, 1992.

Quijano, Aníbal. *Dependencia, urbanizacion y cambio social en Latino America*. Lima: Mosca Azul Editores, 1977.

Rabasa, José. "Of Zapatismo: Reflections on the Folkloric and the Impossible in a Subaltern Insurrection." In *The Politics of Culture in the Shadow of Capital*, ed. Lisa Lowe and David Lloyd, 399–431. Durham, N.C.: Duke University Press, 1997.

Redfield, Robert. *The Little Community and Peasant Society and Culture*. Chicago: University of Chicago Press, 1965.

Reifler Bricker, Victoria. *The Indian Christ, the Indian King: The Historical Substrate of Maya Myth and Ritual*. Austin: University of Texas Press, 1981.

Retamar, Roberto Fernández. "Caliban: Notes towards a Discussion of Culture in Our America." Trans. Lynn Garafola, David Arthur McMurray, and Robert Márquez. *Massachusetts Review* 15 (winter–spring 1974): 7–72.

Rivera, Tomás. *. . . y no se lo tragó la tierra*. Trans. Evangelina Vigil-Piñón. Houston: Arte Publico Press, 1987.

Rodríguez, Ileana. *Women, Guerrillas, and Love: Understanding War in Central America*. Minneapolis: University of Minnesota Press, 1996.

——, ed. *Latin American Subaltern Studies: A Reader*. Durham, N.C.: Duke University Press, 2001.

Rodríguez, Octavio. *La teoría del subdesarrollo de la CEPAL*. Mexico: Siglo Veintiuno, 1980.

Rodriguez, Richard. *Days of Obligation: An Argument with My Mexican Father*. New York: Penguin, 1992.

Rojas, Rosa, and José Gil Olmos. "Piden una profunda reforma del Estado." *La Jornada* (Mexico City, Mexico), 8 January 1996, 1.

——. "Se requiere un Congreso Nacional de los Pueblos Indios: Foro." *La Jornada* (Mexico City, Mexico), 9 January 1996, 9.

Rostow, W. W. *Stages of Economic Growth: A Non-Communist Manifesto*. 1960; Cambridge: Cambridge University Press, 1971.

Ruccio, David. "The State and Planning in Nicaragua." In *The Political Economy of Revolutionary Nicaragua*, ed. Rose J. Spalding, 61–82. Boston: Allen and Unwin, 1987.

Ruiz, Margarito. Interview by author, September 1994.

——. Interview by author, April 1996.

Ruiz, Ramon Eduardo. *Cuba: The Making of a Revolution*. Amherst: University of Massachusetts Press, 1968.

Rus, Jan. "The 'Comunidad Revolucionaria Institucional': The Subversion of Native Government in Highland Chiapas, 1936–1968." In *Everyday Forms of State Formation: Revolution and the Negotiation of Rule in Modern Mexico*, ed. Gilbert

Joseph and Daniel Nugent, 265–300. Durham, N.C.: Duke University Press, 1994.

——. "Introduction." *Latin American Perspectives* 26, no. 6 (November 1999): 5–14.

Sachs, Wolfgang, ed. *The Development Dictionary: A Guide to Knowledge as Power.* London: Zed Books, 1992.

Salazar, Claudia. "Rigoberta's Narrative and the New Practice of Oral History." *Women and Language* 13, no. 1 (fall 1990): 7–8.

Salazar, Inés. "Poetics of Resistance: Discourses of Difference in the Contemporary Writings of African American Women and Chicanas." Ph.D. diss., Stanford University, 1993.

Saldaña-Portillo, María Josefina. "The Discourse of Development and Narratives of Resistance." Ph.D. diss., Stanford University, 1993.

——. "Re-guarding Myself: Rigoberta Menchú's Autobiographical Rendering of the Authentic Other." *Socialist Review* 1–2 (1994): 85–114.

——. "Who's the Indian in Aztlán? Re-writing Mestizaje, Indianism, and Chicanismo from the Lacandon." In *Latin American Subaltern Studies: A Reader,* ed. Ileana Rodríguez, 402–23. Durham, N.C.: Duke University Press, 2001.

Saldívar, Ramón. *Chicano Narrative: The Dialectics of Difference.* Madison: University of Wisconsin Press, 1990.

Sanchez, Javier. Interview by author, September 1994.

Sanford, Victoria. "Between Rigoberta Menchú and La Violencia: Deconstructing David Stoll's History of Guatemala." *Latin American Perspectives* 26, no. 6 (November 1999): 38–46.

Sarmiento, Sergio. Interview by author, September 1994.

Saulniers, Alfred H. "State Trading Organizations in Expansion: A Case Study of ENABAS." In *Nicaragua: Profiles of the Revolutionary Public Sector,* ed. Michael E. Conroy. Boulder, Colo.: Westview Press, 1987.

Scott, James C. *Weapons of the Weak: Everyday Forms of Peasant Resistance.* New Haven, Conn.: Yale University Press, 1985.

——. "Everyday Forms of Resistance." In *Everyday Forms of Peasant Resistance,* ed. Forrest D. Colburn, 3–33. London: M. E. Sharpe, 1989.

Seed, Patricia. *Ceremonies of Possession in Europe's Conquest of the New World, 1492–1640.* New York: Cambridge University Press, 1995.

——. "The Requirement for Resistance: A Critical Comparative History of Contemporary Popular Expectations of Subalternity in the Americas." Paper presented at Cross-Genealogies and Subaltern Knowledges: A Conference, Durham, N.C., Duke University, 15–18 October 1998.

Selsam, Howard, David Goldway, and Harry Martel, eds. *Dynamics of Social Change: A Reader in Marxist Social Science from the Writings of Marx, Engels and Lenin.* New York: International Publishers, 1970.

Sjoberg, G. "Folk and 'Feudal' Societies." In *Political Development and Social Change,* ed. Jason Finkle and Richard W. Gable, 45–53. New York: John Wiley and Sons, 1966.

Sklodowska, Elzbieta. "Spanish American Testimonial Novel: Some Afterthoughts." In *The Real Thing: Testimonial Discourse and Latin America*, ed. Georg M. Gugelberger, 84–100. Durham, N.C.: Duke University Press, 1996.

Smith, Carol A. "Why Write an Exposé of Rigoberta Menchú?" *Latin American Perspectives* 26, no. 6 (November 1999): 15–28.

Sommer, Doris. " 'Not Just a Personal Story': Women's *Testimonios* and the Plural Self." In *Life/Lines: Theorizing Women's Autobiography*, ed. Bella Brodski and Celeste Schneck, 107–30. Ithaca, N.Y.: Cornell University Press, 1988.

———. "Rigoberta's Secrets." *Latin American Perspectives* 18, no. 3 (summer 1991): 32–50.

———. "No Secrets." In *The Real Thing: Testimonial Discourse and Latin America*, ed. Georg M. Gugelberger, 130–60. Durham, N.C.: Duke University Press, 1996.

Spalding, Rose J., ed. *The Political Economy of Revolutionary Nicaragua*. Boston: Allen and Unwin, 1987.

Spillers, Hortense J. "Mama's Baby, Papa's Maybe: An American Grammar Book." *Diacritics* 17, no. 2 (summer 1987): 65–81.

Spivak, Gayatri Chakravorty. "Three Women's Texts and a Critique of Imperialism." In *"Race," Writing, and Difference*, ed. Henry Louis Gates Jr., 262–88. Chicago: University of Chicago Press, 1986.

———. *In Other Worlds: Essays in Cultural Politics*. New York: Methuen, 1987.

———. "Can the Subaltern Speak?" In *Marxism and the Interpretation of Culture*, ed. Cary Nelson and Lawrence Grossberg, 271–316. Urbana: University of Illinois Press, 1988.

———. "Subaltern Studies: Deconstructing Historiography." In *Selected Subaltern Studies*, ed. Ranajit Guha and Gayatri Chakravorty Spivak, 3–34. New York: Oxford University Press, 1988.

Stavenhagen, Rodolfo. "Changing Functions of the Community in Underdeveloped Countries." In *Underdevelopment and Development: The Third World Today*, ed. Henry Bernstein, 83–95. New York: Penguin Books, 1981.

Stoll, David. *Rigoberta Menchú and the Story of All Poor Guatemalans*. Boulder, Colo.: Westview Press, 1999.

———. "Rigoberta Menchú and the Last Resort Paradigm." *Latin American Perspectives* 26, no. 6 (November 1999): 70–80.

Streetan, Paul. *The Frontiers of Development Studies*. London: Macmillan, 1972.

———. "Technology Gaps between Rich and Poor Countries." In *Technology Policy and Development: A Third World Perspective*, ed. Pradip K. Ghosh, 7–26. London: Greenwood Press, 1984.

Szulc, Tad. "Billion in U.S. Aid Stirs Praise and Criticism in Latin America." *New York Times*, 12 March 1962, sec. 1, p. 1.

Tablada, Carlos. *Che Guevara: Economics and Politics in the Transition to Socialism*. Sydney: Pathfinder/Pacific and Asia, 1987.

Tooker, Elisabeth. "The United States Constitution and the Iroquois League." *Ethnohistory* 35, no. 4 (fall 1988): 305–36.

Truman, Harry S. "Inaugural Address, January 20, 1949." In *The Presidents Speak:*

The Inaugural Addresses of the American Presidents from Washington to Clinton, ed. Davis Newton Lott, 292–98. New York: Henry Holt, 1994.

Tucker, Robert, ed. *The Marx-Engels Reader*. New York: W. W. Norton, 1978.

United States Congress. *Hearings of the House Special Committee on Postwar Policy and Planning, 78th Congress, 2d. session*. Washington, D.C.: U.S. Congressional Records, 1944.

United States Treasury Department. *Questions and Answers on the Fund and Bank*. Washington, D.C.: United States Treasury Department, 1945.

Utting, Peter. "Domestic Supply and Food Shortages." In *The Political Economy of Revolutionary Nicaragua*, ed. Rose J. Spalding, 127–48. Boston: Allen and Unwin, 1987.

Valence, Georges. *Les Maîtres du Monde L Allemagne, États-unis, Japon*. Paris: Flammarion, 1992.

Van Deburg, William L. *New Day in Babylon: The Black Power Movement and American Culture, 1965–1975*. Chicago: University of Chicago Press, 1992.

Varese, Stefano. "Una dialécttica negada: Notas sobre la multietnicidad mexicana." In *En torno a la cultura nacional*, ed. José Emilio Pacheco et al., 134–59. Mexico City: Fondo de Cultura Económica, 1982.

Vaughan, Alden T. *The Roots of American Racism: Essays on the Colonial Experience*. New York: Oxford University Press, 1995.

Vilas, Carlos. *The Sandinista Revolution*. New York: Monthly Review Press, 1986.

Viqueira, Juan Pedro. "Los límites del mestizaje cultural en Chiapas." *Historiador mexicano*, CIESAS Sureste 1–2 (1994): 279–303.

Wallerstein, Immanuel. "The Rise and Future Demise of the World Capitalist System." In *The Capitalist World-Economy: Essays by Immanuel Wallerstein*, 1–36. New York: Cambridge University Press, 1979.

——. *After Liberalism*. New York: New Press, 1995.

Warren, Kay B. "Imperialism and Capitalist Industrialization." *New Left Review* 81 (September–October 1973): 3–44.

——. *Imperialism: Pioneer of Capitalism*. London: New Left Books, 1980.

——. *Indigenous Movements and Their Critics: Pan-Maya activism in Guatemala*. Princeton, N.J.: Princeton University Press, 1998.

Waters, Mary Alice. Introduction to *Episodes of the Cuban Revolutionary War, 1956–1958*, by Ernesto "Che" Guevara, 7–39. New York: Pathfinder, 1996.

Weixlmann, Joe, and Chester J. Fontenot, eds. *Studies in Black American Literature*. Vol. 1, *Black American Prose Theory*. Greenwood, Fla.: Penkevill, 1984.

Weixlmann, Joe, Chester J. Fontenot, and Houston A. Baker Jr., eds. *Studies in Black American Literature*. Vol. 3, *Black Feminist Criticism and Critical Theory*. Greenwood, Fla.: Penkevill, 1988.

Weeks, John. "The Mixed Economy in Nicaragua." In *The Political Economy of Revolutionary Nicaragua*, ed. Rose J. Spalding, 43–60. Boston: Allen and Unwin, 1987.

West, Cornel. "Malcolm X and Black Rage." In *Malcolm X: In Our Own Image*, ed. Joe Wood, 48–58. New York: St. Martin's Press, 1992.

Wilbur, Charles K., ed. *The Political Economy of Development and Underdevelopment*. New York: Random House, 1973.

Williams, Gareth. "The Fantasies of Cultural Exchange in Latin American Subaltern Studies." In *The Real Thing: Testimonial Discourse and Latin America*, ed. Georg M. Gugelberger, 225–53. Durham, N.C.: Duke University Press, 1996.

Wolfenstein, Victor. *The Victims of Democracy: Malcolm X and the Black Revolution*. Berkeley: University of California Press, 1981.

Womack, John, Jr. *Zapata and the Mexican Revolution*. New York: Alfred A. Knopf, 1969.

——. *Rebellion in Chiapas: An Historical Reader*. New York: New Press, 1999.

Wood, Joe, ed. *Malcolm X: In Our Own Image*. New York: St. Martin's Press, 1992.

Yúdice, George. "*Testimonio* and Postmodernism." In *The Real Thing: Testimonial Discourse and Latin America*, ed. Georg M. Gugelberger, 42–57. Durham, N.C.: Duke University Press, 1996.

Zimmerman, Marc. "*Testimonio* in Guatemala: Payeras, Rigoberta, and Beyond." In *The Real Thing: Testimonial Discourse and Latin America*, ed. Georg M. Gugelberger, 101–29. Durham, N.C.: Duke University Press, 1996.

Malcolm X, 13–15, 33; relationship to Guevara, 263–67, 269, 270; relationship to Payeras, 265–67, 269. See also *Autobiography of Malcolm X*

Mallon, Florencia, 319 n.12

Marshall, A., 17

Marshall Plan, 23, 294 n.10

Martí, Faribundo, 227. *See also* Faribundo Martí National Liberation Front

Martí, José, 261

Marx, Karl, 17, 22, 31; and colonialism, 35–36, 292 n.1; *A Contribution to the Critique of Political Economy*, 37; *Precapitalist Economic Formations*, 96–97; and race, 36; subjectivity in, 37–40; teleology in, 39, 111

Masculinity: and consciousness, 70–78, 95–98, 130–35, 268; and nationalism, 14, 34–35, 41–43, 66, 71, 73, 78–82, 84, 88–92, 96, 100, 108, 131, 135–36, 152, 259–67, 274, 276–77, 300 n.7, 335 n.1, 337 n.12

Maximilian, Ferdinand-Joseph (emperor of Mexico), 225

McMichael, Philip, 323 n.29

McNamara, Robert Strange, 45–47, 57–58, 296 nn.16–17

Me llamo Rigoberta Menchú y así me nació la conciencia (Rigoberta Menchú): authorial voice in, 153, 155, 157–58, 160–62, 167–71, 182, 188, 223, 260, 310 n.6, 314 nn.17–18, 316 nn.25–26; capitalism in, 176–79, 184–86; colonialism in, 174–76, 178, 180–82, 188–90; conciencia in, 10–11, 154–90, 260–61; and gender, 180–81, 183–84; representation of subaltern in, 152–54, 157, 161, 162, 167–90, 260–61, 286–87, 315 n.24; as representative testimonio, 155–62, 172, 308 nn.1–2, 309 n.3; secrecy in, 172–74, 314 n.21; subjectivity in, 11,

152–54, 162–64, 166–90, 260–61, 286–87

Menchú, Rigoberta, 12, 13, 89, 92, 152–54, 193, 223, 288; interview in *Fem*, 169; relationship to Guevara, 169, 170; relationship to Payeras, 168–70, 177–78, 183. See also *Me llamo Rigoberta Menchú y así me nació la conciencia*

Menger, K., 17

Mestizaje, 12–15, 196–97, 200, 214, 220–21, 252–53, 278–87, 301 n.11, 322 n.25, 338 n.15; consciousness in, 225, 282; relationship to indigenismo, 210–12. *See also* Gamio, Mario: *Forjando Patria*; Indigenismo

Mexican National Coffee Institute (INMECAFE), 218, 324 n.35, 326 n.39

Mexican National Congress, 244

Mexican Workers Confederation (CTM), 220

Mexico: colonization of, 200–205; Constitution of 1857, 203–4; Constitution of 1917 (Article 27 on agrarian reform), 5, 206, 215, 219–22, 226, 320 n.16, 329 n.47; debt crisis in 1982, 213–14, 217, 219; Lerdo Law of 1856, 203–4; oil and agricultural policy in 1970s and 1980s, 13, 203–4, 214–22, 323 nn.30–31, 325 n.38, 326 nn.39–41, 330 n.54, 332 nn.32–35, 333 n.36; Revolution of 1910, 14, 197–98, 205, 219, 224–27, 229, 253, 321 n.18, 328 n.43

MIDINRA. *See* Sandinista National Liberation Front agricultural policy

MIPLAN. *See* Nicaraguan Ministry of Planning

Modernization/modernity. *See* Subjectivity: in discourse of development

Modernization theory, 26–28, 103–4, 294 n.10, 298 n.22. *See also* Rostow, W. W.; Stavenhagen, Rodolfo

Mogel, Reyna, 330 n.53

Mohammed, Elijah, 273, 337 n.10. *See also* Nation of Islam

Moran, Rolando, 90, 91, 153

Moreiras, Alberto, 152–53, 158–59, 173, 308 n.1, 314 n.21

Morelos, José María, 225

Morgenthau, Henry, 20

Morrison, Toni, 153

National Confederation of Popular Organizations (CNOP), 220

National Democratic Convention (CND), 243–46, 252

National Indigenist Institute (INI), 222

National Indigenous Forum (FNI), 246–49, 252

Nationalism: affective ties of, 120; black, 261, 278, 279 (*see also Autobiography of Malcolm X;* Colonialism, internal); and capitalism, 105–6; Chicano, 261, 278, 279 (*see also* Anzaldúa, Gloria; Rivera, Tomás; Rodriguez, Richard); and colonialism, 144–45, 291 n.1, 317 n.1; and consciousness, 91, 100, 104–7, 135; and discourse of development, 4–5, 17–18, 45; and masculinity, 34–35, 41–43, 80; and race (*see* Gamio, Manuel: *Forjando Patria;* Indigenismo; Mestizaje); reactive (*see* Rostow, W. W.: reactive nationalism)

National Peasants Confederation (CNC), 220, 221

National Revolutionary Union of Guatemala, 169, 229, 308 n.2, 310 n.5. See also *Dias de la selva*

National Union of Farmers and Ranchers (UNAG), 113, 143, 146

Nation of Islam, 269, 272–75

Nehru, Jawaharlal, 144

Nicaragua, 10, 114; 1981 agrarian reform law, 126–36, 140. *See also* Sandinista National Liberation Front

Nicaraguan Ministry of Agriculture (MIDINRA). *See* Sandinista National Liberation Front agricultural policy

Nicaraguan Ministry of Planning (MIPLAN), 115, 116, 126

Nicaraguan National Assembly, 136

Nicaraguan Union of National Opposition (UNO), 140

North American Free Trade Agreement (NAFTA), 3, 12, 218, 322 n.25, 327 n.41

North Atlantic Treaty Organization (NATO), 23

Parsons, Talcott, 177

Pasajes de la guerra revolucionaria (Ernesto "Che" Guevara): and colonialism, 86–88, 263; consciousness in, 10–11, 65–67, 70–78, 83–89; and masculinity, 66, 71, 73, 78–82, 84, 88–89, 108, 152, 259–65, 300 n.7; and messianic imagery (*see* subjectivity in); representation of subaltern in, 33, 70, 76, 81–89, 108, 152, 164–65, 269, 270; subjectivity in, 9–10, 66–90, 167, 263, 267

Payeras, Mario, 9, 11, 33, 63, 64, 66–67, 89, 90, 141, 152, 153, 160, 164, 259, 261, 274, 276–77, 282, 284; *Los Pueblos indígenas y la revolución guatemalteca,* 91, 99, 103–8; relation to Guevara, 90–95, 97. See also *Los dias de la selva*

Perry, Bruce, 335 n.2

Pink, Louis Heaton, 292 n.3

Pinochet, Augusto, 109

Plan de Ayala, 221, 328 n.44

Prebisch, Raúl, 49

Pye, Lucien, 26

Quesada Pastrán, Freddy, 137

Rabasa, José, 199

Ramirez, Ricardo. *See* Moran, Rolando

MARÍA JOSEFINA SALDAÑA-PORTILLO is an
associate professor in the English Department and
Ethnic Studies Program at Brown University

Library of Congress Cataloging-in-Publication Data
Saldaña-Portillo, María Josefina.
The revolutionary imagination in the Americas and the
age of development / by María Josefina Saldaña-Portillo.
p. cm. — (Latin America otherwise)
Includes bibliographical references and index.
ISBN 0-8223-3178-0 (cloth : alk. paper)
ISBN 0-8223-3166-7 (pbk. : alk. paper)
1. Revolutions—Latin America. 2. Economic develop-
ment. 3. Latin America—Economic policy. I. Title.
II. Series. JC491.S25 2003
338.98—dc21 2003009458